Sarvepalli Radhakrishnan

BASIC WRITINGS OF S. RADHAKRISHNAN

Edited with an Introduction
by
Robert A. McDermott

JAICO PUBLISHING HOUSE
OMBAY ★ DELHI ★ BANGALORE ★ CALCUTTA
HYDERABAD ★ MADRAS

BASIC WRITINGS OF S. RADHAKRISHNAN
ISBN 81-7224-234-4

Orignally Published by
E.P. Dutton. Inc.
New York

First Jaico Impression : 1972
Second Jaico Impression : 1975
Third Jaico Impression : 1977
Fourth Jaico Impression : 1981
Fifth Jaico Impression : 1987
Sixth Jaico Impression : 1990
Seventh Jaico Impression : 1994

Published by:
Ashwin J. Shah
Jaico Publishing House
121 M. G. Road
Bombay 400 023

Printed by :
Efficient Offset Printers
215, Shahzada Bagh Industrial Complex
Phase II, Delhi-110 035

For Ellen

**Whose affection for India,
especially for its children,
typifies her sensitivity to
life's wonders and tragedies.**

Grateful acknowledgment is made to the following for permission to quote excerpts from copyright material by Sarvepalli Radhakrishnan:

The Brahma-Sūtra: copyright © 1960 by George Allen & Unwin Ltd. Reprinted by permission of George Allen & Unwin Ltd.

East and West in Religion: copyright 1933, © 1958 by George Allen & Unwin Ltd. Reprinted by permission of George Allen & Unwin Ltd., London, and Barnes & Noble, Inc., New York.

Indian Philosophy: copyright 1923, © 1962 by George Allen & Unwin Ltd. Reprinted by permission of George Allen & Unwin Ltd., London, and Humanities Press, Inc., New York.

Mahātmā Gāndhi: copyright 1939, 1949 by George Allen & Unwin Ltd. Reprinted by permission of George Allen & Unwin Ltd., London, and Beacon Press, Boston.

The Principal Upanishads: copyright 1953 by George Allen & Unwin Ltd. Reprinted by permission of George Allen & Unwin Ltd.

The Philosophy of S. Radhakrishnan, ed. Paul Arthur Schilpp: copyright 1952 by The Library of Living Philosophy, Inc. Reprinted by permission of Open Court Publishing Company.

Religion in a Changing World: copyright © 1967 by George Allen & Unwin Ltd. Reprinted by permission of George Allen & Unwin Ltd.

Religion in Transition: copyright 1937 by George Allen & Unwin Ltd. Reprinted by permission of George Allen & Unwin Ltd.

Preface

The work of S. Radhakrishnan has been the most important single factor in the genesis and development of Indian and Western comparative studies. Since shortly after the turn of the century, Radhakrishnan has been working creatively for a greater synthesis of Indian and Western values, and in so doing has helped to establish the data, problems, and a method for the comparative study of Indian and Western philosophical, religious, and cultural ideas. This volume contains a representative selection of Radhakrishnan's most significant writings in these areas.

The Editor's Introduction, in five sections, corresponding to each section of the book, explains the aims, key concepts, and major presuppositions of Radhakrishnan's thought. The initial selection, Radhakrishnan's autobiographical essay, and the corresponding first section of the Introduction explain how Radhakrishnan set out to synthesize the Indian and Western ideas that have absorbed his attention during the past six decades. This first section characterizes Radhakrishnan's "search for truth," and introduces the tasks dealt with in the remaining sections of the book. The other four sections of the book, dealing respectively with Radhakrishnan's interpretation of Indian philosophy, his systematic version of Vedānta, his reinterpretation of Hindu *dharma* and *yoga*, and his consistent plea for a universal synthesis "on the plane of spirit," represent areas in which Radhakrishnan's writings have proven to be extremely significant. As is noted in the concluding section of the Introduction, recent works in comparative philosophy, religion, and culture (the most important of which are listed in the Bibliography), have seriously challenged some of Radhakrishnan's most characteristic claims. Despite the criticisms which can be brought against Radhakrishnan's system, however, his writings are still the best introduction to Indian and comparative philosophy.

The selections have been drawn from volumes that are not readily available to the nonspecialist in Indian studies. Each essay and chapter is reprinted in its entirety; there is no internal editing of Radhakrishnan's text, except for the omission of many footnotes, especially in Chapters 3 and 4. The selections are arranged so as to insure maximum continuity and coherence. The Glossary of Important Names and Terms should provide additional assistance to those unfamiliar with the Indian tradition. It is hoped that the entire volume will be intelligible to the beginning as well as to the accomplished student of Indian and comparative philosophy.

ROBERT A. MCDERMOTT

Rye, New York

Contents

PART IV THE HINDU VIEW: *DHARMA* AND *YOGA*

PART V THE UNIVERSAL VIEW: INDIA AND THE WORLD COMMUNITY

Acknowledgments

Among those who have helped me in a variety of ways, I am grateful to Mr. Joseph E. Cunneen of Holt, Rinehart & Winston, Mr. Thomas C. Miller of Prentice-Hall, Professor Oscar Shaftel of Pratt Institute, and Professors William A. Johnson and Adele M. Fiske of Manhattanville College. I am grateful to Manhattanville College for having encouraged my work in Indian philosophy, including my study of Sanskrit and my participation in the 1966 Summer Institute in Indian Civilization (Fulbright-Hays) and the Syracuse University Faculty Development Seminar on South Asia (Syracuse, summer 1969; India, summer 1970).

I am indebted to Professor Thomas Berry of Fordham University for having introduced me to the splendors of Asian philosophy and religion, and for directing my work in this area with a dedication that is well known to his students and friends. I am also grateful to Professors John H. Lavely and Donald R. Dunbar of Boston University for the characteristic patience and skill with which they directed my dissertation on Radhakrishnan's Comparative Philosophy. My greatest debt is to my brother, John J. McDermott of Queens College, whose singular genius ideally blends practical wisdom, selfless action, and an abiding affection for the varieties of experience.

My wife, Ellen, to whom this edition is dedicated, has been a generous partner in my work on Radhakrishnan and in the larger task of understanding and appreciating India.

The prominent feature of our time
is not so much the wars and the
dictatorships which have disfigured
it, but the impact of different
cultures on one another, their
interaction, and the emergence of
a new civilisation based on the truths
of spirit and the unity of mankind.

S. Radhakrishnan
Fragments of a Confession

Introduction

I

Radhakrishnan's life work as philosopher, interpreter of Hinduism, and exponent of a universal community is traceable to "the challenge of Christian critics" which led him "to make a study of Hinduism and find out what is living and what is dead in it" (p. 40). Radhakrishnan began this study in the first decade of the twentieth century when philosophy in India was exclusively British, primarily neo-Hegelian; but during the two decades between the publication of his master's thesis on the "Ethics of the Vedānta" (1908) and the completion of his two-volume history of Indian philosophy (1923–27), he established the respectability of Indian philosophy not only in India but throughout the philosophical world.

Radhakrishnan's determination to defend Indian philosophy, and the Vedāntic system in particular, provided his work with a coherence and forcefulness that the subject desperately needed at the time, but it also bore an apologetic tone from which his writings are never entirely free. Just as his master's thesis "was intended to be a reply to the charge that the Vedānta system had no room for ethics" (p. 40), virtually all of his subsequent writings are an attempt to establish idealism and Hinduism as a solution to the conflict of philosophical and religious ideals.

Despite its awkwardly self-conscious tone, "My Search for Truth" suggests the basic attitude and broad outline of Radhakrishnan's proposed solution to the conflict of certain philosophical and religious values. Some of the more significant factors in the formation of his system are cited in turn: the pervasive Indian sense of the eternal and the tenuous status of the empirical world, the more humanistic direction of Indian religious thought typified by Rabindranath Tagore, the influence of Bergson's argument for intuition, the ideal of integral experience based on the model of the Indian mystic, and finally the belief in universal salvation. The concluding section of the essay contains some of Radhakrishnan's typical reflections on and hopes for the human condition.

In presenting and extending the idealist and Vedāntist position, Radhakrishnan effectively draws on the works of Rabindranath Tagore and Henri Bergson. Radhakrishnan's first two books, *The Philosophy of Rabindranath Tagore* (1918) and *The Reign of Religion in Contemporary Philosophy* (1920), are not especially insightful on either Tagore or Bergson, but they do signal the author's dual commitment to the humanism and spiritualism of Tagore's poetic vision, and to Bergson's philosophical defense of intuition.[1] Radhakrishnan's major works, such as *An Idealist View of Life*, *Eastern Religions and Western Thought*, and commentaries on the Upanishads and *Brahma-Sūtra*, consistently emphasize the humanistic character of Vedānta and its cognitive certainty based on intuition.

Significantly, in Radhakrishnan's system, intuition is equally the source of philosophical and of religious insight; further, the source and goal of both philosophy and religion are integral experience or the integrated life. Combining the insights of a long line of Indian mystic personalities with Bergson's claims for the role of the religious or integrated personalities in the evolution of consciousness, Radhakrishnan's entire system is based on the ideal of integration within the self, and the integration of the self with the Universal Self or *Ātman*. The philosophical and religious selections in this book are intended to explicate the expression of this ideal.

II

In writing on the difficulties of the historical interpr of philosophy some thirty years after the publication *Indian Philosophy* (1923; 1927), Radhakrishnan acknowledged

[1] For Bergson's theory of intuition, see his *Creative Evolution*, trans. Arthur Mitchell (New York: Random House, 1944), and *Creative Mind* (New York: Philosophical Library, 1946).

that "the writer may at times allow his personal bias to determine his presentation. His sense of proportion and relevance may not be shared by others. His work at best will be a personal interpretation and not an impersonal survey."[2] This caution is warranted in the case of his monumental and highly interpretive two-volume history of Indian philosophy. When Radhakrishnan introduces Indian thought by stating that "philosophy in India is essentially spiritual" (p. 69), he suggests the extent to which he is following the Vedāntist point of view. The same preference for the Vedāntic position, especially the *Advaita* (nondual) Vedānta of Śankara, is operative in his characterization of Indian philosophy:

> If we put the subjective interest of the Indian mind along with its tendency to arrive at a synthetic vision, we shall see how monistic idealism becomes the truth of things. To it the whole growth of Vedic thought points; on it are based the Buddhistic and Brahmanical religions; it is the highest truth revealed to India. Even systems which announce themselves as dualistic or pluralistic seem to be permeated by a strong monistic character (pp. 75–76).

This rendering of the Indian tradition can give the impression that the considerable variety within Indian philosophy consists in variations of the Vedānta system. Radhakrishnan frequently claims to be offering an entirely faithful account of non-Vedāntic systems, but he nevertheless seems to find remarkable corroboration for his own idealistic monism in systems that seem to be emphasizing something quite different.

Specifically, the entire theistic tradition, including the theistic passages in the Upanishads, the predominantly theistic meaning of the *Bhagavadgītā*, and the explicitly theistic philosophy of Rāmānuja, tend to be absorbed into an all-encompassing idealist or Vedāntic synthesis. Similarly, Radhakrishnan does

[2] "Fragments of a Confession," *The Philosophy of S. Radhakrishnan*, ed. Paul Arthur Schilpp (New York: Tudor Publishing Company, 1952), p. 11.

not give sufficient weight to the pluralist and dualist strains in the Indian tradition, and his interpretation of Buddhist philosophy is notoriously inadequate.

By contrast, Radhakrishnan's commentaries on the Upanishads and the *Brahma-Sūtra,* and his exposition of Śankara's Advaita Vedānta (which occupies more than 200 pages in the second volume of his *Indian Philosophy*), are as accurate and as incisive as any interpretation to date. Furthermore, his highly positive reading of the Vedānta position and the rest of the Indian tradition in light of Vedānta have served as the most effective case for the fact that Indian philosophy is not Western nor is it nonsense. Throughout his writings Radhakrishnan has tried to show that the wisest course for Indian thinkers is to synthesize the best of the Indian and Western traditions. With Gāndhi, Tagore, Aurobindo, and Bhagavan Das, Radhakrishnan seeks to draw from the West and from "the fountains of humanist idealism in India's past" (p. 107).

Overall, Radhakrishnan's writings are still the most intelligible introduction to Indian philosophy, especially to the Upanishads, the *Brahma-Sūtra*, and Śankara, the three key elements in Vedānta, the dominant school in Indian philosophy. The selections in the third part of this volume present Radhakrishnan's Indian idealism and the components of the Vedāntic system at their best.

III

As is characteristic of both idealism and Vedānta, Radhakrishnan's epistemology (primarily his theory of intuition) and his metaphysics (primarily his theory of Brahman-*Ātman*) are mutually dependent. Radhakrishnan's case for intuition presupposes the reality of the Absolute or Brahman, the intuition of which is the source and object of all knowledge. Similarly, the metaphysical claims for Brahman, and the levels of reality which it includes, presuppose that great religious personalities, such as the seers (or *ṛishis*) whose insights are expressed in the Upanishads, have overcome *māyā* or the appearance of reality and have achieved the spiritual realization in which all is Brahman. According to Radhakrishnan, recognition of the intuitive experience is precisely what characterizes Indian in contrast to Western philosophy; by valuing intuition over intellect, he is attempting to reverse what he considers to be the characteristically Western preference.[3]

This preference for intuition, however, is not without difficulties. Although he sharply distinguishes immediate or intuitive knowledge from mediated knowledge, Radhakrishnan also has to admit, as Bergson did, that intellect is needed to express the intuitive experience in intelligible and cognitively significant terms:

> The immediacy of intuitive knowledge can be mediated through intellectual definition and analysis. We use intellect to test the validity of intuitions and communicate them to others. Intuition and intellect are complementary. We have, of course, to recognise that intuition transcends the conceptual expressions as reality does not fit into categories.[4]

This passage well summarizes Radhakrishnan's insistence that intuition both transcends conceptual expression and is yet "mixed with layers of interpretation." The incompatibility of these two claims would be diminished if Radhakrishnan were more explicit concerning the transcendence, mediation, and conceptualization of intuition. Radhakrishnan's most consistent general position is probably the following: intuitive experience, whether philosophical or mystical, is expressible and has been expressed countless times, but these expressions are necessarily inadequate. So although intuition cannot be captured by language, only language can preserve the import of intuitive experience and point to the ineffable quality and object of the experience.

To his wise and thoroughly Bergsonian judgment that intuition can best be expressed by myth and image, literature and art, Radhakrishnan could have added that intuition is also

[3] *An Idealist View of Life* (London: George Allen & Unwin, 1962), p. 129.

[4] "Reply to Critics," Schilpp, *op. cit.*, p. 794.

expressed by moral ideals and religious beliefs; but then he cannot hold that intuitive experience is epistemologically true or privileged. Radhakrishnan uses this more appropriate language when he writes:

> The intuitive seer understands the variety of theological doctrines and codes. They are but attempts to express the inexpressible, to translate into human words the music of the divine.[5]

Thus, Radhakrishnan's epistemology and metaphysics both derive from and point to his conception of the integrated or religious personality. The levels of knowledge and reality (in a parallelism that is thoroughly Platonic) are functions of the mystic's vision: "Knowledge of reality is to be won by spiritual effort. One cannot think one's way into reality, but only live into it." [6] And again:

> Though philosophy is a system of thought, the experience it organises must be both rich and comprehensive. The vision of the philosopher is the reaction of his whole personality to the nature of the experienced world. . . . It is a mistake to think that the only qualifications for elucidating truth in the sphere of philosophy are purely intellectual. Only those whose lives are deep and rich light on the really vital syntheses significant for mankind.[7]

Appropriately, Radhakrishnan's theory of reality is the very synthesis that the archetypically "deep and rich" lives in the Vedāntic tradition have spiritually discerned and philosophically expressed.

The philosophical expression of the Upanishadic and Vedāntic vision can be summarized by two models: Brahman-*Ātman* (or the Absolute and Universal Self) and Brahman-*Īśvara* (or the Absolute and God). In both models, *māyā* (the empirical world, or the mysterious relation between Brahman and the world of change) is the polar opposite of Brahman. The following diagram may help to place these categories:

[5] "Spirit in Man," *Contemporary Indian Philosophy*, eds. S. Radhakrishnan and J. H. Muirhead (London: George Allen & Unwin, 1958), p. 503.
[6] *An Idealist View of Life*, p. 128.
[7] *Ibid.*, p. 182.

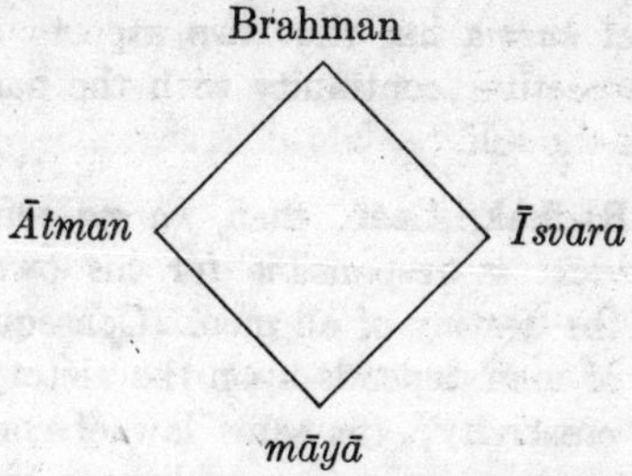

Brahman is all; one without a second. *Māyā* is whatever falls short of Brahman in its absolute oneness. *Ātman* and *Īśvara* are two ways in which Brahman-in-the-world (or *Saguṇa*, in contrast to *Nirguṇa* Brahman) is absolutely one and apparently many, absolutely eternal and apparently temporal. The "apparent" in both cases is the mystery of existence called *māyā*.

Essentially, *māyā* is ignorance (*avidyā*) concerning the structure of reality: "To look upon the world as self-sufficient is to be caught in *māyā*." [8] Or again, *māyā* is failing to realize that the true self is not the empirical self (*jīva*), but is actually *Ātman*—and, ultimately, *Ātman* is Brahman. Note that Radhakrishnan wants to establish a more positive relation between Brahman and the world, and Brahman and the self, than "the general Advaita tradition" had previously postulated. This is Radhakrishnan's expressed aim of interpreting the doctrine of *māyā* "so as to save the world and give it a real meaning." [9]

Similarly, Radhakrishnan interprets the doctrine of *karma* so as to reconcile it with his view of history as creative evolution. In order to reconcile the apparent incompatibility of the Advaitic theory of *karma* with his own emphasis on individual and historical creativity, Radhakrishnan constructs a theory of salvation in which *karma* sets the terms of individual salvation, and evolution sets the terms for historical or universal salvation. In effect, *karma* refers to the conditions or possibilities for the future, both advances and inherent limitations:

> The law of *karma* says that each individual will get the return according to the energy he puts forth. . . . The

[8] Introduction, *Brahma-Sūtra*, p. 137.

[9] "Reply to Critics," Schilpp, *op. cit.*, p. 800.

> principle of *karma* has thus two aspects, a retrospective and a prospective, continuity with the past and creative freedom of the self.[10]

According to Radhakrishnan, then, *karma* refers to the fact that an individual is responsible for his own destiny, and ultimately for the destiny of all men. Consequently, the ultimate triumph of man depends upon the victory of selflessness and historical creativity; the same law of continuity applies to mankind over the entire course of human history as applies to the individual person.

Furthermore, the *karma* of each soul is the primary determinant of the future possibilities for the course of human evolution. Radhakrishnan's ideal, then, is for the individual to identify his own *karma* with the *karma* of all mankind. In accordance with the theory of *Ātman*, the individual is not saved or liberated until he overcomes the distinction between his own salvation and the salvation of all men: "The soul is bound so long as it has a sense of mineness."[11] These liberated souls are the agents of corporate salvation:

> God comes to self-expression through the regenerated individuals. Till the end of the cosmic process is achieved, the individuals retain their distinction though they possess universality of spirit.[12]

Until the *karmas* of every individual are such that no more rebirths are necessary, the salvation of mankind remains an unachieved goal. But Radhakrishnan seems confident that this goal will be achieved. He writes:

> Rebirth is not an eternal recurrence leading nowhere, but a movement from man the animal to man the divine, a unique beginning to a unique end, from wild life in the jungle to a future Kingdom of God.[13]

Radhakrishnan believes that man can and must bring about the conditions that will create this future Kingdom of God,

[10] *An Idealist View of Life*, p. 276.
[11] Introduction, *Brahma-Sūtra*, p. 158.
[12] "Reply to Critics," Schilpp, *op. cit.*, p. 799.
[13] Introduction, *Brahma-Sūtra*, p. 193.

or what he also calls "The World's Unborn Soul." The surest paths toward the realization of this goal are those included in the Hindu view of life.

IV

Even though Radhakrishnan tends to identify the Hindu and Vedāntist points of view, the term Hinduism nevertheless refers to a religious rather than a philosophical position. As Radhakrishnan remarks in his *Hindu View of Life*, "Hinduism is more a way of life than a form of thought." [14] Accordingly, the section on his "Hindu View" treats the concept of *dharma*, or the various religious, ethical, and social duties governing a Hindu's life, and *yoga*, or the various ways and disciplines by which the Hindu seeks the goal of *mokṣa* or release from the chain of rebirth. *Dharma* and *yoga*, when combined with belief in the authority of the Vedas as interpreted by the Brahmins and belief in the doctrine of *karma*, are perhaps the most comprehensive and the most essential aspects of the Hindu tradition.

Radhakrishnan considers *dharma* to be "a word of protean significance,"[15] and explains that it is the concept under which the Hindu "brings the forms and activities which shape and sustain human life." [16] In the narrower sense of the term, *dharma* is one of the four ends of life, along with *artha* (wealth), *kama* (love or pleasure), and *mokṣa* (or spiritual freedom). More comprehensively, *dharma* is "the whole duty of man in relation to the fourfold purposes of life." [17] What is here referred to as "the whole duty" could as accurately be termed "the integral duty" or "the duty of the integrated personality." Following the logical implications of his theory of integral experience, Radhakrishnan conceives of *dharma* as "the com-

[14] *The Hindu View of Life* (New York: Macmillan Company, 1962), p. 58.

[15] S. Radhakrishnan, *Religion and Society* (London: George Allen & Unwin, 1959), p. 105.

[16] *Ibid.*

[17] *Ibid.*, p. 107. See also Introduction, *Brahma-Sūtra*, p. 154: "*Dharma* in a wide sense is used to connote all the means for the achievement of the different ends of life."

plete rule of life, the harmony of the whole man who finds a right and just law of his living" (p. 191).

Just as the ideal personality, according to Radhakrishnan, is integrated both internally and in relation to his environment, *dharma* "has two sides: the social and the individual, the *varna dharma* and the *āśrama dharma*" (p. 193). Further, Radhakrishnan relates his theory of *dharma* to the theory of reality, especially to the theory of the universal self:

> *Dharma* tells us that while our life is in the first instance for our own satisfaction, it is more essentially for the community and most of all for that universal self which is in each of us and all beings (p. 191).

Thus, *dharma* is the obligation to become a universal self; it is also the realization of the Brahman-*Ātman* unity in a cultural as well as in an individual context. In this sense, *dharma* comes to mean the ideal of the *summum bonum* of human life. In Radhakrishnan's view, the ideals of civilization are generated and prescribed by *dharma*. He writes:

> The difference between the half-civilised and the civilised is all the distance between a narrow self-regarding individualism controlled by the animal impulses of self-preservation, self-assertion, and self-satisfaction and the self-forgetful universalism devoted to the good of the whole. It is the transformation of the individual into the universal outlook, the linking up of our daily life with the eternal purpose that makes us truly human.[18]

What Radhakrishnan here calls "the truly human" presupposes the Upanishadic or Vedāntic theory of man, and the possibility of realizing that "eternal purpose" presupposes the various ways or disciplines called *yogas*.

Radhakrishnan's interpretive version of *yoga* resembles his theory of *dharma* in that both of these concepts are assumed to be both Indian and universal. Although he presents *yoga* as a universal rather than as an exclusively Indian discipline,

[18] S. Radhakrishnan, *Kalki—or the Future of Civilisation* (Bombay: Hind Kitabs, 1956), p. 31.

Radhakrishnan nevertheless attributes the greatest advances in this discipline to the Hindu tradition. He suggests that *yoga* harnesses man's energies "by the most intense concentration of personality," and thereby forces "the passage from the narrow ego to the transcendental personality."[19] The basis for this theory of *yoga* is Radhakrishnan's metaphysics of the integrated personality, and the function of *yoga*, like the function of metaphysics, is the realization of the unity of *Ātman* and Brahman. Man is not necessarily liberated by *yoga* or *dharma* any more than by metaphysics; but *yoga*, like *dharma*, is the discipline that makes Radhakrishnan's metaphysics a means to liberation. Radhakrishnan notes: "Man is not saved by metaphysics. Spiritual life involves a change of consciousness."[20] There are at least three ways, *mārgas* or *yogas*, by which this change of consciousness can be effected, but according to Radhakrishnan, all of these lead to *jñāna-yoga* or the way of knowledge:

> We can distinguish certain broad ways to man's realisation, the *karma-mārga*, the way of work, *bhakti-mārga*, the way of devotion, the *dhyāna-mārga*, the way of meditation. All these lead to *jñāna*, wisdom or enlightenment. All *yoga* is one and includes the different aspects of work, devotion and knowledge (p. 222).

For each of these *mārgas*, the model is the exceptional personality, whether the exemplar of the faithful performance of one's duty, the religious devotee, or the contemplative; in each case, the goal is the kind of knowledge which is conducive to, and ultimately identical with, *mokṣa* or liberation. To a greater or lesser extent, each personality in the long line of Indian *avatāras*, holy men, and contemporary leaders, exemplifies one or more *mārgas*. In some respects, Radhakrishnan's presentation of contemporary personalities such as Tagore, Gāndhi, and Nehru is more revealing than his accounts of traditional figures such as Gautama Buddha, Śankara, Rāmānuja, or Ramana Maharshi.

[19] Introduction, *Bhagavadgītā* (London: George Allen & Unwin, 1953), p. 50.

[20] Introduction, *Brahma-Sūtra*, p. 107.

V

Radhakrishnan's ideals of the integrated personality and the syntheses of the Indian and universal, the spiritual and humanistic, are variously personified by Rabindranath Tagore, Mahātmā Gāndhi, and Jawaharlal Nehru. In each of these figures Radhakrishnan finds a particular set of laudable qualities roughly corresponding to the Idealist, the Hindu, and the world-cultural points of view. Tagore's music, art, and literature celebrate a spiritual and transcendental view of the world that combines traditional Indian values and contemporary Western humanism. Gāndhi's life and thought are archetypically Hindu in their commitment to *dharma* and discipline. Nehru represents "the age to come, the age of world men with world compassion" (p. 284). To each in his own way the text which Radhakrishnan invokes for Gāndhi might be applied to the others as well: "Whatever being there is endowed with glory and grace and vigour, know that to have sprung from a fragment of My splendor" (p. 277).

What is perhaps most significant about Radhakrishnan's treatment of these figures (and many others [21]) is that he finds them to be exemplars of the Indian habit of attempting to synthesize conflicting philosophical, religious, and cultural ideals. Obviously, Radhakrishnan's emphasis on the synthetic and universal relies on very broad philosophical, religious and cultural ideals; his task is to find ideals that are broad enough to be universal without being abstract or empty. Figures like Tagore, Gāndhi, and Nehru help to give content to some of the ideals espoused in Radhakrishnan's Idealist and Hindu views of life.

Similarly, Radhakrishnan tries to conceive of religion in a way that does justice both to its universal and to its parochial aspects. His essays on "Religion and Religions" (1952) and "Creative Religions" (1956) presuppose both the diversity of religious traditions and something that he considers to be essential to all religion; this element, as noted in "My Search for

[21] See Radhakrishnan's essays on Bhagavan Sri Ramana and Sri Ramakrishna in *Great Indians*, ed. D. S. Sarma (Bombay: Hind Kitabs. 1949).

Truth," is concerned not with creeds or codes, but with "an insight into reality" (p. 51). Radhakrishnan conceives of the Hindu tradition more as a way of life than as a form of thought, but in light of his conception of religion, the Hindu view of life clearly involves a commitment to the ultimate unity of the self and the rest of the created world within Brahman. What Radhakrishnan considers to be the essence of religion would seem to be scarcely distinguishable from the view of reality and disciplines that characterize the Idealist and Hindu views.

It is a short step from Radhakrishnan's Idealist and Hindu views to his vision of a world community. As he explains: "Human progress lies in an increasing awareness of the universal working in man."[22] According to Radhakrishnan, the universal is realized through the labors of fallible but selfless men such as Tagore, Gāndhi, and Nehru. He views these three as exemplars of his own conviction that "man is not a detached spectator of a progress immanent in human history, but an active agent remoulding the world nearer to his ideals. Every age is much what we choose to make it" (p. 50). Thus, we can understand his conviction that "Hinduism is more a way of life than a form of thought" (p. 21). It is in this context that Radhakrishnan understands and offers an appreciation of Tagore, Gāndhi, and Nehru.

[22] *An Idealist View of Life*, p. 273.

Chronology

1888	Born, September 5, near Madras.
1905–09	Voorhees College and Madras Christian College.
1908	Master's Thesis: "Ethics of Vedānta."
1909–18	Assistant Professor, Professor of Philosophy, Presidency College, Madras.
1915	Met Mahātmā Gāndhi.
1918	Met Rabindranath Tagore. *The Philosophy of Rabindranath Tagore.*
1918–21	Professor of Philosophy, Mysore University.
1920	*The Reign of Religion in Contemporary Philosophy.*
1921–31	George V Professor of Philosophy, Calcutta University.
1923	*Indian Philosophy*, Vol. I.
1925–37	Chairman, Indian Philosophical Congress.
1926	*The Hindu View of Life* (based on the Upton Lectures delivered at Manchester College, Oxford, 1926). Haskel Lecturer in Comparative Religion, University of Chicago. "The Role of Philosophy in the History of Civilization," an address at the Sixth International Congress of Philosophy, Harvard University.
1928	Met Jawaharlal Nehru.
1932	*An Idealist View of Life* (based on the Hibbert Lectures at the University of London and Manchester College, 1929).
1933	*East and West in Religion* (based on lectures at Manchester College, 1929–30).

1936–39 Spalding Professor of Eastern Religion and Ethics at Oxford University.

1939 Elected Fellow of the British Academy.
Eastern Religions and Western Thought.
Mahātmā Gāndhi: Essays and Reflections on His Life and Work.

1939–48 Vice-Chancellor, Benares Hindu University.

1944 *India and China* (based on lectures delivered in China, May, 1944).

1946–52 Leader, Indian Delegation, UNESCO.

1947 *Religion and Society.*

1948 *The Bhagavadgītā.*

1949–52 Ambassador of India to U.S.S.R.

1950 *The Dhammapada.*

1952 "The Religion of the Spirit and the World's Need: Fragments of a Confession," and "Reply to Critics," in Schilpp, ed., *The Philosophy of S. Radhakrishnan.*

1952–62 Vice-President of India.

1952–54 President, General Conference of UNESCO.

1953–62 Chancellor, University of Delhi.

1953 *The Principal Upanishads.*

1955 *Recovery of Faith.*

1956 *East and West.*

1957 *Source Book in Indian Philosophy.*

1958 "Spirit in Man," in Radhakrishnan and Muirhead, eds., *Contemporary Indian Philosophy.*

1959 *The Brahma-Sūtra.*

1962–67 President of India.

1967 *Religion in a Changing World.*

Editor's Note

The Editor has assumed extreme discretionary power in eliminating most of the footnotes from the selections in chapters III and IV. Those notes which substantially affect the argument of the text and those which seem to be especially revealing or interesting to the reader have been retained; the vast majority of the notes, however, are not of immediate import to the nonspecialist. It is assumed that the scholar will want to work with the original texts, and the serious student is likewise urged to consult the original editions of the works in question, *The Principal Upanishads*, *Eastern Religions and Western Thought*, and *The Brahma-Sūtra*, and to make full use of Radhakrishnan's scholarly and suggestive references to Indian and Western sources.

Abbreviations

B.U.	Bṛhad-āraṇyaka Upanishad
B.S.	Brahma-Sūtra
C.U.	Chāndogya Upanishad
E.T.	English Translation
Katha	Kaṭha Upanishad
K.U.	Kauṣītakī Upanishad
Maitri	Maitrī Upanishad
Ma.U.	Māṇḍūkya Upanishad
Praśna	Praśna Upanishad
R.V.	Ṛg Veda
S.U.	Śvetāśvatara Upanishad
T.U.	Taittirīya Upanishad

PART I. AUTOBIOGRAPHICAL

My Search for Truth *

I. EARLY YEARS

I was born on September 5, 1888, at a small place, Tirutani, forty miles to the north-west of Madras, in South India, the second child of Hindu parents, who were conventional in their religious outlook. I have not had any advantages of birth or of wealth. The early years of my life till twelve were spent in Tirutani and Tirupati, both famous as pilgrim centres. I cannot account for the fact that from the time I knew myself I have had firm faith in the reality of an unseen world behind the flux of phenomena, a world which we apprehend not with the senses but with the mind, and even when I was faced by grave difficulties, this faith has remained unshaken. A meditative frame of mind is perhaps responsible for my love of loneliness. Side by side with my outward activities, there is in me an inner life of increasing solitude in which I love to linger. Books, the vistas they unveil, and the dreams they awaken, have been from the beginning my constant and unfailing companions. I am not quite at home in the conventional social functions by which life's troubles are tempered to most of us. When I am in company, unless it be with one or two who know me well, it is with an effort that I get along. But I have an almost uncanny knack of putting myself *en rapport* with any individual, high or low, old or young, if the need arises. While I am essentially shy and lonely, I pass for a social and sociable man. My withdrawn nature and social timidity have given me a reputation that I am difficult to know. Again, I am said to be cold and strong-willed, while I know that I am the opposite of it. I am capable of strong and profound emotions, which I generally tend to conceal. I am

* From Vergilius Ferm, ed. *Religion in Transition* (London: George Allen & Unwin, 1937), pp. 11–59.

nervously organised, sensitive, and highstrung. If with an unstable, sensitive nature and ordinary intellectual gifts I have not yet made a mess of this life, and if the editor thinks it worth his while to ask me to contribute an autobiographical essay to this volume, it is due to good luck. When Napoleon's eagle eye flashed down the list of officers proposed for promotion to higher rank, he used to scribble in the margin of a name 'Is he lucky?' I have luck, and it is this that has protected me thus far. It is as if a great pilot had been steering my ship through the innumerable rocks and shoals on which other barks had made shipwreck. The major guidance. I think, decisions of my life have been taken under a sort of plan, and prepare, and yet when the choice is made, I have a feeling that an invisible hand has been guiding me for purposes other than my own. I do not, however, pretend that I enjoy the special care of providence. Such a feeling, if it means more than the simple truth that the Supreme has an individual interest in and a delicate care for human beings, that its love is individual, immediate, and intimate, is an irrational prejudice. While I attribute the little success I have achieved to this luck or guidance, I do not want to shift the blame for my failures to ill luck or circumstances. My achievements are not entirely my own, but my mistakes are in large part due to my own folly or weakness.

II. HOME LIFE

I have often been reminded in later years of Hegel's saying that a man has made up his account with this life when he has work that suits him and a wife whom he loves. While men fill their feverish days with politics and business, love affairs and worldly careers, and drain to its dregs the enchanting cup of life, women, who are less sophisticated and so closer to reality, perceive that the true meaning of life is not exhausted by its obvious routine. They cling to the deeper and more ultimate reality in the light of which life no longer seems contingent and mediocre. In the battle between the naturalists and the idealists, between those who affirm that only those things are real which can be touched and handled and those who believe, in addition, in the reality of eternal values, the women of India are found conspicuously fighting on the side of the latter. By example rather than by precept, by their life rather than by their words, they lend an importance and depth of meaning to the passing events which form so large a part of our daily life. Though many of my class and generation were married earlier than it is usual in Western countries, these early marriages were not unsuccessful. The Hindu ideal of a wife, exalted and exacting, still has a strong hold on unsophisticated Hindu women. 'If he is faithless, I must be faithful. If he is shaken, I must abide. If he sees another, I must await his return'. If there is a taint in this blind devotion, then there is a taint in the Eternal who loves us with the same love, awaiting us patient and unwearied, when we return, weary with false pleasures, to him. A pure unquestioning love that triumphs over the weaknesses of the loved one is perhaps the greatest gift of heaven. Full of tenderness and deep affection as Indian married life is, its value can be greatly increased by suitable changes in the social institutions which have become stabilised by the unwillingness of legislatures to interfere with social customs. The only security which Indian women have against the breaking of their bodies and minds is the goodwill of their husbands and this is not enough in our present conditions.

III. PHILOSOPHY AND RELIGION

I had my school and college career in Christian missionary institutions. At an impressionable period of my life, I became familiar not only with the teaching of the New Testament, but with the criticisms levelled by Christian missionaries on Hindu beliefs and practices. My pride as a Hindu roused by the enterprise and eloquence of Swami Vivekananda was deeply hurt by the treatment accorded to Hinduism in missionary institutions. It was difficult for me to concede that Hindu ascetics and teachers who preserved for our world a living contact with the classical culture of India, which is at the root of much that we know and almost all that we practise, were not truly religious. Even the poor illiterate villagers with their ancient household traditions and religious observances seemed to me to be more familiar with the spiritual mystery enveloping this world than the emancipated, comfort-minded intellectuals eager for life and adventure. They were aware of the ancient truths and maxims which the spectacle of human life has suggested to thinking minds in all ages. Life is short and happiness uncertain. Death comes to all, prince and peasant alike. True knowledge is to know one's own ignorance. Contentment is better than riches, and a mind at peace with itself is worth more than the applause of assemblies. The superstitious Indian woman may have her haunting fears but, thanks to centuries of training, she has a noble dignity, a tender refinement, and a mental poise and magnanimity which many of her more intellectual contemporaries lack. The village pilgrim who spends all his earnings to have a bath in the Ganges or a *darśan* of the deity at Puri, who undertakes weary marches through toil and suffering to Benares or Kailas, has an innate conviction that man does not live by bread alone. Our age is a sophisticated one. In its superior fashion it laughs at gods and ghosts, values and ideals. It is too clever to take these outworn superstitions seriously, but the illiterate Hindus who are foolish enough to perceive that these things are the symbols of thoughts beyond the reach of our rational minds do not merit our derision. I know that the people of India are the victims of paralysing superstitions, but I cannot believe that they are devoid of religious sense. Every mother teaches her child that if he is to grow up religiously, he must love God, abstain from sin, and be full of sympathy and help to those who are in trouble. We have invented innumerable ways of spending the time allotted to us. May it not be that the way of the primitive Hindu is not the least wise of these? To dwell on the contemplation of eternal ideas, to struggle to behold the divine with the eye of the mind and to feed on the shadows of perfection, is that an ignoble life?

My religious sense did not allow me to speak a rash or a profane word of anything which the soul of man holds or has held sacred. This attitude of respect for all creeds, this elementary good manners in matters of spirit, is bred into the marrow of one's bones by the Hindu tradition, by its experience of centuries. Religious tolerance marked the Hindu culture from its very beginnings. When the Vedic Aryans came into contact with people professing other creeds, they soon adjusted themselves to the new elements. The Vedic religion received incalculable material and impulse for the determining of its own unique character through the re-shaping of its foreign elements. The famous Hindu scripture, *Bhagavadgītā*, declares that if one has faith and devotion to the other gods, it is faith and devotion to the supreme One, though not in the prescribed way. The end of religion is an essential knowledge of God. Doctrines about God are only guides to the seekers who have not reached the end. They represent God under certain images, as possessing certain attributes and not as He is in himself. For example, in Christendom, God the Father gave place to God the Mother in the Middle Ages as in Mariolatry when she was said to be 'Queen of Heaven, who can do all that she wills'. No formula can confine God. Besides, the knowledge we are capable of receiving depends on the stage of our development. A great truth cannot be imparted to one who possesses a narrower one answering to the measure of his capacity. If the life is deepened, the imperfect truth gives place to the more perfect one. The true teacher helps us to deepen our insight, not alter our view. He gives us a better access to our own scriptures for 'the path men take from every side is mine'. The different religions are not rival or competing forces, but fellow labourers in the same great task. 'God has not left Himself without witness among any people. Clement of Alexandria allows that there was always a natural manifestation of the one Almighty God amongst all right-thinking men. Bred in such beliefs, I was somewhat annoyed that truly religious people—as many Christian missionaries undoubtedly were—could treat as subjects for derision doctrines that others held in deepest reverence. This unfortunate practice has, in my opinion, little support in the teaching or example of Jesus, though some of his later followers encouraged it. Religious truth outside the biblical revelation was according to Augustine a work of the devil, a caricature perpetrated by demons. Serious students of comparative religion are impressed by the general revelation of God. All truth about God has its source in God. The conception of a unique revelation, of a chosen people is contrary to the love and justice of God. It is a pet fancy of the pious that their own religion is the flower of the development of religion, its final end into which all others converge. In the new world order such a view of spiritual monopolies has no place.

The challenge of Christian critics impelled me to make a study of Hinduism and find out what is living and what is dead in it. The spirit of the times, in which India, so to say, was turning in its sleep, strengthened this resolve. The philosophy courses for the B.A. and the M.A. degrees in the Madras University did not demand any acquaintance with the Indian systems of thought and religion. Even to-day Indian philosophy forms a very minor part of philosophical studies in Indian Universities. In partial fulfilment of the conditions for the M.A. degree examination, I prepared a thesis on the *Ethics of the Vedānta*, which was intended to be a reply to the charge that the Vedānta system had no room for ethics. At the time (1908) when I was only a young student of twenty, the publication of a book with my name on the title-page excited me a great deal, though now, when I look back upon the juvenile and rhetorical production, I am ashamed that I ever wrote it. My great surprise, however, was that my distinguished teacher, Professor A. G. Hogg, the present Principal of the Madras Christian College, a thinker of great penetration in theological matters, awarded me a testimonial, which I still treasure, in which he expressed himself thus: 'The thesis which he prepared in the second year of his study for this degree shows a remarkable understanding of the main aspects of the philosophical problem, a capacity for handling easily a complex argument besides more than the average mastery of good English'. All the same, that little essay indicates the general trend of my thought. Religion must establish itself as a rational way of living. If ever the spirit is to be at home in this world and not merely a prisoner or a fugitive, secular foundations must be laid deep and preserved worthily. Religion must express itself in reasonable thought, fruitful action, and right social institutions.

From April, 1909, when I was appointed to the Department of Philosophy in the Madras Presidency College, I have been a teacher of Philosophy and engaged in the serious study of

Indian philosophy and religion. I soon became convinced that religion is an autonomous form of experience which cannot be confused with anything else, not even with morality, though it cannot help expressing itself in a high code of morality. Religion is essentially a concern of the inner life. Its end is to secure spiritual certainty which lifts life above meaningless existence or dull despair. It must be judged by its own standard, whether it gives security to values, meaning to life, confidence to adventure. Its roots lie in the spirit of man deeper than feeling, will, or intellect. The deepest depths of the soul reflect the divine, when they are kept undimmed. 'God has put eternity into the heart of man', says the Preacher. The sense of the infinite is the basis of religion. This sense is not satisfied with what the eyes see or the ears hear. When cultivated, it introduces us into a higher world than the material. A man may be highly moral, practise virtue scrupulously, but if faith and hope in the spiritual direction of the universe are not there, he is not a religious man. Religion is that knowledge of the essential nature of reality, that insight or penetration which satisfies not only a more or less powerful intellectual impulse in us, but that which gives to our very being the point of contact which it needs for its vital power, for the realisation of its true dignity, for its saving. To this end intense spiritual labour and moral activity are needed. To have a vision of God requires a pure heart. To know the truth, not learning but the heart of a child is needed. The ethical has a prominent place in the process of the purification of the mind by which communion with God is brought about. When the goal is reached, the spirit shines through and illuminates the whole life, filling it with ethical character and vital energy.

Whatever may be the Hindu practice, Hindu religion cannot be regarded as unworldly or otherworldly. According to it, the aim of religion is to attain a knowledge or a vision of God and the aim of ethics is to remake human life into the mould of the unseen. The two are bound up with each other. The consciousness of the infinite spirit is the impulse to the ideal. It expresses itself in a burning passion for righteousness and purity. The sense of the spiritual and the longing for righteousness go together.

A verse in the *Mahābhārata* says that the mark of the Aryan is not learning, not religion, but conduct alone. Philosophy in India is not an abstract study remote from the life of man. It is intimately woven into the texture of human existence. The civilisation of India is an effort to embody philosophical wisdom in social life. My occasional contributions to learned magazines like the *International Journal of Ethics*, *Monist*, *Quest*, had for their objective the establishing of the ethical character of the Hindu religion. Spiritual values are realised on earth through the empiric means of family love, of love and friendship, of loyalty and reverence. To the truly religious, all life is a sacrament. Modern attempts to improve the general condition of the community, to transform society so that hope and happiness might be brought within the reach of the needy and the down-trodden, are not inconsistent with the Hindu religion but are demanded by it.

It is urged often that belief in the illusory character of the world associated with the Hindu religion conflicts with ethical seriousness: It is wrong to interpret the meaning of the doctrine of *māyā* in a way that affects the urgency of the ethical demand. The doctrine of *māyā* declares that the world is dependent on and derived from the ultimate reality. It has the character of perpetual passing away, while the real is exempt from change. It has therefore a lower status than the Supreme itself. In no case is its existence to be confused with illusory being or non-existence. Even Śankara, who advocates the theory of *māyā*, carefully distinguishes the phenomenal existence of the world from the being of Brahman and the non-being of dreams, illusions, etc. Besides, many other interpreters of the Vedānta repudiate the doctrine of *māyā* even in this limited sense.

In regard to my views on Hindu ethics and the doctrine of *māyā*, I found great support in the writings of Rabindranath Tagore. The results of my study of his works (translated into English) are embodied in a book which Macmillan (London) brought out in 1918. This book, which has all the faults of immature youth, secured on the whole a friendly reception. The poet himself was extremely generous. He wrote in December 1918: 'Though my criticism of a book that concerns me may not be seriously accepted, I can say that it has surpassed my expectation. The earnestness of your endeavour and your penetration have amazed me, and I am thankful to you for the literary grace of its language which is so beautifully free from all technical jargon and a mere display of scholarship'.

In 1918 I was appointed Professor of Philosophy in the new University of Mysore. My previous studies inclined me to accept a spiritual, non-dogmatic view of religion. It is not a private revelation or what is imposed by public authority, but what springs naturally from the light of reason and the insight of experience. I was persuaded that philosophy led us to a spiritual or, what I then called, an absolutist view of religion. If philosophy is employed to lend support to a pluralistic idealism which looks upon God as the President of the Immortals and human individuals as eternal spirits who will retain for all time their unique irreplaceable significance, it is influenced by our religious prepossessions. I published a series of articles in *Mind* on M. Bergson's philosophy, pointing out that he was an absolutist. From a similar standpoint I examined the philosophical views of Leibniz, James Ward, William James, Rudolf Eucken, Hastings Rashdall, Bertrand Russell, Lord Balfour, etc., and pointed out that their implicit support of pluralism or pluralistic theism is traceable to the interference of religion with the pursuit of philosophy. This thesis was set forth in an ambitious work on *The Reign of Religion in Contemporary Philosophy* (Macmillan, 1920). It had a very warm reception. Noted critics praised it beyond its merits. Apart from many favourable reviews by men of established reputation in philosophy like J. H. Muirhead, J. S. Mackenzie, and J. M. E. McTaggart, among others, Professor Hinman of America in his presidential address to the American Philosophical Association selected for treatment "Two Representative Idealists, Bosanquet and Radhakrishnan". To be coupled with Bosanquet is an honour which more eminent men would covet. The book was used by students in metaphysics not only in Indian universities, but in several British and American ones, and I became somewhat known as a writer on philosophy.

In 1921 I was appointed to the most important philosophy

chair in India, King George V Chair of Mental and Moral Science in the University of Calcutta. Professor J. H. Muirhead, to whom I owe more than I can tell, invited me to write a systematic and readable account of Indian philosophy, for his famous 'Library of Philosophy'. I put together my studies on this subject, which occupied me from 1908, and published the two volumes which are now in their second edition. The task of bringing together a multitude of minute particulars into a creative and cumulative relationship is not an easy one. My ambition in this work was not only to chronicle but to interpret, to show the interconnection of the different views, to render the vibration of life. Besides, in all philosophical interpretation the right method is to interpret thinkers at their best, in the light of what they say in their moments of clearest insight. There is no reason why philosophical writers should not be judged as other creative artists are, at least in the main, on the basis of their finest inspirations. To understand a great thinker, we must have enough sympathy to imagine ourselves as standing in his place, possessing his information, cherishing his beliefs, feeling his emotions. So long as we keep reminding ourselves that we are modern and that these ancients had faults and passions that we do not share, we can never achieve more than caricatures of these thinkers. Humility is the mother of all writing, even though that writing may relate to the history of philosophy. I am happy that I helped, to some extent, in the endeavour to take Hindu thought again into the general stream of human thought. There was a time when it was regarded as something quaint, strange, antiquated, incapable of playing a part in the world's spiritual awakening. But that impression is slowly disappearing. Ancient Indians do not belong to a different species from ourselves. We find from an actual study of their views that they ask questions and find answers analogous in their diversity to some of the more important currents in modern thought. Indian philosophy is now recognised as an important branch of study and even the editors of the *Encyclopaedia Britannica* (14th ed.) found some space for it and asked me to write the article on 'Indian Philosophy'.

Through my articles in the *Hibbert Journal*, I was brought

into contact with its editor, Dr. L. P. Jacks, late Principal of Manchester College, Oxford, who graciously invited me to give the Upton Lectures on *The Hindu View of Life*, in 1926, in his college. I was enabled to accept his invitation, as the University of Calcutta deputed me to represent it at the Congress of the Universities of the British Empire in June, 1926, and the International Congress of Philosophy at the Harvard University in September, 1926. This was my first visit to Europe and America and I have the most pleasant recollections of it. The very warm reception which I had in Oxford and Cambridge, in Harvard and Princeton, in Yale and Chicago, and many other places, is fixed in my mind.

In the lectures on *The Hindu View of Life* I represent Hinduism as a progressive historical movement still in the making. Its adherents are not custodians of a deposit, but runners carrying a lighted torch. The weaknesses of the Hindu faith which have drawn the institution into disgrace and are to-day blocking the way for social advance are due to a confusion between tradition and truth. We must preserve the spirit of truth which will guide us into all truth. God does not say 'I am Tradition', but he says 'I am Truth'. Truth is greater than its greatest teachers. We must realise that the history of the race is strewn with customs and institutions which were invaluable at first and deadly afterwards. Gross abuses which still survive require to be cut off with an unsparing hand. Hinduism insists on the upward striving, not only in the sphere of morals but in that of intellect. It is not to be regarded as either pessimistic or fatalistic. The law of *karma* affirms the implicit presence of the past in the present. When we unconsciously or mechanically follow the impulses of the past, we are not exercising our freedom. But we are free when our personal subject becomes the ruling centre. It is not necessary for me to refer to the different criticisms urged against the Hindu faith since the chief of them are considered in that book.

At the Philosophical Congress held at Harvard University in September, 1926, the lack of spiritual note in modern civilisation was the theme of my address to the general meeting, an idea which I set forth in some detail in a small book called *Kalki—or the Future of Civilisation.* In the last few decades the world has been transformed so rapidly and completely at any rate in its superficial aspects. Science helps us to build up our outer life, but another discipline is necessary to strengthen and refine the living spirit. Though we have made enormous progress in knowledge and scientific inventions, we are not above the level of past generations in ethical and spiritual life. In some respects we have perhaps declined from their standards. Our natures are becoming mechanised; void within, we are reduced to mere atoms in a community, members of a mob. Behaviourist psychology teaches us that man has no inwardness and can be understood completely from the standpoint of the observer.

Some of the recent attempts at the re-planning of society are attended with this danger. Though man has compelled the world to minister to his needs, though the application of modern science to production and distribution enables us to provide the possibilities of material well-being for all and make poverty an anachronism, still large numbers of men are suffering from poverty and starvation. This chaotic condition is due to a lack of fellowship and co-operation. The Russian experiment, whatever we may think of it, is at least an honest attempt to secure for all an equal share in things which constitute the physical basis of life. The glaring contrasts of poverty and wealth are not accepted by them as inevitable. Even Fascism is labouring to build up a true communal life and effect a more equitable distribution of power, wealth, and opportunity. Only the unfortunate result of these attempts is mutual conflict and suppression of individual liberty. There is a standardisation of souls, a loss of self-confidence, a tendency to seek salvation in herds. Not only is the individual robbed of his freedom to order his life as he wills, he is also deprived of the liberty to think as he will and express his thoughts and opinions. Society has become a prison. That there is a real feeling for humanity in these desperate attempts to check the economic exploitation of the masses, one can readily admit. But if it is to be achieved by the other exploitation of the baser passions of human nature, its selfishness and hatred, its insolence and fanaticism, the ideal order will be an inhuman one. Let us by all means establish a just economic order, but let us also note that the economic man is not the whole man. For a complete human being, we require the cultivation of the grace and joy of souls overflowing in love and devotion and free service of a regenerated humanity. If we wish to realise the reign of law and justice in this world, it is to enable the soul to gain inward peace. Physical efficiency and intellectual alertness are dangerous if spiritual illiteracy prevails. Aldous Huxley's *Brave New World* gives us a picture of perfect adaptation of means to ends which will mean at the same time the breeding of men and women in bottles, the disappearance of all family life, of art and literature, of philosophy and religion, the death of all things of the spirit. The elimination of the inner world of personal experience is not a sign of progress. The present crisis of civilisation is the direct result of the loosening hold of ethical and spiritual ideals.

We see things happening in the civilised world to-day that recall the worst phases of the Dark Ages. New gods of race and nation are set up in the place of God who is dethroned. The souls of men are poisoned and perverted by collective myths. They control their loyalties, present apocalyptic hopes, demand an intense and passionate devotion to a goal outside and greater than the self and serve as religions which have the power to give luminous meaning to life and stir the will to action. The few who have the perception of the unity of mankind and feel the happiness and misery of a neighbouring people as though it were their own are swamped by the millions who are taught to accustom themselves to the idea of humanity as an assemblage of combatant communities whose strength is tested through war. The perilous rivalries of national states are accompanied by a furious competition in armaments. It is no use deceiving ourselves that armaments are not meant to be used. We cannot help using them any more than an animal eating food can help throwing out filth. At the rate at which preparations for war are proceeding and men's passions are stirred, a catastrophe compared with which the last war was only a picnic seems to be drawing near.

It is not, however, the part of wisdom to accept the collapse as inevitable and abandon all struggle against it. It would be the surest way of bringing it about. Nothing is inevitable in human affairs except peace. It is the world's desperate need. Many leading scientists devote their lives to the study of the hidden causes of natural cataclysms such as earthquakes, which man is powerless to overcome. Wars are human phenomena, and it is our duty to investigate their causes.

There is something fundamentally defective in the present organisation of society. It is not sufficiently democratic. The basis of democracy is the recognition of the dignity of human beings. It affirms that no individual is good enough to be trusted with absolute power over another and no nation is good enough to rule another. But the present organisation of society, national and international, works on the principle that the strong do what they can and the weak suffer what they must. The clashing standards of value and the contradictory schemes of life embodied in the nation state and the Communist doctrine are crude and cumbrous attempts to shape a better future for the menaced groups and individuals. A deep, uncontrollable restlessness stirs the illiterate and down-trodden millions the world over. They are coming into a new consciousness of their rights and are clamouring to wrest them from the hands of their exploiters. Those who are giving material and moral support to dictatorships in Europe were born into and grew up in a world of strife, suffering, and confusion, and, in the case of Germany, of political humiliation, with the memories of defeat and disaster in their minds and hearts. Dictatorships are political devices born of despair.

The League of Nations has been tried in the balance and found wanting. It has turned out an instrument in the hands of the stronger nations to maintain the status quo and oppose those who demand change. Nominally international, it is worked by people who think and act nationally. These speak of peace and collective security, integrity of small nations, and the plighted word when it serves their interest. The desire of the dominant powers to secure their colonial possessions, of the victorious powers to hang on to the spoils of victory, is dressed up as love of peace and superiority to nationalism. The high priests at Geneva are like the patriarchs of the past, conservative, dogmatic defenders of established injustices, and not reshapers of the world in the light of justice and freedom for all. History is revolutionary, and the League as it works at present is a negation of history. It does not take account of the movement of mind, the stream of ideas, the pace and direction in which life and time are flowing. Dynamic and ambitious nations eager to effect changes in the status quo withdraw from the League to resume unrestrained liberty of political action. They declare that justice comes first and peace second. The League consists of the satisfied powers and the weaker nations.

More than the economic factor, the psychological element of prestige operates in the matter of the possession of colonies. While they are for their owners a source of profit, they provoke the envious resentment of others. The determination of some nations to hold on to what they have and defend it at all costs, and the equal determination of others to wrest it from them, are the causes of wars. If only the great powers are willing to make in advance a small part of the sacrifices which each of them will have to make, should a war start, the terrible menace which threatens us to-day could be warded off. The lead in this matter can be taken by Great Britain, whose political realism is not unmixed with idealism. Britain is aiming at transforming its empire into a free partnership of nations which enter into it of voluntary accord. The inferior status of India in it is a source of weakness and makes it an object of envy to others. So long as India is a dependency and not a dominion, Great Britain cannot complain if Italy and Germany wish to take their share in what the Britisher in other moods called the white man's burden. She has no moral authority to question Japan's adventures in the Far East or Italy's in Africa. Things are never settled until they are settled right. If we go behind the give and take of politics to the ultimate question of right and wrong, we see that the instability of the world is due to the outrage on the moral law in which powerful nations are acquiescing. It is time we restore the supremacy of law and organise the world for an enduring peace.

Civilisation is an act of spirit, not of body or of mind. Achievements of knowledge and power are not enough; acts of spirit and morality are essential. Man must become an active, purposeful force. He must cease to believe in an automatic law of progress which will realise itself irrespective of human ideals and control. Man is not a detached spectator of a progress immanent in human history, but an active agent remoulding the world nearer to his ideals. Every age is much what we choose to make it. The trouble with our civilisation is that in our anxiety to pursue the things of time, we are neglecting the things that are not of time, the enduring and the eternal. The significance of man's life is not exhausted by his service of the earthly kingdom. The whole complex range of human life becomes shallow, aimless, and unsatisfying if it is not shot through with a sense of the eternal. We must build all relationships on a basis of understanding fellowship, remembering the controlling principle that life on earth is meaningless apart from its eternal background. Growth of civilisation is marked by an increase of genuineness, sincerity, and unselfishness. The only effective way of altering society is the hard and slow one of changing individuals. If we put first things first, through patient effort and struggle, we will win power over circumstances and mould them. Only a humanity that strives after ethical and spiritual ideals can use the great triumphs of scientific knowledge for the true ends of civilisation.

I had an opportunity of expressing this view in its philosophical setting when in 1929 I was invited to take the post vacated by Principal J. Estlin Carpenter in Manchester College, Oxford. This invitation gave me an opportunity to lecture to the students of the University of Oxford on Comparative Religion. During this visit, I had the privilege of giving the Hibbert Lectures on *An Idealist View of Life* to large audiences at the Universities of London and of Manchester. These lectures state my views on some of the ultimate problems of philosophy. They take into account the changes in the intellectual climate of the world, the crisis through which religion and social life are passing. The days of external ceremonial religion which can co-exist with a deceitful paganism are over. Men are asking for reality in religion. They want to penetrate to the depths of life, tear away the veils that hide the primordial reality and learn what is essential for life, for truth, and righteousness. The decay of dogmatic, mechanical religion led to the rise of a number of substitutes of modes of escape, but they do not show an adequate appreciation of the natural profundity of the human soul. Secular wisdom is not a substitute for religion.

Modern civilisation seemed to me to suffer from the same defect of being soulless. Politics and economics do not take their direction from ethics and religion. If the lost 'soul' is to be restored to human life, a new vital religion which does not require us to surrender the rights of reason, which even wholly free and disillusioned spirits can adopt, must be developed.

Religion is not a creed or a code but an insight into reality. If we confuse it with an intellectual view, we will justify the ancient practice of armed societies fighting for different versions of God's nature. The founders of religion, the saints and sages, have all been prophetic souls, who had direct acquaintance with spiritual reality, in and behind that which our senses perceive.

Spiritual certainty is conveyed by spiritual knowledge, which is not merely perceptual or conceptual. This knowledge is not a-logical but super-logical. It is called integral insight or intuitive knowledge. Hegel and the rationalists are not quite right in giving the supreme position to reason in the sense of critical intelligence. The drift of our age and its ruling methods of work support a scientific rationalism. The demands of our civilisation direct the attention of its workers so energetically and exclusively to that which is nearest at hand, to the investigation and practical application of our material resources. Such intensive concentration on the empirical and the technical is perhaps unique in the history of civilisation. That it has benefited mankind enormously is beyond question. But even those who adopt the methods and conceptions of exact and descriptive sciences are obliged to raise the further question of the limitations and value of scientific knowledge itself. While the theories of science are useful as tools for the control of nature, they cannot be said to reveal what reality is. Electrons and protons do not clear up the mystery of reality. Besides, God and soul cannot be treated as mathematical equations. Our deepest convictions, for which we are sometimes willing to die, are not the results of rational calculation.

The decisive experiences of personal life cannot be comprehended in formulas. Their driving power is in those urgent and intimate contacts with reality which convey to us deep certainties which transform our lives. Even a scientific rationalism requires us to admit the actuality of such experiences, and the phenomenal and incomplete character of merely scientific knowledge. The fact of this integral or intuitive knowledge tells us that we are not helplessly shut out from an insight into reality by the constitution of our minds.

The whole course of Hindu philosophy is a continuous affirmation of the truth that insight into reality does not come through analytical intellect, though it is accessible to the human mind in its integrality. In this conviction Hindu thinkers are supported by many others, including Plato and Plotinus, St. Paul and St. Augustine, Luther and Pascal. The very nature of the cosmic process as a perpetual creation of novelty, which is adopted by modern science, points to the need of intuition. Life is not a simple geometrical pattern. The essence of life is creativity. It is a living creation of something new, not a dead connection of cause and effect. The inner compulsion which lies behind that which is visible to our eyes is an urge to create, to generate. to make alive, to bring forth something new out of the hidden treasure of being. We shall never be able to analyse the sources of the creative spirit. If the real is a genuine becoming, then the highest knowledge can only be an insight. Yet there is enough of rationality in this insight. There is no break in the chain of real connection, though our limited vision may not be able to penetrate to the series of causes and effects. The world is creative activity but a continuous one and a rational one. While the rationality of the world is transparent to the intellect, its mysteriousness can be grasped only by intuition.

Intuitive knowledge, however, is not opposed to intellectual knowledge as Bergson sometimes makes us believe. Intuition is not a sensual thrill or an emotional debauch. In intuitive knowledge, intellect plays a considerable part. If intuition is unsupported by intellect, it will lapse into self-satisfied obscurantism. Intuition assumes the continuity and unity of all experience. An intellectual search for the ultimate cause may lead us to an idea of God. Intuition tells us that the idea is not merely an idea but a fact. The prophet souls, the religious geniuses intuit cosmic truths which cannot be communicated except imperfectly. The intellectual creeds are such imperfect expressions and therefore sometimes seem to be conflicting one with another.

The end of man is to let the spirit in him permeate his whole being, his soul, flesh, and affections. He attains his deepest self by losing his selfish ego. Man is not a mere sum of his instincts and desires. He seeks to be a single indivisible unity or organism. Dissatisfaction and unrest accompany every breach in organic wholeness. There is always a tension between what we are and what we wish to become. The human self is a temporary unstable organisation oscillating between the matter which offers the possibility of existence and the spirit which moulds it into significant being. It strives after integration.

Integrated lives are the saved ones. They possess the joy unspeakable, the peace that passeth understanding. Our earthly joys would pale before that spiritual bliss like electric lamps before the morning sun.

The new society will be built by those who have deepened their personalities and integrated their lives. The imperfect social order is a challenge to those who have achieved inner strength and integrity. They by their self-sacrificing will contribute to the reign of God, of love and of virtue on earth. No individual is really saved until society is perfected. If the historical process is a burden from which the soul attempts to free itself, it can free itself only when the historical process reaches its fulfilment. The stronger individuals help the weaker ones until all are saved. Universal salvation is the aim of the historical process, and when the goal is reached the process disappears. The temporal becomes the eternal.

During the course of history, which is the translation of one specific possibility of the Infinite Spirit, the latter is envisaged by us as the Divine principle controlling the course of this historical succession. God is not the great silent sea of infinity in which the individuals lose themselves but the Divine person who inspires the process first, last, and without ceasing.

To say that God created the world is an understatement. He is creating now and for all time. History is in this sense the epic of the Divine will, a revelation of God. The Divine works and shines through the earthly medium. In Hindu religion the Divine is said to be the Kavi or the Poet, the maker or the creator. God as person is deeply concerned in the affairs of this world. He is the friend, judge, and the redeemer of mankind. God is the Absolute spirit, timeless and unchanging, from the cosmic or human end. He is the way in which the Absolute not only appears to and is known by us, but also the way in which it works in the cosmic process. The Absolute is at once the sum and source of limitless possibilities. One of these possibilities is being actualised in the cosmic process. To this possibility which is in course of accomplishment, the Absolute assumes the form of a God who is guiding the world with a previous knowledge of its general plan and direction. God is not a figment of our minds. God is a real symbol of the Absolute reality, an aspect of the Absolute in its relation to this specific possibility which is being actualised. He is not a distorted reflection of the Absolute but, as Leibniz says, a phenomenon well founded in the reality. When there is a complete identity between God and the world, that is, when God's purpose is fulfilled, when all individual spirits are perfected, God Himself will relapse into the Absolute, 'creation being thus at once ransomed and annulled by the cessation of the impulse to individuate'. The lapse of the world does not take away from the infinite reality of the Absolute spirit.

This, in brief, is the view that I set forth at some length in my Hibbert Lectures, and I am grateful for the very warm reception that they had. Distinguished philosophers of Europe and America, including Samuel Alexander and Bertrand Russell, J. H. Muirhead and J. S. Mackenzie, W. R. Inge and L. P. Jacks, Rabindranath Tagore and Sir Herbert Samuel, welcomed it in the most generous terms.

Some of the sermons and occasional addresses which I gave while I was at Oxford are brought together in a small book *East and West in Religion.* The main theme of these addresses is that religion consists in doing justice, in loving mercy, and in making our fellow-creatures happy. A saint is not a stained glass image but one who works for his fellow-men and endeavours to establish a new relation of loving-kindness among them. He regards an individual's need as a sufficient claim on his generosity. We must believe in the equality of men not only in the soul but in the flesh. It is true that we cannot fall in love with a telephone directory. Love of humanity must be defined in terms of the men and women with whom we are brought into contact.

It was a great experience for me to preach from Christian pulpits in Oxford and Birmingham, in Manchester and Liverpool. It heartened me to know that my addresses were liked by Christian audiences. Referring to my sermon on *Revolution Through Suffering*, an Oxford daily observed, 'Though the Indian preacher had the marvellous power to weave a magic web of thought, imagination, and language, the real greatness of his sermon resides in some indefinable spiritual quality which arrests attention, moves the heart, and lifts us into an ampler air'.

IV. LIFE'S PROBLEMS

Those to whom life has been kind should not accept this good fortune as a matter of course. If one is allowed to lead a secure life while so many around who deserve better are confined to miserable surroundings and subjected to tragic blows, it is one's duty to think continually of those who were denied the privileges one had. My position as a teacher brought me into close relations with young men and women in the plastic years of their lives. The subject of philosophy, which is not primarily utilitarian in its aim, is a great instrument of liberal education. Its aim is one of elevating man above worldliness, of making him superior to circumstances, of liberating his spirit from the thraldom of material things. Philosophy claims to implant in the minds of those who are of a nature to profit by its teachings and influence a taste for those things which the world cannot give and cannot take away. If properly pursued, it arms us against failure, against sorrow and calamity, against boredom and discouragement. It may not prepare us for success if we mean by it accumulation of material wealth. But it helps us to love those aims and ideals, the things beyond all price on which the generality of men who aim at success do not set their hearts. To form men is the object of philosophy.

In the hours I was privileged to spend with my pupils, it was my ambition to educate them to a belief in a spiritual and ethical universe. If the central truths of mysticism and charity, inwardness and love are brought home to our hearts and thoughts, the temptations to irreligion which assail us in later life will have little power to overcome us. It is essential to awaken in one's pupils a feeling of need for a silent hour, a time of pure refreshment for heart and spirit, for self-communion, which will help them to collect their thoughts, reassemble their personalities and find themselves. In that silence we hear the still voices of the soul with its plaintive cry of the prisoner for freedom, of the wanderer for home, the cry of the finite for the infinite. Religion is what we do with ourselves when we are alone. In every one of us is a secret shrine where no one could intrude, to which we must retire as often as possible and discover what our true self is as distinct from the appearance we present to the world outside. Most of us are self-deceivers and constant examination alone can save us. Silent communion is an essential part of all worship. The Book of Revelation has a striking phrase that, as the seer watched the angels worshipping before the throne of God, suddenly 'there was silence in Heaven for the space of half an hour'. The strains of music ceased; the voices of the heavenly choir were stilled. That silence was not a dead one but pulsing with life, when the angels ceased to speak but waited in silence to hear the voice of spirit. In that stillness we come close to reality, become aware of how best we could make our life an offering to the Divine.

Worship does not consist in fasts and prayers, but in the offering of a pure and contrite heart. The musk is in the deer but it thinks that the fragrance comes from outside and so hunts for it restlessly. God is in us and we have only to turn within to realise the truth. There is a Sanskrit verse which says that the thoughtless man dives into deep lakes, penetrates into jungles, ascends steep hills in search of flowers for the worship of God while the one lotus which he can offer is his own mind. Man must make himself a living sacrifice. We cannot offer anything unclean or impure, maimed or mutilated to God. 'The temple of God is holy which temple ye are'. Out of the confusion around us we have to devise a destiny and make it manifest through all the twists and turns of accident. Otherwise life becomes a meaningless succession of irrelevant episodes unconnected with any specific purpose, springing from nothing and returning to nothing. What gives value and meaning to life is a purpose steadily pursued through the obstacles that hinder its living growth. Interest, meaning, purpose, value, are qualities given to events by the individual mind, while chance provides the occasions for the application of these values. In these silent hours of self-communion we strive to free ourselves from the suffocating routine, from the masks and mummeries of existence, cleanse our thoughts, and create within ourselves a clean heart and a single mind. *Yoga*, which has for its aim the achievement of the closest correspondence between the inner mind and the outer life, uses as its means silence, meditation, self-recollection.

I have been privileged to learn that my work has not been altogether in vain. A few men and women were enabled to regard the fundamental truth as something to be absorbed into one's thought, incorporated into one's being. Only humanity which expresses itself in peace of mind and patience with all makes human life worth living, and is of more value than health or wealth. The truly great are not those who have more money or brains or higher social position. God does not think less of people because they are poor or unintelligent. What matters is whether we have been kind to others and honest and sincere with ourselves and in our intimate relations with others. People richly endowed with physical health and material possessions are seen wrestling with care and suffering. They may appear in drawing-rooms with smiles pinned to their faces while their hearts are broken with pain. They use their power and wealth to hide from themselves their real state and by concentrating on outer achievements satisfy certain of their impulses. But deep down they understand that something is amiss with them. They feel it to be a particular unkindness of the universe that no one should stick to them, that they should become estranged from their own children, that they never succeed in forming a permanent centre and that as they grow older, they grow more and more lonely. Soon they find that life is meaningless to them, and their eyes show that dumb, wondering fear which we sometimes see in the eyes of animals, indicating a deep melancholy, an ultimate sadness. We see in their eyes, in spite of their lively gestures and shrill voices, a harassed look, as if this world were not their real home, as if they had come from some far-off place and could not get back. A nameless sadness weighs them down and they seem to grow indifferent to every feeling except a faint yearning to be at peace and dead. To the eye that has learnt to read the heart, their frivolous excitement, their gaiety and laughter is only a mask. The fact that they are ill at ease indicates a state of unbalance. They suffer, because they struggle to escape from the incoherent, the unmeaning, the enslaving to coherence, significance, and freedom. The nearer we are to the awakening, the more desolate do we feel. The soul is laden with the sense of guilt, of the feeling that one ought to have done better, and with a longing for liberation. The sadness tends to set in the direction of seeking a possible solution, a true friend, who can guide the soul, as parents guide their children. Blessed are they that mourn; that suffer and weep. The heart that aches is the heart which loves. The more tender it is, the more does it suffer. The grief of the large-hearted is too deep even for tears. We can buy immunity from suffering only by giving up life's greatest good, by hardening the heart. The story of the saint with a crown of gold has a point. When he went to heaven and saw there all the other saints wearing their jewelled crowns, while he himself was given a crown of gold without any jewels, he asked, 'Why has my crown no jewels'? The angel replied, 'Because you provided none. Those jewels are the tears that saints have shed on earth. You shed none'. 'How could I', he asked, 'when I was so happy in the love of God'? 'It is much', said the angel. 'Here is your crown, and it is made of gold; but jewels are for those who wept'. It is by suffering that we understand. The condition of true human life is to suffer pain and endure loneliness. Only those who live outward lives without being touched to their inward depths can escape suffering.

Often suffering is not punishment but discipline. When the great blow falls, when we stand in our darkest hour, shocked, baffled, defeated for the moment, when life has completely lost its savour, when we are tempted to cry 'O God, art thou dead?' or with one mightier, 'My God, why hast thou forsaken me?' when we hear no response even to such a cry of despair, when utter silence faces us, when the foundations slip away and the world seems to be cracking all about us, we have to bear it all, face the storm, cling to hope and believe in love. All this means suffering and it is through suffering that we learn and grow. By enduring pain we show the triumph of mind over matter, and the suffering becomes a means for growth in grace. When once anchorage is secured and life disciplined, and permitted by spirit, suffering is turned into bliss. The fear of suffering gives place to the courage to suffer. The path to bliss is found to be through pain which man consents to take upon himself.

The life of each one of us touches the lives of others at many points. We draw health and strength, comfort and encouragement from our intercourse with them. There are some to whom we have never turned in vain for sympathy and help. Such people who light fires in dark rooms are the salt of the earth. All too often we take their love and friendship for granted. We do not realise how much we owe to them, though there can be no repayment for tenderness, for sympathy, for gratitude. It asks for no reward or return. Where genuine love is present, a person desires but to give, not to sell, to receive as a pure gift, not to earn. In terms of spiritual currency, love is greater than justice, who is only a blind goddess. If the beloved sees the slightest merit in it, one would give away all he has and is and be ready to be misunderstood, ridiculed, reviled, persecuted, and wounded to the core. No devotion, no sacrifice, is too great. When the soul seems dead and all the world a wilderness, when our hearts are dry and brains barren, what brings us hope and solace is not analysis or criticism but love and friendship. It is these that sweep men into new courses of life. They are greater than wealth, greater than fame, far greater than culture. Even the mighty of the earth can do no more while the poorest are capable of them. They do not depend on power or riches. They need neither hands nor feet. They shine through the eyes and give warmth through a word or a smile. The touch of a compassionate hand often illuminates one like a lightning-flash in the darkness. Profound influences are wrought by creative minds by a light gesture or a brief conversation. The fund of humanity and idealism, locked up in human hearts unreleased or scarcely released, is released and overflows.

This human and intimately personal life seemed to me to be more important than that of a pedantic scholar or a dull dispenser of thought. An instinct to stand by the weak and the helpless must always be an essential part of a refined nature. No man knows another. How, then, can he judge what he does not know or understand? We know only the words and actions of others. We cannot read their thoughts, their subconscious mind. We have no clue to the secret recesses of the soul, the silent passions with which their hearts are bursting. Unless a man lives through another's experience, he cannot realise what it is like. Besides, whose life is so clean, whose character is so spotless that he can sit in judgement on others? Few will escape punishment if a method of spiritual vivisection is applied to all men. Most of us find ourselves in absurd positions when some overmastering passion reduces us to unreason. We are like birds of the forest, beating our wings in vain against the bars of the cage. Judgement is what is most hateful. Jesus, when he was confronted by the woman taken in adultery, turned not from her, but from those who sought to condemn her. He was disgusted at the foulness of their minds, at the sensuousness of their souls, at the indecency of their attitude to the poor human being. In the presence of all that vileness, that cruel malignant criticism, the only thing that was real was his love. Nothing shall tempt true men to feel contempt for any or superior to any. Deep down in one's heart one knows that one is quite as other men are, as futile and as human. Most men will be criminal when tempted or heroes when inspired. We are moulded into strange shapes through ignorance and circumstances. Not all men are capable of loosening themselves from organic urges which seem to master them, though man alone, among the creatures we know of, is capable of liberating himself by means of spiritual initiative from the blind primordial urges. Most of us are the slaves of our passions. When under their control it is impossible for us to see objects in their true light. We believe whatever accords with our feelings. It is therefore the duty of every genuine soul to insist on the good side and ignore the opposite. There is an unquenched spark of the divine fire in the worst villain. The secrets of eternity are found in all though they become manifest in some.

A friend of mine, who has known me well for over twenty years, made a comment rather sarcastically that I am incapable of indignation, that I am foolproof, that I suffer gladly not only fools but the 'sinful'. I am afraid that this observation is not untrue. It is not easy to know the difference between good men and bad. Ideas may be theoretically divided into good and bad, but not men and women, for each of us contains, in himself or herself, in varying degrees, the good and the bad, the high and the low, the true and the false. Besides, society has queer notions about right and wrong. Unorthodox personal relationships are wrong, while acts involving whole nations in war are right. Cruelty, treachery, and exploitation are condoned, while loving the wrong person not wisely but too well is condemned, though the latter is only a misfortune, not a crime. It is easier to make saints out of libertines than out of prudes and Pharisees. The infinite pathos of life calls for infinite understanding. What the 'sinful' need is not abuse and criticism. They yearn to be understood; they long for a little comfort, for respect and rest. When they stand bewildered, when their nerves are stretched to the breaking-point by the strain of their own misdeeds and the contempt of the world, what they need is someone in whom they could trust wholeheartedly. Human affection is indispensable to them. Not compassion, which is a form of contempt, but a tender regard which can overlook the past and help the future. There is no need to tread the road to ruin to the end. By a change in mental and spiritual disposition, we can check the rapid decline and prepare for ourselves a new destiny. It depends on us whether we take the rake's line downhill to destruction or the pilgrim's progress upward. I have every confidence in the power of love to evoke the right change. The friend takes the place of an analyst, who succeeds in removing the blind urges and fixations by exposing them to view. Some are silent, because they have nothing to say; others are silent because they have no one to say it to. To a true friend, even the most perverse will pour out their hearts and thus get relieved. He is not afraid to face the dismal reality and see it as it really is. For the soul of man is essentially a lovable thing. No human being is innately wicked or incapable of improvement. No one can succeed in stifling the soul or drugging or deceiving it for all time. The best side of a human being is his real side, his true self. Such an attitude to life makes one turn a blind eye to human inertia and weakness. 'Love', says St. Paul, 'is never glad when others go wrong, love is gladdened by goodness, always slow to expose, always eager to believe the best, always hopeful, always patient'.

It is one of the hardest things to criticise the actions of those of whom we are fond, but it is what one expects and longs for from true friendship. Every time the courage is found, the bond becomes stronger. A true friend not only seeks and inquires, but probes and pierces, digs his fists into the heart, though this process of ruthless unveiling or pitiless exposure is most painful and costing. But then the only way to attain peace of mind and inward harmony is by means of knowledge and adjustment. We must be completely sincere with ourselves and then adjust ourselves to circumstances. We must never lie to ourselves. If it is true that we do not know perfectly until we love perfectly, it is also true that we do not love perfectly until we know perfectly. A sense of shame holds us back. We feel that we would be giving ourselves away, would be disclosing our own disastrous inadequacy, would be betraying ourselves, but such feelings are out of place in true love, which to the conventional will appear strange, peculiar, exacting, hard at times to recognise as love. It is no use to feel awkward or constrained. So long as that feeling is there, one is not quite oneself. A friend's view is not a critical or a hostile judgement. The things we suffer from lose their power when once they are given utterance. So long as we do not get at the truth, we will lose ourselves in the outer and lie empty within. To surrender our vanity and love of ourselves and expose the naked ribs of reality may mean anguish and sacrifice but it is worth it. Truth, according to the *Mahābhārata*, is penance and sacrifice of a high order. It says: 'Truth is always natural with the good. Truth is eternal duty. One should reverentially bow unto truth. Truth is the highest refuge. Truth is duty, truth is penance, truth is *yoga*. Truth is the eternal Brahman. Truth is said to be—sacrifice of a high order. Everything rests on Truth'. Truth and reality, not falsehood and semblance, are the foundations of lasting friendship, of spiritual life. These friendly revelations have little in common with the exhibitions of spiritual nudism where the sinner speaks exultingly of the depths of sin from which he has emerged to emphasise the heights to which he has attained.

It is the good fortune of some to get the confidence of a few of the unhappy men, the lonely ones, the misfits, who are found in abundance in this world. Those persecuted by society, those reeds shaken by the wind are more appealing than the successful, for we see in them the mystery, the beauty, and the sadness of life. Though there is no special virtue in the hopeless and the outcast, we see in them the struggle of the unconquerable spirit of man with fate or circumstance. The spirit is never broken, however much it may be bent or beaten. We do not know what confidence is, where it comes from, the head or the heart, through what channels it communicates with others. We do not know whether it is visible in the eye or audible in the spoken word. It cannot be acquired through much study and thought. It is a magic gift granted to one and denied to another. I soon discovered that a small particle of this invaluable gift had been granted to me through no merit of mine. There is a queer impression that Hindus, especially those who talk about philosophy, are more domesticated in the world of spirit. Thanks to it, my correspondence includes letters asking advice and help in every conceivable perplexity. Some of these letters are absurd, some pathetic, and some both. Cranks and faddists fond of their own remedies for the ills of this world are a good many of these correspondents. But now and again one chances on long letters from some old friends, others who through communications have come near, still others who are complete strangers, about their own travails or those of their friends. My relations have little to do with distinctions of age, class or calling, rank or education. It pleases me to know that to some lonely or enslaved souls I was perhaps the only or the first person to show any sympathy or understanding. At times my interest in other people has been so strong and spontaneous that it was misunderstood. There have been cases where the results I expected never arose in spite of my best endeavours. They only indicate that I have not been able to handle these problems with either wisdom or adequacy.

Yet withal, I am happy that I have been brought into human contact with quite a number of my fellow-men. I do not believe that there is any such thing as chance or mere coincidence. Desires work unseen through forces of nature. Apparently unimportant happenings sometimes play an unexpected part in our lives. There is such a thing as spiritual gravitation. We can never wholly tell why certain people attract us. We cannot help responding to them and finding them interesting. Beauty can never understand itself, says Goethe. Attraction also is only partly explained. Certain persons attach with devotion and why they do so cannot be accounted for. The real causes of our likes and dislikes are usually hidden deep down in the obscure recesses of our nature. They have little to do with reason or logic and we cannot account for them. Wonderful have been the experiences vouchsafed me in this life. Through them the deeps of my own nature have been opened to me in a surprising manner. Through them my life has become more intimately connected with the surrounding social order, more complicated, more difficult, and yet far richer and fuller. They have forged links of human affection and regard, given me high joys as well as deep sorrows, and have become inextricably interwoven with the fabric of my life. They in a sense made for genuine fulfilment of destiny.

I have had my own share of anxiety, trouble, and sorrow, but I have had blessings, too, more than I deserve, the chief being the affection and kindness which I receive in abundance from other people. For all these a thank-offering is due. Truly religious souls from Buddha and Christ down to lesser mortals, in spite of gross defects of nature, of mind and heart, have striven to lighten the load of humanity, to strengthen the hopes without which it would have fainted and fallen in its difficult journey. If we are to imitate in some small measure their example, we must help the weak and comfort the unhappy. The perception that casts a shadow over one's existence is that one is not able to take a larger share of the burden of pain that lies upon the world, with its poor and lowly, with its meek and suffering. It does not matter if one has to live one's days in silence, if only it is given in them to smile at a child sometimes, to comfort another human soul in a way that will cheer him and put new hope into his heart.

PART II. THE HISTORICAL VIEW: INDIAN PHILOSOPHY

Indian Philosophy: General Characteristics *

Philosophy in India is essentially spiritual. It is the intense spirituality of India and not any great political structure or social organisation that it has developed, that has enabled it to resist the ravages of time and the accidents of history. External invasions and internal dissensions came very near crushing its civilisation many times in its history. The Greek and the Scythian, the Persian and the Mogul, the French and the English have in turn attempted to suppress it, and yet it has its head held high. India has not been finally subdued, and its old flame of spirit is still burning. Throughout its life it has been living with one purpose. It has fought for truth and against error. It may have blundered, but it did what it felt able and called upon to do. The history of Indian thought illustrates the endless quest of the mind, ever old, ever new.

The spiritual motive dominates life in India. Indian philosophy has its interest in the haunts of men, and not in supralunar solitudes. It takes its origin in life, and enters back into life after passing through the schools. The great works of Indian philosophy do not have that ex cathedra character which is so prominent a feature of the later criticisms and commentaries. The *Bhagavadgītā* and the Upaniṣads are not remote from popular belief. They are the great literature of the country, and at the same time vehicles of the great systems of thought. The *Purāṇas* contain the truth dressed up in myths and stories, to suit the weak understanding of the majority. The hard task of interesting the multitude in metaphysics is achieved in India.

The founders of philosophy strive for a socio-spiritual refor-

* From the Introduction, *Indian Philosophy* I (London: George Allen & Unwin, 1923), pp. 24–49.

mation of the country. When the Indian civilisation is called a Brāhmanical one, it only means that its main character and dominating motives are shaped by its philosophical thinkers and religious minds, though these are not all of Brāhmin birth. The idea of Plato that philosophers must be the rulers and directors of society is practised in India. The ultimate truths are truths of spirit, and in the light of them actual life has to be refined.

Religion in India is not dogmatic. It is a rational synthesis which goes on gathering into itself new conceptions as philosophy progresses. It is experimental and provisional in its nature, attempting to keep pace with the progress of thought. The common criticism that Indian thought, by its emphasis on intellect, puts philosophy in the place of religion, brings out the rational character of religion in India. No religious movement has ever come into existence without developing as its support a philosophic content. Mr. Havell observes: 'In India, religion is hardly a dogma, but a working hypothesis of human conduct, adapted to different stages of spiritual development and different conditions of life'. Whenever it tended to crystallise itself in a fixed creed, there were set up spiritual revivals and philosophic reactions which threw beliefs into the crucible of criticism, vindicated the true, and combated the false. Again and again, we shall observe, how when traditionally accepted beliefs become inadequate, nay false, on account of changed times, and the age grows out of patience with them, the insight of a new teacher, a Buddha or a Mahāvīra, a Vyāsa, or a Śaṁkara supervenes, stirring the depths of spiritual life. These are doubtless great moments in the history of Indian thought, times of inward testing and vision, when at the summons of the spirit's breath, blowing where it listeth and coming whence no one knows, the soul of man makes a fresh start and goes forth on a new venture. It is the intimate relation between the truth of philosophy and the daily life of people that makes religion always alive and real.

The problems of religion stimulate the philosophic spirit. The Indian mind has been traditionally exercised over the questions of the nature of Godhead, the end of life, and the relation of the individual to the universal soul. Though philosophy in India has not as a rule completely freed itself from the fascinations of religious speculation, yet the philosophical discussions have not been hampered by religious forms. The two were not confused. On account of the close connection between theory and practice, doctrine and life, a philosophy which could not stand the test of life, not in the pragmatistic but the larger sense of the term, had no chance of survival. To those who realise the true kinship between life and theory, philosophy becomes a way of life, an approach to spiritual realisation. There has been no teaching, not even the Sāṁkhya, which remained a mere word of mouth or dogma of schools. Every doctrine is turned into a passionate conviction, stirring the heart of man and quickening his breath.

It is untrue to say that philosophy in India never became self-conscious or critical. Even in its early stages rational reflection tended to correct religious belief. Witness the advance of religion implied in the progress from the hymns of the Veda to the Upaniṣads. When we come to Buddhism, the philosophic spirit has already become that confident attitude of mind which in intellectual matters bends to no outside authority and recognises no limit to its enterprise, unless it be as the result of logic, which probes all things, tests all things, and follows fearlessly wherever the argument leads. When we reach the several *darśanas* or systems of thought, we have mighty and persistent efforts at systematic thinking. How completely free from traditional religion and bias the systems are will be obvious from the fact that the Sāṁkhya is silent about the existence of God, though certain about its theoretical indemonstrability. Vaiśeṣika and Yoga, while they admit a supreme being, do not consider him to be the creator of the universe, and Jaimini refers to God only to deny his providence and moral government of the world. The early Buddhist systems are known to be indifferent to God, and we have also the materialist *Cārvākas*, who deny God, ridicule the priests, revile the Vedas, and seek salvation in pleasure.

The supremacy of religion and of social tradition in life does not hamper the free pursuit of philosophy. It is a strange paradox, and yet nothing more than the obvious truth that while the social life of an individual is bound by the rigours of caste, he is free to roam in the matter of opinion. Reason freely questions and criticises the creeds in which men are born. That is why the heretic, the sceptic, the unbeliever, the rationalist and the freethinker, the materialist and the hedonist all flourish in the soil of India. The *Mahābhārata* says: 'There is no *muni* who has not an opinion of his own'.

All this is evidence of the strong intellectuality of the Indian mind which seeks to know the inner truth and the law of all sides of human activity. This intellectual impulse is not confined to philosophy and theology, but extends over logic and grammar, rhetoric and language, medicine and astronomy, in fact all arts and sciences, from architecture to zoology. Everything useful to life or interesting to mind becomes an object of inquiry and criticism. It will give an idea of the all comprehensive character of intellectual life, to know that even such minutiae as the breeding of horses and the training of elephants had their own *śāstras* and literature.

The philosophic attempt to determine the nature of reality may start either with the thinking self or the objects of thought. In India the interest of philosophy is in the self of man. Where the vision is turned outward, the rush of fleeting events engages the mind. In India '*Ātmānam viddhi*', know the self, sums up the law and the prophets. Within man is the spirit that is the centre of everything. Psychology and ethics are the basal sciences. The life of mind is depicted in all its mobile variety and subtle play of light and shade. Indian psychology realised the value of concentration and looked upon it as the means for the perception of the truth. It believed that there were no ranges of life or mind which could not be reached by a methodical training of will and knowledge. It recognised the close connexion of mind and body. The psychic experiences, such as telepathy and clairvoyance, were considered to be neither abnormal nor miraculous. They are not the products of diseased minds or inspiration from the gods, but powers which the human mind can exhibit under carefully ascertained conditions. The mind of man has the three aspects of the subconscious, the conscious, and the superconscious, and the 'abnormal' psychic phenomena, called by the different names of ecstasy, genius, inspiration, madness, are the workings of the superconscious mind. The Yoga system of philosophy deals especially with these experiences, though the other systems refer to them and utilise them for their purposes.

The metaphysical schemes are based on the data of the psychological science. The criticism that Western metaphysics is one-sided, since its attention is confined to the waking state alone, is not without its force. There are other states of consciousness as much entitled to consideration as the waking. Indian thought takes into account the modes of waking, dreaming, and dreamless sleep. If we look upon the waking consciousness as the whole, then we get realistic, dualistic, and pluralistic conceptions of metaphysics. Dream consciousness when exclusively studied leads us to subjectivist doctrines. The state of dreamless sleep inclines us to abstract and mystical theories. The whole truth must take all the modes of consciousness into account.

The dominance of interest in the subjective does not mean that in objective sciences India had nothing to say. If we refer to the actual achievements of India in the realm of positive science, we shall see that the opposite is the case. Ancient Indians laid the foundations of mathematical and mechanical knowledge. They measured the land, divided the year, mapped out the heavens, traced the course of the sun and the planets through the zodiacal belt, analysed the constitution of matter, and studied the nature of birds and beasts, plants and seeds.[1] 'Whatever conclusions we may arrive at as to the original source of the first astronomical ideas current in the world, it is probable that to the Hindus is due the invention of algebra and its application to astronomy and geometry. From them also the Arabs received not only their first conceptions of algebraic analysis, but also those invaluable numerical symbols

[1] We may quote a passage which is certainly not less than 2,000 years before the birth of Copernicus, from the *Aitareya Brāhmaṇa:* 'The sun never sets nor rises. When people think to themselves the sun is setting, he only changes about after reaching the end of the day, and makes night below and day to what is on the other side. Then when people think he rises in the morning, he only shifts himself about after reaching the end of the night, and makes day below and night to what is on the other side. In fact he never does set at all'. Haug's Edition, iii. 44; C.U. III, II. 1–3. Even if this be folklore, it is interesting.

and decimal notation now current everywhere in Europe, which have rendered untold service to the progress of arithmetical science'.[2] 'The motions of the moon and the sun were carefully observed by the Hindus, and with such success that their determination of the moon's synodical revolution is a much more correct one than the Greeks ever achieved. They had a division of the ecliptic into twenty-seven and twenty-eight parts, suggested evidently by the moon's period in days and seemingly their own. They were particularly conversant with the most splendid of the primary planets; the period of Jupiter being introduced by them, in conjunction with those of the sun and the moon into the regulation of their calendar in the form of the cycle of sixty years, common to them and the Chaldeans'. It is now admitted that the Hindus at a very early time conceived and developed the two sciences of logic and grammar. Wilson writes: 'In medicine, as in astronomy and metaphysics, the Hindus once kept pace with the most enlightened nations of the world; and they attained as thorough a proficiency in medicine and surgery as any people whose acquisitions are recorded, and as indeed was practicable, before anatomy was made known to us by the discoveries of modern inquirers'. It is true that they did not invent any great mechanical appliances. For this a kind Heaven, which gave them the great water-courses and abundant supplies of food, is responsible. Let us also remember that these mechanical inventions belong, after all, to the sixteenth century and after, by which time India had lost her independence and become parasitic. The day she lost her freedom and began to flirt with other nations, a curse fell on her and she became petrified. Till then she could hold her own even in arts, crafts, and industries, not to speak of mathematics, astronomy, chemistry, medicine, surgery, and those branches of physical knowledge practised in ancient times. She knew how to chisel stone, draw pictures, burnish gold, and weave rich fabrics. She developed all arts, fine and industrial, which furnish the conditions of civilised existence. Her ships crossed the oceans and her wealth brimmed over to Judea, Egypt and Rome. Her conceptions of man and society, morals and religion were remarkable for the time. We

[2] Monier Williams, *Indian Wisdom*, p. 184.

cannot reasonably say that the Indian people revelled in poetry and mythology, and spurned science and philosophy, though it is true that they were more intent on seeking the unity of things than emphasising their sharpness and separation.

The speculative mind is more synthetic, while the scientific one is more analytic, if such a distinction be permitted. The former tends to create cosmic philosophies which embrace in one comprehensive vision the origin of all things, the history of ages and the dissolution and decay of the world. The latter is inclined to linger over the dull particulars of the world and miss the sense of oneness and wholeness. Indian thought attempts vast, impersonal views of existence, and makes it easy for the critic to bring the charge of being more idealistic and contemplative, producing dreamy visionaries and strangers in the world, while Western thought is more particularist and pragmatistic. The latter depends on what we call the senses, the former presses the soul sense into the service of speculation. Once again it is the natural conditions of India that account for the contemplative turn of the Indian who had the leisure to enjoy the beautiful things of the world and express his wealth of soul in song and story, music and dance, rites and religions, undisturbed by the passions of the outer world. 'The brooding East', frequently employed as a term of ridicule, is not altogether without its truth.

It is the synthetic vision of India that has made philosophy comprehend several sciences which have become differentiated in modern times. In the West during the last hundred years or so several branches of knowledge till then included under philosophy, economics, politics, morals, psychology, education have been one by one sheared away from it. Philosophy in the time of Plato meant all those sciences which are bound up with human nature and form the core of man's speculative interests. In the same way in ancient Indian scriptures we possess the full content of the philosophic sphere. Latterly in the West philosophy became synonymous with metaphysics, or the abstruse discussions of knowledge, being, and value, and the complaint is heard that metaphysics has become absolutely theoretical, being cut off from the imaginative and the practical sides of human nature.

If we put the subjective interest of the Indian mind along

with its tendency to arrive at a synthetic vision, we shall see how monistic idealism becomes the truth of things. To it the whole growth of Vedic thought points; on it are based the Buddhistic and the Brāhmanical religions; it is the highest truth revealed to India. Even systems which announce themselves as dualistic or pluralistic seem to be permeated by a strong monistic character. If we can abstract from the variety of opinion and observe the general spirit of Indian thought, we shall find that it has a disposition to interpret life and nature in the way of monistic idealism, though this tendency is so plastic, living, and manifold that it takes many forms and expresses itself in even mutually hostile teachings. We may briefly indicate the main forms which monistic idealism has assumed in Indian thought, leaving aside detailed developments and critical estimates. This will enable us to grasp the nature and function of philosophy as understood in India. For our purposes monistic idealism is of four types: (1) Non-dualism or Advaitism; (2) Pure Monism; (3) Modified Monism; and (4) Implicit Monism.

Philosophy proceeds on the facts of experience. Logical reflection is necessary to ascertain whether the facts observed by one individual are accepted by all, or are only subjective in their character. Theories are accepted if they account for facts satisfactorily. We have already said that the facts of mind or consciousness were studied by the Indian thinkers with as much care and attention as the facts of the outer world are studied by our modern scientists. The philosophical conclusions of Advaitic monism are based on the data of psychological observation.

The activities of the self are assigned to the three states of waking, dreaming, and dreamless sleep. In dream states an actual concrete world is presented to us. We do not call that world real, since on waking we find that the dream world does not fit in with the waking world; yet relatively to the dream state the dream world is real. It is discrepancy from our conventional standards of waking life, and not any absolute knowledge of truth as subsisting by itself, that tells us that dream states are less real than the waking ones. Even waking reality is a relative one. It has no permanent existence, being only a correlate of the waking state. It disappears in dream and sleep. The waking consciousness and the world disclosed to it are related to each other, depend on each other as the dream consciousness and the dream world are. They are not absolutely real, for in the words of Śaṁkara, while the 'dream-world is daily sublated, the waking world is sublated under exceptional circumstances'. In dreamless sleep we have a cessation of the empirical consciousness. Some Indian thinkers are of the opinion that we have in this condition an objectless consciousness. At any rate this is clear, that dreamless sleep is not a complete non-being or negation for such a hypothesis conflicts with the later recollection of the happy repose of sleep. We cannot help conceding that the self continues to exist, though it is bereft of all experience. There is no object felt and there can be none so long as the sleep is sound. The pure self seems to be unaffected by the flotsam and jetsam of ideas which rise and vanish with particular moods. 'What varies not, nor changes in the midst of things that vary and change is different from them'. The self which persists unchanged and is one throughout all the changes is different from them all. The conditions change, not the self. 'In all the endless months, years and small and great cycles, past and to come, this self-luminous consciousness alone neither rises nor ever sets'. An unconditioned reality where time and space along with all their objects vanish is felt to be real. It is the self which is the unaffected spectator of the whole drama of ideas related to the changing moods of waking, dreaming, and sleeping. We are convinced that there is something in us beyond joy and misery, virtue and vice, good and bad. The self 'never dies, is never born—unborn, eternal, everlasting, this ancient one can never be destroyed with the destruction of the body. If the slayer thinks he can slay, or if the slain thinks he is slain, they both do not know the truth, for the self neither slays nor is slain'.

In addition to the ever-identical self, we have also the empirical variety of objects. The former is permanent, immutable, the latter impermanent and ever changing. The former is absolute, being independent of all objects; the latter changes with the moods.

How are we to account for the world? The empirical variety is there bound in space, time, and cause. If the self is the one, the universal, the immutable, we find in the world a mass of particulars with opposed characters. We can only call it the not-self, the object of a subject. In no case is it real. The principal categories of the world of experience, time, space, and cause are self-contradictory. They are relative terms depending on their constituents. They have no real existence. Yet they are not non-existent. The world is there, and we work in it and through it. We do not and cannot know the why of this world. It is this fact of its inexplicable existence that is signified by the word *māyā*. To ask what is the relation between the absolute self and the empirical flux, to ask why and how it happens, that there are two, is to assume that everything has a why and a how. To say that the infinite becomes the finite or manifests itself as finite is on this view utter nonsense. The limited cannot express or manifest the unlimited. The moment the unlimited manifests itself in the limited, it itself becomes limited. To say that the absolute degenerates or lapses into the empirical is to contradict its absoluteness. No lapse can come to a perfect being. No darkness can dwell in perfect light. We cannot admit that the supreme, which is changeless, becomes limited by changing. To change is to desire or to feel a want, and it shows lack of perfection. The absolute can never become an object of knowledge, for what is known is finite and relative. Our limited mind cannot go beyond the bounds of time. space, and cause, nor can we explain these, since every attempt to explain them assumes them. Through thought, which is itself a part of the relative world, we cannot know the absolute self. Our relative experience is a waking dream. Science and logic are parts of it and products of it too. This failure of metaphysics is neither to be wept over nor to be laughed over, neither to be praised nor blamed, but understood. With a touching humility born of intellectual strength, a Plato, or a Nāgārjuna, a Kant or a Śamkara, declares that our thought deals with the relative, and has nothing to do with the absolute.

Though the absolute being is not known in the logical way, it is yet realised by all who strain to know the truth, as the reality in which we live, move, and have our being. Only through it can anything else be known. It is the eternal witness of all knowledge. The non-dualist contends that his theory is based on the logic of facts. The self is the inmost and deepest reality, felt by all, since it is the self of all things known and unknown too, and there is no knower to know it except itself. It is the true and the eternal, and there is nought beside it. As for the empirical ramifications which also exist, the non-dualist says, well, they are there, and there is an end of it. We do not know and cannot know "why". It is all a contradiction, and yet is actual. Such is the philosophical position of Advaita or non-dualism taken up by Gauḍapāda and Śaṁkara.

There are Advaitins who are dissatisfied with this view, and feel that it is no good covering up our confusion by the use of the word *māyā*. They attempt to give a more positive account of the relation between the perfect being absolutely devoid of any negativity, the immutable real, felt in the depths of experience and the world of change and becoming. To preserve the perfection of the one reality we are obliged to say that the world of becoming is not due to an addition of any element from outside, since there is nothing outside. It can only be by a diminution. Something negative like Plato's non-being or Aristotle's matter is assumed to account for change. Through the exercise of this negative principle, the immutable seems to be spread out in the moving many. Rays stream out of the sun which nevertheless did not contain them. *Māyā* is the name of the negative principle which lets loose the universal becoming, thereby creating endless agitation and perpetual disquiet. The flux of the universe is brought about by the apparent degradation of the immutable. The real represents all that is positive in becoming. The things of the world ever struggle to recover their reality, to fill up what is lacking in them, to shake off their individuality and separateness, but are prevented from doing so by their inner void, the negative *māyā* constituted by the interval between what they are and what they ought to be. If we get rid of *māyā*, suppress the tendency to duality, abolish the interval, fill up the deficit, and allow the disturbance to relax, space, time, and change reach back into pure being. As long as the original insufficiency of *māyā* prevails, things are condemned to be existent in space–time–cause world. *Māyā* is not a human construction. It is prior to our intellect and independent of it. It is verily the generator of things and intellects, the immense potentiality of the whole world. It is sometimes called the *prakṛti*. The alternations of generation and decay, the ever-repeated cosmic evolutions, all represent this fundamental deficit in which the world consists. The world of becoming is the interruption of being. *Māyā* is the reflection of reality. The world-process is not so much a translation of immutable being as its inversion. Yet the world of *māyā* cannot exist apart from pure being. There can be no movement, if there were not immutability, since movement is only a degradation of the immutable. The truth of the universal mobility is the immobile being.

As becoming is a lapse from being, so is *avidyā* or ignorance a fall from *vidyā* or knowledge. To know the truth, to apprehend reality, we have to get rid of *avidyā* and its intellectual moulds, which all crack the moment we try to force reality into them. This is no excuse for indolence of thought. Philosophy as logic on this view persuades us to give up the employment of the intellectual concepts which are relative to our practical needs and the world of becoming. Philosophy tells us that, so long as we are bound by intellect and are lost in the world of many, we shall seek in vain to get back to the simplicity of the one. If we ask the reason why there is *avidyā*, or *māyā*, bringing about a fall from *vidyā* or from being, the question cannot be answered. Philosophy as logic has here the negative function of exposing the inadequacy of all intellectual categories, pointing out how the objects of the world are relative to the mind that thinks them and possess no independent existence. It cannot tell us anything definite about either the immutable said to exist apart from what is happening in the world, or about *māyā*, credited with the production of the world. It cannot help us directly to the attainment of reality. It, on the other hand, tells us that to measure reality we have to distort it. It may perhaps serve the interests of truth when once it is independently ascertained. We can think it out, defend it logically, and help its propagation. The supporters of pure monism recognise a higher power than abstract intellect which enables us to feel the push of reality. We have to sink ourselves in the universal consciousness and make ourselves co-extensive with all that is. We do not then so much *think* reality as *live* it, do not so much *know* it as *become* it. Such an extreme monism, with its distinctions of logic and intuition, reality and the world of existence, we meet with in some Upanisads, Nāgārjuna and Saṁkara in his ultra-philosophical moods, Śrī Harsa and the Advaita Vedāntins, and echoes of it are heard in Parmenides and Plato, Spinoza and Plotinus, Bradley and Bergson, not to speak of the mystics, in the West.[3]

Whatever the being, pure and simple, may be to intuition, to intellect it is nothing more or less than an absolute abstraction. It is supposed to continue when every fact and form of existence is abolished. It is the residue left behind when abstraction is made from the whole world. It is a difficult exercise set to the thought of man to think away the sea and the earth, the sun and the stars, space and time, man and God. When an effort is made to abolish the whole universe, sublate all existence, nothing seems to remain for thought. Thought, finite and relational, finds to its utter despair that there is just nothing at all when everything existent is abolished. To the conceptual mind the central proposition of intuition, 'Being only is', means that there is just nothing at all. Thought, as Hegel said, can only work with determinate realities, concrete things. To it all affirmation implies negation, and vice versa. Every concrete is a becoming, combining being and non-being, positive and negative. So those who are not satisfied with the intuited being, and wish to have a synthesis capable of being attained by thought which has a natural instinct for the concrete, are attracted to a system of objective idealism. The concrete idealists try to put together the two concepts of pure being and apparent becoming in the single synthesis of God. Even extreme monists recognise that becoming depends on

[3] In the Sāṁkhya philosophy we have practically the same account of the world of experience, which does not in the least stain the purity of the witness self. Only a pluralistic prejudice which has no logical basis asserts itself, and we have a plurality of souls. When the pluralism collapses, as it does at the first touch of logic, the Sāṁkhya theory becomes identical with the pure monism here sketched.

being, though not vice versa. We get now a sort of refracted absolute, a God who has in Him the possibility of the world, combines in His nature the essence of all being, as well as of becoming, unity as well as plurality, unlimitedness and limitation. The pure being now becomes the subject, transforming itself into object and taking back the object into itself. Position, opposition, and composition, to use Hegelian expressions, go on in an eternal circular process. Hegel rightly perceives that the conditions of a concrete world are a subject and an object. These two opposites are combined in every concrete. The great God Himself has in Him the two antagonistic characters where the one is not only through the other, but is actually the other. When such a dynamic God eternally bound in the rotating wheel is asserted, all the degrees of existence, from the divine perfection up to vile dust, are automatically realised. The affirmation of God is the simultaneous affirmation of all degrees of reality between it and nothing. We have now the universe of thought constructed by thought, answering to thought and sustained by thought, in which subject and object are absorbed as moments. The relations of space, time, and cause are not subjective forms, but universal principles of thought. If on the view of pure monism we cannot understand the exact relation between identity and difference, we are here on better ground. The world is identity gone into difference. Neither is isolated from the other. God is the inner ground, the basis of identity; the world is the outer manifestation, the externalisation of self-consciousness.

Such a God, according to the theory of pure monism, is just the lapse from the absolute, with the least conceivable interval separating him from pure being or the absolute. It is the product of *avidyā* which is separated from *vidyā* by the least conceivable extent. In other words, this concrete God is *the highest product of our highest intelligence.* The pity is, that it is a *product* after all, and our intelligence, however near it approximates to *vidyā*, is not yet *vidyā*. This God has in him the maximum of being and the minimum of defect—still a defect. The first touch of *māyā*, the slightest diminution of absolute being, is enough to throw it into space and time, though this space and this time will be as near as possible to the absolute unextendedness and eternity. The absolute one is converted into the Creator God existent in some space, moving all things from within without stirring from His place. God is the absolute objectivised as something somewhere, a spirit that pushes itself into everything. He is being–non-being, Brahman-*Māyā*, subject-object, eternal force, the motionless mover of Aristotle, the absolute spirit of Hegel, the (absolute-relative) *Viśiṣṭādvaita* of Rāmānuja, the efficient as well as the final cause of the universe. The world is beginningless and endless, since the energising of God could not have begun and could never come to an end. It is its essential nature to be ever at unrest.

There is no doubt that this is the highest conception which thought can reach. If we follow to the end the natural movement of our intellect which tries to unify the things of the world and synthesise opposites, a principle of explanation which is neither pure being nor pure non-being, but something which combines both, is what we get. This concept is constructed by a compression of all things into the whole. Philosophy on this view is constructive in character, and is therefore positive in its nature and synthetic in its function. Even here logical understanding playing with abstractions shuts us from the concrete in which alone the abstractions live, move, and have their being. Thought as reason gets over the difficulties of logical understanding. Starting from the world of experience, we go up to the ultimate principle of God, and from the conception of the whole so gained we descend into details and review the parts. All logical dogmatisms which have confidence in the power of thought end with this conception of the world. The difficulty arises if we doubt the absoluteness of thought. May not our knowledge be relative to the requirements of the mind which unifies and divides? Perhaps for a mind differently shaped, knowledge may be different from what it is. Our present knowledge makes us think that all knowledge will be of this type, but when there are critics who dispute such an assertion, it is difficult to defend the position. Admitting that the conceptual plan of reality revealed to thought is true, still, it is sometimes urged, thought is not identical with reality. By compressing all concepts in o one, we do not go beyond concepts. A relation is only a part of the mind that relates. Even an infinitely superior mind is yet a mind and of the same mould as man's. The theory of modified monism is adopted by some Upaniṣads, and the *Bhagavadgītā*, some followers of Buddhism and Rāmānuja, if not Bādarāyaṇa. In the West Aristotle and Hegel stand out as witnesses to it.

According to the first view perfect being is real; unreal becoming is actual, though, we do not know why. According to the second, the world becoming is a precipitation (apparent) of pure being into space and time by the force of diminution or *māyā*. According to the third, the highest product we have is a synthesis of pure being and not-being in God. We are immediately under a logical necessity to affirm all intermediate degrees of reality. If pure being is dismissed as a concept useless so far as the world of experience is concerned and we also disregard as illogical the idea of a Creator God, then what exists is nothing more than a mere flux of becoming, ever aspiring to be something else than what it is. The main principle of Buddhism results. In the world of existence, on the hypothesis of modified monism, the specific characters of the degrees of intermediate reality are to be measured by the distance separating them from the integral reality. The common characters of all of them are existence in space and time. Closer attention reveals to us more and more special attributes. Admit the distinction between thinking reals and unthinking objects, and we have the dualistic philosophy of Madhva. Even this is fundamentally a monism so long as the reals are dependent (*paratantra*) on God, who alone is independent (*svatantra*). Emphasise the independence of the thinking beings, and we have pluralism according to Sāṁkhya, if only we do not worry about the existence of God which cannot be demonstrated. Add to it the plurality of the objects of the world, we have pluralistic realism, where even God becomes one real, however great or powerful, among others. In the discussions about the intermediate degrees of reality the unit of individuality seems to depend upon the fancy of the philosopher. And whether a system turns out atheistic or theistic is determined by the attention paid to the absolute under the aegis of which the drama of the universe is enacted. It sometimes shines out brilliantly with its light focussed in a God and at other times fades out. These are the different ways in which the mind of man reacts to the problems of the world according to its own peculiar constitution.

There is a cordial harmony between God and man in Indian thought, while the opposition between the two is more marked in the West. The mythologies of the peoples also indicate it. The myth of Prometheus, the representative man, who tries to help mankind by defending it against Zeus who desires to destroy the human race and supplant it with a new and better species, the story of the labours of Hercules who tries to redeem the world, the conception of Christ as the Son of Man, indicate that man is the centre of attention in the West. It is true that Christ is also called the Son of God, the eldest begotten who is to be sacrificed before a just God's anger can be appeased. Our point here is that the *main* tendency of Western culture is an opposition between man and God, where man resists the might of God, steals fire from him in the interests of humanity. In India man is a product of God. The whole world is due to the sacrifice of God. The *Puruṣa-sūkta* speaks of such an eternal sacrifice which sustains man and the world. In it the whole world is pictured as one single being of incomparable vastness and immensity, animated by one spirit, including within its substance all forms of life.

The dominant character of the Indian mind which has coloured all its culture and moulded all its thoughts is the spiritual tendency. Spiritual experience is the foundation of India's rich cultural history. It is mysticism, not in the sense of involving the exercise of any mysterious power, but only as insisting on a discipline of human nature, leading to a realisation of the spiritual. While the sacred scriptures of the Hebrews and the Christians are more religious and ethical, those of the Hindus are more spiritual and contemplative. The one fact of life in India is the Eternal Being of God.

It is the ultimate presupposition of all philosophy that nothing real can be self-contradictory. In the history of thought it takes some time to realise the importance of this presupposition, and make a conscious application of it. In the Ṛg Veda there is an unconscious acceptance of the validity of ordinary knowledge. When we reach the stage of the Upaniṣads, dialectical problems emerge and the difficulties of knowledge are felt. In them we find an attempt made to mark the limits of knowledge and provide room for intuition, but all in a semi-philosophical way. When faith in the power of reason was shaken, scepticism supervened, and materialists and nihilists came upon the scene. Admitting the Upaniṣad position that the unseen reality cannot be comprehended by the logical intellect, Buddhism enforced the unsubstantiality of the world. To it, contradiction is of the nature of things, and the world of experience is nothing more than a tension of opposites. We cannot know if there is anything more than the actual, and this cannot be real since it is self-contradictory. Such a conclusion was the end of the Buddhistic development. We have in the theory of Nāgārjuna a philosophically sustained statement of the central position of the Upaniṣads. There is a real, though we cannot know it; and what we know is not real, for every interpretation of the world as an intelligible system breaks down. All this prepared the way for a self-conscious criticism of reason. Thought itself is self-contradictory or inadequate. Differences arise when the question is put, why exactly is it incapable of grasping reality. Is it because it deals with parts and not the whole, or is it because of its structural incapacity or innate self-contradictoriness? As we have seen, there are those who hold to the rationality of the real with the reservation that reality is not mere reason. So thought is incapable of giving us the whole of reality. The 'that' exceeds the 'what' in Bradley's words. Thought gives us knowledge of reality, but it is only knowledge, and not reality. There are others who feel that the real is self-consistent, and whatever is thought is self-contradictory. Thought works with the opposition of subject and object, and the absolute real is something in which these antitheses are annulled. The most concrete thought, in so far as it tries to combine a many in one, is still abstract, because it is self-contradictory, and if we want to grasp the real, we have to give up thought. On the first hypothesis, what thought reveals is not opposed to reality, but is revelatory of a part of it. Partial views are contradictory only because they are partial. They are true so far as they go, but they are not the whole truth. The second hypothesis tells us that reality can be apprehended by a form of feeling or intuition. The first view also insists on a supplementing of thought by feeling, if reality is to be attained in its fullness. We seem to require another element in addition to thought, and this is suggested by the term *darśana,* which is used to describe a system of philosophy, doctrine, or *śāstra.*

The term *darśana* comes from the word *dṛś,* to see. This seeing may be either perceptual observation or conceptual knowledge or intuitional experience. It may be inspection of facts, logical inquiry or insight of soul. Generally, *darśanas* mean critical expositions, logical surveys, or systems. We do not find the word used in this reference in the early stages of philosophical thought, when philosophy was more intuitional. It shows that *darśana* is not an intuition, however much it may be allied to it. Perhaps the word is advisedly used, to indicate a thought system acquired by intuitive experience and sustained by logical argument. In the systems of extreme monism philosophy prepares the way for intuitional experience by giving us an idea of the impotence of thought. In the systems of moderate monism, where the real is a concrete whole, philosophy succeeds at best in giving an ideal reconstruction of reality. But the real transcends, surrounds, and overflows our miserable categories. In extreme monism it is intuitional experience that reveals to us the fullness of reality; in concrete monism, it is insight, where knowledge is penetrated by feeling and emotion. Conceptual constructions do not possess the certainty of experienced facts. Again, an opinion or logical view becomes truth only if it stands the test of life.

Darśana is a word which is conveniently vague, as it stands for a dialectical defence of extreme monism as well as the intuitional truth on which it is based. Philosophically *darśana* is putting the intuition to proof and propagating it logically. Even in other systems it applies to the logical exposition of the truth that could be had in conceptual terms with or without the aid of any vivifying intuition. *Darśana* so applies to all views of reality taken by the mind of man, and if reality is one, the different views attempting to reveal the same must agree with each other. They cannot have anything accidental or contingent, but must reflect the different view-points obtained of the one real. By a close consideration of the several views our mind gets by snap-shotting reality from different points, we rise to the second stage of a full rendering of reality in logical terms. When we realise the inadequacy of a conceptual account to reality, we try to seize the real by intuition, where the intellectual ideas are swallowed up. It is then that we are said to get the pure 'being' of extreme monism from which we get back to the logical real of thought, which again we begin to spell letter by letter in the different systems themselves. ***Darśana*** as applicable to this last means any scientific account of reality. It is the one word that stands for all the complex inspiration of philosophy by its beautiful vagueness.

A *darśana* is a spiritual perception, a whole view revealed to the soul sense. This soul sight, which is possible only when and where philosophy is lived, is the distinguishing mark of a true philosopher. So the highest triumphs of philosophy are possible only to those who have achieved in themselves a purity of soul. This purity is based upon a profound acceptance of experience, realised only when some point of hidden strength within man, from which he cannot only inspect but comprehend life, is found. From this inner source the philosopher reveals to us the truth of life, a truth which mere intellect is unable to discover. The vision is produced almost as naturally as a fruit from a flower out of the mysterious centre where all experience is reconciled.

The seeker after truth must satisfy certain essential conditions before he sets out on his quest. Śaṁkara, in his commentary on the first Sūtra of the Vedānta Sūtras, makes out that four conditions are essential for any student of philosophy. The first condition is a knowledge of the distinction between the eternal and the non-eternal. This does not mean full knowledge, which can come only at the end, but only a metaphysical bent which does not accept all it sees to be absolutely real, a questioning tendency in the enquirer. He must have the inquiring spirit to probe all things, a burning imagination which could extract a truth from a mass of apparently disconnected data, and a habit of meditation which will not allow his mind to dissipate itself. The second condition is the subjugation of the desire for the fruits of action either in the present life or a future one. It demands the renunciation of all petty desire, personal motive, and practical interest. Speculation or enquiry to the reflective mind is its own end. The right employment of intellect is understanding the things, good as well as bad. The philosopher is a naturalist who should follow the movement of things without exaggerating the good or belittling the evil on behalf of some prejudice of his. He must stand outside of life and look on it. So it is said that he must have no love of the present or the future. Only then can he stake his all on clear thinking and honest judgement and develop an impersonal cosmic outlook with devotedness to fact. To get this temper he must suffer a change of heart, which is insisted on in the third condition, where the student is enjoined to acquire tranquillity, self-restraint, renunciation, patience, peace of mind, and faith. Only a trained mind which utterly controls the body can enquire and meditate endlessly so long as life remains, never for a moment losing sight of the object, never for a moment letting it be obscured by any terrestrial temptation. The seeker after truth must have the necessary courage to lose all for his highest end. So is he required to undergo hard discipline, spurn pleasure, suffer sorrow and contempt. A spiritual discipline which includes pitiless self-examination will enable the seeker to reach his end of freedom. The desire for *mokṣa* or release is the fourth condition. The metaphysically minded man who has given up all his desires and trained his mind has only one devouring desire to achieve the end or reach the eternal. The people of India have such an immense respect for these philosophers who glory in the might of knowledge and the power of intellect, that they worship them. The prophetic souls who with a noble passion for truth strive hard to understand the mystery of the world and give utterance to it, spending laborious days and sleepless nights, are philosophers in a vital sense of the term. They comprehend experience on behalf of mankind, and so the latter are eternally grateful to them.

Reverence for the past is another national trait. There is a certain doggedness of temperament, a stubborn loyalty to lose nothing in the long march of the ages. When confronted with new cultures or sudden extensions of knowledge, the Indian does not yield to the temptations of the hour, but holds fast to his traditional faith, importing as much as possible of the new into the old. This conservative liberalism is the secret of the success of Indian culture and civilisation. Of the great civilisations of the world, hoary with age, only the Indian still survives. The magnificence of the Egyptian civilisation can be learnt only from the reports of the archaeologists and the readings of the hieroglyphics; the Babylonian Empire, with its marvels of scientific, irrigation, and engineering skill, is to-day nothing more than a heap of ruins; the great Roman culture, with its political institutions and ideals of law and equality, is, to a large extent, a thing of the past. The Indian civilisation, which even at the lowest estimate is 4,000 years old, still survives in its essential features. Her civilisation, dating back to the period of the Vedas, is young and old at the same time. She has been renewing her youth whenever the course of history demanded it. When a change occurs, it is not consciously felt to be a change. It is achieved, and all the time it professes to be only a new name for an old way of thinking. In the Ṛg Veda we shall see how the religious consciousness of the Aryan invaders takes note of the conceptions of the people of the soil. In the Atharva Veda we find that the vaguer cosmic deities are added to the gods of the sky and sun, fire and wind, worshipped by the Aryan peoples from the Ganges to the Hellespont. The Upaniṣads are regarded as a revival or rather a realisation of something found already in the Vedic hymns. The *Bhagavadgītā* professes to sum up the teachings of the Upaniṣads. We have in the epics the meeting-point of the religious conceptions of the highest import with the early nature worship. To respect the spirit of reverence in man for the ancient makes for the success of the new.[4] The

[4] Cf. 'This claim of a new thing to be old is, in varying degrees, a common characteristic of great movements. The Reformation professed to be a return to the Bible, the Evangelical movement in England a return to the Gospels, the High Church movement a return to the Early Church. A large element even in the French Revolution, the greatest of all breaches with the past, had for its ideal a return to Roman republican virtue or to the simplicity of the natural man' (Gilbert Murray, *Five Stages of Greek Religion*, p. 58).

old spirit is maintained, though not the old forms. This tendency to preserve the type has led to the fashionable remark that India is immobile. The mind of man never stands still, though it admits of no absolute breach with the past.

This respect for the past has produced a regular continuity in Indian thought, where the ages are bound each to each by natural piety. The Hindu culture is a product of ages of change wrought by hundreds of generations, of which some are long, stale, and sad, and others short, quick, and joyous, where each has added something of quality to the great rich tradition which is yet alive, though it bears within it the marks of the dead past. The career of Indian philosophy has been compared to the course of a stream which, tumbling joyfully from its source among the northern mountain tops, rushes through the shadowy valleys and plains, catching the lesser streams in its imperious current, till it sweeps increased to majesty and serene power through the lands and peoples whose fortunes it affects, bearing a thousand ships on its bosom. Who knows whether and when this mighty stream which yet flows on with tumult and rejoicing will pass into the ocean, the father of all streams?

There are not wanting Indian thinkers who look upon the whole of Indian philosophy as one system of continuous revelation. They believe that each civilisation is working out some divine thought which is natural to it.[5] There is an immanent teleology which shapes the life of each human race towards some complete development. The several views set forth in India are considered to be the branches of the self-same tree. The short cuts and blind alleys are somehow reconciled with the main road of advance to the truth. A familiar way in which the six orthodox systems are reconciled is to say that just as a mother in pointing out the moon to the baby speaks of it as the shining circle at the top of the tree, which is quite intelligible to the child, without mentioning the immense distance separating the earth from the moon which would have bewildered it, even so are different views given to suit the varying weakness of human understanding. The *Prabodhacandrodaya*, a philosophic drama, states that the six systems

[5] The Greeks call this special quality of each people their 'nature', and the Indians call it their '*dharma*'.

of Hindu philosophy are not mutually exclusive, but establish from various points of view the glory of the same uncreate God. They together form the living focus of the scattered rays that the many-faceted humanity reflects from the splendid sun. Mādhava's *Sarvadarsanasaṁgraha* (A.D. 1380) sketches sixteen systems of thought so as to exhibit a gradually ascending series, culminating in the Advaita Vedānta (or non-dualism). In the spirit of Hegel, he looks upon the history of Indian philosophy as a progressive effort towards a fully articulated conception of the world. The truth is unfolded bit by bit in the successive systems, and complete truth is reflected only when the series of philosophies is completed. In the Advaita Vedānta are the many lights brought to a single focus. Vijñānabhiksu, the sixteenth-century theologian and thinker, holds that all systems are authoritative, and reconciles them by distinguishing practical from metaphysical truth, and looks upon Sāṁkhya as the final expression of truth. Madhusūdana Sarasvatī in his *Prasthānabheda* writes: 'The ultimate scope of all the *munis*, authors of these different systems, is to support the theory of *māyā*, and their only design is to establish the existence of one supreme God, the sole essence, for these *munis* could not be mistaken, since they were omniscient. But as they saw that men, addicted to the pursuit of external objects, could not all at once penetrate into the highest truths, they held out to them a variety of theories in order that they might not fall into atheism. Misunderstanding the object which the *munis* thus had in view, and representing that they even designed to propound doctrines contrary to the Vedas, men have come to regard the specific doctrines of these several schools with preference, and thus became adherents of a variety of systems'. This reconciliation of the several systems is attempted by almost all the critics and commentators. The difference is only about what they regard as the truth. Defenders of Nyāya like Udayana look upon Nyāya, and theists like Rāmānuja consider theism to be the truth. It is in accordance with the spirit of Indian culture to think that the several currents of thought flowing in its soil will discharge their waters into the one river whose flood shall make for the City of God.

From the beginning the Indian felt that truth was many-sided, and different views contained different aspects of truth which no one could fully express. He was therefore tolerant and receptive of other views. He was fearless in accepting even dangerous doctrines so long as they were backed up by logic. He would not allow to die, if he could help it, one jot or tittle of the tradition, but would try to accommodate it all. Several cases of such tolerant treatment we shall meet with in the course of our study. Of course there are dangers incident to such a breadth of view. Often it has led the Indian thinkers into misty vagueness, lazy acceptance, and cheap eclecticism.

Indian Philosophy: Past and Present

PHILOSOPHICAL DEVELOPMENT

Throughout the history of Indian thought, the ideal of a world behind the ordinary world of human strivings, more real and more intangible, which is the true home of the spirit, has been haunting the Indian race. Man's never-ceasing effort to read the riddle of the sphinx and raise himself above the level of the beast to a moral and spiritual height finds a striking illustration in India. We can watch the struggle for four millennia (or longer, if the recent archaeological finds in Sind and the Punjab, which are withdrawing the shroud that hid the remote past, are to be taken into account). The naïve belief that the world is ruled by the gods of Sun and Sky, who watch from on high the conduct of men, whether it is straight or crooked; the faith that the gods who can be persuaded by prayer or compelled by rites to grant our requests are only the forms of the one Supreme; the firm conviction that the pure stainless spirit, to know whom is life eternal, is one with the innermost soul of man; the rise of materialism, scepticism, and fatalism, and their supersession by the ethical systems of Buddhism and Jainism, with their central doctrine that one can free oneself from all ill only by refraining from all evil, in thought, word, and deed—God or no God; the liberal theism of the *Bhagavadgītā,* which endows the all-soul with ethical in addition to metaphysical perfections; the logical scheme of the Nyāya, which furnishes the principal categories of the world of knowledge which are in use even to-day; the Vaiśeṣika interpretation of nature; the Sāṁkhya speculations in science and psychology; the Yoga scheme of the pathway to perfection; the ethical and social regulations of the Mīmāṁsā and the religious interpretations of the Supreme reality, as put forward by Śaṁkara, Rāmānuja, Madhva, Nimbārka, Vallabha, and Jīva Gosvāmi—form a remarkable record of philosophical development in the history of the human race. Type succeeds type, school follows on school, in logical sequence. The life of the Indian was ever on the move, shaping itself as it grew, and changing from time to time in relation to its physical, social, and cultural contexts. In the early stages the ancient Indians were doing everything for the first time. They had practically no wisdom of the past to fall back upon. They had, moreover, enormous difficulties to contend with, which are now almost things of the past. In spite of these, their achievement in the realm of thought and practice is a considerable one. But the cycle is not complete, and the range of possible forms is not exhausted; for the sphinx still smiles. Philosophy is yet in its infancy.

The survey of Indian thought, as of all thought, impresses one with the mystery and the immensity of existence as well as the beauty and the persistence of the human effort to understand it. The long procession of thinkers struggled hard to add some small piece to the temple of human wisdom, some fresh fragment to the ever incomplete sum of human knowledge. But human speculation falls short of the ideal, which it can neither abandon nor attain. We are far more conscious of the depth of the surrounding darkness than of the power to dispel it possessed by the flickering torches that we have the privilege to carry as the inheritors of a great past. After all the attempts of philosophers, we stand to-day in relation to the ultimate problems very near where we stood far away in the ages—where perhaps we shall ever stand as long as we are human, bound Prometheus-like to the rock of mystery by the chains of our finite mind. The pursuit of philosophy is not, however, a vain endeavour. It helps us to feel the grip and the clanging of the chains. It sharpens the consciousness of human imperfection, and thus deepens the sense of perfection in us, which reveals the imperfection of our passing lives. That the world is not so transparent to our intellects as we could wish is not to be wondered at, for the philosopher is only the lover of wisdom and not its possessor. It is not the end of the voyage that matters, but the voyage itself. To travel is a better thing than to arrive.

At the end of our course, we may ask whether the known facts of history support a belief in progress. Is the march of human thought a forward movement, or is it one of retrogression? The sequence is not capricious and unmeaning. India believes in progress, for, as we have already said, the cycles are bound together by an organic tie. The inner thread of continuity is never cut. Even the revolutions that threaten to engulf the past help to restore it. Backward eddies serve rather to strengthen than retard the current. Epochs of decadence, like the recent past of this country, are in truth periods of transition from an old life to a new. The two currents of progress and decline are intermingled. At one stage the forces of progress press forward with a persistent sweep, at another the line sways to and fro, and sometimes the forces of retrogression seem to overwhelm those of progress, but on the whole the record is one of advance. It would be idle to deny that much has perished in the process. But few things are more futile than to rail against the course which the historical past has taken or weep over it. In any case, some other kind of development would have been worse. The more important thing is the future. We are able to see further than our predecessors, since we can climb on their shoulders. Instead of resting content with the foundations nobly laid in the past, we must build a greater edifice in harmony with ancient endeavour as well as the modern outlook.

THE UNITY OF ALL SYSTEMS

The twin strands which in one shape or another run through all the efforts of the Indian thinkers are loyalty to tradition and devotion to truth. Every thinker recognises that the principles of his predecessors are stones built into the spiritual fabric, and, if they are traduced, one's own culture is defamed. A progressive people with a rich tradition cannot afford to neglect it, though it may contain elements which are not edifying. The thinkers try hard to explain, allegorise, alter, and expurgate the traditional lore, since men's emotions are centred round it. The later Indian thinkers justify the different philosophical interpretations of the universe advanced by the earlier ones, and regard them as varying approximations to the truth as a whole. The different views are not looked upon as unrelated adventures of the human mind into the realm of the unknown or a collection of philosophical curiosities. They are regarded as the expression of a single mind, which has built up the great temple, though it is divided into numerous walls and vestibules, passages and pillars.

Logic and science, philosophy and religion, are related organically. Every fresh epoch in the progress of thought has been inaugurated by a reform in logic. The problem of method, involving as it does an insight into the nature of human thought, is of great value. The Nyāya points out that no stable philosophy can be built except on the foundations of logic. The Vaiśesika warns us that all fruitful philosophy must take into account the constitution of physical nature. We cannot build in the clouds. Though physics and metaphysics are clearly distinct and cannot be blended, still a philosophic scheme must be in harmony with the results of natural science. But to extend to the universe at large what is true of the physical world would be to commit the fallacy of scientific metaphysics, and the Sāṁkhya asks us to beware of that danger. The resources of nature cannot generate consciousness. We cannot reduce nature and consciousness the one to the other, as scientific and psychological metaphysics attempt to do. Reality appears not only in science and in human life, but in religious experience, which is the subject matter of the *yoga* system. The *Pūrva Mīmāṁsā* and the Vedānta lay stress on ethics and religion. The relation between nature and mind is the supreme problem of philosophy which the Vedānta takes up. The saying, that the saints do not contradict one another, is true of philosophies also. The Nyāya-Vaiseṣika realism, the Sāṁkhya-Yoga dualism and the Vedānta monism do not differ as true and false but as more or less true. They are adapted to the needs of the slow-witted (*mandādhikāri*), the average intellect (*madhyamādhikāri*) and the strong-minded (*uttamādhikāri*) respectively. The different views are hewn out of one stone and belong to one whole, integral, entire, and self-contained. No scheme of the universe can be regarded as complete, if it has not the different sides of logic and physics, psychology and ethics, metaphysics and religion. Every system of thought developed in India offered its own theory of knowledge, interpretation of nature and mind, ethics and religion. Our knowledge of the universe has grown enormously under the guidance of the natural sciences, and we cannot afford to be satisfied with any restricted outlook on life. The future attempts at philosophic construction will have to relate themselves to the recent advances of natural science and psychology.

PHILOSOPHY AND LIFE

Philosophy has for its function the ordering of life and the guidance of action. It sits at the helm and directs our course through the changes and chances of the world. When philosophy is alive, it cannot be remote from the life of the people. The ideas of thinkers are evolved in the process of their life history. We must learn not only to reverence them, but to acquire their spirit. The names of Vaśiṣṭha and Viśvāmitra, Yājñavalkya and Gārgī, Buddha and Mahāvīra, Gautama and Kaṇāda, Kapila and Patañjali, Bādarāyaṇa and Jaimini, Śaṁkara and Rāmānuja, are not merely themes for the historian but types of personality. With them philosophy is a world-view based on reflection and experience. Thought, when it thinks itself out to the end, becomes religion by being lived and tested by the supreme test of life. The discipline of philosophy is at the same time the fulfilment of a religious vocation.

THE DECLINE OF PHILOSOPHY IN THE RECENT PAST

The evidence brought together in this work does not support the general criticism that the Indian mind has a fear of thinking. We cannot dismiss the whole progress of Indian thought with a sapient reference to the Oriental mind, which is not sufficiently dry and virile to rise above grotesque imagination and puerile mythology. Yet there is much in the thought-history of the last three or four centuries to lend countenance to this charge. India is no longer playing her historic rôle as the vanguard of higher knowledge in Asia.[1] It seems to some that the river that has flowed down the centuries so strong and full is likely to end in a stagnant waste of waters. The philosophers, or rather the writers on philosophy of this period of decadence, profess to be votaries of truth, though they understand by it merely the pious sophistries or the sacrosanct hair-splittings of this or that school of dogmatics. These professional dialecticians imagine that the small brook by their side, trickling away in the sand or evaporating in the fog, is the broad river of Indian philosophy.

A variety of causes have contributed to this result. The political changes brought about by the establishment of the Mohammadan supremacy turned men's minds into conservative moulds. In an age when individual self-assertion and private judgement threatened at every point to dissolve into anarchy the old social order and all stable conviction, the need for authoritative control was urgently felt. The Mohammadan conquest, with its propagandist work, and later the Christian missionary movement, attempted to shake the stability of Hindu society, and in an age deeply conscious of instability, authority naturally became the rock on which alone it seemed that social safety and ethical order could be reared. The Hindu, in the face of the clash of cultures, fortified himself with conventions and barred all entry to invading ideas. His society, mistrusting reason and weary of argument, flung itself passionately into the arms of an authority which stamped all

[1] Regarding China's debt to India, Professor Liang Chi Cho says: 'India taught us to embrace the idea of absolute freedom, that fundamental freedom of mind, which enables it to shake off all the fetters of past tradition and habit as well as the present customs of a particular age—that spiritual freedom which casts off the enslaving forces of material existence. . . . India also taught us the idea of absolute love, that pure love towards all living beings which eliminates all obsessions of jealousy, anger, impatience, disgust and emulation, which expresses itself in deep pity and sympathy for the foolish, the wicked and the sinful—that absolute love which recognises the inseparability between all beings'. He goes on to explain the contributions of India to Chinese literature and art, music and architecture, painting and sculpture, drama, poetry, and fiction, astronomy and medicine, educational method and social organisations. See *Viśvabhārati Quarterly* (October, 1924). The influence of India on Burma and Ceylon, Japan and Korea, is well known.

free questioning as sin. Since then it has failed in loyalty to its mission. There were no longer any thinkers, but only scholars who refused to strike new notes, and were content to raise echoes of the old call. For some centuries they succeeded in deceiving themselves with a supposedly final theory. Philosophy became confused with the history of philosophy when the creative spirit had left her. It abdicated its function and remained wrapped up in its illusions. When it ceased to be the guide and the guardian of the general reason, it did a great wrong to itself. Many believed that their race had travelled long and far towards a goal at which it had at length arrived. They felt rather tired and inclined to rest. Even those who knew that they had not arrived, and saw the large tract of the country stretching into the future, were afraid of the unknown and its ordeals. The silences and the eternities cannot be questioned without peril by the weak of heart. The dizziness of the inquiry into the infinite is a vertigo which even mighty minds try to avoid, if they can. The strongest of human forces are subject to intervals of lethargy, and the philosophic impulse has had in these three or four centuries an attack of lethargy.

THE PRESENT SITUATION

To-day the great religions of the world and the different currents of thought have met on Indian soil. The contact with the spirit of the West has disturbed the placid contentment of recent times. The assimilation of a different culture has led to the impression that there are no official answers to ultimate problems. It has shaken the faith in the traditional solutions, and has, in some degree, helped to a larger freedom and flexibility of thought. Tradition has become fluid again, and while some thinkers are busy rebuilding the house on ancient foundations, others want to remove the foundations altogether. The present age of transition is as full of interest as of anxiety.

During the recent past, India was comfortably moored in a backwater outside the full current of contemporary thought, but she is no longer isolated from the rest of the world. The historian of three or four centuries hence may have much to say on the issues of the intercourse between India and Europe, but as yet they lie hidden from our view. So far as India is concerned, we notice the broadening of men's range of experience, the growth of the critical temper and a sort of distaste for mere speculation.

But there is another side to the picture. In the field of thought, as well as in that of action, the spirit of man is doomed to decay as much in anarchy as in bondage. There is not much to choose between the two, so far as culture and civilisation are concerned. Anarchy may mean material discomfort, economic ruin, and social danger and bondage material comfort, economic stability, and social peace. But it would be incorrect to confuse the standards of civilisation with economic welfare and maintenance of social order. It is easy to understand the feeling of the Indians of the beginning of the nineteenth century, who after generations of public strife and private suffering welcomed the British rule as the dawn of a golden age; but it should be equally easy to sympathise with the Indian feeling of the present day that the spirit of man craves, not comfort, but happiness, not peace and order, but life and liberty, not economic stability or equitable administration, but the right to work out one's own salvation even at the cost of infinite toil and tribulation. Even non-political virtues do not thrive in the absence of political autonomy. British rule has given India peace and security, but they are not ends in themselves. If we are to put first things first, then we must admit that economic stability and political security are only means, however valuable and necessary, to spiritual freedom. A bureaucratic despotism which forgets the spiritual ends, for all its integrity and enlightenment, cannot invigorate the peoples beneath her sway, and cannot therefore evoke any living response in them. When the founts of life are drying up, when the ideals for which the race stood for millennia, the glow of consciousness, the free exercise of faculty, the play of life, the pleasure of mind, and the fullness of peace, *prāṇārāmam, mana-ānandam, śānti-samṛddham,* are decaying, it is no wonder that the Indian is conscious only of the crushing burden and not of the lifted weight. It is no use speaking to him of the magnitude of Britain's work, for the verdict of history is passed on the spiritual quality of the achievement. If the leaders of recent generations have been content to be mere echoes of the past and not independent voices, if they have been intellectual middlemen and not original thinkers, this sterility is to no small extent due to the shock of the Western spirit and the shame of subjection. The British are aware of the deep-rooted causes of the present attitude of India, whatever it may be called, unrest, revolt, or challenge. They tried to bring their civilisation, which they naturally regard as higher, to touch the Indians, and they felt that they should press on in the task of enlightenment and education, good in themselves, without any hesitation or cessation of effort. But India has no sympathy with this policy of cultural imperialism. She tenaciously clings to her ancient customs which helped her to check the swell of passion, the blindness of temper, and the thrust of desire. One who is acquainted with the history of her past can sympathise with her anxiety to dwell in her own spiritual house, for 'each man is the master of his own house'. Political subjection which interferes with this inner freedom is felt as a gross humiliation. The cry for *swarāj* is the outer expression of the anxiety to preserve the provinces of the soul.

Yet the future is full of promise. If India gains freedom within, then the Western spirit will be a great help to the Indian mind. Hindu thought never developed a Monroe Doctrine in matters of culture. Even in the ancient times when India grew enough spiritual food to satisfy her own people, there is no recorded age when she was not ready and eager to appreciate the products of other people's imagination. In her great days India conformed to the wisdom of the Athenians, of whom Pericles said: 'We listen gladly to the opinions of others and do not turn sour faces on those who disagree with us'. Our fear of outside influence is proportioned to our own weakness and want of faith in ourselves. To-day, it is true, we bear lines of sorrow in our face and our hair is grey with age. The thoughtful among us have a brooding uneasiness of soul, some are even steeped in pessimism, and so have become intellectual hermits. The non-cooperation with Western culture is a passing episode due to unnatural circumstances. In spite of it, there are attempts to understand and appreciate the spirit of Western culture. If India assimilates the valuable elements in the Western civilisation, it will be only a repetition of parallel processes which happened a number of times in the history of Indian thought.

Those who are untouched by the Western influence are for a large part intellectual and moral aristocrats, who are indifferent to political issues, and adopt a gospel not of confident hope but of resignation and detachment. They think that they have little to learn or to unlearn, and that they do their duty with their gaze fixed on the eternal *dharma* of the past. They realise that other forces are at work, which they cannot check or control, and ask us to face the storms and disillusionment of life with the unruffled calm of self-respect. This was the class which in better times was more elastic and was ever renewing the attempts to reconcile rational philosophy with revealed religion. It had always explained and defended the faith in the face of heretics and unbelievers, and had recourse to the allegorical method as the instrument of theological interpretation. Religion, for it, embraced within its scope the whole nature of man, his intelligence as much as his practical and emotional aspirations. If to-day the representatives of the ancient learning had the inspiration of the past, they would, instead of non-cooperating with other forces, build a fresh scheme with originality and freedom and in the strength of the legacy of ancient wisdom. But they have an exaggerated respect for authority in thought and action, in things spiritual and things secular, and have thus exposed themselves to the charges of mental servility and obscurantism. While, in pre-Mohammadan times, appeal to authority was no bar to intellectual independence, and while men were able and ready to offer rational grounds for allegiance to the authorities of their choice, be they the Vedas or the āgamas, and while authority was made to speak in the voice of reason by means of a critical selection and philosophical interpretation, now reverence for authority has become the imprisonment of the human spirit. To question the belief of the scriptures is to question the authority of the great dead. To accept them is a sign of loyalty. Enquiry and doubt are silenced by the citation of ancient texts, scientific truths are slighted, if they cannot be fitted into the Procrustean bed of established belief. Passivity, docility, and acquiescence become the primary intellectual virtues. No wonder the philosophical writings of recent times are far below the level of the best work of the past ages. If thought had been less strained, it would have been more spacious.

The thinkers of India are the inheritors of the great tradition of faith in reason. The ancient seers desired not to copy but to create. They were ever anxious to win fresh fields for truth and answer the riddles of experience, which is ever changing and therefore new. The richness of the inheritance never served to enslave their minds. We cannot simply copy the solutions of the past, for history never repeats itself. What they did in their generation need not be done over again. We have to keep our eyes open, find out our problems, and seek the inspiration of the past in solving them. The spirit of truth never clings to its forms but ever renews them. Even the old phrases are used in a new way. The philosophy of the present will be relevant to the present and not to the past. It will be as original in its form and its content as the life which it interprets. As the present is continuous with the past, so there will be no breach of continuity with the past.

One of the arguments of the conservatives is that truth is not affected by time. It cannot be superseded, any more than the beauty of the sunset or a mother's love for a child. Truth may be immutable, but the form in which it is embodied consists of elements which admit of change. We may take our spirit from the past, for the germinal ideas are yet vital, but the body and the pulse must be from the present. It is forgotten that religion, as it is to-day, is itself the product of ages of change; and there is no reason why its forms should not undergo fresh changes so long as the spirit demands it. It is possible to remain faithful to the letter and yet pervert the whole spirit. If the Hindu leaders of two thousand years ago, who had less learning and more light, could come on earth again after all these centuries, they would seldom find their true followers among those who have never deviated from the most literal interpretations of their views.[2] To-day a great mass of accretions have accumulated, which are choking up the stream and the free life of spirit. To say that the dead forms, which have no vital truth to support them, are too ancient and venerable to be tampered with, only prolongs the suffering of the patient who is ailing from the poison generated by the putrid waste of the past. The conservative mind must open itself to the necessity of change. Since it is not sufficiently alive to this need, we find in the realm of philosophy a strange mixture of penetrating sagacity and unphilosophical confusion. The chief energies of the thinking Indians should be thrown into the problems of how to disentangle the old faith from its temporary accretions, how to bring religion into line with the spirit of science, how to meet and interpret the claims of temperament and individuality, how to organise the divergent influences on the basis of the ancient faith. But, unfortunately, some of the *pariṣads* are engaged not with these problems but those suited for the Society of Antiquarians. It has become the tilting-ground of the specialists. The religious education of the nation is not undertaken on broad lines. It is not seen that the spiritual inheritance cannot be any longer the monopoly of a favoured few. Ideas are forces, and they must be broadcasted, if the present aging to death is to be averted. It would be indeed strange if the spirit of the Upanisads, the *Bhagavadgītā*, and the Dialogues of Buddha, that could touch the mind to such fine issues, should have lost its power over man. If, before it is too late, there is a reorganisation of national life, there is a future for Indian thought; and one cannot tell what flowers may yet bloom, what fruits may yet ripen on the hardy old trees.

While those who have not yet been subjected to the influence of Western culture are conservatives in all matters of

[2] Cf. Aurobindo Ghose: 'If an ancient Indian of the time of the Upanisad, of the Buddha, or the later classical age were to be set down in modern India . . . he would see his race clinging to forms and shells and rags of the past and missing nine-tenths of its nobler meaning . . . he would be amazed by the extent of the mental poverty, the immobility, the static repetition, the cessation of science, the long sterility of art, the comparative feebleness of the creative intuition' (*Ārya*, v. p. 424).

thought and practice, there are some among those educated in Western ways of thinking who adopt a despairing philosophy of naturalistic rationalism and ask us to get rid of the weight of the past. These are intolerant of tradition and suspicious of the alleged wisdom of age. This attitude of the 'progressives' is easily understood. The spiritual heritage of the race has not protected India from the invader and the spoiler. It seems to have played her false and betrayed her into the present state of subjection. These patriots are eager to imitate the material achievements of Western states, and tear up the roots of the ancient civilisation, so as to make room for the novelties imported from the West. Till the other day Indian thought was not a subject of study in the Indian universities, and even now its place in the philosophical curricula of the universities is insignificant. Suggestions of the inferiority of Indian culture permeate the whole educational atmosphere. The policy inaugurated by Macaulay, with all its cultural value, is loaded on one side. While it is so careful as not to make us forget the force and vitality of Western culture, it has not helped us to love our own culture and refine it where necessary. In some cases, Macaulay's wish is fulfilled, and we have educated Indians who are 'more English than the English themselves', to quote his well-known words. Naturally some of these are not behind the hostile foreign critic in their estimate of the history of Indian culture. They look upon India's cultural evolution as one dreary scene of discord, folly, and superstition. One of their number recently declared that, if India is to thrive and flourish, England must be her 'spiritual mother' and Greece her 'spiritual grandmother'. Albeit, since he has no faith in religion, he does not propose the displacement of Hinduism by Christianity. These victims of the present age of disillusion and defeat tell us that the love of Indian thought is a nationalist foible, if not a pose of the highbrows.

It is a bewildering phenomenon that, just when India is ceasing to appear grotesque to Western eyes, she is beginning to appear so to the eyes of some of her own sons. The West tried its best to persuade India that its philosophy is absurd, its art puerile, its poetry uninspired, its religion grotesque, and its ethics barbarous. Now that the West is feeling that its judgement is not quite correct, some of us are insisting that it was wholly right. While it is true that it is difficult in an age of reflection to push men back into an earlier stage of culture and save them from the dangers of doubt and the disturbing power of dialectic, we should not forget that we can build better on foundations already laid than by attempting to substitute a completely new structure of morality, of life, and of ethics. We cannot cut ourselves off from the springs of our life. Philosophical schemes, unlike geometrical constructions, are the products of life. The heritage of our history is the food that we have to absorb on pain of inanition.

The conservatives are convinced of the glory of the ancient heritage and the godlessness of modern culture; the radicals are equally certain of the futility of the ancient heritage and the value of naturalistic rationalism. There is much to be said for these views; but the history of Indian thought, when rightly studied, will lead us to regard the two as equally defective. Those who condemn Indian culture as useless are ignorant of it, while those who commend it as perfect are ignorant of any other. The radicals and the conservatives, who stand for the new hope and the old learning, must come closer and understand each other. We cannot live by ourselves in a world where aircraft and steamships, railways and telegraphs, are linking all men together into a living whole. Our system of thought must act and react on the world progress. Stagnant systems, like pools, breed obnoxious growths, while flowing rivers constantly renew their waters from fresh springs of inspiration. There is nothing wrong in absorbing the culture of other peoples; only we must enhance, raise, and purify the elements we take over, fuse them with the best in our own. The right procedure regarding the fusing together of the different elements tossed from outside into the national crucible, is indicated roughly in the writings of Gāndhi and Tagore, Aurobindo Ghose and Bhagavan Das. In them we see the faint promise of a great future, some signs of a triumph over scholasticism, as well as a response to the discovery of a great culture. While drawing upon the fountains of humanist idealism in India's past, they show a keen appreciation of Western thought. They are anxious to re-seek the ancient fountainhead and direct its waters to irrigate, through pure and uncontaminated conduits, lands which hunger and thirst. But the future which we wish to see is practically non-existent. With the slackening of the political excitement, which is absorbing the energies of some of the best minds of India, with the increasing insistence on the study of Indian thought in the new universities, which the old ones are following most reluctantly, the dawn may break. The forces of the conservatism, which prefers the life that was to the life that will be, are not likely to gain any strength in the days to come.

The problem facing Indian philosophy to-day is whether it is to be reduced to a cult, restricted in scope and with no application to the present facts, or whether it is to be made alive and real, so as to become what it should be, one of the great formative elements in human progress, by relating the immensely increased knowledge of modern science to the ancient ideals of India's philosophers. All signs indicate that the future is bound up with the latter alternative. Loyalty to the spirit of the previous systems of thought, as well as the mission of philosophy, requires us to possess an outlook that always broadens. Indian philosophy acquires a meaning and a justification for the present only if it advances and ennobles life. The past course of Indian philosophic development encourages us in our hope. The great thinkers, Yājñavalkya and Gārgī, Buddha and Mahāvīra, Gautama and Kapila, Śaṁkara and Rāmānuja, Madhva and Vallabha, and scores of others are India's grandest title to existence, a clear testimony of her dignity as a nation with a soul, the proof that she may yet rise above herself and the pledge of this supreme possibility.

PART III. THE IDEALIST VIEW OF LIFE: THE UPANISADS AND VEDĀNTA

The Upaniṣads as the Vedānta *

The Vedānta meant originally the Upaniṣads, though the word is now used for the system of philosophy based on the Upaniṣads. Literally, Vedānta means the end of the Veda, *vedasya antaḥ*, the conclusion as well as the goal of the Vedas. The Upaniṣads are the concluding portions of the Vedas. Chronologically they come at the end of the Vedic period. As the Upaniṣads contain abstruse and difficult discussions of ultimate philosophical problems, they were taught to the pupils at about the end of their course. When we have Vedic recitations as religious exercises, the end of these recitals is generally from the Upaniṣads. The chief reason that the Upaniṣads are called the end of the Veda is that they represent the central aim and meaning of the teaching of the Veda. The content of the Upaniṣads is *vedānta vijñānam*, the wisdom of the Vedānta. The *Saṁhitās* and the *Brāhmaṇas*, which are the hymns and the liturgical books, represent the *karma-kāṇḍa* or the ritual portion, while the Upaniṣads represent the *jñāna-kāṇḍa* or the knowledge portion. The learning of the hymns and the performance of the rites are a preparation for true enlightenment.

The Upaniṣads describe to us the life of spirit, the same yesterday, to-day, and for ever. But our apprehensions of the life of spirit, the symbols by which we express it, change with time. All systems of orthodox Indian thought accept the authoritativeness of the Vedas,[1] but give themselves freedom

* From the Introduction, *The Principal Upanishads* (London: George Allen & Unwin, 1953), pp. 24–27.

[1] Even the Buddhists and the Jainas accept the teaching of the Upaniṣads, though they interpret it in their own ways. See Introduction to *Dhammapada* and *Viśeṣāvaśyaka Bhāṣya*, *Yaśovijaya Jaina Granthamālā* No. 35.

in their interpretation. This variety of interpretation is made possible by the fact that the Upaniṣads are not the thoughts of a single philosopher or a school of philosophers who follow a single tradition. They are the teachings of thinkers who were interested in different aspects of the philosophical problem, and therefore offer solutions of problems which vary in their interest and emphasis. There is thus a certain amount of fluidity in their thought which has been utilised for the development of different philosophical systems. Out of the wealth of suggestions and speculations contained in them, different thinkers choose elements for the construction of their own systems, not infrequently even through a straining of the texts. Though the Upanisads do not work out a logically coherent system of metaphysics, they give us a few fundamental doctrines which stand out as the essential teaching of the early Upanisads. These are recapitulated in the *Brahma-Sūtra*.

The *Brahma-Sūtra* is an aphoristic summary of the teaching of the Upanisads, and the great teachers of the Vedānta develop their distinctive views through their commentaries on this work. By interpreting the sūtras which are laconic in form and hardly intelligible without interpretation, the teachers justify their views to the reasoning intelligence.

Different commentators attempt to find in the Upanisads and the *Brahma-Sūtra* a single coherent doctrine, a system of thought which is free from contradictions. Bhartṛprapañca, who is anterior to Śaṁkara, maintains that the selves and the physical universe are real, though not altogether different from Brahman. They are both identical with and different from Brahman, the three together constituting a unity in diversity. Ultimate Reality evolves into the universal creation *sṛṣṭi* and the universe retreats into it at the time of dissolution, *pralaya*.

The advaita of Śaṁkara insists on the transcendent nature of non-dual Brahman and the duality of the world including *Īśvara* who presides over it. Reality is Brahman or Ātman. No predication is possible of Brahman as predication involves duality and Brahman is free from all duality. The world of duality is empirical or phenomenal. The saving truth which redeems the individual from the stream of births and deaths is the recognition of his own identity with the Supreme. 'That thou art' is the fundamental fact of all existence.[2] The multiplicity of the universe, the unending stream of life, is real, but only as a phenomenon.

Rāmānuja qualifies the non-dual philosophy so as to make the personal God supreme. While Brahman, souls, and the world are all different and eternal, they are at the same time inseparable. Inseparability is not identity. Brahman is related to the two others as soul to body. They are sustained by Him and subject to His control. Rāmānuja says that while God exists for Himself, matter and souls exist for His sake and subserve His purposes. The three together form an organic whole. Brahman is the inspiring principle of the souls and the world. The souls are different from, but not independent of, God. They are said to be one only in the sense that they all belong to the same class. The ideal is the enjoyment of freedom and bliss in the world of Nārāyaṇa, and the means to it is either *prapatti* or *bhakti*. The individual souls, even when they are freed through the influence of their devotion and the grace of God, retain their separate individuality. For him and Madhva, God, the author of all grace, saves those who give to Him the worship of love and faith.

For Madhva there are five eternal distinctions between (1) God and the individual soul, (2) God and matter, (3) soul and matter, (4) one soul and another, (5) one particle of matter and another. The supreme being endowed with all auspicious qualities is called Viṣṇu, and Lakṣmī is His power dependent on Him. *Mokṣa* is release from rebirth and residence in the abode of Nārāyaṇa. Human souls are innumerable, and each of them is separate and eternal. The divine souls are destined for salvation. Those who are neither very good nor very bad are subject to *saṁsāra*, and the bad go to hell. Right knowledge of God and devotion to Him are the means to salvation. Without divine grace there can be no salvation.

Baladeva adopts the view of *acintya-bhedābheda*. Difference and non-difference are positive facts of experience and yet cannot be reconciled. It is an incomprehensible synthesis of opposites. Rāmānuja, Bhāskara, Nimbārka and Baladeva believe that there is change in Brahman, but not of Brahman.

[2] C.U. VI. 8. 7; B.U. 4. 10.

Ultimate Reality: Brahman *

To the pioneers of the Upaniṣads, the problem to be solved presented itself in the form, what is the world rooted in? What is that by reaching which we grasp the many objects perceived in the world around us? They assume, as many philosophers do, that the world of multiplicity is, in fact, reducible to one single, primary reality which reveals itself to our senses in different forms. This reality is hidden from senses but is discernible to the reason. The Upaniṣads raise the question; what is that reality which remains identical and persists through change?

The word used in the Upaniṣads to indicate the supreme reality is Brahman. It is derived from the root *bṛh.* 'to grow, to burst forth'. The derivation suggests gushing forth, bubbling over, ceaseless growth, *bṛhattvam.* Śaṁkara derives the word 'Brahman' from the root *bṛhati* to exceed, *atiśayana* and means by it eternity, purity. For Madhva, Brahman is the person in whom the qualities dwell in fullness, *bṛhanto hy·asmin guṇāḥ.* The real is not a pale abstraction, but is quickeningly alive, of powerful vitality. In the Ṛg Veda, Brahman is used in the sense of 'sacred knowledge or utterance, a hymn or incantation',[1] the concrete expression of spiritual wisdom. Sometimes *vāc* is personified as the One.[2] *Viśva-karman,* the All-Maker is said to be the lord of the holy utterance.[3] Brahman is *mantra* or prayer. Gradually it acquired the meaning of power or potency of prayer. It has a mysterious power and contains within itself the essence of the thing denoted. Bṛhaspati, Brahmaṇaspati are interpreted as the lord of prayer.

* From the Introduction, *The Principal Upanishads* (London: George Allen & Unwin, 1953), pp. 52–104.

[1] R.V. VII. 1ff.

[2] X. 125.

[3] X. 81. 7; X. 71.

In the *Brāhmaṇas*, Brahman denotes the ritual and so is regarded as omnipotent. He who knows Brahman knows and controls the universe. Brahman becomes the primal principle and guiding spirit of the universe. 'There is nothing more ancient or brighter than this Brahman'.

In later thought, Brahman meant wisdom or Veda. As divine origin was ascribed to the Veda or Brahman, the two words were used with the same meaning. Brahman or sacred knowledge came to be called the first created thing, *brahma prathamajam* and even to be treated as the creative principle, the cause of all existence.

The word suggests a fundamental kinship between the aspiring spirit of man and the spirit of the universe which it seeks to attain. The wish to know the Real implies that we know it to some extent. If we do not know anything about it, we cannot even say that it is and that we wish to know it. If we know the Real, it is because the Real knows itself in us. The desire for God, the feeling that we are in a state of exile, implies the reality of God in us. All spiritual progress is the growth of half-knowledge into clear illumination. Religious experience is the evidence for the Divine. In our inspired moments we have the feeling that there is a greater reality within us, though we cannot tell what it is. From the movements that stir in us and the utterances that issue from us, we perceive the power, not ourselves, that moves us. Religious experience is by no means subjective. God cannot be known or experienced except through his own act. If we have a knowledge of Brahman, it is due to the working of Brahman in us.[4] Prayer is the witness to the spirit of the transcendent divine immanent in the spirit of man. The thinkers of the Upaniṣads based the reality of Brahman on the fact of spiritual experience, ranging from simple prayer to illuminated experience. The distinctions which they make in the nature of the Supreme Reality are not merely logical. They are facts of spiritual experience.

[4] Cf. St. Anselm: 'I cannot seek Thee except Thou teach me, nor find Thee except Thou reveal Thyself'; *Rūmī:* 'Was it not I who summoned Thee to long service; was it not I who made Thee busy with my name? Thy calling "Allāh" was my "Here am I".'

The thinkers of the Upaniṣads attempt to establish the reality of God from an analysis of the facts of nature and the facts of inner life.

> Who knows and who can declare what pathway leads to the gods?
> Seen are their lowest dwelling-places only;
> What pathway leads to the highest, most secret regions?[5]

The Upaniṣads assume that it is a distorted habit of mind which identifies 'the highest, most secret regions' with the 'lowest dwelling-places'. The Real is not the actual. The Upaniṣads ask, 'What is the *tajjalān* from which all things spring, into which they are resolved and in which they live and have their being'.[6]

The Bṛhad-āraṇyaka Upaniṣad maintains that the ultimate reality is *being, san-mātraṁ hi brahma.* Since nothing is without reason there must be a reason why something exists rather than nothing. There is something; there is not nothing. The world is not self-caused, self-dependent, self-maintaining. All philosophical investigation presupposes the reality of being, *astitva-niṣṭhā.* The theologian accepts the first principle of being as an absolute one; the philosopher comes to it by a process of mediation. By logically demonstrating the impossibility of not-being in and by itself, he asserts the necessity of being. Being denotes pure affirmation to the exclusion of every possible negation. It expresses simultaneously God's consciousness of himself and his own absolute self-absorbed being. We cannot live a rational life without assuming the reality of being. Not-being is sometimes said to be the first principle. It is not absolute non-being but only relative non-being, as compared with later concrete existence.

Even as the *nyagrodha* tree is made of the subtle essence which we do not perceive, so is this world made of the infinite Brahman. 'It is at the command of that Imperishable that the sun and the moon stand bound in their places. It is at the command of that Imperishable that the heaven and the earth stand each in its own place. It is at the command of that

[5] R.V. III. 54.
[6] C.U. III. 14. 1.

Imperishable that the very moments, the hours, the days, the nights, the half-months, the months, the seasons and the years have their appointed function in the scheme of things. It is at the command of that Imperishable that some rivers flow to the east from the snow-clad mountains while others flow to the west'. When Bālāki defines Brahman as the person in the sun (*āditye puruṣaḥ*) and successively as the person in the moon, in lightning, in ether, in wind, in fire, in the waters, also as the person in the mind, in the shadow, in echo, and in the body, King Ajātaśatru asks, 'Is that all?' When Bālāki confesses that he can go no farther, the king says, 'He who is the maker of all these persons, he, verily, should be known'. Brahman is *satyasya satyam*, the Reality of the real, the source of all existing things.[7]

In some cosmological speculations the mysterious principle of reality is equated with certain naturalistic elements. Water is said to be the source of all things whatsoever.[8] From it came *satya*, the concrete existent. Others like Raikva look upon air as the final absorbent of all things whatsoever, including fire and water.[9] The Kaṭha Upaniṣad tells us that fire, having entered the universe, assumes all forms. The Chāndogya Upaniṣad, however, makes out that fire is the first to evolve from the Primaeval Being and from fire came water and from water the earth. At the time of dissolution, the earth is dissolved in water, and water in fire and fire in the Primaeval Being. *Ākāśa*, ether, space, is sometimes viewed as the first principle.

In regard to the development of the universe, the Upaniṣads look upon the earliest state of the material world as one of extension in space, of which the characteristic feature is vibration represented to us by the phenomenon of sound. From *ākāśa*, *vāyu*, air arises. Vibration by itself cannot create forms unless it meets with obstruction. The interaction of vibrations is possible in air which is the next modification. To sustain the different forces, a third modification arises, *tejas*, of which light and heat are the manifestations. We still do not have

[7] B.U. II. 1.

[8] B.U. V. 5. 1.

[9] C.U. IV. 3. 1–2.

stable forms and so the denser medium of water is produced. A further state of cohesion is found in earth. The development of the world is a process of steady grossening of the subtle *ākāśa* or space. All physical objects, even the most subtle, are built up by the combination of these five elements. Our sense experience depends on them. By the action of vibration comes the sense of sound; by the action of things in a world of vibrations the sense of touch, by the action of light the sense of sight, by the action of water the sense of taste, by the action of earth the sense of smell.

In the Taittirīya Upaniṣad the pupil approaches the father and asks him to explain to him the nature of Brahman. He is given the formal definition and is asked to supply the content by his own reflection. 'That from which these beings are born, that in which when born they live, and that into which they enter at their death is Brahman'. What is the reality which conforms to this account? The son is impressed by material phenomena and fixes on matter (*anna*) as the basic principle. He is not satisfied, for matter cannot account for the forms of life. He looks upon life (*prāṇa*) as the basis of the world. Life belongs to a different order from matter. Life, again, cannot be the ultimate principle, for conscious phenomena are not commensurate with living forms. There is something more in consciousness than in life. So he is led to believe that consciousness (*manas*) is the ultimate principle. But consciousness has different grades. The instinctive consciousness of animals is quite different from the intellectual consciousness of human beings. So the son affirms that intellectual consciousness (*vijñāna*) is Brahman. Man alone, among nature's children has the capacity to change himself by his own effort and transcend his limitations. Even this is incomplete because it is subject to discords and dualities. Man's intellect aims at the attainment of truth but succeeds only in making guesses about it; there must be a power in man which sees the truth unveiled. A deeper principle of consciousness must emerge if the fundamental intention of nature, which has led to the development of matter, life, mind, and intellectual consciousness, is to be accomplished. The son finally arrives at the truth that spiritual freedom or delight (*ānanda*), the ecstasy of fulfilled existence is the ultimate principle. Here the search ends, not simply because the pupil's doubts are satisfied but because the pupil's doubts are stilled by the vision of Self-evident Reality. He apprehends the Supreme Unity that lies behind all the lower forms. The Upaniṣad suggests that he leaves behind the discursive reason and contemplates the One and is lost in ecstasy.[10] It concludes with the affirmation that absolute Reality is *satyam*, truth, *jñānam*, consciousness, *anantam*, infinity.

There are some who affirm that *ānanda* is the nearest approximation to Absolute Reality, but is not itself the Absolute Reality. For it is a logical representation. The experience gives us peace, but unless we are established in it we have not received the highest.

In this account, the Upaniṣad assumes that the naturalistic theory of evolution cannot be accepted. The world is not to be viewed as an automatic development without any intelligent course or intelligible aim. Matter, life, mind, intelligence are different forms of existence with their specific characteristics and modes of action, each acting on the other but not derived from each other. The evolution of life in the context of matter is produced not by the material principle but by the working of a new life principle which uses the conditions of matter for the production of life. Life is not the mechanical resultant of the antecedent co-ordination of material forces, but it is what is now called an emergent. We cannot, by a complete knowledge of the previous conditions, anticipate the subsequent result. There is an element of the incalculable. Life emerges when the material conditions are available, which permit life

[10] Cf. Jalāl-uddīn Rūmī:

I died a mineral and became a plant.
I died a plant and rose an animal,
I died an animal and I was man.
Why should I fear? When was I less by dying?
Yet once more I shall die as man, to soar
With the blessed angels; but even from angelhood
I must pass on. All except God perishes.
When I have sacrificed my angel soul,
I shall become that which no mind ever conceived.
O, let me not exist! for Non-existence proclaims,
'To him we shall return'.

to organise itself in matter. In this sense, we may say matter aspires for life, but life is not produced by lifeless particles. So also life may be said to be aspiring for or be instinct with mind, which is ready to emerge when conditions enable it to organise itself in living matter. Mind cannot be produced from things without mind. When the necessary mental conditions are prepared, intelligence qualifies the mental living creature. Nature is working according to this fundamental intention, which is being accomplished because it is essentially the instrument of the Supreme Being.

The world is not the result of meaningless chance. There is a purpose working itself out through the ages. It is a view which modern science confirms. By interpreting the fragmentary relics of far remote times, science tells us how this earth in which we live was gradually adapted to be a place where life could develop, how life came and developed through uncounted centuries until animal consciousness arose and this again gradually developed, until apparently, man with self-conscious reason appeared on the scene. The long record of the development of the human race and the great gifts of spiritual men like the Buddha, Socrates, Jesus make out that man has to be transcended by God-man.

It cannot be argued that, when material particles are organised in a specific way, life arises. The principle of organisation is not matter. The explanation of a thing is to be sought in what is above it in the scale of existence and value and not below it. Matter cannot raise itself. It moves to a higher level by the help of the higher itself. It cannot undergo inner development without being acted upon by something above it. The lower is the material for the higher. Life is the matter for mind and form for physical material: so also intellect is form for the mind and matter for the spirit. The eternal is the origin of the actual and its nisus to improvement. To think of it as utterly transcendent or as a future possibility is to miss its incidence in the actual. We cannot miss the primordiality of the Supreme. 'Verily, in the beginning this world was Brahman'.[11] There is the perpetual activity of the Supreme in the world.

[11] B.U. I. 4. 10–11; Maitrī VI. 17.

The Upaniṣad affirms that Brahman on which all else depends, to which all existences aspire, Brahman which is sufficient to itself, aspiring to no other, without any need, is the source of all other beings, the intellectual principle, the perceiving mind, life, and body. It is the principle which unifies the world of the physicist, the biologist, the psychologist, the logician, the moralist, and the artist. The hierarchy of all things and beings from soulless matter to the deity is the cosmos. Plato's world-architect, Aristotle's world-mover belong to the cosmos. If there is ordered development, progressive evolution, it is because there is the divine principle at work in the universe.

Cosmic process is one of universal and unceasing change and is patterned on a duality which is perpetually in conflict, the perfect order of heaven and the chaos of the dark waters. Life creates opposites, as it creates sexes, in order to reconcile them. 'In the beginning the woman (Ūrvaśī) went about in the flood seeking a master'. Indra, for example, divided the world into earth and sky. He 'produced his father and mother from his own body'. This conflict runs through the whole empirical world, and will end when the aim of the universe is accomplished. Creation moves upward towards the divine. When the union between the controlling spirit and the manifesting matter is completed, the purpose of the world, the end of the evolutionary process, the revelation of spirit on earth is accomplished. The earth is the foothold of God, the mother of all creatures whose father is heaven.[12]

[12] The Chinese believe that Chien (Heaven) is the father and Khun (Earth) is the mother of all terrestrial existence. Zeus as Sky-father is in essential relation to Earth-mother. The two are correlative. See A. B. Cook, *Zeus*, Vol. I (1914), p. 779.

Zoroaster reaches the conception of a single spiritual God, Ormuzd or Ahura Mazda, in whom the principle of good is personified, while the evil principle is embodied in Ahriman, or Angra Mainyu, who limits the omnipotence of Ahura Mazda. The whole creation is a combat between the two. The two principles strive eternally in life, and in this struggle men take part. Man is responsible for his actions, good or bad. If he struggles against evil, confesses God, and cares for the purity of his body and soul, then after four periods of three thousand years each in the world's history a time shall arrive for the final victory of good over evil, of Ormuzd over Ahriman. The general resurrection of the dead and the

The conflict is not final. The duality is not a sterile dualism. Heaven and earth, God and matter have the same origin.

As regards the primordial God *Hiraṇya-garbha*, a circular process is found. The primal being spontaneously produces the primaeval water; from this comes the primordial God as the first born of the divine Order, the golden germ of the world 'who was the first seed resting on the navel of the unborn'.[13] *Hiraṇya-garbha* who is the World-soul expresses his spirit through the environment. He manifests the forms contained within himself. The world is fixed in him as are the spokes in the hub of a wheel. He is the thread, *sūtrātman*, on which all beings and all worlds are strung like the beads of a necklace. He is the first-born, *prathama-ja*. He is also called Brahmā and these Brahmās are created from world to world.

In the Ṛg Veda, *Hiraṇya-garbha* is the golden germ which enters into creation after the first action of the creator. In the Sāṁkhya, *prakṛti* is treated as unconscious and develops on account of the influence of the multitude of individual subjects, and the first product of development is *mahat*, the great one, or *buddhi*, the intellect. It is the development of cosmic intelligence or *Hiraṇya-garbha*. On the subjective side, *buddhi* is the first element of the *liṅga* or the subtle body. It is the essence of the individual spirit. *Buddhi* serves as the basis for the development of the principle of individuation, *ahaṁkāra*, from which are derived, on the one hand, mind and the ten sense organs, five of perception and five of action and, on the other hand, the subtle elements from which arise in their turn the gross elements. *Sattva* is *buddhi*, the innermost of the three circles, the outer being *rajas* and *tamas* which are identified with *ahaṁkāra* and *manas*, which are the emanations of *rajas*

---

last judgment will take place then, assuring him of his place among the saved and the righteous.

The Jews adopted the two principles of good and evil and they were taken over by Christianity. When Blake speaks of the marriage of Heaven and Hell, Heaven represents the one clear light over all and Hell the dark world of passion and the senses. Divided, both are equally barren, but from their union springs joy. 'Oh that man would seek immortal moments! Oh that men could converse with God' was Blake's cry.

[13] R.V. X. 82; IV. 58. 5.

and *tamas*. The *sattva* or the *buddhi* is the *bīja*, the seed of the living individual, since it contains the seeds of *karma* which develop at each birth into a sense-organism. The *sattva* or *liṅga* is called the ego, the *jīva*. As the *buddhi* is the *sūtrātman* of the individual, so is *Hiraṇya-garbha* the *sūtrātman*, the thread-controller of the world.

In the Kaṭha Upaniṣad, in the development of principles the great self stands after the undeveloped and the primaeval spirit. *Hiraṇya-garbha*, the World-soul is the first product of the principle of non-being influenced by the Eternal Spirit, *Īśvara*. The *puruṣa* of the Sāṁkhya is the Eternal Spirit made many. *Hiraṇya-garbha* is the great self, *mahān ātmā*, which arises from the undiscriminated, the *avyakta*, which corresponds to the primitive material or waters of the *Brāhmaṇas*, or the *prakṛti* of the Sāṁkhya. We have the Supreme Self, the Absolute, the Supreme Self as the eternal subject observing the eternal object, waters or *prakṛti* and the great self which is the first product of this interaction of the eternal subject and the principle of objectivity. The Supreme Lord, *Īśvara*, who eternally produces, outlasts the drama of the universe. Śaṁkara begins his commentary on the *Bhagavadgītā* with the verse: '*Nārāyaṇa* is beyond the unmanifest. The golden egg is produced from the unmanifest. The earth with its seven islands and all other worlds are in the egg'. The names and forms of the manifested world are latent in the egg as the future tree is in the seed.

Hiraṇya-garbha answers to the Logos, the Word of Western thought. For Plato, the Logos was the archetypal idea. For the Stoics it is the principle of reason which quickens and informs matter. Philo speaks of the Divine Logos as the 'first born son', 'archetypal man', 'image of God', 'through whom the world was created'. Logos, the Reason, 'the Word was in the beginning and the Word became flesh'. The Greek term, Logos, means both Reason and Word. The latter indicates an act of divine will. Word is the active expression of character. The difference between the conception of Divine Intelligence or Reason and the Word of God is that the latter represents the will of the Supreme. *Vāc* is Brahman. *Vāc*, word, wisdom, is treated in the Ṛg Veda as the all-knowing. The first-born of Ṛta is *vāc: yāvad brahma tiṣṭhati tāvatī vāk.*[14] The Logos is conceived as personal like *Hiraṇya-garbha.* 'The Light was the light of men'. 'The Logos became flesh'.[15]

The Supreme is generally conceived as light, *jyotiṣāṁ jyotiḥ,* the light of lights. Light is the principle of communication. *Hiraṇya-garbha* is organically bound up with the world. Himself, a creature, the first-born of creation, he shares the fate of all creation in the end.[16] But *Īśvara* is prior to the World-soul. The principle of process applies to God. While he is the expression of the non-temporal he is also the temporal. *Īśvara,* the eternal Being functions in the temporal *Hiraṇya-garbha.* Rāmānuja who looks upon *Īśvara* as the supreme transcendent Reality above all world events treats Brahmā as the demi-urge of creation who forms the lower world in the name and bidding of God.

Why is the universe what it is, rather than something else? Why is there this something, rather than another? This is traced to the divine will. This world and its controlling spirit are the expressions of the Supreme Lord. While the World-soul and the world are organically related and are interdependent, there is no such relationship between the Supreme Lord and the world, for that would be to subject the infinite to the finite. The relationship is an 'accident' to use Whitehead's expression. This word 'accident' implies two different considerations: (1) that Divine Creativity is not bound up with this world in such a way that the changes which occur in the world affect the integrity of the Divine; and (2) that the world is an accidental expression of the Divine principle. Creativity is not bound to express itself in this particular form. If the choice were necessary it would not be free. Creation is the free expression of the Divine mind, *icchā-mātram.* The world is the *manifestation* of *Hiraṇya-garbha* and the *creation* of *Īśvara.* The world is the free self-determination of God. The power of self-determination, self-expression, belongs to God. It is

[14] R.V. X. 114. 8.

[15] John 1:4, 5.

[16] 'When all things are subjected to him then the Son himself will also be subjected to him who put all things under him, that God may be everything to everyone'. I Cor. 15:28.

not by itself. It belongs to the Absolute which is the abode of all possibilities, and by its creative power one of these possibilities is freely chosen for accomplishment. The power of manifestation is not alien to being. It does not enter it from outside. It is in being, inherent in it. It may be active or inactive. We thus get the conception of an Absolute-God, Brahman—*Īśvara*, where the first term indicates infinite being and possibility, and the second suggests creative freedom.[17] Why should the Absolute Brahman perfect, infinite, needing nothing, desiring nothing, move out into the world? It is not compelled to do so. It may have this potentiality but it is not bound or compelled by it. It is free to move or not to move, to throw itself into forms or remain formless. If it still indulges its power of creativity, it is because of its free choice.

In *Īśvara* we have the two elements of wisdom and power, *Śiva* and *Śakti*. By the latter the Supreme who is unmeasured and immeasurable becomes measured and defined. Immutable being becomes infinite fecundity. Pure being, which is the free basis and support of cosmic existence, is not the whole of our experience. Between the Absolute and the World-soul is the Creative Consciousness. It is *prajñāna-ghana* or truth-consciousness. If *sat* denotes the primordial being in its undifferenced unity, *satya* is the same being immanent in its differentiations. If the Absolute is pure unity without any extension or variation, God is the creative power by which worlds spring into existence. The Absolute has moved out of its primal poise and become knowledge-will. It is the all-determining principle. It is the Absolute in action as Lord and Creator. While the Absolute is spaceless and timeless potentiality, God is the vast self-awareness comprehending, apprehending every possibility.[18]

[17] In the Taoist *Tao Tê Ching*, *Tao*, literally 'Way', stands for the Absolute, the divine ground and *Tê* for 'power', for the unfolding of the divine possibilities. Cf. also *tathatā* or suchness and *ālaya-vijñāna* the all-conserving or receptacle consciousness.

[18] Eckhart says: 'God and Godhead are as different as heaven from earth. . . . God becomes and unbecomes'. 'All in Godhead is one, and of this naught can be said. God works, but Godhead works not. There is no work for it to do and no working in it. Never did it contemplate anything of work. God and Godhead differ after the manner of working and

Brahman is not merely a featureless Absolute. It is all this world. *Vāyu* or air is said to be manifest Brahman, *pratyakṣam brahma*. The Śvetāśvatara Upaniṣad makes out that Brahman is beast, bird, and insect, the tottering old man, boy, and girl. Brahman sustains the cosmos and is the self of each individual. Supra-cosmic transcendence and cosmic universality are both real phases of the one Supreme. In the former aspect the Spirit is in no way dependent on the cosmic manifold; in the latter the Spirit functions as the principle of the cosmic manifold. The supra-cosmic silence and the cosmic integration are both real. The two, *nirguṇa* and *saguṇa* Brahman, Absolute and God, are not different. Jayatīrtha contends that Śaṁkara is wrong in holding that Brahman is of two kinds—*brahmaṇo dvairūpyasya aprāmāṇikatvāt*. It is the same Brahman who is described in different ways.

The personality of God is not to be conceived on the human lines. He is not to be thought of as a greatly magnified person. We should not attribute to the Divine human qualities as we know them.[19] We have (1) the Absolute, (2) God as Creative power, (3) God immanent in this world. These are not to be regarded as separate entities. They are arranged in this order because there is a logical priority. The Absolute must be there with all its possibilities before the Divine Creativity can choose one. The divine choice must be there before there can be the Divine immanent in this world. This is a logical succession

---

not working. . . . When I come into the Ground, into the depths, into the flow and fount of Godhead, none will ask me whence I have come or whither I go. None will have missed me; God passes away'. *Sermon* LVI. Evans' E.T.

[19] Aquinas says: 'Things said alike of God and of other beings are not said either in quite the same sense or in a totally different sense but in an analogous sense'. *Summa Contra Gentiles* XXXIV. God is not good or loving in the human sense. 'For who hath known the mind of the Lord?' Romans 11:34. God is personal, but, as Karl Barth says, 'personal in an *incomprehensible* way in so far as the conception of His personality surpasses all our views of personality. This is so, just because He and He alone is a true, real and genuine person. Were we to overlook this and try to conceive God in our own strength according to our conception of personality, we should make an idol out of God'. *The Knowledge of God and the Service of God* (1938), pp. 31ff.

and not a temporal one. The world-spirit must be there before there can be the world. We thus get the four poises or statuses of reality,[20] (1) the Absolute, Brahman, (2) the Creative Spirit, *Īśvara*, (3) the World-Spirit, *Hiraṇya-garbha*, and (4) the World. This is the way in which the Hindu thinkers interpret the integral nature of the Supreme Reality. Māṇḍūkya Upaniṣad says that Brahman is *catuṣ-pāt*, four-footed, and its four principles are Brahman, *Īśvara*, *Hiraṇya-garbha*, and *Virāj*.

The conception of *tri-suparṇa* is developed in the fourth section of the Taittirīya Upaniṣad. The Absolute is conceived as a nest from out of which three birds have emerged, viz. *virāj*, *Hiraṇya-garbha*, and *Īśvara*. The Absolute conceived as it is in itself, independent of any creation, is called Brahman. When it is thought of as having manifested itself as the universe, it is called *virāj;* when it is thought of as the spirit moving everywhere in the universe, it is called *Hiraṇya-garbha;* when it is thought of as a personal God creating, protecting, and destroying the universe, it is called *Īśvara*. *Īśvara* becomes *Brahmā*, *Viṣṇu*, and *Śiva* when his three functions are taken separately. The real is not a sum of these. It is an ineffable unity in which these conceptual distinctions are made. These are fourfold to our mental view, separable only in appearance. If we identify the real with any one definable state of being, however pure and perfect, we violate the unity and divide the indivisible. The different standpoints are consistent with each other, complementary to each other and necessary in their totality for an integral view of life and the world. If we are able to hold them together, the conflicting views which are emphasised exclusively by certain schools of Indian Vedānta become reconciled.

Absolute being is not an existing quality to be found in the things. It is not an object of thought or the result of production. It forms an absolute contrast to, and is fundamentally different from, things that are, as is in its way nothingness. It can be expressed only negatively or analogically. It is that from which our speech turns back along with the mind, being unable to comprehend its fullness. It is that which the tongue of man

[20] [See original, 65 n[2], for a comparison of the Upanishadic stages of reality with Plotinus' scheme.—Ed.]

cannot truly express nor human intelligence conceive. Śaṁkara in his commentary on the *Brahma-Sūtra* refers to an Upaniṣad text which is not to be found in any of the extant Upaniṣads. Bāhva, asked by Bāṣkali to expound the nature of Brahman, kept silent. He prayed, 'Teach me, sir'. The teacher was silent, and when addressed a second and a third time he said: 'I am teaching but you do not follow. The self is silence'.

We can only describe the Absolute in negative terms. In the words of Plotinus, 'We say what he is not, we cannot say what he is'. The Absolute is beyond the sphere of predication. It is the *śūnyatā* of the Buddhists. It is 'not gross, not subtle, not short, not long, not glowing, not shadowy, not dark, not attached, flavourless, smell-less, eye-less, ear-less, speech-less, mind-less, breath-less, mouth-less, not internal, not external, consuming nothing and consumed by nothing'.[21] It cannot be truly designated. Any description makes It into something. It is nothing among things. It is non-dual, Advaita. It denies duality. This does not mean, however, that the Absolute is non-being. It means only that the Absolute is all-inclusive and nothing exists outside it.

Negative characters should not mislead us into thinking that Brahman is a nonentity. While it is non-empirical, it is also inclusive of the whole empirical world. The Absolute is described as 'full both of light and not-light, of desire and not-desire, of anger and not-anger, of law and not-law, having verily filled all, both the near and the far off, the this and the that'.[22] Negative and positive characterisations are given to affirm the positivity of being.

To say that the nature of Brahman cannot be defined does not mean that it has no essential nature of its own. We cannot define it by its accidental features, for they do not belong to its essence. There is nothing outside it. As no enquiry into its nature can be instituted without some description, its *svarūpa* or essential nature is said to be *sat* or being, *cit* or consciousness, and *ānanda* or bliss. These are different phrases for the same being. Self-being, self-consciousness, and self-

[21] B.U. II. 8. 8. [See original, 67 n[1], for texts on the Infinite by Plotinus, Pseudo-Dionysius, Lao-Tzu, and Chuang-Tzu.—Ed.]

[22] B.U. IV. 4. 5.

delight are one. It is absolute being in which there is no nothingness. It is absolute consciousness in which there is no non-consciousness. It is absolute bliss in which there is no suffering or negation of bliss. All suffering is due to a second, an obstacle; all delight arises from the realisation of something withheld, by the overcoming of obstacles, by the surpassing of the limit. It is this delight that overflows into creation. The self-expression of the Absolute, the creation of numberless universes is also traced to Brahman. All things that exist are what they are, because of the nature of Brahman as *sat*, *cit*, and *ānanda*. All things are forms of one immutable being, variable expressions of the invariable reality. To describe Brahman as the cause of the world is to give its *taṭastha* or accidental feature. The defining characteristics are in both cases due to our logical needs. When the Absolute is regarded as the basis and explanation of the world, he is conceived as the lord of all, the knower of all, the inner controller of all.[23] God has moved out everywhere: *sa paryagāt*. The Śvetāśvatara Upaniṣad speaks of the one God, beside whom there is no second, who creates all the worlds and rules with His powers, and at the end of time rolls them up again.[24] He lives in all things and yet transcends them. The Universal Self is like the sun who is the eye of the whole universe and is untouched by the defects of our vision. He is said to fill the whole world and yet remain beyond its confines. 'Verily motionless like a lone tree does the God stand in the heaven, and yet by Him is this whole world filled'.[25]

The distinction between Brahman in itself and Brahman in the universe, the transcendent beyond manifestation and the transcendent in manifestation, the indeterminate and the determinate, *nirguṇo guṇī*, is not exclusive.[26] The two are like two sides of one reality. The Real is at the same time being realised.

[23] Mā.U. 6.

[24] III. 2. 3; VI. 1–12.

[25] S.U. III. 9.

[26] Cf. Eckhart: 'The Godhead gave all things up to God. The Godhead is poor, naked and empty as though it were not; it has not, wills not, wants not, works not, gets not. It is God who has the treasure and the bride in him, the Godhead is as void as though it were not.'

In the metrical Upaniṣads, as in the *Bhagavadgītā*, the personal is said to be superior to the superpersonal: *puruṣān na paraṁ kiñcit*, there is nothing beyond the person. It is doubtful whether the author of the *Brahma-Sūtra* accepted the distinction of *saguṇa* and *nirguṇa* in regard to Brahman. Even the *Nirguṇa* Brahman is not without determinations. The *Sūtrakāra* makes a distinction between the super-personal (*apuruṣa-vidha*) and the personal (*puruṣa-vidha*), i.e., between Brahman and *Īśvara.* The latter is not a human fancy or a concession to the weak in mind. The *nirākāra* (formless), and the *sākāra* (with form), are different aspects of the same Reality. The seeker can choose either in his spiritual practices. In *Brahma-Sūtra* III. 3, we find that the author maintains that the *akṣara* texts which describe Brahman negatively as 'not this, not this' are 'not useful for meditation'. He holds that Brahman is unaffected by the different states, of waking, dream, sleep. The view that Brahman undergoes changes is refuted on the ground that they relate to the effects due to the self-concealment of Brahman. Bādarāyaṇa denies reality to a second principle.

Hiraṇya-garbha, the World-soul is the divine creator, the supreme lord *Īśvara* at work in this universe. A definite possibility of the Absolute is being realised in this world. In the Upaniṣads the distinction between *Īśvara* and *Hiraṇya-garbha*, between God and the World-soul is not sharply drawn. If the World-soul is ungrounded in *Īśvara,* if he is exclusively temporal, then we cannot be certain of the end of the cosmic process. When the Upaniṣads assert that the individual ego is rooted in the universal self or *Ātman*, it would be preposterous to imagine that the World-soul is unrelated to *Īśvara* or Brahman. *Hiraṇya-garbha* who has in him the whole development in germ acts on the waters. As we have seen, the image of waters is an ancient one by which human thought attempts to explain the development of the universe. The waters are initially at rest and so free from waves or forms. The first movement, the first disturbance, creates forms and is the seed of the universe. The play of the two is the life of the universe. When the development is complete, when what is in germ is manifest, we have the world-consummation. *Hiraṇya-garbha* creates the world according to the eternal Veda, which has within itself eternally the primary types of all classes of things; even as the God of the mediaeval Scholastics creates according to the eternal archetype of Ideas which He as the eternal Word eternally possesses. Brahman is the unity of all that is named. *Hiraṇya-garbha* or Brahmā is the World-soul and is subject to changes of the world. He is *kārya* Brahmā or effect, Brahman as distinct from *Īśvara* who is *kāraṇa* Brahman or causal Brahman. *Hiraṇya-garbha* arises at every world-beginning and is dissolved at every world-ending. *Īśvara* is not subject to these changes. For both Saṁkara and Rāmānuja, *Hiraṇya-garbha* has the place of a subordinate and created demi-urge. *Īśvara* is the eternal God who is not drawn into but directs the play of the worlds that rise and perish and is Himself existing transcendentally from all eternity. The Vedic deities are subordinate to *Īśvara* and hold a similar position to Him in the formation and control of the world that the angelic powers and directors maintain in the heavenly hierarchy of Scholasticism and of Dante.

We have thus the four sides of one whole: (1) the transcendental universal being anterior to any concrete reality; (2) the causal principle of all differentiation; (3) the innermost essence of the world; and (4) the manifest world. They are co-existent and not alternating poises where we have either a quiescent Brahman or a creative Lord. These are simultaneous sides of the one Reality.

Ultimate Reality: *Atman*

The word *ātman* is derived from *an* 'to breathe'. It is the breath of life. Gradually its meaning is extended to cover life, soul, self, or essential being of the individual. Śaṁkara derives *ātman* from the root which means 'to obtain' 'to eat or enjoy or pervade all'. *Ātman* is the principle of man's life, the soul that pervades his being, his breath, *prāṇa*, his intellect, *prajñā*, and transcends them. *Ātman* is what remains when everything that is not the self is eliminated. The Ṛg Veda speaks of the unborn part, *ajo bhāgaḥ*.[1] There is an unborn and so immortal element in man, which is not to be confused with body, life, mind, and intellect. These are not the self but its forms, its external expressions. Our true self is a pure existence, self-aware, unconditioned by the forms of mind and intellect. When we cast the self free from all outward events, there arises from the inward depths an experience, secret and wonderful, strange and great. It is the miracle of self-knowledge, *ātma-jñāna*. Just as, in relation to the universe, the real is Brahman, while name and form are only a play of manifestation, so also the individual egos are the varied expressions of the One Universal Self. As Brahman is the eternal quiet underneath the drive and activity of the universe, so *ātman* is the foundational reality underlying the conscious powers of the individual, the inward ground of the human soul. There is an ultimate depth to our life below the plane of thinking and striving. The *ātman* is the superreality of the *jīva*, the individual ego.

The Chāndogya Upaniṣad gives us a story, where gods and demons both anxious to learn the true nature of the Self approach Prajā-pati who maintains that the ultimate self is

[1] R.V. X. 16. 4.

free from sin, free from old age, free from death and grief, free from hunger and thirst, which desires nothing and imagines nothing. It is the persisting spirit, that which remains constant in all the vicissitudes of waking, dream, and sleep, death, rebirth, and deliverance. The whole account assumes that there is consciousness even in the apparently unconscious states, when we sleep, when we are drugged or stunned. The gods sent Indra and the demons Virocana as their representatives to learn the truth. The first suggestion is that the self is the image that we see in the eye, in water, or in a mirror. The conception of the self as the physical body is inadequate. To indicate that what we see in another's eye, a pail of water, or a mirror is not the true self, Prajā-pati asked them to put on their best clothes and look again. Indra saw the difficulty and said to Prajā-pati that as this self (the shadow in the water) is well adorned when the body is well adorned, well dressed when the body is well dressed, well cleaned when the body is well cleaned, so that self will also be blind if the body is blind, lame if the body is lame, crippled if the body is crippled, and will perish in fact as soon as the body perishes. Such a view cannot be accepted. If the self is not the body, may it be the dreaming self? The second suggestion is that the true self is 'he who moves about happy in dreams'. Again a difficulty was felt. Indra says that, though it is true that this dreaming self is not affected by the changes of the body, yet in dreams we feel that we are struck or chased, we experience pain and shed tears. We rage in dreams, storm with indignation, do things perverted, mean, and malicious. Indra feels that the self is not the same as dream-consciousness. The self is not the composite of mental states, however independent they may be of the accidents of the body. Dream states are not self-existent. Indra again approaches Prajā-pati who gives him another suggestion that the self is the consciousness in deep sleep. Indra feels that, in that state, there is consciousness neither of the self nor of the objective world. Indra feels that he does not know himself nor does he know anything that exists. He is gone to utter annihilation. But the self exists even in deep sleep. Even when the object is not present, the subject is there. The final reality is the active universal consciousness, which is not to be confused with either the bodily, or the dreaming consciousness or the consciousness in deep sleep. In the state of deep, dreamless sleep, the self wrapped round by the intellect has no consciousness of objects, but is not unconscious. The true self is the absolute self, which is not an abstract metaphysical category but the authentic spiritual self. The other forms belong to objectified being. Self is life, not an object. It is an experience, in which the self is the knowing subject and is at the same time the known object. Self is open only to self. The life of the self is not set over against knowledge of it as an objective thing. Self is not the objective reality, nor something purely subjective. The subject-object relationship has meaning only in the world of objects, in the sphere of discursive knowledge. The Self is the light of lights, and through it alone is there any light in the universe. It is perpetual, abiding light. It is that which neither lives nor dies, which has neither movement nor change and which endures when all else passes away. It is that which sees and not the object seen. Whatever is an object belongs to the not-self. The self is the constant witness-consciousness.

The four states stand on the subjective side for the four kinds of soul, *Vaiśvānara*, the experiencer of gross things, *Taijasa*, the experiencer of the subtle, *Prājña*, the experiencer of the unmanifested objectivity, and the *Turīya*, the Supreme Self. The Māṇḍūkya Upaniṣad, by an analysis of the four modes of consciousness, waking, dream, deep sleep, and illumined consciousness, makes out that the last is the basis of the other three. On the objective side we have the cosmos, *Virāj*, the World-soul *Hiraṇya-garbha*, the Supreme God, *Īśvara*, and the Absolute, Brahman. By looking upon *Īśvara* as *prājña*, it is suggested that the supreme intelligence who dwells in the sleeping state holds all things in an unmanifested condition. The divine wisdom sees all things, not as human reason does in parts and relations, but in the original reason of their existence, their primal truth and reality. It is what the Stoics call *spermatikos* or the seed Logos which is manifested in conscious beings as a number of seed logoi.

In treatises on *yoga*, the potential all-consciousness of the state of sleep is represented in the form of a radiant serpent called *Kuṇḍalinī* or *Vāg-devī*. We come across this representation in earlier treatises also. In the Ṛg Veda, *vāc* is said to be the serpent queen, *sarpa-rājñī*. The process of *yoga* consists in rousing the radiant serpent and lifting it up from the lowest sphere to the heart, where in union with *prāṇa* or life-breath its universal nature is realised and from it to the top of the skull. It goes out through an opening called *brahma-randhra* to which corresponds in the cosmic organism the opening formed by the sun on the top of the vault of the sky.

Brahman as *Ātman*

In the early prose Upaniṣads, *ātman* is the principle of the individual consciousness and Brahman the superpersonal ground of the cosmos. Soon the distinction diminishes and the two are identified. God is not merely the transcendent numinous other, but is also the universal spirit which is the basis of human personality and its ever-renewing vitalising power. Brahman, the first principle of the universe, is known through *ātman*, the inner self of man. In the *Śatapatha Brāhmaṇa*[1] and the Chāndogya Upaniṣad[2] it is said: 'Verily this whole world is Brahman', and also 'This soul of mine within the heart, this is Brahman'. 'That person who is seen in the eye, He is *ātman*, that is Brahman'.[3] God is both the wholly other, transcendent and utterly beyond the world and man, and yet he enters into man and lives in him and becomes the inmost content of his very existence.[4]

[1] X. 6. 3.

[2] III. 14. 1.

[3] B.U. I. 4. 10. Cf. Keith: 'It is impossible to deny that the Ātman-Brahman doctrine has a long previous history in the Brāhmaṇas and is a logical development of the idea of unity of the Ṛg Veda'. *The Religion and Philosophy of the Veda and the Upaniṣads*, p. 494. Heraclitus says 'I searched myself'. The Logos is to be sought within, for man's nature is a microcosm and represents the nature of the whole.

Cf. Plotinus: 'One that seeks to penetrate the nature of the Divine Mind must see deeply into the nature of his own soul, into the Divinest point of himself. He must first make abstraction of the body, then of the lower soul which built up that body, then of all the faculties of sense, of all desires and emotions and every such triviality, of all that leans towards the mortal. What is left after this abstraction is the part which we describe as the image of the Divine Mind, an emanation preserving some of that Divine Light'. *Enneads* V. 3. 9.

[4] C.U. IV. 15.

Nārāyaṇa is the God in man who lives in constant association with *nara*, the human being. He is the immortal dwelling in the mortals.[5] The human individual is more than the universe. He lives independently in his own inexpressible infinity as well as in the cosmic harmonies. We can be one with all cosmic existence by entering into the cosmic consciousness. We become superior to all cosmic existence by entering into the world-transcending consciousness. Answering to the four grades of consciousness, waking, dream, deep sleep, spiritual consciousness, we have the four states of the individual, *sthūla* (gross), *sūkṣma* (subtle), *kāraṇa* (causal), and the pure self. As *Īśvara* is the cause of the world, so the causal self is the source of the development of the subtle and the gross bodies.[6]

[5] R.V. IV. 2. 1.

[6] The first *tattva* is the root of manifestation, called *mahat* or the great principle. In *ahaṁkāra* we find individual consciousness which proceeds from the intellectual principle by an individualising determination. Sometimes, *citta* is said to be the first product of *prakṛti*, with its triple character of *buddhi* or discrimination, *ahaṁkāra* or self-sense and *manas* or mind.

The Status of the World: *Māyā* and *Avidyā*

The ecstasy of divine union, the bliss of realisation tempts one to disregard the world with its imperfections and look upon it as a troubled and unhappy dream. The actual fabric of the world, with its loves and hates, with its wars and battles, with its jealousies and competitions as well as its unasked helpfulness, sustained intellectual effort, intense moral struggle seems to be no more than an unsubstantive dream, a phantasmagoria dancing on the fabric of pure being. Throughout the course of human history, men have taken refuge from the world of stresses, vexations, and indignities in the apprehension of a spirit beyond. The prayer to 'lead us from unreality to reality, from darkness to light, from death to immortality' assumes the distinction between reality, light, and immortality and unreality, darkness, and death. The Katha Upaniṣad warns us not to find reality and certainty in the unrealities and uncertainties of this world. The Chāndogya Upaniṣad tells us that a covering of untruth hides from us the ultimate truth even as the surface of the earth hides from us the golden treasure hidden under it. The truth is covered by untruth, *anṛta*. The Bṛhad-āraṇyaka and the Īśa Upaniṣads speak to us of the veiling of truth by a disc of gold and invoke the grace of God for removing the veil and letting us see the truth. According to the Śvetāśvatara Upaniṣad, we can achieve the cessation of the great world-illusion, *viśva-māyā-nivṛttiḥ* by the worship of God.[1] If this aspect of spiritual experience were all, the world we live in, that of ignorance, darkness, and death would be quite different from the world of underlying reality, the world of truth, light, and life. The distinction would be-

[1] I. 10.

come one of utter opposition between God and the world. The latter would be reduced to an evil dream from which we must wake up as soon as possible.

Indifference to the world is not, however, the main feature of spiritual consciousness. Brahman, the completely transcendent, the pure silence has another side. Brahman is apprehended in two ways. Saṁkara says: *dvirūpaṁ hi brahmāvagamyate, nāma-rūpa-vikāra-bhedopādhi-viśiṣṭam, tad viparītaṁ sarvopādhi-varjitam.* Both the Absolute and the Personal God are real; only the former is the logical prius of the latter. The soul when it rises to full attention knows itself to be related to the single universal consciousness, but when it turns outward it sees the objective universe as a manifestation of this single consciousness. The withdrawal from the world is not the conclusive end of the spiritual quest. There is a return to the world accompanied by a persistent refusal to take the world as it confronts us as final. The world has to be redeemed and it can be redeemed because it has its source in God and final refuge in God.

There are many passages where the world of duality is suggested to be only seeming. The existence of duality is not admitted to be absolutely real. In the passage of the Chāndogya Upaniṣad regarding the modifications of the three fundamental constituents of being, fire, water, and food, it is said that just as all that is made of clay, copper, or iron is only a modification, a verbal expression, a simple name, the reality being clay, copper, or iron, even so all things can be reduced to three primary forms of reality. It is suggested that all things are reducible to reality, being mere modifications. All this is to be understood as meaning that the Absolute stands above becoming and passing away which it transcends.

In the Maitrī Upaniṣad, the Absolute is compared to a spark, which, made to revolve, creates apparently a fiery circle, an idea expanded by Gauḍapāda in his *Kārikā* on the Māṇḍūkya Upaniṣad. This may suggest that the world is a mere appearance. Even here the intention may well be to contrast the reality of the Absolute with empirical reality without making the latter an illusion.

The assertion that with the knowledge of the Self all is known [2] does not exclude the reality of what is derived from the Self. When the Aitareya Upaniṣad asserts that the universe is founded in consciousness and guided by it, it assumes the reality of the universe and not merely its apparent existence. To seek the one is not to deny the many. The world of name and form has its roots in Brahman, though it does not constitute the nature of Brahman. The world is neither one with Brahman nor wholly other than Brahman. The world of fact cannot be apart from the world of being. From one being no other being is born. It exists only in another form, *saṁsthānāntareṇa*.

Māyā in this view states the fact that Brahman without losing his integrity is the basis of the world. Though devoid of all specifications, Brahman is the root cause of the universe. 'If a thing cannot subsist apart from something else, the latter is the essence of that thing'. The cause is logically prior to the effect. Questions of temporal beginning and growth are subordinate to this relation of ground and consequent. The world does not carry its own meaning. To regard it as final and ultimate is an act of ignorance. So long as the erroneous view of the independence of the world does not disappear, our highest good will not be realised.

The world is the creation of God, the active Lord. The finite is the self-limitation of the infinite. No finite can exist in and by itself. It exists by the infinite. If we seek the dynamic aspect we are inclined to repudiate the experience of pure consciousness. It is not a question of either pure consciousness or dynamic consciousness. These are the different statuses of the one Reality. They are present simultaneously in the universal awareness.

The dependence of the world on God is explained in different ways. In the Chāndogya Upaniṣad, Brahman is defined as *tajjalān* as that (*tat*) which gives rise to (*ja*), absorbs (*lī*), and sustains (*an*) the world. The Bṛhad-āraṇyaka Upaniṣad argues that *satyam* consists of three syllables, *sa, ti, yam,* the first and the last being real and the second unreal, *madhyato anṛtam*. The fleeting is enclosed on both sides by an eternity which is

[2] B.U. II. 4. 5, 7, 9; C.U. VI. 1. 2; M.U. I. 1. 3.

real. The world comes from Brahman and returns to Brahman. Whatever exists owes its being to Brahman. The different metaphors are used to indicate how the universe rises from its central root, how the emanation takes place while the Brahman remains ever-complete, undiminished 'As a spider sends forth and draws in (its thread), as herbs grow on the earth, as the hair (grows) on the head and the body of a living person, so from the Imperishable arises here the universe'. Again, 'As from a blazing fire sparks of like form issue forth by the thousands even so, many kinds of beings issue forth from the Immutable and they return thither too'. The many are parts of Brahman even as waves are parts of the sea. All the possibilities of the world are affirmed in the first being, God. The whole universe before its manifestation was there. The antecedent of the manifested universe is the non-manifested universe, i.e., God. God does not create the world but becomes it. Creation is expression. It is not a making of something out of nothing. It is not making so much as becoming. It is the self-projection of the Supreme. Everything exists in the secret abode of the Supreme. The primary reality contains within itself the source of its own motion and change.

The Śvetāśvatara Upaniṣad mentions the different views of creation held at the time of its composition, that it is due to time, to nature, to necessity, to chance, to the elements, to the person or the combination of these. It repudiates all these views and traces the world to the power of the Supreme.

The Śvetāśvatara Upaniṣad describes God as *māyin*, the wonder-working powerful Being, who creates the world by His powers.[3] Here *māyā* is used in the sense in which the Ṛg Veda employs it, the divine art or power by which the divinity makes a likeness of the eternal prototypes or ideas inherent in his nature. Indra is declared to have assumed many shapes by his *māyā*. *Māyā* is the power of *Īśvara* from which the world arises. He has made this world, 'formed man out of the dust of the ground and breathed into him a living soul'. All the works of the world are wrought by Him. Every existence contained in time is ontologically present in creative eternity. The Supreme is both transcendent and immanent. It is the

[3] III. 10.

one, breathing breathless, *tad ekam, anīd avātam.* It is the manifest and the unmanifest, *vyaktāvyaktāḥ*, the silent and the articulate, *śabdāśabdāḥ.* It is the real and the unreal, *sad-asat.*[4]

While the world is treated as an appearance in regard to pure being, which is indivisible and immutable, it is the creation of *Īśvara* who has the power of manifestation. *Māyā* is that which measures out, moulds forms in the formless. God has control of *māyā;* he is not subject to it. If God were subject to *māyā* he would not be infinite supreme existence. Any being compelled to manifest itself is not free. *Iśvara* has in him the power of manifestation, non-manifestation, and other-manifestation, *kartum, a-kartum, anyathā-kartum.* Brahman is logically prior to *Īśvara* who has the power of manifestation, and takes him over into His transcendental being when He is not manifesting His nature.

This dual nature of the Supreme provides the basis for the reality of personality in God and man, and so for authentic religious experience. This world, far from being unreal, is intimately connected with the Divine Reality. This complex evolving universe is a progressive manifestation of the powers of the Supreme Spirit from matter to spiritual freedom, from *anna* to *ānanda.* The purpose of the cosmic evolution is to reveal the spirit underlying it. God lives, feels, and suffers in every one of us, and in course of time His attributes, knowledge, beauty, and love will be revealed in each of us.

When the Kaṭha Upaniṣad says that the Supreme Lord experiences the results of deeds, it suggests that we are the images and likenesses of God, and when we experience the results of our deeds, He does also. There is an intimate connexion between God and the world of souls.

Deussen holds that the idealistic monism of Yājñavalkya is the main teaching of the Upaniṣads and the other doctrines of theism, and cosmogonism are deviations from it caused by the inability of man to remain on the heights of pure speculative thought. The view which regards the universe as actually real, the *Ātman* as the universe which we know, and the theistic

[4] R.V. X. 5. 7; M.U. II. 2. 1.

developments are said to be departures from the exalted idealism of Yājñavalkya. It is not necessary to look upon the theism emphasised in the Kaṭha and the Śvetāśvatara Upaniṣads as a declension from the pure monistic idealism. It is in the direct line of development of Upaniṣad thought.

The Absolute is not a metaphysical abstraction or a void of silence. It is the absolute of this relative world of manifestation. What is subject to change and growth in the world of becoming reaches its fulfilment in the world of the Absolute. The Beyond is not an annulling or a cancellation of the world of becoming, but its transfiguration. The Absolute is the life of this life, the truth of this truth.

If the world were altogether unreal, we could not progress from the unreal to the Real. If a passage is possible from the empirical to the Real, the Real is to be found in the empirical also. The ignorance of the mind and the senses and the apparent futilities of human life are the material for the self-expression of that Being, for its unfolding. Brahman accepts world existence. The Ultimate Reality sustains the play of the world and dwells in it. That is why we are able to measure the distance of the things of the world from the Absolute and evaluate their grades of being. There is nothing in this world which is not lit up by God. Even the material objects which lack the intelligence to discover the nature of the divine ground of their being are the emanations of the creative energy of God and they are able to reveal to the discerning eye the divine within their material frames. What is not possible for inanimate and non-rational beings is open to the rational human being. He can attain to a knowledge of the divine ground of his being. He is not coerced into it, but has to attain it by the exercise of his choice. The unchangeableness of the Supreme does not mean that the universe is a perfectly articulated mechanism in which everything is given from the beginning. The world is real as based on Brahman; it is unreal by itself.

Cosmic existence partakes of the character of the real and the unreal. It is aspiring to become completely real. The Chāndogya Upaniṣad rejects the view that the world was originally *a-sat* or non-being, and from it all existence was produced. It affirms: 'In the beginning this world was just being, one only without a second'.[5]

The Supreme is described as a *kavi*, a poet, an artist, a maker or creator, not a mere imitator. Even as art reveals man's wealth of life, so does the world reveal the immensity of God's life. The *Brahma-Sūtra* refers to the creation of the world as an act of *līlā*, play, the joy of the poet, eternally young.

If immutability is the criterion of reality, then the world of manifestation has no claim to reality. Change is the pervading feature of the world. Changing things imply non-existence at the beginning and non-existence at the end. They are not constantly present. Mortality is imprinted on all beings who are subject to birth, decay, dissolution, and death. This very planet will decline and dissolve. While change is the mark of the relative world, this changing world reaches its fulfilment in the Absolute. What is incomplete in the relative world of becoming is completed in the absolute world of being.

Māyā is also used for *prakṛti*, the objective principle which the personal God uses for creation. All nature, even in the lowest, is in ceaseless movement, aspiring to the next higher stage, of which it is itself an image or lower manifestation. *Prakṛti*, not-self, matter all but cast out from the sphere of being, is tending feebly to get back to the self, receives form and is thus linked up with Absolute Being. Even matter is Brahman. *Prakṛti* by itself is more a demand of thought than a fact of existence. Even the lowest existence has received the impress of the Creative Self. It is not utter non-existence. Absolute non-being is non-existent. It is impossible in a world which flows freely from the bounty of being. *Prakṛti* is called non-being. It is not strictly correct. This description indicates its distance from being. It is the ultimate possibility on the side of descent from the Divine, almost non-being, but not utter non-being.

While *prakṛti* is said to be the *māyā* of God, its forms seem to us individual souls to be external to us. It is the source of our ignorance of its real nature.

While the world is created by the power of *māyā* of *Īśvara*,

[5] VI. 2. 2.

the individual soul is bound down by *māyā* in the sense of *avidyā* or ignorance. The manifestation of Primordial Being is also a concealment of His original nature. The self-luminous moves about clothed in the splendours of the cosmic light which are not His real nature. We must tear the cosmic veil and get behind the golden brightness which *Savitṛ* has diffused. The Upaniṣad says: 'Two birds, inseparable friends cling to the same tree. One of them eats the sweet fruit, the other looks on without eating. On the same tree man sits, grieving, immersed, bewildered by his own impotence (*an-īśa*). But when he sees the other lord (*īśa*), contented and knows his glory, then his grief passes away'. We mistake the multiplicity for ultimate reality. If we overlook the unity, we are lost in ignorance.

When we get to the concept of *prakṛti* we are in the realm of *Hiraṇya-garbha.* The similes employed by the Upaniṣads, salt and water, fire and sparks, spider and thread, flute and sound assume the existence of an element different from being. Into the original stillness of *prakṛti*, *Hiraṇya-garbha* or Brahmā sends sound, *nāda-brahma.* By his ecstatic dance the world evolves. This is the meaning of the symbol of *Naṭa-rāja.* His dance is not an illusion. It is a timeless fact of the Divine Reality. The forms are manifestations of the Real, not arbitrary inventions out of nothing. Form, *rūpa,* is the revelation of the formless *a-rūpa. Nāma,* name, is not the word by which we describe the object, but it is the power or the character of reality which the form of a thing embodies. The Infinite is nameless for it includes all names. The emphasis right through is on the dependence of the world on Brahman. The relative rests in the Absolute. There can be no echo without a noise. The world is not self-explanatory; it is not the cause of itself. It is an effect. The Īśa Upaniṣad indicates that the basic reality is the One, and the derivative and dependent reality is the many. When the Kena Upaniṣad says that Brahman is the mind of mind, the life of life, it does not assert the unreality of mind and life, but affirms the inferiority, the incompleteness of our present existence. All that we find in the world is an imperfect representation, a divided expression of what is eternally in the Absolute Being.

The world depends on Brahman, and not Brahman on the world. 'God is the dwelling-place of the universe; but the universe is not the dwelling-place of God' is a well-known Rabbinic dictum. The world of experience with its three states of waking, dream, and deep sleep is based on the subject-object relation. This duality is the principle of all manifestation. The objects are perceived in both dream and waking and the distinction of seer and seen is present in both. The world of manifestation is dependent on the Absolute. The Absolute Spirit which transcends the distinction between the subject and the object is logically prior to the manifested world. The world is a process of becoming; it is not being.

The Upaniṣads make it clear that the waking state and the dream state are quite distinct. The objects of the dream state are illusory; not so those of waking experience. 'There are no chariots in that state (of dreaming), no horses, no roads. He himself creates chariots, horses, roads'. Imaginary objects exist only during the time we imagine them, *kalpana-kāla*, but factual objects exist not only when we perceive them but also when we do not perceive them, *bāhyāś ca dvaya-kālāḥ*. The spatio-temporal order is a fact, not a state of mind or a phase of consciousness.

Avidyā is mentioned in the Upaniṣads as the source of delusion. The Kaṭha Upaniṣad speaks of people living in ignorance and thinking themselves wise, who move about wandering in search of reality, like blind men following the blind. If they had lodged themselves in *vidyā*, wisdom, instead of *avidyā*, ignorance, they would easily have seen the truth. The Chāndogya Upaniṣad distinguishes between *vidyā* or knowledge which is power and *avidyā* or ignorance which is impotence. While *māyā* is more cosmic in significance, *avidyā* is more subjective. We are subject to *avidyā* when we look upon the multiplicity of objects and egos as final and fundamental. Such a view falsifies the truth. It is the illusion of ignorance. The world of multiplicity is out there, and has its place, but if we look upon it as a self-existing cosmos, we are making an error. While the world process reveals certain possibilities of the Real, it also conceals the full nature of the Real. *Avidyā* breeds selfishness and becomes a knot in the heart which we should untie before we can get possession of the Self in the recesses of our heart. The Praśna Upaniṣad tells us that we cannot reathe world of Brahman unless we have shaken off the crookedness in us, the falsehood (*anṛtam*) in us, the illusion (*māyā*) in us.

The world has the tendency to delude us into thinking that it is all, that it is self-dependent, and this delusive character of the world is also designated *māyā* in the sense of *avidyā*. When we are asked to overcome *māyā*, it is an injunction to avoid worldliness. Let us not put our trust in the things of this world. *Māyā* is concerned not with the existence of the world but with its meaning, not with the factuality of the world but with the way in which we look upon it.

There are passages in the Upaniṣads which make out that the world is an appearance, *vācārambhaṇaṁ vikāro ṅāmadheyam*, while Reality is pure being. There are others which grant reality to the world, though they maintain that it has no reality apart from Brahman. Śaṁkara tells us that the former is the true teaching of the Upaniṣads, while the latter view is put forward only tentatively as a first step in the teaching to be later withdrawn.. The reality conceded to the world is not ultimate. It is only empirical.

If we keep in mind the fourfold character of the Supreme, we shall avoid confusion in regard to the status of the world. If we concentrate attention on Brahman, the Absolute, we feel that the world is not independent of Brahman but rests in Brahman. The relationship between the two cannot be logically articulated. If we turn to the personal *Īśvara*, we know that the world is the creation of Brahman and not its organic expression. The power of creation is called *māyā*. If we turn to the world process which is a perpetual becoming, it is a mixture of being and non-being, *sat* and *asat*, the divine principle and *prakṛti*. *Hiraṇya-garbha* and his world are both subject to time, and should be distinguished from the eternal. But the temporal becoming is by no means false.

As to why the Supreme has this fourfold character, why it is what it is, we can only accept it as the given reality. It is the ultimate irrationality in the sense that no logical derivation of the given is possible. It is apprehended by us in spiritual consciousness, and accounts for the nature of experience in all its aspects. It is the only philosophical explanation that is possible or necessary.

The Individual Self

Jīva is literally, 'that which breathes', from *jīv* 'to breathe'. It referred originally to the biological aspect of man's nature which goes on throughout life, in waking, dream, and sleep. It is called *puruṣa* in the sense of *puri-śaya* or 'that which dwells in the citadel of the heart'. This means that the biological serves the ends of another, the soul or psyche. It is this soul which reaps the fruits of deeds and survives the death of the physical body. It is the *bhoktṛ*, the enjoyer, *kartṛ*, the doer. It is the *vijñāna-māyā ātmā*. The *jīva* consists of a material body, the principle of breath (*prāṇa*), regulating the unconscious activities of the individual, and the principle of conscious activities (*manas*) which uses the five sensory organs (*indriyas*) of sight, hearing, touch, smell, and taste and the five organs of action, viz. speech, hands, feet, excretory, and generative organs. All these are organised by *vijñāna* or *buddhi*. The basis of the individuality of the ego is *vijñāna* or intelligence which draws round itself mind, life, and body. The ego belongs to the relative world, is a stream of experience, a fluent mass of life, a centre round which our experiences of sense and mind gather. At the back of this whole structure is the Universal Consciousness, *Ātman*, which is our true being.

The human individual is a complex of five elements, *anna*, *prāṇa*, *manas*, *vijñāna*, and *ānanda*. The Highest Spirit which is the ground of all being, with which man's whole being should get united at the end of his journey, does not contribute to his self-sense. Life and matter are organised into the gross physical body, *sthūla-śarīra*, mind and life into the subtle body, *sūkṣma-śarīra*, intelligence into the causal body, *kāraṇa-śarīra*, and *Ātman*, the Universal Self is the supreme being sustaining the others. The ego is the manifestation of the Universal Self using memory and moral being which are changing formations. *Puruṣa* is sometimes used for the *ātman* which is higher than *buddhi*. *Buddhi* belongs to the objective hierarchy of being. *Puruṣa* is the subjective light of consciousness that is reflected in all beings.

The natural sciences, physics and chemistry, anatomy and physiology, psychology and sociology, treat man as an object of inquiry. They show that man is a link in the chain of living beings, one among many. He has a body and a mind which belong to him, but his self is not derived from any of these, though it is at the root of them all. All empirical causalities and biological processes of development apply to his outer being, but not to his self. The physical, the biological, the psychological, and the logical aspects are aspects of his nature, his *kośas*, as the Taittirīya Upaniṣad calls them. There are great possibilities of empirical investigation, but man is more than what he knows about himself.

The ego is a unity of body, life, mind, and intelligence. It is not a mere flux, as some early Buddhists and Hindus thought. Intelligence which is the unifying principle gives us the ego-consciousness. Memory is one factor which helps to preserve the continuity of the ego which is also influenced by a number of factors which are not present to our memory and are hardly grasped by our surface consciousness. The subconscious plays a great part in it. The nature of the ego depends on the principle of organisation and the experience to be organised. As we have an enormous variety of experiences with which we can identify ourselves, an infinite number of objects which we can pursue, fame, career, possessions, or power, we have an infinite number of individuals marked out by their past and present experiences, their education and environment. What we are depends on what we have been. The ego is a changing formation on the background of the Eternal Being, the centre round which our mental and vital activities are organised. The ego is perpetually changing, moving up and down, up towards union with the divine godhead or down to the fiendish extremes of selfishness, stupidity, and sensuality. The self-transcending capacity of the *jīva* is the proof that it is not the limited entity it takes itself to be.

The hierarchies of existence and value correspond. The order of phenomena which has the lowest degree of reality in the existential scale has the lowest degree of value in the ethical or spiritual scale. The human individual is higher than the animal, plant, or mineral.

What is the relation of the Universal Self to the individual selves? Different views are held on the matter. Śaṁkara believes that the Universal Self is identical with the individual self. The individual self is eternally one with and also different from the Universal Self, says Rāmānuja. The individual self is eternally different from the Universal Self according to Madhva.

When the soul is said to be an *aṁśa* or fragment of the Divine mind, it is to indicate that it is subsequent to the Divine mind, as a recipient of the Divine idea. The souls therefore serve as matter for the Divine Forms. This is the truth indicated in the Sāṁkhya theory of the multiplicity of selves. Though the self is one in all, in the manifested world, there is an *aṁśa*, fragment, part, or ray of the self which presides over the movements of our personal lives through the ages. This persistent divine form is the real individuality which governs the mutations of our being. This is not the limited ego, but the Infinite Spirit reflecting itself in our personal experience. We are not a mere flux of body, life, and mind thrown on the screen of a Pure Spirit which does not affect us in any way. Behind this flux there is the stable power of our being through which the Infinite Spirit manifests itself. The Divine has many modes of manifestation, and at many levels, and the fulfilment of the purposes of these modes constitutes the supreme scope of the eternal kingdom. In the world of manifestation the ground of created being is God's idea of it, which, because it is divine, is more real than the creature itself. The soul, therefore, represents an idea of the divine mind, and the different souls are the members of the Supreme. The soul draws its idea of perfection from the Divine Creator who has given it existence. The soul's substantial existence derives from the Divine mind, and its perfection consists in the vision of the Divine mind, in its effectuating the divine pattern for it in its consciousness and character.

There does not seem to be any suggestion that the individual egos are unreal. They all exist only through the Self and have no reality apart from It. The insistence on the unity of the Supreme Self as the constitutive reality of the world and of the individual souls does not negate the empirical reality of the latter. The plurality of individual souls is admitted by the Upaniṣads. The individuals do not resolve themselves in the Universal Absolute so long as the world of manifestation is functioning. The released individuals know themselves as the Self and not as the psycho-physical vehicles which are animated by the Self and so are incarnations of the Self. These vehicles are causally determined and are subject to change.

The individual is, in a sense, created by God after His own image and in His own likeness, but he has his creaturely form. We do not know our own possibilities. The individual ego is subject to *avidyā* or ignorance when it believes itself to be separate and different from all other egos. The result of this separatist ego-sense, *ahaṁkāra,* is failure to enter into harmony and unity with the universe. This failure expresses itself in physical suffering and mental discord. Selfish desire is the badge of subjection or bondage. When the individual shakes off this *avidyā,* he becomes free from all selfishness, possesses all, and enjoys all.

The unity of the Self does not make the distinctions of the individual souls irrelevant. There is no mixing up of the fruits of action, as the different individual selves are kept distinct by their association with *buddhi.* Our lives become meaningful in so far as they partake of the divine logos. The logos is seen in close connection with the logical or rational element in us. The Divine Reason is immanent in our reason. The ego's possession of intelligence gives it the capacity for moral choice. It may either turn to the Indwelling Spirit or pursue the separate interests of the ego. It may open itself to the Self or shut itself away from It. One leads to light and life, the other to darkness and death. We have the seeds of both in us. We may live a life controlled by flesh and blood and earth-born intellect or we may lay ourselves open to God and let Him work in us. As we choose the one or the other, we are led to death or immortality. When we forget our true nature and lose ourselves in the things of the world, we have evil and suffering.

Alienation from our true nature is hell, and union with it is heaven. There is a perpetual strain in human life, an effort to reach from the arbitrary into an ideal state of existence. When we divinise our nature, our body, mind, and spirit work flawlessly together and attain a rhythm which is rare in life.

Without the individual there is neither bondage nor liberation. The Eternal in His transcendent form as Brahman or cosmic being as *Īśvara* does not arrive at immortality. It is the individual who is subject to ignorance and who rises to self-knowledge. The self-expression of the Supreme through the individuals will continue until it is completed. The Divine possesses always its unity, and Its aim in the cosmic process is to possess it in an infinite experience through many conscious selves. So long as we are subject to ignorance, we stand away from God and are immersed in our limited egos. When we rise to self-knowledge, we are taken up into the Divine Being and become aware of the Infinite, Universal Consciousness in which we live.

Intellect and Intuition: *Vidyā* (Knowledge) and *Avidyā* (Ignorance)

If *buddhi, vijñāna*, intelligence, has its being turned towards the Universal Self it develops intuition or true knowledge, Wisdom. But ordinarily, intelligence is engaged in discursive reasoning and reaches a knowledge which is, at best, imperfect, through the processes of doubt, logic, and skilful demonstration. It reflects on the data supplied by *manas* or the sense-mind with its knowledge rooted in sensations and appetites. At the intellectual level we grope with an external vision of things, where objects are extrinsically opposed to one another. We are besieged by error and incapacity. Integral knowledge possesses its object truly and securely. Nothing is external to it. Nothing is other than itself. Nothing is divided or in conflict within its all-comprehensive self-awareness. It is the means of knowledge and knowledge itself.

Intuitive knowing is immediate as distinct from the discursive and mediate knowledge. It is more immediate than sensory intuition, for it overcomes the distinction between the knower and the known which subsists in sense-intuition. It is the perfect knowledge, while all other knowledge is incomplete and imperfect in so far as it does not bring about an identification between subject and object. All other knowledge is indirect and has only symbolic or representative value. The only generally effective knowledge is that which penetrates into the very nature of things. But in lower forms of knowledge this penetration of the subject into the object is limited and partial. Scientific understanding assumes that an object can be known only if it is broken up into its simpler constituents. If anything organic is handled in this manner, its significance is lost. By employing intuitive consciousness we know the object with less distortion and more actuality. We get close to perceiving the thing as it is.

Knowledge presupposes unity or oneness of thought and being, a unity that transcends the differentiation of subject and object. Such knowledge is revealed in man's very existence.[1] It is unveiled rather than acquired. Knowledge is concealed in ignorance and when the latter is removed the former manifests itself. What we are, that we behold, and what we behold, that we are. Our thought, our life, and our being are uplifted in simplicity and we are made one with truth. Though we cannot understand or describe, we taste and we possess. We become new.[2] When the beatific vision of Absolute Being has once dawned on the dazzled beholder, the savour of the phenomenal is gone for it is seen to be steeped in the noumenal.

The report which the mind and the senses give, so long as they are unenlightened by the spirit in us, is a misleading report. Yet that report is the basis from which we have to proceed. What the world and the individual seem to be are a distortion of what they really are, and yet through that distortion we arrive at the reality. Even as the conclusions of common sense are corrected by those of scientific understanding, the conclusions of the latter require to be corrected by the light of the spirit in us. The abstractions of the intellect require to be converted into the actuality of spiritual experience and the concrete vision of the soul.

If the real is misconceived as an object of knowledge, it cannot be known. Empirical objects may be known by outer observation or inner introspection. But the self cannot divide itself into the knower and the known. Logical reasoning is incapable of comprehending the living unity of God and man,

[1] Eckhart says: 'God in the fullness of His Godhead dwells eternally in His image (the soul itself)'. Rudolf Otto, *Mysticism: East and West* (1932), p. 12.

[2] Cf. Plotinus: 'And one that shall know this vision—with what passion of love shall he not be seized, with what pang of desire, what longing to be molten into one with this, what wondering delight! If he that has never seen this Being must hunger for It as for all his welfare, he that has known must love and reverence It as the very Beauty; he will be flooded with awe and gladness stricken by a salutary terror; he loves with a veritable love, with sharp desire; all other loves than this he must despise, and disdain all that once seemed fair'. *Enneads* E. T. MacKenna, Vol. I (1917), p. 86.

the absolute and the relative. Logical incapacity is not evidence of actual impossibility. Reality unites what discursive reason is incapable of holding together. Every atom of life is a witness to the oneness and duality of God and the world. Being can never be objectified or externalised. It is co-inherent and co-existent in man. It is unknowable because we identify existence with objectivity. This is true, to a limited extent, of purely external things like tables and chairs. They are not to be reduced to sensations or concepts arising in the knowing mind. But spiritual reality is not revealed in the way in which objects of the natural world or principles of logic are apprehended. Yājñavalkya tells us that the self is its own light when the sun has set, when the moon has set, when the fire is put out, *ātmaivāsya jyotir bhavati*. It is our deepest being behind the vestures of body, life, mind, and intellect. Objectivity is not the criterion of reality, but the criterion is reality itself revealed in our very being. We ask for a criterion of knowledge on the assumption of a duality between the knowing subject and the known object. If the object appears alien and impenetrable, then the question of knowing it becomes a problem. But no object can be set in opposition to the spirit and so the question of criterion does not arise. True knowledge is an integral creative activity of the spirit which does not know anything external at all. For it everything is its own life. Here there is identity, possession, absorption of the object at the deepest level. Truth in spiritual life is neither the reflection nor the expression of any other reality. It is reality itself. Those who know the truth become the truth. *brahma-vid brahmaiva bhavati*. It is not a question of having an idea or a perception of the real. It is just the revelation of the real. It is the illumination of being and of life itself. It is *satyam, jñānam*. Knowledge and being are the same thing, inseparable aspects of a single reality, being no longer even distinguishable in that sphere where all is without duality.

Where there is duality, there one sees another, hears another. We have objective knowledge. While *vijñāna* deals with the world of duality, *ānanda* implies the fundamental identity of subject and object, non-duality. Objectification is estrangement. The objective world is the 'fallen' world, disintegrated and enslaved, in which the subject is alienated from the object of knowledge. It is the world of disruption, disunion, alienation. In the 'fallen' condition, man's mind is never free from the compulsion exercised by objective realities. We struggle to overcome disunion, estrangement, to become superior to the objective world with its laws and determinations.

We cannot, however, become aware of the true life in its unity and multiplicity, in its absoluteness and relativity, if we do not free ourselves from the world of divided and isolated objects. In the objective world where estrangement and limitations prevail, there are impenetrable entities, but in the knowledge where we have fullness and boundlessness of life, nothing is external, but all is known from within. Intellect moves from object to object. Unable to comprehend them all it retains their multiplicity. Intellectual knowledge is a scattered, broken movement of the one undivided infinite life which is all-possessing and ever satisfied. Intuitive knowing is unimprisoned by the divisions of space, successions of time or sequences of cause and effect. Our intellectual picture is a shadow cast by the integral knowledge which possesses the object truly and securely.

Reality is a fact, and facts are apprehended by intuition, whether perceptual or non-perceptual. The divine primordial reality is not a fact of the empirical world, and yet as the central spiritual fact we must have a direct apprehension of it. Our logical knowledge can give us indirect approximation to it but not a direct grasp of it. The seers of the Upaniṣads not only have deep vision but are able to translate their visions into intelligible and persuasive speech. They can do so only through hints and images, suggestions and symbols, for they are not susceptible of adequate expression.

The Upaniṣads distinguish between *a-parā vidyā*, lower knowledge and *parā vidyā* or higher wisdom. While the former gives us knowledge of the Vedas and the sciences, the latter helps us to gain the knowledge of the Imperishable. The first principle disguises itself. In the Bṛhad-āraṇyaka Upaniṣad, the self is seen as the reality of reality. The reality of the world is the empirical; the true reality is the *ātman*, the self which the empirical reality conceals. A distinction is made between the knower of texts and the knower of the self in the Chāndogya

Upaniṣad. Svetaketu cannot understand the question of rebirth, despite much Vedic learning. The Taittirīya Upaniṣad reduces the knowledge of the Vedas to an inferior position by assigning it to *mano-maya* (mind-made) self which has to be surmounted before final truth is attained. The self is perceived, according to the Kaṭha Upaniṣad, not by logical reason but by spiritual contemplation, *adhyātma-yoga*. The real is not attained by force of intellect or by much learning but is revealed to the aspirant whose will is at rest in Him. We realise God by the clarity of illumination, *jñāna-prasādena.*

The Bṛhad-āraṇyaka Upaniṣad teaches that, while those who put their trust in the intellect cannot attain to a knowledge of Brahman, yet there is an apprehension of His being by those who are childlike. *Bālya* includes humility, receptivity, or teachableness and an earnest search. The writer asks us to give up the pride of learning, *pāṇḍitya.* A self-denial which includes our intellectual pride and power is demanded. Purity of intellect is different from congestion of it. To attain purity of vision, we require a childlike nature which we can get by tranquillising the senses, simplifying the heart, and cleaning the mind.

It is through quietening the strivings of the will and the empirical intellect that the conditions are realised for the revelation of the Supreme in the individual soul. 'Therefore having become calm, subdued, quiet, patiently enduring and collected, one sees the Self just in the self'.

Even as we have an intellectual discipline for the theoretical understanding of the world, we have a moral and spiritual discipline for the direct apprehension of truth. Even as we cannot understand the art of swimming by talking about it and can learn it only by getting into the water and practising swimming, so also no amount of theoretical knowledge can serve as a substitute for the practice of the life of spirit. We can know God only by becoming godlike. To become godlike is to become aware of the light in us, by returning consciously to the divine centre within us, where we have always been without our knowing it. Detachment (*vairāgya*) is the essential means for the attainment of wisdom (*jñāna*). Only the pure in heart can see God.

We must cultivate a religious disposition. God is revealed only to those who believe that He is. When in doubt, later tradition asks us to give the benefit of the doubt to the theist. For if there is no God, there is no harm in believing in Him; if there is, the atheist would suffer. Faith, as trust in the universe, in its reliability, in its essential soundness and decency, is the starting-point of spiritual development.

Spiritual inclination is essential for the pursuit of spiritual life. In the Bṛhad-āraṇyaka Upaniṣad, Yājñavalkya offers to divide all his earthly possessions between his two wives, Kātyāyanī and Maitreyī. The latter asks whether the whole world filled with wealth can give her life eternal. Yājñavalkya says: 'No, your life will be just like that of people who have plenty of things, but there is no hope of life eternal through wealth'. Maitreyī spurns the riches of the world remarking, 'What shall I do with that which will not make me immortal'? Yājñavalkya recognises the spiritual fitness of his wife and teaches her the highest wisdom.

Ethical preparation is insisted on. If we do not abstain from wrong-doing, if we are not composed in our minds, we cannot attain to spiritual wisdom. Our moral being must be purged of all evil. The Śvetāśvatara Upaniṣad tells us that we should cleanse our natures to reach the goal, since even a mirror can reflect an image properly only if it is cleansed of its impurities. We must renounce selfish desire, surrender material possessions, become bereft of egotism. The path is 'sharp as the edge of a razor and hard to cross, difficult to tread'.

A teacher who has attained the goal may help the aspiring soul. Truth has not only to be demonstrated but also communicated. It is relatively easy to demonstrate a truth, but it can be communicated only by one who has thought, willed, and felt the truth. Only a teacher can give it with its concrete quality. He that has a teacher knows, *ācāryavān puruṣo veda.* Only he must be a proper teacher who embodies truth and tradition. Only those who have the flame in them can stir the fire in others.

The individual should develop the habit of introversion, of abstracting from the outside world and looking within himself. By a process of abstraction we get behind knowing, feeling, and willing to the essential Self, the God within. We must silence our speech, mind, and will. We cannot hear the voice of the still spirit in us, so long as we are lost in vain talk, mental rambling, and empty desires. The mind must strip away its outer sheaths in complete detachment, return to its inward quiet and fix its attention on the essential Self which is the ground and reality of the whole universe. The Muṇḍaka Upaniṣad brings out the need for concentrated attention and undistracted effort. An ordered, disciplined training of all our powers, a change of mind, heart, and will is demanded.

Several forms of meditation are advised. Symbols (*pratīka*) are used as supports for meditation. We are free to use the symbols which are most in conformity with our personal tendencies. Meditation on the *praṇava* is suggested in the Māṇḍūkya Upaniṣad.

It is said that the Self cannot be realised except by those whom the Self chooses. Self-realisation is possible through the grace of the Divine. God-vision is the fruit of strenuous effort and Divine grace. Only the Spirit in us can raise us to the spiritual status. The Real, which is the basis of this manifold world of things and minds, can be apprehended directly and immediately only by those who fulfil certain conditions and submit to the leadings of the spirit. We do not so much hold the idea of the Real as the idea holds us. We are possessed by it.

Vidyā and *avidyā* are two ways of apprehending Reality. Both are forms of relative knowledge and belong to the manifested universe. Knowledge formulated logically is not equivalent to a direct and immediate apprehension of the Real. Whatever words we use, whatever concepts we employ, fall short of reality.[3] The *anubhava* is beyond all manifestation and is complete in itself. *Vidyā* stresses the harmony and interconnections of elements which make up the world; *avidyā* the separateness, mutual independence, and strife. *Vidyā* helps us to appreciate intellectually the intelligible ideas about the nature of the Divine ground and the nature of the direct experience of it in relation to other experiences. It indicates the means by which we can attain Brahman. Such a system of

[3] When Al Ghazzāli or, two centuries later, Thomas Aquinas refused to proceed with the consideration of truths about God, when once they attained direct apprehension of the Divine Reality, they refer to this inadequacy of verbal or logical expressions.

theological doctrine points out that there is nothing intrinsically self-contradictory about the postulate of religion, viz. the divine reality, and that it is also empirically verifiable if only we are willing to submit to a discipline. The theological knowledge or *vidyā* is different from the experience or *anubhava* of it. The experience is recorded as a pure and direct intellectual intuition in *śruti*. When we reflect on the experiences or their records and reduce them to a rational order we have *smṛti*. While the first is the domain of metaphysical principles, the second applies these principles to individual and social conduct. *Vidyā* is nearer the truth than *avidyā*.

But *vidyā* is also understood as *jñāna* which is of the essential nature of the Divine Reality. It is then eternal wisdom which is not the knowledge possessed by any individual. It is the wisdom hidden beneath the sheaths of ignorance. It is one with the Supreme Self, which is self-evident and needs no proof, *svataḥ-siddha*, self-valid certainty.

Though intuitive wisdom is different from knowledge of the senses or anything we can achieve by logical reflection, it is not to be confused with occultism, obscurantism, or extravagant emotion. It is not magical insight or heavenly vision, or special revelation obtained through supernatural powers. What we attain by vision, empirical or trans-empirical, belongs to the objective world. It is a distinction within the objective world, between the physical and the super-physical, between what we reach by the five senses and a sixth sense. Wisdom is pure reason, capacity for fundamental truth. It is the possession of the soul or it is the soul that penetrates into its own ground and depth and becomes essential being. It springs from it of necessity when it meditates on itself. This wisdom is eternal, universal, and necessary for Śaṁkara. It cannot be destroyed though it may be obscured.

All the same, the tradition of thought has been strong in the Upaniṣads. We lead up to experience through intellectual knowledge. For those who are incapable of integral insight, perception and inference are the only available means. Even men of experience do not contradict rational thought, though they go beyond it.

Ethics

The Upaniṣads insist on the importance of ethical life. They repudiate the doctrine of the self-sufficiency of the ego and emphasise the practice of moral virtues. Man is responsible for his acts. Evil is the free act of the individual who uses his freedom for his own exaltation. It is fundamentally the choice which affirms the finite, independent self, its lordship and acquisitiveness, against the universal will. Evil is the result of our alienation from the Real. If we do not break with evil, we cannot attain freedom.

Man is of the divine race, but he has in him the element of non-being, which exposes him to evil. As a spiritual being he can burst the revolving circle of nature and become a citizen of another world in unity with Absolute Being who is his creative source. Man is the mediator between God and nature and has to complete the work of creation by the incarnation of wisdom. He must illumine what is dark and strengthen what is weak in him. His entire being should labour to become one with the Divine. Our fallen nature, sunk in sin, is felt as contrary to the Real and yet as existent. The self feels itself to be in contradiction to all that is supremely real. There is the pain of discord between the existent and the Real. In moral life the self feels itself divided against itself. And yet the struggle itself is impossible unless we look upon the desire for the divine and the consciousness of rebellion as belonging to the same self. The felt contradiction is possible only through the reality which is above the discord. The antithesis between what we wish to be and what we are is implicitly their unity. The divine consciousness and will must become our consciousness and will. This means that our actual self must cease to be a private self; we must give up our particular will, die to our ego, by surrendering its whole nature, its consciousness, and character to the Divine.

The freedom of the human individual is assumed, though the limitations of *karma* are mentioned. 'He fetters himself by himself, as a bird by its nest'. The freedom of the individual increases to the extent to which he identifies himself with the Absolute in him. the *antar-yāmin.* If we leave the world after having known the true self, then our life in all worlds is the life of freedom.

Some theistic Upaniṣads say that the inner power, the Divine, caused the man whom He will lead on high from these worlds to do good works and He causes the man whom He will lead downwards to do evil works. In theism the stress is on Divine providence. In the Śvetāśvatara Upaniṣad, the Self is the overseer of all actions, who apportions to each person his qualities, who executes justice, who restrains the evil, allots good fortune, and brings to maturity the actions of the individual souls.[1]

The general impression that the Upaniṣads require world-denial is not quite correct. They insist on a spirit of detachment, *vairāgya,* which is not indifference to the world. It is not abandonment of objects but non-attachment to them. We do not raise ourselves above the world by contempt for the world. It is the spirit of equanimity which is insisted on. To be tranquil is to envy no man, to have no possessions that another can take from us, to fear none. When the Hindu thinkers ask us to adopt *saṁnyāsa* or relinquishment of home and possessions, to accept the three great renunciations, consecrated in the three vows, evangelical counsels of poverty, obedience, and chastity, they point to self-denial as the root of spiritual life.

Spirit of renunciation does not mean neglect of social duties. *Saṁnyāsa* does not mean that we owe no duties to the world; we free ourselves only from ritualistic duties. Rare fruits of spirit ripen on the soil of detachment.[2] There is a popular verse

[1] VI. 11. 12. 4; V. 5ff.

[2] When Ernest Renan described St. Francis as 'the one perfect Christian' it was felt to be an exaggeration. Hardly anyone else in the Christian world comes so close to the ideal set forth in the Gospels. 'He that renounceth not everything that he hath, he cannot be my disciple'. We feel

which makes out that one should give up attachment, but if one is not capable of it, let him cultivate attachment; only it should be attachment to all.

We should release ourselves from selfish likes and dislikes. The Divine cannot use our mind and body so long as we wish to use them for our own ends.[3]

Detachment is opposed to attachment, not to enjoyment. Enjoy through renunciation is the advice of the Īśa Upaniṣad.[4] Good and evil do not depend on the acts one does or does not, but on the frame of mind one has. The good man is he who concurs with the divine purpose, and the bad man is he who resists it. If one's mind is good, one's acts will be good. Our attempt should be not so much external conformity as inward cleansing. From goodness of being good will and good works flow.[5] When the soul is at peace, the greatest sorrows are borne lightly. Life becomes more natural and confident. Changes in outer conditions do not disturb. We let our life flow of itself as the sea heaves or the flower blooms.

Work by itself does not give us liberation. It cleanses the mind, purifies the heart, and produces the illumination which is the immediate condition of salvation. Śaṁkara argues that

---

that these demands are excessive and even fantastic. We excuse ourselves by saying that Jesus did not mean all that he is reported to have said or that his words were not of general application. We make compromises, while St. Francis did not allow any compromises.

[3] Cf. St. John of the Cross: 'The soul that is attached to anything, however much good there may be in it, will not arrive at the liberty of divine union. For whether it be a strong wire rope or a slender and delicate thread that holds the bird, it matters not, if it really holds it fast; for until the cord be broken the bird cannot fly. So the soul, held by the bonds of human affections, however slight they may be, cannot, while they last, make its way to God'.

[4] Eckhart tells us: 'It is permissible to take life's blessings with both hands, provided thou dost know thyself prepared in the opposite event to leave them just as gladly'.

[5] Cf. Eckhart: 'Men should not think so much of what they ought to do, as of what they ought to be. Think not to lay the foundation of thy holiness upon doing, but rather upon being. For works do not sanctify us, but we should sanctify the works. Whoever is not great in his essential being will achieve nothing by works, whatever he may do'. Rudolf Otto, *Mysticism: East and West*, p. 126.

the knowledge of Brahman, as it relates to an existent being, cannot be contingent on what a person does or does not.

Contemplation is the way to cleanse one's mind and heart. It means rest, suspension of mental activity, withdrawal into the interior solitude in which the soul is absorbed in the fruitful silence of God. We cannot stop there; we must overflow with a love that communicates what it knows to others. Saints with abundant power and tireless energy work for the transfiguring of men and the changing of the course of secular history. Different methods are suited for different temperaments, and they are all permitted.

The ethical virtues we are called upon to adopt are mentioned in several passages. Life is compared to a sacrifice where the fee shall be asceticism, liberality, integrity, non-injury to life, and truthfulness. The Taittirīya Upaniṣad gives a list of students' duties. He should not be negligent of truth, virtue, welfare, prosperity, study, and teaching. He should perform only those acts which are irreproachable. In case of doubt concerning any act of conduct, the student should follow the practice of those *Brāhmaṇas* who are competent to judge, apt, devoted, not harsh lovers of virtue. In one passage all the virtues are brought together under the three *da*'s which are heard in the voice of the thunder, namely, *dama*, or self-restraint, *dāna* or self-sacrifice, and *dayā* or compassion. Prajā-pati conveys it to the three classes of his creation, gods (*deva*), men (*manuṣya*) and demons (*asura*). Śaṁkara makes out that gods have desires (*kāma*), men suffer from greed (*lobha*) and demons from anger (*krodha*). By the practice of the three injunctions we free ourselves from the sway of craving, greed, and anger. When the Buddha asks us to put out in our hearts the monstrous fires of infatuation, greed, and resentment, he is emphasising the three virtues enjoined by the Upaniṣads.

Dama is self-control. We should reduce our wants and be prepared to suffer in the interests of truth. Austerity, chastity, solitude, and silence are the ways to attain self-control.

Tapas is severe self-discipline undertaken for spiritual ends. It is exercised with reference to the natural desires of the body and the distractions of the outer world. It consists of exercises of an inward kind, prayers offered in the heart, self-analysis, and outer acts like fasting, self-mortification, sexual abstinence, or voluntary poverty. Strength is developed by a resisting force. The power gained by resisting one temptation helps us in overcoming the next. To evade discipline is to empty life of its significance. Nothing is more tranquil than to be unshaken by the troublous motions of the flesh. Renunciation, *nyāsa*, is superior to *tapas* or austerity or asceticism. The latter is a means to the former. It is not to be made into an end in itself. Ethical life includes moral uprightness though many minds feel only the need for mechanical ritual.

Brahmacarya is not sex-destruction. There is no gulf between flesh and spirit, but only between the fallen and the transfigured flesh. Ancient Indian thinkers were of the opinion that the seed within man and woman is intended for the purpose of creating a body by which another soul may come into physical embodiment. When thus controlled, *brahmacarya* helps creative work of every description. When the seed is wasted in sex excesses, the body becomes weak and crippled, the face lined, the eyes dull, hearing impaired, and the brain inactive. If *brahmacarya* is practised, the physical body remains youthful and beautiful, the brain keen and alert, the whole physical expression becomes the image and likeness of the Divine.

Mauna or silence is advised as leading the soul forward to contemplation.[6] By the discipline of silence we curb the excesses which flow from the tongue, heresy, backbiting, flattery. We cannot listen to the voice of God when our minds are dissipated, given to restless activity, and are filled externally and internally with noise. Progress in silence is progress to the realisation of spirit. When silence descends on the soul, its activities are joined to the silent creative power of God.

Dāna enjoins gifts. It is negatively freedom from greed and positively assistance to those in need. 'There is no hope of

[6] Cf. Isaiah: 'The tillage of righteousness is silence'. 'In silence and in hope shall be your strength'.

immortality by wealth'.[7] Possessiveness is condemned. The Taittirīya Upaniṣad regulates the art of giving. One should give with faith, one should not give without faith, one should give liberally, with modesty, with fear, with sympathy.

Dayā is *karuṇā*, compassion. We should try to be at peace with all, abhor all cruelty and ill-will. Enmity means misunderstanding. A forgiving attitude frees the individual. We should grudge none, forgive all. So long as we remember an injustice, we have not forgiven either the person or the action. If only we know that there is more suffering than wickedness in the world, we would be kindly. It is by compassion, which shrinks from no sacrifice, that we can overcome the ravages of selfishness. We must be patient. God himself is unimaginably patient. Tolerance, long suffering, patience are the fruits of spirit.

The ethical individual is required to become like a child. The perfect man is a divine child, accepting the divine play, without fear or reserve, care or grief, in utter purity. A child is not entangled with things that seem important to grown-ups, whose occupations are mainly paltry and whose professions petrified. A child's wise incomprehension is linked with living and is more than defensiveness or disdain. We cannot return to childhood. We have to gain the state which is unconstricted by temporal purpose, but purposeful, a state in which time and eternity coincide.

When it is said that the Upaniṣads adopt a spiritual view of life, it does not mean that they despise body, life, and mind. The latter are the conditions or instruments for the life of spirit in man. They are not ends in themselves, but are means or

[7] B.U. II. 4. 2. Cf. Jalāl-Uddīn Rūmī:

Once the noble Ibrahim, as he sat on his throne,
Heard a clamour and noise of cries on the roof,
Also heavy footsteps on the roof of his palace.
He said to himself, 'Whose heavy feet are these'?
He shouted from the window, 'Who goes there'?
The guards, filled with confusion, bowed their heads, saying,
'It is we going the rounds in search'.
He said, 'What seek ye'? They said 'Our camels'.
He said, 'Whoever searched for camels on a housetop'?
They said, 'We follow thy example,
Who seekest union with God, while sitting on a throne'.

opportunities for the expression of the Universal Spirit in us. Spirit and life are not to be separated.

The ritualistic practices are reinterpreted. They are to prepare the mind for spiritual realisation, to spur it on to pierce the veil of the finite and to seek deliverance in identification with the Supreme Reality. If rites are performed without the knowledge of their meaning, they are not only useless but dangerous. The presumptuous performer may have his head cut off. He who knows a particular rite and he who knows it not both perform a rite, but when performed with knowledge the act becomes more effective. Meditation on the meaning of the sacrifice sometimes took the place of the actual sacrifice. 'Suppose', Janaka asks Yājñavalkya, 'you had no milk or rice or barley to perform the fire-sacrifice, *agnihotra*, with what would you sacrifice'? 'With the fruits of trees and whatever herbs there were'. 'If there were none'? 'Then with water'. 'If there were no water'? 'Then, indeed, there would be nothing here, yet, this would be offered, the truth in faith'. When the heart is fully persuaded, there is little sense of sacrifice. Sacrificial life becomes a natural manifestation of the new spirit. Self-conscious sacrifice, with its burden of self-righteousness and expectation of reward, is not of much use.

The caste divisions are mentioned in some of the Upaniṣads.[8] They did not, however, harden into a rigid social system. In the Chāndogya Upanisad five learned Brāhmins who approach Uddālaka Āruṇi for instruction in regard to *Vaiśvānara Ātman* are taken by him to King Aśvapati Kaikeya, who gives them instruction after first demonstrating the imperfections of their views. Ajātaśatru of Kāśi teaches Gārgya Bālāki the nature of Brahman, after pointing out the defects of the twelve views which Gārgya Bālāki sets forth. Ajātaśatru observes that it is not usual for a Brāhmin to approach a Kṣatriya for instruction. The doctrine of rebirth is taught by Pravāhaṇa Jaivali to Āruṇi with the remark that the Brāhmins had never before had this knowledge. Among the students of the Upaniṣads is Satyakāma, of unknown origin, whose mother Jabālā could not tell who his father was.

[8] B.U. I. 4. 15.

The four *āśramas* or stages of life are recognised. While the usual rule is that one has to pass through successive stages of life, exceptions are permitted. Jābāla Upaniṣad asks us to renounce whenever we feel a call to it. Besides, even in a householder's stage one can attain spiritual freedom.

Karma and Rebirth

Until we negate the ego and get fixed in the Divine Ground we are bound to the endless procession of events called *saṁsāra*. The principle which governs this world of becoming is called *karma*. There are moral and spiritual laws as well as physical laws. If we neglect the laws of health, we injure our health; if we neglect the laws of morality, we wreck our higher life. Any rational conception of the universe, any spiritual conception of God requires us to recognise the utter and unquestionable supremacy of law in shaping our conduct and character.

The law of *karma* is not external to the individual. The judge is not without but within. The law by which virtue brings its triumph and ill-doing its retribution is the unfolding of the law of our being.[1] The world order is a reflection of the Divine Mind. The Vedic gods were regarded as the maintainers of the order, *ṛta* of the world. They were the guardians of *ṛta*. God, for the Śvetāśvatara Upaniṣad, is the ordainer of *karma*, *karmādhyakṣaḥ*, God is law as well as love. His love is through law.. The working of *karma* is wholly dispassionate, just, neither cruel nor merciful. Though we cannot escape from the workings of this principle, there is hope, for if man is what he has made himself, he may make himself what he will. Even the soul in the lowest condition need not abandon all hope. If we miss the

[1] Cf. the words of a fine fragment of the lost *Melanippe* of Euripides.

Dream you that men's misdeeds fly up to Heaven
And then some hand inscribes the record of them
Upon God's tablets; and God, reading them,
Deals the world justice? Nay, the vault of Heaven
Could not find room to write the crimes of earth,
Nor God himself avail to punish them:
Justice is *here on earth*, had ye but eyes.

right path, we are not doomed to an eternity of suffering. There are other existences by which we can grow into the knowledge of the Infinite Spirit with the complete assurance that we will ultimately arrive there. If there is a fundamental difference between Christianity and Hinduism, it is said that it consists in this, that while the Hindu to whatever school he belongs believes in a succession of lives, the Christian believes that 'it is appointed to men once to die, but after this the judgment'.

Belief in rebirth has persisted, at any rate, from the time of the Upaniṣads. It is a natural development from the views of the Vedas and the *Brāhmaṇas* and receives articulate expression in the Upaniṣads.[2] After mentioning the dispersal of the members of the human body at death—the eye of man goes to the sun, the breath to the wind, speech to fire, the mind to the moon, the ear to the quarters of heaven, the body to the earth, the soul to the ether, the hair to the plants and trees, the blood and seed to the waters—Yājñavalkya is asked as to what remains of the individual. He takes the questioner apart, discusses with him in secret about the nature of work. In truth, a man becomes good by good works and evil by evil works. Our lives incarnate our characters.

The future of the soul is not finally determined by what it has felt, thought, and done in this one earthly life. The soul has chances of acquiring merit and advancing to life eternal. Until the union with the timeless Reality is attained, there will be some form of life or other, which will give scope to the individual soul to acquire enlightenment and attain life eternal. Even as non-being is only an abstract lower limit of the existential order, absolute evil is also such a lower limit. Non-being, if it existed in itself diametrically opposed to being, would be completely destroyed. Such non-being is non-existent. Therefore as every existent thing has the form of the Divine, it has also the promise of good.

The Upaniṣads give us detailed descriptions of the manner in which a man dies and is born again.[3] The transition is illus-

[2] See R.V. X. 16. 3.

[3] See B.U. IV. 3. 37–38; IV. 4. 1–5 and 9. 7. See Kaṭha I. 1. 5–6.

trated by certain examples. As a grasshopper, when it has come to the end of a blade of grass, finds another place of support, and then draws itself towards it, similarly this self, after reaching the end of this body, finds another place of support and then draws himself towards it. As a goldsmith, after taking a piece of gold, gives it another, newer and more beautiful shape, similarly does this self, after having thrown off this body, and dispelled ignorance, take another, newer and more beautiful form, whether it be of the manes, or demigods or gods or of Prajā-pati or Brahmā or of any other beings.[4] These passages bring out several aspects of the theory of rebirth. The soul finds out its future body before it leaves the present one. The soul is creative in the sense that it creates a body. At every change of body, the soul takes a newer form. The state of each existence of the soul is conditioned and determined by its knowledge (*vidyā*), its conduct (*karma*) in the previous existence. From the Bṛhad-āraṇyaka Upaniṣad it appears that all the organs accompany the departing soul, which enters into the *saṁjñāna* and becomes possessed of knowledge and consciousness *vijñāna*. The results of learning and conduct cling to the soul.[5]

The ignorant, the unenlightened go after death to sunless demoniac regions. The good are said to go up to regions which are sorrowless, through the air, sun, and moon. The Chāndogya Upaniṣad speaks of two ways open to mortals, the bright and the dark, the way of the gods and the way of the fathers. Those who practise penance and faith enter the path of light, and they never return to the cycle of human existence. Those who are only ethical, performing works of public utility, travel by the path of smoke, dwell in the world of the fathers till the time comes for them to fall down, then they are born again according to their deserts.[6] The descriptions may be fictitious, but the principle of the ascent and the descent of the soul is

[4] B.U. IV. 4. 3–5.

[5] Cf. with this the Buddhist view that the migrating soul consists of *vijñāna* and the other four *skandhas* of *vedanā*, feeling, *saṁjñā*, perception, *saṁskāra* or dispositions, and *rūpa* or corporeal form.

[6] C.U. V. 10. 1–6.

what the Upaniṣads insist on. Beautiful characters attain covetable births and ugly ones miserable births. Heaven and hell belong to the world of time.

Rebirth is the lot of man until he obtains true knowledge. By virtuous acts he furthers his evolution. The reward of goodness is to grow in goodness. The reward of growing in purity of heart is to gain a clearer vision of reality. Knowledge of reality leads to salvation.

It is sometimes suggested that the soul, before undergoing rebirth, experiences reward or punishment for its deeds in appropriate places. The original Vedic belief of reward in heaven or punishment gets mixed up with the doctrine of rebirth.

The soul is said to be a very minute entity residing in the cavity of the heart and resembling in every respect, except size, the visible man.

Life Eternal

The fact that the individual consciousness has for its essential reality the Universal Self implies the possibility that every human being can rend the veil of separateness and gain recognition of his true nature and oneness with all beings. The Upaniṣads develop this character of life eternal.

In the Ṛg Veda, what is aimed at is length of days on earth and life in the world of heaven in the company of gods. In the *Brāhmaṇas*, the performers of various rites are promised the reward of community of being, companionship, and fellowship with the gods. When the Absolute Brahman was recognised, the gods became intermediaries through whose influence the end of unity with the Absolute is obtained. When Brahman and *Ātman* are identified, the highest goal is declared to be unity with the Self. Deliverance is different from existence in *svarga* or paradise. The latter is a part of the manifested world. The soul may live there for ages and yet return to earth, an heir to its deeds. Deliverance, on the other hand, is a state of permanent union with the Highest Self. Life in paradise is a prolongation of self-centered life, while life eternal is liberation from it. While the former is time extended, the latter is time transcended.

Enlightenment does not mean a departure in space to a new abode. Arrival and departure have no meaning in the context of liberation. The passages where the soul is said to go by the veins to the rays of the sun and to the sun or from the moon through the worlds of fire, wind, Varuṇa, Indra, and Prajā pati, to Brahman speak of the soul on the pathway to perfection. The Chāndogya Upaniṣad states that the soul of the emancipated, at death, goes out by the hundred and first vein through the crown of the head, fire, wind, and sun to Brahman.

He who knows Brahman becomes Brahman.[1] Perfection is a state of mind, not contingent on change of time or place. It is an experience of the present, not a prophecy of the future. Temporal distinctions do not apply to it, but if any temporal terms are to be used, they will be words like 'now', 'presently', 'When all desires that dwell in the human heart are cast away, then a mortal becomes immortal and (even) here he attaineth to Brahman'. Freedom is not a future state on whose coming we wait in expectation. It is life in the spirit, in God who is the foundation and power of life.

Is *mokṣa* or liberation life with the Supreme Person whom we love and worship in this life?[2] Is it personal immortality with absolute likeness to God in the world of Brahmā?[3] Is it an impersonal absorption in the Divine Transcendent?[4] All these views are to be found in the Upaniṣads. There are four aspects of release distinguished as *sāmīpya* or intimacy with the divine, *sārūpya* or *sādharmya*, similarity of nature with the divine, reflecting his glory, *sālokya* or conscious co-existence with the divine in the same world, and *sāyujya* or communion with the divine bordering on identity.

There are certain general characteristics of the state of *mokṣa* or freedom. It is conceived as freedom from subjection to time. As birth and death are the symbols of time, life eternal or *mokṣa* is liberation from births and deaths. It is the fourth state of consciousness beyond the three worlds, what the *Bhagavadgītā* calls *paramam brahma* or *brahma-nirvāṇa.* It is freedom from subjection to the law of *karma.* The deeds, good or bad, of the released cease to have any effect on him. Even as a horse shakes its mane, the liberated soul shakes off his sin; even as the moon comes out entire after having suffered an eclipse from *Rāhu*, so does the liberated individual free himself from mortal bondage. His works consume themselves like a reed stalk in the fire. As water does not stop on the lotus leaf, works do not cling to him. Works have a meaning only for a self-centred individual. Liberation is the destruction

[1] B.U. IV. 4. 9; M.U. III. 2. 9.
[2] C.U. III. 20. 2.
[3] M.U. III. 1. 3; III. 2. 6–8.
[4] Praśna VI. 5.

of bondage, which is the product of ignorance. Ignorance is destroyed by knowledge and not by works. Freedom is not a created entity; it is the result of recognition.

Knowledge takes us to the place where desire is at rest, *a-kāma*, where all desires are fulfilled, *āpta-kāma*, where the self is the only desire, *ātma-kāma*. He who knows himself to be all can have no desire. When the Supreme is seen, the knots of the heart are cut asunder, the doubts of the intellect are dispelled and the effects of our actions are destroyed. There can be no sorrow or pain or fear when there is no other. The freed soul is like a blind man who has gained his sight, a sick man made whole. He cannot have any doubt for he is full and abiding knowledge. He attains the highest bliss for which a feeble analogy is married happiness. He can attain any world he may seek.

The law of *karma* prevails in the world of *saṁsāra*, where our deeds lead us to higher or lower stations in the world of time. If we obtain knowledge of the eternal reality, Brahman or *Ātman*, deeds have no power over us. The state of life eternal is said to be beyond good and evil. The knower of the self ceases to be stained by action. He goes beyond the ethical, though rooted in it,[5] *anyatra dharmāt, anyatrādharmāt.* The path of virtue and vice is a means, not an end. The end is beyond the law of injunction and prohibition of good and evil. 'Our activities, being inspired by the divine cannot be wrong'; 'Nous is never wrong', says Aristotle.[6] The life of a free spirit is not bound by any formulas. It breaks its bonds and finds its own way to a development of its own which could never have been charted in advance. The liberated spirit conforms spontaneously to the ethical rules. 'To one who has knowledge of the self, non-hatred, and other virtues come off naturally without any effort'. Every religion sets before us the goal of

[5] Kaṭha: II. 14; see also C.U. VIII. 4. 1; M.U. III. 1. 3; K.U. I. 4.

Cf. The Buddha. *Majjhima Nikāya* I. 135. 'If you understand the parable of the raft, you must discard dharma, and adharma'.

John 3:9. 'Whoever is born of God, cannot sin'.

Galatians 5:18. 'If you are led by the Spirit, you are not under the law'.

[6] *De Anima* III. 10. 433. A.

liberation, which has a sense of exaltation, a sense of freedom and victory over the world, over evil and death.

When we are delivered in life, our condition is that of the *jīvan-mukta*, who is freed from the bonds of conditioned existence. His appearance continues without much outer change. His embodied state does not affect the being whom it clothes, as he has complete control over the bodily frame and knows its externality. Though tossed in the welter he retains his vision. While *jīvan-mukti* is deliverance during life, *videha-mukti* is deliverance after death, when out of bodily form. In either case the soul is freed from conditioned existence.

There is the suggestion about *karma-mukti* or gradual release. When the release is only partial and temporary, the individual soul descends again into the egoistic life and the higher consciousness is withdrawn from him. The memory of that experience, however, will work its way, until the impurities are removed.

The different emphases we find in the Upaniṣads, in regard to the state of freedom, can be understood if we bear in mind the integral or fourfold character of Brahman. In some passages oneness with Brahman is stressed; in others communion with the Supreme Person and in still others devotion to the Cosmic Spirit and participation in the work of the world. Union with God may take many forms. When the outer self is hushed, the deeper layers of consciousness are released into activity, the self may enter into the silence of the Absolute Brahman or into communion with the Eternal Person or be transported into the beatific embrace of the Cosmic Spirit. The soul may pass through various realms of spirit, bathing in their light and feeding on their bliss.

Yājñavalkya centres his attention on oneness with the Absolute Brahman, a state where there is no desire, there is no passion, not even any consciousness, *pretya saṁjñā nāsti*.[7] When honey is prepared by the collection of various juices, the latter cannot discriminate from which trees they were drawn; even so when the souls are merged in the Real, they cannot discriminate from which bodies they come. The self rises above the distinction of subject and object which characterises all empirical consciousness. It is altogether time-transcending.

[7] B.U. II. 4. 12; IV. 5. 13.

This is impersonal immortality where the soul achieves absoluteness, unconditioned being. It is illumined consciousness and not oblivion of consciousness. It is not a void of immobile peace where all is lost and everything is extinct. This is only one aspect of deliverance.

There is also the account where the self becomes one with the Supreme Person. He who knows 'I am *Brahman*', becomes the universe. Even the gods cannot prevent him from becoming the universe for he is its soul.[8] Man has potential universality which he actualises in the state of liberation. We are one with the indeterminate pure silence in essence and with the personal Lord in the liberty of cosmic manifestation. Out of the peace and poise of Brahman arises the free activity of the liberated individual. Essential unity with God is unity with one another through God. In the sense of heightened awareness we do not forget the world, which seems strangely of one piece. We are lifted out of provincialism into perspective, as we become aware of something vaster, profounder, more ultimate than the world. Rule over oneself, *svārājya*, becomes rule over the world, *sāmrājya*. Salvation is *sarvātma-bhāva*.

When the mind assumes the form of the Supreme through the power of meditation we have *samprajñāta-samādhi*, when the individual is aware that his consciousness has assumed the nature of Brahman. But when all consciousness of external objects in the waking state due to the function of the senses, of internal objects in the dream state due to the functioning of mind, or of the unmanifested in the state of dreamless sleep is absent, we have *a-samprajñāta-samādhi*. While in the former our awareness is of God, in the latter it is of the Absolute.

There are passages which suggest that the released self retains its own form freed from the imperfections of the empirical ego and untouched by worldly pleasure and pain. Yet other passages affirm the presence of such qualities. They cannot therefore be incompatible with pure intelligence. Such is the view of Bādarāyaṇa. The liberated self's desires are fulfilled by its mere will. The self is spoken of as sinless and one with the highest Person. Non-separation or *avibhāga* from Brahman is suggested in many passages. Non-separation is not absolute identity. The liberated self has no other overlord, *anyādhipatiḥ*.

[8] B.U. I. 4. 10.

There are passages where the self is said to possess adjuncts, which make for individuality and others where these are denied. Bādarāyaṇa reconciles the two views by affirming that the assumption or non-assumption of individual form is entirely a matter of option for the released soul. It can, if it so chooses, enter into many bodies created by its own will even as the flame of a lamp can convert itself into several flames.

In the *Aitareya Āraṇyaka* it is said that Vāmadeva ascended from this world and attained immortality in yonder world of heaven. The Kauṣītakī Upaniṣad gives us an account of the world of Brahmā with the Aparājita palace, the tree Ilya, the Sālajya city and the sea Ara. The passages of the Upaniṣads which make out that the reward of enlightenment is heaven in one form or another have in mind co-residence with Brahmā or *Hiraṇya-garbha*. The *Brahma-Sūtra* discusses the question whether those who go by the path of the gods reach the world of *Hiraṇya-garbha Brahmā* or become one with *Īśvara*. Bādari holds that they reach the world of *Hiraṇya-garbha*, for only to his world is going possible. Śaṁkara says, 'The created Brahmā has a specific locality and so can be the goal of a journey but not the Supreme Brahman who is present everywhere and is the inner self of the travelling individual selves'. When we reach *brahma-loka*, we continue to function there until the end of the process, when along with Brahmā, we enter the Supreme Brahman. Śaṁkara thinks that all this refers to gradual release, *karma-mukti*. Jaimini holds that the liberated souls enter the highest Brahman. Bādarāyaṇa is of the view that those who meditate on symbols go to the world of the symbols and not to the world of Brahmā.

Even as we have the fourfold nature of the Supreme, the liberated individual has different aspects of utter peace, pure energy, devotion to the Cosmic Spirit, and participation in the world. He looks at the world and is lost in it, as it is a perpetual striving to raise itself above itself.[9]

[9] Communing in this sort through earth and heaven
With every form of creature, as it looked
Towards the Uncreated with a countenance
Of adoration, with an eye of love.

Wordsworth

When we refer to Absolute Brahman, we emphasise the illumined quiescence, the non-objective consciousness in which there is a total extinction of sorrow and evil, the pure bliss infinitely surpassing all human joys, far exceeding the power of man to conceive. This very insight makes the self one with the Supreme and all existences. Only we are no more bound to them in a false relation. In our transfigured consciousness where our egoistic individuality is absent, we are not divided from others but feel one with them. Our real self is no more the individual, mental being, but is one with the Self behind the mental forms of all other selves. Our body, life, mind are no more binding, but become the transparent vehicle of our divine consciousness. When that end is reached we are a true becoming of the Divine, a free movement of the Universal Spirit. Our body, life, and mind, we feel, are one with the cosmic body, life, and mind. Our spirit fills the whole world. By knowing the eternal we understand the true nature of God, the world and the individual.

Spiritual wisdom (*vidyā*) does not abolish the world, but removes our ignorance (*avidyā*) of it. When we rise to our true being, the selfish ego falls away from us and the true integral self takes possession of us. We continue to live and act in the world, though with a different outlook. The world also continues, though it is no more alien to us. To live permanently in this new consciousness is to live in eternity.

Possessing the immortality of non-birth, the redeemed self still assumes, by free volition an individual form in the manifested world. Birth is a becoming of the Supreme in the cosmic being. This becoming is not inconsistent with Being. It becomes a means and not an obstacle to the enjoyment of life eternal. To be released from the chain of birth and death is not to flee from the world of becoming. Bondage does not consist in the assumption of birth or individuality, but in the persistence of the ignorant sense of the separate, selfish ego. It is not the embodiment that creates the bondage but the frame of mind. To the free spirit life has no terrors. He wishes to conquer life for God. He uses the world as the mould and condition for the manifestation of his spiritual freedom. He may assume birth for the purpose of helping the world.

There will be individualisation without an ego-sense. The play of the individual consciousness can take many forms, assume many aspects and poises. All through, however, he lives in the truth of the cosmic play with no delusion, released from ego, in full control of the manifested being.

The individual soul is eternal. It endures throughout the cosmic process. It commences at birth as the inheritor of the previous person and survives physical death in an altered form. For the self that has realised perfection the body ceases to be a burden. He lives in the flesh but not after the flesh.

The individual is an aspect of the Transcendent in the universe and when liberated from all limitations, he acts with his centre in the Supreme. The inner peace is manifested in the joyous freedom of outer activity. He will be at work in the world though he cannot wish to do any evil. He can do any action, for he does it disinterestedly. The desires of those whose thoughts are fixed on the Supreme do not bind. The freed soul does not aim at the improvement of humanity, but his life itself is a service. His renunciation has become the natural consequence of his wisdom. The Chāndogya Upaniṣad distinguishes desires that bind from the desires that liberate, and speaks of the Supreme Self as desiring and purposing truth.

Śaṁkara argues that the co-existence of *karma* or work, involving, as it does, the distinction of doer and the thing done, with the knowledge of the identity of the individual self with the Supreme, which negatives all such distinctions, is inconceivable. It is only self-centred action that becomes impossible. The liberated individual becomes active in God. God is born in us, i.e., becomes active in us, when all powers of the soul, which hitherto have been bound and imprisoned, become liberated and set free. 'For we are his offspring'. God becomes the centre of the free man's life so that love is radiated and good works spring forth spontaneously. He is as unconscious of the power of his life as life itself, which springs, blossoms, and puts forth its life's work in a free outpouring with no reflection on the why or the wherefore. He lives out of his own depths, and life wells up out of itself. In a sense, he is not the doer. He has become one with the Universal Self, possessed by the

Transcendent; he is *udāsīna* or unattached. The Universal Self has taken sovereign possession of the individual soul. When the individual soul ascends into the silence it becomes vast, tranquil, actionless. It observes the actions of *prakṛti* without taking part in them. There is no personal factor, and therefore there is no bondage.

Those who have attained life eternal live and wander about in the world, to all appearance, like ordinary mortals. They wear no special signs. Only their activities are centred in the highest being and are completely under their control, which is not so for those who live in the world of *saṁsāra*. They are tolerant, sympathetic, and respectful to the unliberated who are struggling with unsatisfied minds to diminish the evil and imperfection in the world. These are helped by the seers who accept the conventions with the idea of refining them. They live and suffer and rejoice and die as other mortals do, but they have no doubt in their minds, no fear in their hearts. For the liberated soul, *saṁsāra* and *mokṣa* or *nirvāṇa* as the Buddhists call it, time and eternity, the phenomenal and the real, are one. Though the liberated soul lives in the world of becoming, he lives with his consciousness centred in the Divine ground of all being. As a matter of fact, his consciousness, because it is centred in God, is intensified, and so his life in the world is more vital. Holy calm, supreme self-mastery, and righteous action characterise the lives of saints. They become a light, a power of the Truth to which they have struggled and attained, and help the development of others. They will be engaged in the work of the world, sustained by their rare vision, until the struggle with evil and imperfection is altogether overcome and the world is restored to spirit.

Whether after liberation one takes an active interest in the world or renounces it is a matter of temperament. Yājñavalkya chooses to retire to the forest, while Janaka rules a state. Whatever they do, they help those like us who are lost in the world of sorrow and suffering. Though embodiment or disembodiment makes no difference to the liberated souls, as they are filled with compassion, they take up the burden of the world. According to *Viveka-cūḍamaṇi:* 'Themselves having crossed over, they remain out of compassion for men and in order to help them also to make the crossing'. Until all people are redeemed, the liberated work in the world assuming individual forms which are the vestures of spiritual life. Spirit and material existence, *ānanda* and *anna*, are the highest and lowest rungs of a continuous series. There is a link between the two. Even as the eternal Divine is able to hold the whole universe within itself while remaining pure spirit, the soul that is one with the Eternal possesses the same poise, with reference to the individual setting. It is no more ignorantly immersed in the mutable creation. It exists consciously in its true being while using the psycho-physical apparatus, which it does not any more mistake for its true being. While the liberated retain the consciousness of the transcending, self-existent, timeless, they identify their being with the Infinite God in whom all existences dwell.

Again and again, the Upaniṣads stress that we should see all existences in the Self and the Self in all existences. Even as the Supreme is all these existences, we also should acquire the right relation to the world. Perfect fulfilment of our individuality means the perfect fulfilment of our relations with the world and the other individuals. We are called upon to overcome not only our separate egoistic existence but also our life in a paradise of self-absorbed bliss. The perfected soul cannot look with indifference on the sufferings of the imperfect, for they are also his own self. He would work to lift them into freedom. It is not now a function of altruism but is the life divine, the integral way. He will work until all beings in the manifested world are fulfilled. The liberated individuals are released from their individuality at the close of creation.

Brahma-loka is the widest possible integration of cosmic experience, the farthest limit of manifested being. Brahmā is the soul that ensouls this great dwelling. He is the true life of every being. He endures during the whole period of the cosmos. Beyond it there is nothing in the manifested world. It is not the eternal beyond the empirical. It is the farthest limit of manifestation. When the world receives its consummation, when it is delivered from time to eternity, then there is the flight of the alone to the Alone. The plan of God for the world, which was before creation, is carried out, for He is the beginning and the end of the world. The Cosmic Lord has his exteriorised existence and his interior life. When he turns outward the cosmos is evolved; when he turns his attention inward, the cosmos retreats into latency and the manifested world terminates. When the world is redeemed, the Supreme Lord becomes the Absolute One, alone, and knows nothing else.

In the *Brahma-loka* the liberated individuals present to each other as one. They are manifold in the cosmic process. Their consciousness of the Supreme which is lodged in the *buddhi* is one and not divided among the bodily forms. This identical consciousness is associated with different bodies. This manifoldness does not take away from the unity of the divine being. Until the final return of the whole universe into the Absolute, until the purpose of God before the creation is carried out, the individuals, freed from bondage to matter, will retain their distinctiveness without being sundered by boundaries. When the two poles of being are reconciled, when all individuals rise above the plane of quality, with its ego sense, struggling aspiration, and imperfect love, the world lapses into the Absolute.

PART IV. THE HINDU VIEW: *DHARMA* AND *YOGA*

Dharma: The Individual and the Social Order in Hinduism *

I

The last fifty years have seen the most revolutionary changes of any period in human history.[1] The inventions of science have put an end to human isolation and provided marvellous opportunities for the realisation of the dream of ages, the building of a great society on earth, whose vision has inspired the seers and prophets of all races and nations. The social and ethical issues raised by the spread of science and technology and the new contacts of races and cultures are common to both East and West. We must now learn to live together and understand one another.

The chief obstacle to mutual understanding has been an almost mystical faith in the superiority of this or that race and the historic missions of nations. Napoleonic France felt called to sow the seeds of revolution in the soil of Europe, Imperialistic Britain to carry the white man's burden of civilising, for a consideration, the backward peoples, Soviet Russia to liberate the proletariat from bondage to capitalism, and Nordic Germany to save the world from the antichrist of communism. This conceit of the legendary destinies of nations is not confined to the West. There are Indians who believe that true spirituality has never appeared anywhere in the world save on the sacred soil of India. There are Chinese who imagine that they alone are civilised. Public men in Japan often use the language of the Shinto divine Hirata of a hundred years ago, that the Japanese are the descendants

* From *Eastern Religions and Western Thought* (New York: Oxford University Press, 1959), pp. 349–385.

[1] 'From the stone age to the death of Queen Victoria is one era; we are now living in the second'. Gerald Heard, *These Hurrying Years* (1933), p. 1.

of the gods, different in kind rather than degree from all other nations, and the Mikado, the son of heaven, is entitled to rule them all. If in ancient times the groups claimed to be under special divine protection, they now employ scientific jargon by declaring that they are in line with the development of evolution, with the unrolling of history. They solemnise their desires and organise their hatreds by propounding the theory of the predestination of races. This pernicious doctrine of fundamental racial differences and national missions is preventing the development of a true human community in spite of the closer linking up of interests and the growing uniformity of customs and forms of life. Science, however, supports the very different view that the fundamental structure of the human mind is uniform in all races. The varied cultures are but dialects of a single speech of the soul. The differences are due to accents, historical circumstances, and stages of development. If we are to find a solution for the differences which divide races and nations to-day, it must be through the recognition of the essential oneness of the modern world, spiritually and socially, economically and politically.

Some of those whose tradition and training are limited to the European are apt to imagine that before the great Greek thinkers, Socrates, Plato, and Aristotle, there was a crude confusion of thought, a sort of chaos without form and void. Such a view becomes almost a provincialism when we realise that systems of thought which influenced countless millions of human beings had been elaborated by people who never heard the names of the Greek thinkers. The Hindu sages had formulated systems of philosophy and conduct, the Jews had developed a lofty monotheism, Zarathustra had proclaimed the universe to be an ever increasing kingdom of righteousness, and Buddha had taught the way of enlightenment. The Chinese had records of a civilisation that was even then two thousand years old, and the pyramids of Egypt and the palaces of Babylon were antiquities in the eyes of men of that period. If we leave aside the great civilisations of Egypt, Assyria, Knossos, and others whose influence on the modern world is more indirect than direct, the outstanding developments prior to 500 B.C. were the emergence of the prophetic school in Israel, of Confucianism in China, and of Brahmanism and Buddhism in India. The present state of the world is largely conditioned by the philosophies of life that had been worked out by then. The opportunities for these different tendencies to weave themselves into the warp and woof of world history are now available. Even if some of them are unsuited to modern conditions, the story of man's gradual rise and progress cannot be without its interest to all those who have faith in the solidarity of man. It is therefore a matter of significance that in these lectures we are taking up one important problem and viewing it from different historical standpoints.

II

In dealing with any social organisation we must inquire into the essential ideas on which it is founded, the conception of life which inspires it, and the forms which these ideas of life assume. The inspiring ideas are always larger than the historical forms which embody them. The Hindu view of the individual and his relation to society can be best brought out by a reference to the synthesis and gradation of (1) the fourfold object of life (*puruṣārtha*), desire and enjoyment (*kāma*), interest (*artha*), ethical living (*dharma*), and spiritual freedom (*mokṣa*); (2) the fourfold order of society (*varna*), the man of learning (Brāhmin), of power (Kṣatriya), of skilled productivity (Vaiśya), and of service (Śūdra); and (3) the fourfold succession of the stages of life (*āśrama*), student (*brahmacāri*), householder (*grihastha*), forest recluse (*vānaprastha*), and the free supersocial man (*saññyāsin*). By means of this threefold discipline the Hindu strives to reach his destiny, which is to change body into soul, to discover the world's potentiality for virtue, and derive happiness from it. It used to be said that God created the universe in order that He might apprehend Himself. Whatever we may feel about it, it is beyond question that the world exists in order that we may apprehend ourselves, attaining our full selfhood through response to whatever in it corresponds to the developing personality. The approach to this goal must not be too sudden and immediate for all individuals. It has to be reached through a progressive training, a gradual enlarging of the natural life accompanied by an uplifting of all its motives. The rule, the training, and the result differ with the type of the individual, his bent of life and degree of development. Life is much too complex for an ideal simplicity.

1. *Mokṣa.* The chief end of man is the development of the individual. The Upaniṣad tells us that there is nothing higher than the person. But man is not an assemblage of body, life, and mind born of and subject to physical nature. The natural half-animal being with which he confuses himself is not his whole or real being. It is but an instrument for the use of spirit which is the truth of his being. To find the real self, to exceed his apparent, outward self, is the greatness of which man alone of all beings is capable. 'Verily, O Gārgī, he who departs from this world without knowing this Imperishable one is a vile and wretched creature'.[2] To inquire into his true self, to live in and from it, to determine by its own energy what it shall be inwardly and what it shall make of its outward circumstances, to found the whole life on the power and truth of spirit, is *mokṣa* or spiritual freedom. To be shut up in one's own ego, to rest in the apparent self and mistake it for the real, is the root of all unrest to which man is exposed by reason of his mentality. To aspire to a universality (*sarvātma-bhāva*) through his mind and reason, through his heart and love, through his will and power, is the high sense of his humanity.

2. *Kāma.* Is this perfection consistent with normal living? There is a prevalent idea that the Hindu view concedes no reality to life, that it despises vital aims and satisfactions, that it gives no inspiring motive to human effort. If spirit and life were unrelated, spiritual freedom would become an unattainable ideal, a remote passion of a few visionaries. There is little in Hindu thought to support the view that one has to attain spiritual freedom by means of a violent rupture with ordinary life. On the other hand, it lays down that we must pass through the normal life conscientiously and with knowledge, work out its values, and accept its enjoyments. Spiritual

[2] B. U. III. 8. 10.

life is an integration of man's being, in its depth and breadth, in its capacity for deep meditation as well as reckless transport. *Kāma* refers to the emotional being of man, his feelings and desires. If man is denied his emotional life, he becomes a prey to repressive introspection and lives under a continual strain of moral torture. When the reaction sets in, he will give way to a wildness of ecstasy which is ruinous to his sanity and health.

3. *Artha.* The third end relates to wealth and material well-being. Though it is not its own end, it helps to sustain and enrich life. There was never in India a national ideal of poverty or squalor. Spiritual life finds full scope only in communities of a certain degree of freedom from sordidness. Lives that are strained and starved cannot be religious except in a rudimentary way. Economic insecurity and individual freedom do not go together.

4. *Dharma.* While the spontaneous activities of interest and desire are to be accepted, their full values cannot be realized if their action is unrestrained. There must be a rule, a guidance, a restraint. *Dharma* gives coherence and direction to the different activities of life. It is not a religious creed or cult imposing an ethical or social rule. It is the complete rule of life, the harmony of the whole man who finds a right and just law of his living. Each man and group, each activity of soul, mind, life, and body, has its *dharma*. While man is justified in satisfying his desires, which is essential for the expression of life, to conform to the dictates of his desires is not the law of his being. He will not get the best out of them if he does not conform to the *dharma* or the rule of right practice. A famous verse of the *Mahābhārata* says: 'I cry with arm uplifted, yet none heedeth. From righteousness (*dharma*) flow forth pleasure and profit. Why then do ye not follow righteousness?' *Dharma* tells us that while our life is in the first instance for our own satisfaction, it is more essentially for the community and most of all for that universal self which is in each of us and all beings. Ethical life is the means to spiritual freedom, as well as its expression on earth.

The *dharma* and its observance are neither the beginning

nor the end of human life, for beyond the law is spiritual freedom, not merely a noble manhood but universality, the aim which ennobles the whole life of the individual and the whole order of society. Man's whole life is to be passed in the implicit consciousness of this mysterious background.

The four ends of life point to the different sides of human nature, the instinctive and the emotional, the economic, the intellectual and the ethical, and the spiritual. There is implanted in man's fundamental being a spiritual capacity. He becomes completely human only when his sensibility to spirit is awakened. So long as man's life is limited to science and art, technical invention, and social programmes, he is incomplete and not truly human. If we are insolent and base, unfair and unkind to one another, unhappy in personal relationships, and lacking in mutual understanding, it is because we remain too much on the surface of life and have lost contact with the depths. When the fountains of spirit from which the creative life of the individual and society is fed dry up, diseases of every description, intellectual, moral, and social, break out. The everlasting vagrancy of thought, the contemporary muddle of conflicting philosophies, the rival ideologies which cut through national frontiers and geographical divisions, are a sign of spiritual homelessness. The unrest is in a sense sacred, for it is the confession of the failure of a self-sufficient humanism with no outlook beyond the world. We cannot find peace on earth through economic planning or political arrangement. Only the pure in heart, by fostering the mystical accord of minds, can establish justice and love. Man's true and essential greatness is individual. The scriptures could point out the road but each man must travel it for himself. The law of *karma* affirms the responsibility of each individual for his life. 'The sins ye do by two and two, ye shall pay for one by one', as Kipling called Beelzebub to remark. There is no salvation by proxy or in herds. In primitive societies there is collective responsibility, but on the hypothesis of rebirth, the guilt of an action attaches to its author. The punishment must fall on the individual, if not in this life, then in the next or perhaps in a later. The dignity and responsibility of the individual soul are recognised.

III. THE FOUR CLASSES [3]

The aim of *dharma* is to take the natural life of man and subject it to control without unduly interfering with its largeness, freedom, and variety. It has two sides: the social and the individual, the *varna dharma*, which deals [illegible] the duties assigned to men's position in society as de[illegible] by their character (*guna*) and function (*karma*); the *āśrama dharma*, which deals with the duties relevant to the stage of life, youth, manhood, or old age. We may deal with the theory of the four classes from three different standpoints, the spiritual-social, the ethical-psychological, and the conventional.

1. The earliest reference to the four classes is in the *Puruṣa-sūkta* of the Ṛg Veda,[4] where they are described as having sprung from the body of the creative spirit, from his head, arms, thighs, and feet. This poetical image is intended to convey the organic character of society. Man is not only himself, but is in solidarity with all of his kind. The stress of the universal in its movement towards the goal of the world is the source of man's sociality. Society is not something alien, imposed on man, crushing him, against which he rebels in knowledge and action. There is a profound integration of the social destiny with that of the individual. Human society is an attempt to express in social life the cosmic purpose which has other ways of expression in the material and the supramaterial planes.

Between the individual and the totality of mankind are set up smaller groups as aids, though they often turn out obstacles, to the larger unity of mankind. The difficulties of distance and organisation, the limitations of the human heart, as well as the variety and richness of life, are responsible for the smaller groups, which are meant to be used as means to a larger universality. Even if humanity becomes a more manageable unit of life, intermediate groups are bound to exist for the development of varying tendencies in the total human aggregate. The family, the tribe, the clan, the nation, are

[3] See Bhagavan Das, *Hindu Social Organization* (1932); Aurobindo Ghose, *The Psychology of Social Development*; G. H. Mees, *Dharma and Society* (1935).

[4] X. 90.

successive stages in this constant approach to universality. The individual thus belongs not only to humanity but to a class or country, race or religion. The group, which is midway between the individual and humanity, exists not merely for itself but for the one and the other, helping them to fulfil each other.

If the limited group, religious, political, or economic, regards itself as absolute and self-sufficient and demands the total service and life of the individual for its own development, it arrogates to itself claims which it does not possess. Even as the individual has no right to look upon himself as the final end of existence and claim the right to live for himself, without taking into account the needs of society, the social group has no right to demand the absolute surrender of the individual's rights. The two principles which must govern all group life are the free and unfettered development of the individual and the healthy growth of society. The individual and the society are interdependent. The sound development of the individual is the best condition for the growth of the society, and a healthy condition of society is the best condition for the growth of the individual. An ant-heap or a beehive is not the model for a human commonwealth. No harmony is to be achieved by the enslavement of the individual.

Man is not an abstract individual. He belongs to a certain social group by virtue of his character, behaviour, and function in the community. When the fourfold division of society is regarded as the ordinance of God or the dispensation of the spirit, the suggestion is that spiritual wisdom, executive power, skilled production, and devoted service are the indispensable elements of any social order. It is the function of the wise to plan the social order, of the powerful to sanction it, i.e., back it by authority which has force behind it, of the skilled to execute it or carry it out with the help of the devoted workers. The fourfold classification is conceived in the interests of world progress. It is not intended specially for the Hindus, but applies to the whole human race, which has one destiny which it seeks and increasingly attains through the countless millennia of history. The true object of all human action is *lokasaṁ-*

graha or the holding together of the human race in its evolution. In pursuance of such a view, Hindu leaders accepted primitive societies and foreign settlers such as the Greeks and the Scythians into the Hindu fold and recognized their priestly families as Brāhmins and their fighting men as Kṣatriyas.

2. As the individual is a social being, society is the necessary means by which he attains the development of his personality. A secure place must be found for him in the community so that he can derive the utmost help from it. By his nature, man falls into four types, the man of learning and knowledge, the man of power and action, the skilled craftsman, and the labourer. The types are determined by the prominent elements of man's active nature.

Those who are pre-eminently intellectual are the Brāhmins, whose function it is to seek and find knowledge, communicate it to others, and make it prevail in the world. Their activity is not the pursuit of practical aims in the narrow sense. They seek their joy in the practice of an art, a science, or a philosophy and set an example of attachment to disinterested pursuits of the mind. The perversions of this type are a mere intellectuality or curiosity for ideas without an accompanying ethical elevation, a narrow specialisation without the requisite openness of mind, a thirst for novelty, a tendency to imitate current fashions, an ineffective idealism without any hold on life. The true Brāhmin is said to be one who has sensed the deepest self and acts out of that consciousness. He is expected to embody the law of self-dedicating love, the grace and joy of souls in the consciousness of the service, free, high, and daring, of the humanity of the future, where hate, violence, and fanaticism will be unknown. The Brāhmins give moral guidance. They reveal but do not enforce. Practical administration is not their task. They keep clear of the love of power as well as the pressure of immediate needs. Plato affirms that kings must be philosophers. In the allegory of the Cave the wise man who has escaped into the daylight must not stay there but must go back to teach others. 'We shall compel him to go back though we do him an injustice'. The Hindu believes that any one immediately and deeply concerned with the exercise of power cannot be completely objective. The rulers will be concerned with government and the thinkers with values. If society is not to be led by the blind, we must have the contemplative thinkers at the top. Every society needs to have a class which is freed from material cares, competitive life, and is without obligations to it. Freedom is of the essence of the higher life and the great values cannot be achieved under a compulsion or a sense of duty.

A dry spirit of detachment and disconnexion from immediate surroundings are essential qualities for those engaged in the pursuit of truth. An invincible patience, a contempt of all little and feeble enjoyments, humility without any baseness, an infinite hope, and a high fearlessness are the qualities that mark the seeker of truth. These, which fit them for their vocation, unfit them for success in life. If their claims on society are not sufficiently safeguarded, they will be doomed to loneliness and not seldom to starvation. Their very strength prevents them from compromising with the things they despise. A class of disinterested seekers of truth supported by society, influencing it, and placed above the corrupting tendency of power, is the very life of social stability and growth. After all, civilisation is based on a vision.

If a Brāhmin class was found necessary even in those less organised and complicated times, it is much more necessary to-day, when there is a widespread tendency to confuse national interests with objective truth. Our intellectuals to-day with rare exceptions are camp followers of political rulers. When Hegel saw Napoleon on horseback at the head of his army, he said, 'I saw the world soul riding'. The thinkers betray their function when they descend to the market-place to serve the passions of race, class, or nation. When they let their spirits get enclosed in the mentality of politics, when they fail to give to society a vision of humanity and civilisation, the whole social structure will totter. Those who belong to the spiritual ministry of society must guard their integrity of mind as a sacred possession, be completely masters of themselves, and proclaim the truth that all cities, all states, all kingdoms are mortal, and only the spirit of man immortal. Thucydides contemplates the image of a world in which Athens should have ceased to exist. Polybius shows us the conqueror of Carthage meditating over the burning town. 'And Rome too shall meet her fateful hour'.

The Brāhmins will now be considered to be receivers of unearned income. Even as it is the function of the state to support schools and colleges, museums and picture-galleries, it must also support a leisured class. In the world to-day the leisured are those who inherit wealth, though there is no reason to suppose that the children of rich parents are exceptionally intelligent and sensitive. In China, boys and girls used to be selected for this class on the results of competitive examinations. But the special training cannot be postponed till the age of examinations. If the training is to start early enough we must choose the members soon after birth. Is it to be by lot? The Hindu assumed that birth in a family which had the traditions of the leisured class might offer the best solution.

While it is the business of the Brāhmin to lay down the science of values, draw out the blueprints for social reconstruction, and persuade the world to accept the high ends of life, it is the business of the Kṣatriya to devise the means for gaining the ends. Not only in the ancient epics but in the recent history of Rajput chivalry do we find Kṣatriya princes cast in the heroic mould, the limits of whose fame are the stars, men whom no fear could terrify, no difficulty could daunt, men for whom retreat was more bitter than death. The qualities that mark the Kṣatriya type are a heroic determination from which no danger or difficulty can distract them, a dynamic daring which shrinks from no adventure, a nobility of soul which would do nothing sordid or mean, and an unflinching resistance to injustice and oppression. The worshippers of power, the men of brute force, the selfish tyrants are the perversions of this type. The qualities of the Kṣatriya are as necessary as those of the Brāhmin for the perfection of human nature.

The political is not the highest category. The state exists in order that its members may have a good life. It is a social convenience. It is not the judge of its own conduct. Though righteousness depends on force, 'it is wrong to say that it is the will of the strong'.[5] The state is not above ethics. It exists essentially for the good of the individual and has therefore no right to demand the sacrifice of the individual, though it has every right to demand the conditions essential for the performance of its task. The worship of the God-State with which we are familiar to-day, that the State is the creator of right and wrong, that reasons of state justify any crime, that ethics are a purely individual matter, are flatly opposed to the Hindu view. Rāma tells Lakṣmaṇa: 'I bear arms for the sake of truth. It is not difficult for me to gain this whole universe but I desire not even the suzerainty of the heavens if it is to be through unrighteousness'.[6] The state finds its justification according to the measure in which it pursues and protects the full development of the human person. The end is personal liberty and happiness, and all government is a convenient means to this end.

The Hegelian theory that what is is right, and that the Prussian military state is the highest form of 'the Spirit' on earth, is in practice a denial of moral authority. It confuses the good with the real and reduces the distinction between right and wrong to one of strong and weak. Force is what counts, and not right, which is only another name for superior force. On this view, no government has any moral authority, and conflicts between classes and nations can only be decided by force. The League of Nations is suspected to be another power system, not an alternative to war but only an excuse for a holy war. The League has failed not because it was lacking in armed force but because it had no moral authority. Only an earnest application of the democratic tradition in the relations between states and a rearrangement of the world on that basis can give the needed authority to the League. The great task of our generation is to embody real democracy in the material structure of our civilisation, to work for a world community far richer in its cultural opportunities for all men, and far more brotherly in its relationships.

The Hindu scheme permits the use of force for the maintenance of order and enforcement of law, occasionally even

[5] *Mahābhārata*, III. 134. 3.

[6] *Rāmāyaṇa*, II. 97. 6–7.

to the point of the destruction of human life. In a perfect society where every one is naturally unselfish and loving, there would be no need for government or force, but so perfect a condition is perhaps not suited to mere men. In the actual imperfect conditions the state will have to exercise force on recalcitrant individuals. The need for force is, however, a sign of imperfection. In principle anything which has the taint of coercion is to that extent lacking in perfection, as the *Mahābhārata* has it. We may feel that we are justified in using force to restrain the evil-doer. This very necessary coercion results in two disadvantages. It tempts the user to its unrighteous use and causes resentment in those against whom it is used. While we cannot obviate the necessity for the use of coercion in political arrangements, so long as sinful ambition, pride, lust, and greed are operative in human nature, it is essential to guard against its abuses and remember that there is a higher obligation of love that transcends the requirements of mere justice, in the light of which all codes of justice are to be judged. The ideal is the Brāhminic one of non-resistance, for the means are as important as the end. In this imperfect world, however, the non-resisters are able to practise their convictions only because they owe their security to the maintenance by others of the principles which they repudiate.

The use of force is limited to occasions where it is the only alternative and is applied for the sake of creating a more suitable environment for the growth of moral values and not for activities which can hardly fail to result in social chaos. Force, when unavoidable, must be employed in an ethical spirit. The use of force does not become permissible simply because it has an ethical aim. It must be applied in an ethical way. The users of force are not the ones to judge the causes for which it has to be employed. The Ksatriyas rule only as the guardians and servants of the law. They have an executive power over the community which is valid only so long as they carry out the law, which is placed under the control of the Brāhmins and the seers and protected from interference by political or economic power. The function of the state is limited to the protection of the law and defence. People were allowed to manage their affairs in accordance with the traditional rules and customs. They did not care who the rulers were so long as their lives were undisturbed. One flag was as good as another, if social life was carried on in the same way. This attitude has made the country a prey to invaders. The enforcement of moral laws is what gives a king his glory. This is evident from the description of the king who could say: 'In my realm there is neither thief nor miser, nor drunkard, nor one who is altarless, nor any ignoramus, nor any unchaste man or woman'.

As in all ancient societies, only the fighting classes took part in wars. The motive was more monarchical loyalty than national pride. Even when tribes were at war, the non-combatants were little affected. Megasthenes writes: 'If the Indians are at war with one another, it is not customary for them to touch those who are tilling the land, but the one group may be engaged in battle . . . but the other is peacefully engaged in ploughing or reaping or pruning or mowing nearby'. These principles were laid down at a time when wars were fought according to strict rules by small professional armies. In modern wars whole populations are involved and there are no non-combatants. The forces must act with efficiency and indiscrimination. They may kill and maim, starve and ruin millions of human beings who are absolutely innocent. An indiscriminate massacre of masses will be disastrous to the whole society, and by no stretch of the imagination can it be said that it will protect the interests of the community. There is much to be said for those who believe that complete pacifism is the only attitude to wars under modern conditions that can be adopted by those who have faith in the fundamental unity of all being. Yet we live, not in a perfect universe, but only in an improving one at best.

The third class of Vaiśyas brings into relief the tendency of life to possess and enjoy, to give and take. In its outward action, this power appears as the utilitarian, practical mind engaged in commerce and industry. Though bent on the efficient exploitation of the natural resources, this type is also marked by humanity and ordered benevolence. Though the members of this class are engaged in pursuits where the temptations to the acquisition of wealth are real, they are expected to develop qualities of humanity and neighbourly service. If they are keen on wealth for its own sake, they are to be 'detested'. It is not their main function to contribute to the spiritual welfare of society or its political power, yet we cannot have these without their co-operation. Practical intelligence and adaptive skill are their chief marks. The perversions of this type are familiar to us, as our age is pre-eminently a commercial one. Armament manufacturers foment discords between nations for the sake of profits. The records of the League of Nations show how merchants, European and Asiatic, have been making millions through the sale of vile drugs that destroy the body, mind, and soul of the people. In some countries those who purchase the drug are given free the hypodermic syringe with which to inject it. For the lust of gold man hurls his fellow-men over these precipices of war between races and nations, of drunkenness, and drug-addiction. Commerce and industry, which are the life-blood of the human race, are perverted from their proper use by a false standard of values. Property, according to the Hindu view, is a mandate held by its possessors for the common use and benefit of the commonwealth. The *Bhāgavata* tells us that we have a claim only to so much as would satisfy our hunger. If any one desires more, he is a thief deserving punishment. To gain wealth and power at the expense of society is a social crime. To destroy surplus products simply because we cannot sell them for profit is an outrage on humanity.

A fourth variety of human nature finds its outlet in work and service. Labour is the basis of all human relations. While the first three classes are said to be twice born, the fourth is said to be once born and so inferior. It only means that the activities of the members of the fourth class are instinctive and not governed by ideals of knowledge, strength, or mutual service. While the seeker of wisdom works for the joy of the search, the hero of action works from a sense of honour, the artist and the skilled craftsman are impelled by a love of their art, and even the lowest worker has a sense of the dignity of labour. Though all these are impressed by the social code with a sense of their social value, the lowest classes are not generally aware of the plan of the social order and their place in it. They fulfil their duties for the satisfaction of their primary needs, and when these are gratified, they tend to lapse into a life of indolence and inertia. An instinctive obedience and a mechanical discharge of duty are their chief contributions.

It is not to be assumed that the qualities which are predominant in each of the four classes are exclusive of one another. As a matter of fact there is no individual who does not possess all these essentials. Classes are marked as wise or heroic, skilled or unskilled, according as one or the other predominates in them. None of these can be regarded as complete. The Brāhmin cannot serve truth with freedom if he has not moral courage and heroism, if he has not the practical sense to adapt the highest truth to the conditions of actual life and the needs of the different classes of society, if he has not the sense of service to humanity. Even the man of action, though he is not engaged in the pursuit of wisdom, has a sense of the direction of society, the aims it has, and the way in which he has to sanction the details essential for the realisation of those aims. He uses his power for the service of the society. The man of practical ability is called upon to devote his skill and possessions to the good of society. He has a general idea of the nature of the social good, has the courage and the enterprise essential for the exploitation of natural resources, and is anxious to improve the material conditions of life in every conceivable way. Even the man of labour is not a social drudge. As a part of the social order, he strives to serve society through his special function with knowledge, honour, and skill. The fourfold spirit is present in every member of society and its fruitful development is the test of each one's efficiency. There is no life, in so far as it is human, which is not at the same time an enquiry into truth, a struggle with forces inward and outward, a practical adaptation of the truth to the conditions of life and a service of society. Every one in his own way aims at being a sage, a hero, an artist, and a servant. But the conditions of life demand specialisation within limits. Each one cannot develop within his single life the different types of excellence. As a rule one type of excellence or perfection is attainable only at the expense of another. We cannot erect on the same site both a Greek temple and a Gothic cathedral, though each has its own loveliness. 'The ascetic virtues cannot flourish side by side with the social and the domestic. If you choose to be an anchorite, you cannot be a statesman'. A hermit does not know what human love is. A social worker cannot devote his strength to the advancement of knowledge. But wherever we may start, it is open to us to reach the highest perfection, and man reaches perfection by each being intent on his own duty.[7] 'Men of all classes, if they fulfil their assigned duties, enjoy the highest imperishable bliss'.

While, from a spiritual standpoint, all work has in it the power to lead to perfection, a natural hierarchy binding the position in society with the cultural development of the individual arises. Life is a staircase with steps leading to a goal and no man can rest satisfied until he reaches the top. Not the stage reached but the movement upwards is of importance. The road is better than the resting-place. Hierarchy is not coercion but a law of nature. The four classes represent four stages of development in our manhood. Every human being starts with a heavy load of ignorance and inertia. His first stage is one of toil demanded by the needs of the body, the impulse of life, and the law of society. Manu tells us that all men are born Śūdras and become Brāhmins by regeneration through ethical and spiritual culture. From the lowest stage we rise into a higher type when we are driven by the instinct for useful creation. We have here the vital man. At a higher level, we have the active man with ambition and will power. Highest of all is the Brāhmin, who brings a spiritual rule into life. Though something of all these four is found in all men in different degrees of development, one or the other tends to predominate in the dealings of the soul with its embodied nature, and that becomes the basis for future development. As he unfolds and grows, man changes his status and class.[8] Growth is ordinarily gradual. Nature

[7] *Bhagavadgītā*, XVIII. 45.

[8] 'A man whether he be a Brāhmin, Kṣatriya, Vaiśya or Śūdra is such by nature. By evil deed does a twice-born man fall from his position. The Kṣatriya or a Vaiśya who lives in the condition of a Brāhmin by practising the duties of one attains to Brāhminhood' (*Mahābhārata*, Anuśāsanaparva, 143. 6).

cannot be rushed. The seer's vision is the ideal for the active man; while he can trust the seer, the lower ones may not be able to do so. They look to the practical men. We can only understand and follow those who are just a step beyond ourselves. The distant scene is practically out of sight. The social order is intended to produce the type and provide for growth beyond it.

If one who is of a lower nature desires to perform the social tasks of a higher class, before he has attained the answering capacities, social order will be disturbed. To fight is a sin for a Brāhmin but not for a Kṣatriya, whose function is to fight without ill will for a righteous cause, when there is no other course.[9] Arjuna in the *Bhagavadgītā* is required to follow his own nature. To follow the law of another's nature is dangerous. The bent of Arjuna's nature was to fight; to run away from the battle-field would be a flight from his nature. Man cannot ordinarily transcend his psychological endowment. In the actual social order, there may be people who consider it right to fight and others to abstain, and both are justified. The fourfold classification is against modern notions of conscription where every one is obliged to take to military service, or universal suffrage where ruling power is distributed among all. In the natural hierarchy there cannot be one moral standard for all. The higher a person is in the social scale, the greater are the obligations. The tendency to judge others by our own standards must be tempered by a greater understanding of each one's special work and place in society.

Individuals and classes were bound to one another by what is called the spirit of status and not terminable contract. Every man had his place in society and fixed duties attached to it. The social organism expected from each man his duties but guaranteed to each subsistence and opportunity for self-expression. The spirit of competition was unknown. Regulated control, even if coercive, is less tyrannical than blind competition. It secures for the largest number of individuals effective freedom in non-economic and cultural spheres. Regulation in

[9] 'If thou wilt not carry on this righteous warfare, then casting away thine own *dharma* and thine honour, thou wilt incur sin' (*Bhagavadgītā*, II. 33).

the interests of a fuller measure of freedom is not the same as the total subjection of the individual to the state.

In a real sense, the fourfold scheme is democratic. Firstly, it insists on the spiritual equality of all men. It assumes that within every human creature there is a self which has the right to grow in its own way, to find itself, and make its life a full and satisfied image and instrument of its being. Secondly, it makes for individuality in the positive sense. Individuality is attained not through an escape from limitations but through the willing acceptance of obligations. It is erroneous to assume that only the aberrant or the anarchical is the true individual. Thirdly, it points out that all work is socially useful and from an economic standpoint equally important. Fourthly, social justice is not a scheme of rights but of opportunities. It is wrong to assume that democracy requires all men to be alike. Society is a pattern or an organism in which different organs play different parts. Excellence is specific and cannot be universal. Equality refers to opportunity and not to capacity. While it recognises that men are unequal in scale and quality, it insists that every human being shall have the right and the opportunity to contribute to human achievement, as far as his capacity goes. Society must be so organised as to give individuals sufficient scope to exercise their natural energies without being interfered with by others. Even Marx does not accept the view that all men are born equal with an inherent right to identical shares in the commodities produced by the community. An assertion of abstract equality is not the same as the principle from each according to his capacity and to each according to his requirements. There is no attempt to equalise capacities or level up the requirements.[10] Fifthly,

[10] Stalin, in his address to the Seventeenth Congress of the Communist Party, defines the position thus: 'By equality Marxism means not only equality in personal requirements and personal life, but the abolition of class, i.e. (*a*) the equal emancipation of all toilers from exploitation, after the capitalists have been overthrown and expropriated; (*b*) the equal abolition for all of private property in the means of production, after they have been transformed into the property of the whole society; (*c*) the equal duty of all to work according to their ability and the equal right of all toilers to receive according to the amount of work they have done (socialist society); (*d*) the equal duty of all to work according to their

the essence of democracy is consideration for others. Freedom for the individual means restrictions on absolute power. No one class can make unlimited claims. The State, the Church, and other organisations must limit themselves and leave room for those who neither think nor feel as they do. Spiritual power, political power, and economic power must be properly adjusted in a well-ordered society. Democracy is not to be confused with mutual rivalries. Kauṭilya's *Artha-śāstra* discusses the theory of social contract to enforce the duties and rights of the state and the individual. While the rulers are obliged to abide by the rules of *dharma*, the citizens pay the taxes in return for the protection they receive. Monarchy was not the only type of government. Republican constitutions were well known. Representative self-governing institutions operated in India even by the time of Megasthenes. Village communities presided over by councils of elders chosen from all castes and representing all interests maintained peace and order, controlled taxation, settled disputes, and preserved intact the internal economy of the country. Trade-guilds were also managed on similar lines, protecting the professional interests and regulating working hours and wages. The peasant worked the land to maintain himself and the family and contribute a little to the community. The craftsman fashioned the tools and the clothing necessary for the community, and was in turn provided with the food and shelter necessary. This system prevailed even after the British rule started. Sir William Hunter observed: 'The trade guilds in the cities, and the village community in the country, act, together with caste, as mutual assurance societies, and under normal conditions allow none of their members to starve. Caste, and the trading or agricultural guilds concurrent with it, take the place of a poor law in India'. Land became a commodity to be bought and sold for the first time in the administration of Warren Hastings. The new economy of the private ownership of land,

---

ability and the equal right of all toilers to receive according to their requirements (communist society). And Marxism starts out with the assumption that people's abilities and requirements are not, and cannot be, equal in quality or in quantity, either in the period of socialism or in the period of communism'. Webb, *Soviet Russia* (1936), vol. ii, p. 702.

with the zamindar as the permanent landlord, a sort of middleman between the state and the peasant, the divorce of industry from agriculture, and large-scale production in factories have brought about a social revolution. Under the centralised administration of the British, local self-government and autonomous village organisation disappeared. A strange impression prevails that in India caste prevented the development of democratic institutions. In the administration of villages and towns, caste and trade-guilds, provinces and even federations, the democratic principle where every individual is both sovereign and subject is affirmed. Even such details as the rules of elections, division into electoral units, rules of procedure and debate do not escape notice. Representative democracy or the *pañchāyat* system is native to the Indian temperament. Sixthly, the general tendency of men of all classes to strive to the summit is due to the impression that the position at the top is one of pleasure, profit, and power. To obtain these, every one wishes to climb the social ladder. But in the Hindu scheme life becomes more difficult as we rise higher. A Brāhmin should do nothing for the sake of enjoyment. If we realise the increase of social responsibility and the diminution of the personal enjoyments of life as we rise in the social ladder, we will be more satisfied with our own place and work in society. Those who seek the higher place will lead a life of simplicity and self-denial.

Within this fourfold scheme each individual has to follow his own nature and arrive at his possible perfection by a growth from within. The individual is not a mere cell of the body or a stone of the edifice, a mere passive instrument of its collective life. Man is not a thing or a piece of machinery which can be owned. The question of property, of the man over the woman, of the father over the child, of the state over the individual must be given up. The individual's action must be determined by his own essential quality. Through the fulfilment of his nature he contributes to the good of the society, though he may not intend it. We must avoid the cant of the preacher who appeals to us for the deep-sea fishermen on the ground that they are daily risking their lives that we may have fish for our breakfasts and dinners. They are doing nothing of the kind. They go to sea for themselves and their families, not for our breakfasts and dinners. Our convenience happily is a by-product of their labours.

True law which develops from within is not a check on liberty but its outward image, its visible expression. Human society progresses really and vitally only when law becomes the expression of freedom. It will reach its perfection when man having learned to know becomes spiritually one with his fellow-men. The law of society exists only as the outward mould of his inner nature. The true man conforms to law simply because he cannot help it. When Draupadī blames her husband for obeying the law when it has led him into difficulties, he replies that he does not observe it in expectation of any reward but because his mind has become fixed on it. Man helps the world by his life and growth only in proportion as he can be more freely himself, using the ideals and the opportunities which he finds in his way. He can use them effectively only if they are not burdens to be borne by him, but means towards his growth. By gathering the materials from the minds and lives of his fellow-men and making the most of the experience of humanity's past ages, he expands his own mind and pushes society forward. Social order (*kṣema*) and progress (*yoga*) are thus safeguarded.

3. When birth acquired greater importance classes degenerated into castes. The chief features of caste are: (i) *Heredity:* One cannot change one's caste. (ii) *Endogamy:* Every member of a caste must marry a member of the same caste and may not marry outside it. (iii) *Commensal restrictions:* Regulations are imposed regarding the acceptance of food and drink from members of other castes. The caste scheme recognises the individuality of the group. When aboriginal deities were taken over into the Hindu pantheon, the priesthoods attached to them were accepted as Brāhmins even as the ruling families of the tribe were accepted as Kṣatriyas. Hence arose innumerable subdivisions. The beliefs and practices which the different groups developed in the course of ages were recognised as valid and relations among groups regulated in accordance with them.

In the period of the Vedic hymns (1500 B.C. to 600 B.C.),

there were classes and not castes. We do not find any reference to connubial or commensal restrictions. The occupations were by no means hereditary. There is, however, a marked differentiation between the fair-skinned Aryans and the dark-skinned Dasyus. This racial distinction faded into the background in the early Buddhist times (600 B.C. to 300 B.C.). In the *Jātakas* the four classes are mentioned and the Kṣatriyas are said to be the highest. Any one who took to the priestly way of life became a Brāhmin. There were no endogamous restrictions. According to one *Jātaka*, Buddha himself though a Kṣatriya married a poor farmer's daughter. Though marriages within the same class were encouraged, intermarriages were by no means unusual or forbidden. Function in the trade-guilds became, before long, hereditary. Megasthenes tells us that there were seven castes, that intermarriages between them were forbidden, and that function was hereditary though the philosophers were exempt from these restrictions. His observations can be accepted only with caution. Chandragupta himself was of mixed descent. Megasthenes' account shows, however, that mixed marriages were exceptional even in the fourth century B.C., though they continued to occur in later times. Caste in its rigour became established by the time of Manu and the *Purāṇas*, which belong to the period of the Gupta kings (A.D. 330 to 450). The great invaders, the Sakas, the Yavanas, the Pahlavas, and the Kushans, were accepted as Hindus. It is said in *Mudrārākṣasā* that Chandragupta was opposed by a force under the command of 'the great monarch of the barbarian tribes' who had in his army members of the foreign tribes. Yuan Chwang's account of the bloodthirsty Hunnish tyrant Mihiragula shows that the Huns were savages from the central Asian steppes. When these tribes were taken over into Hinduism an unusually strong disinclination to intermarriage developed. The endogamous custom which was encouraged in the Buddhist period and became the usual practice in the time of Megasthenes was made the rule by Manu, who carefully regulated exceptions to it. Caste was the Hindu answer to the challenge of society in which different races had to live together without merging into one. The difficulty of determining the psychological basis led to the acceptance of birth as the criterion. Society, being a machine, inclines to accept an outer sign or standard. The tendency of a conventional society is to fix firmly and formalise a system of grades and hierarchies. Besides, as the types fix themselves, their maintenance by education and tradition becomes necessary and hereditary grooves are formed.

While there are only four classes, the castes are innumerable. We have tribal, functional, sectarian castes, as well as outcastes. There are references to the untouchables in the *Jātakas.* Fa Hien, the Chinese pilgrim (A.D. 405 to 411), describes how the Caṇḍālas had to live apart and give notice of their approach on entering a town by striking a piece of wood. The untouchables mainly included some who were on the outskirts of civilisation and were left unabsorbed by the Hindu faith and others who performed duties which were regarded as low. In the class scheme there was no fifth class of untouchables.

The substitution of the principle of birth for virtue and valour has been the main factor in the process of social crystallisation and caste separatism. Birth is said to indicate real, permanent differences in the mental attitudes of men though they cannot be easily measured by the rough and ready methods of anthropologists. The theory of rebirth by which man's inborn nature and course of life are determined by his own past lives gives additional support to the view that man is born to the social function which is natural to him. It is not realised that the fact of ancestry, parentage, and physical birth may not always indicate the true nature of the individual. When the obligations of the classes do not spring spontaneously from their inner life, they become mere conventions, departing largely from the maintenance of ethical types. The son of a Brāhmin is always a Brāhmin though he may have nothing of the Brāhmin in him. The individual does not fall naturally into his place in society but is thrust into it by an external power. Any system where an abstract power, caste, or church decides a person's profession and place is an unnatural one. As the individuals are esteemed high or low, not by the degree of their sociality but by their profession, wealth, or power, class conflicts arise where all desire power and privilege. In the class scheme the social duty of the individual is insisted on, not his personal rights. In caste, privilege is more important. In the class order any one who has the courage to undergo the discipline, the strength to deny himself the pleasures of life, and the capacity to develop his powers is free to rise to the top; not so in the caste scheme, which does not allow for the free play of man's creative energies. While the man of the higher caste is left to his sense of duty and conscience, the weaker ones with their anti-social tendencies are made to feel the weight of punishment. In actual practice the setting up of different standards of punishment for offenders of different castes is the weakest part of the system. In fairness to the lawgivers, it may be said that they made out that the higher the caste the greater is the offence when moral rules are violated.

The disparity between the hereditary function and the individual's nature was reduced to some extent by education and training. And so the scriptures while recognising the hereditary practice insist that character and capacity are the real basis and without them the social status is meaningless.

When the Brāhmin looked upon his position as one of easy privilege and not arduous obligation, protests were uttered. Manu and others contrast the ideal Brāhmin who has the ethical quality with the actual who bases his claim on birth. In *Śuddhārthacintāmani* it is said that the three features of a Brāhmin are austerity, learning, and birth, and one who has the third and not the first two qualities is only a Brāhmin by caste. Again, Kauśika received instruction from a meat-seller and said to him: 'In my opinion you are a Brāhmin even in this life. Because a Brāhmin who is haughty and who is addicted to degrading vices is no better than a Śūdra, and a Śūdra who restrains his passions and is ever devoted to truth and morality I look upon as a Brāhmin, inasmuch as character is the basis of Brāhminhood'. Chāṇdogya Upaniṣad gives the story of Satyakāma, the son of Jābālā who approached Gautama Haridrumata and said to him, 'I wish to become a student with you, sir; may I come to you'? He said to him, 'Of what family are you, my friend'? He replied, 'I do not know, sir, of what family I am. I asked my mother and she answered,

"In my youth when I had to move about much as a servant, I conceived thee. I do not know of what family thou art. I am Jābālā by name and thou art Satyakāma", therefore I am Satyakāma Jābālā, sir'. He said to him, 'No one but a true Brāhmin would thus speak out. Go and fetch fuel, friend. I shall initiate you; you have not swerved from the truth'.[11] Even after caste became conventional, Kavaṣa, the son of a slave girl, was accepted as a Brāhmin. To minimise th rigours of caste the relative character of caste distinctions is frequently emphasised. The *Rāmāyaṇa* tells us that there were only Brāhmins in the Kritayuga and all people were of one class.

Though theistic movements from the Āḷvārs and Rāmānuja, though Rāmānanda and Kabīr, Nānak and Caitanya, Nāmdev and Eknāth protest against caste inequalities, they have not disappeared as yet. Even Christian churches in their anxiety to propagate their faith compromise with it. Pope Gregory XV published a bull sanctioning caste regulations in the Christian Church of India.[12] The general effect of the impact of the West has been in the direction of liberalising the institution The rise of nationalism is the direct result of the incorporatior of Western ideals in the thought and life of the country. The hostile judgement on British rule in India is based on con ceptions of justice and freedom for which the British are, i the main, responsible. The Britisher's interest in India i more the permanence of his rule than the reform of India society. His attitude and policy are best expressed in th statement of James Kerr, the principal of the Hindu Colleg at Calcutta, who said as far back as 1865, 'It may be doubte if the existence of caste is on the whole unfavourable to th permanence of our rule. It may even be considered favourabl to it, provided we act with prudence and forbearance. I spirit is opposed to national union'.[13] The recent constitution changes stereotype communal divisions and caste distinction Though measures which provide for the special representatio of certain classes of people are adopted in the name of soci

[11] IV. 4. 1–5.

[12] *Encyclopaedia Britannica*, 11th ed., Vol. V, p. 468.

[13] Ghurye, *Caste and Race in India* (1932), p. 164.

justice, they are calculated to retard the growth of national unity. Hindu reform movements are impelled by the conviction that caste is an anachronism in our present conditions, and that it persists through sheer inertia.

Those who defy caste rules are outcasted, and this punishment till recently made the influence of caste virtually irresistible. The freedom of the individual, however, was not completely suppressed. The rules of caste were quite flexible. There was no attempt to crystallise morals. Those who demand a radical reform might form themselves into a new caste. The laws were there, but they were admitted to be relative and susceptible to change. The law books declare that the sources of *dharma* are the scriptures, the sayings and doings of those who know the scripture, the practice of the virtuous, and the approval of the enlightened conscience. The texts indicate the framework, and within their limits ample liberty of interpretation is allowed. As the texts themselves are often conflicting, one is obliged to use one's own reason and conscience. Men of moral insight and uprightness could depart from the established usage and alter customary law. Āpastamba says, 'Right and wrong do not go about proclaiming "here we are"; nor do gods, angels and the manes say "this is right and that is wrong", but right is what the Aryans praise and wrong is what they blame'. In the Taittirīya Upaniṣad the teacher gives the young man at the end of years of study a general rule of conduct.

> Speak the truth, practise virtue; neglect not the sacrifices due to gods and manes: let thy mother be to thee as a divinity, also thy father, thy spiritual teacher and thy guest; whatever actions are blameless, not others, shouldst thou perform; good deeds, not others, shouldst thou commend; whatsoever thou givest give with faith, with grace, with modesty, with respect, with sympathy.

How is the student to know what is right? Ordinarily custom is a sufficient guide, but in cases of doubt the young man is invited to take as his model what is done in similar circumstances by Brāhmins 'competent to judge, apt and devoted, but not harsh lovers of virtue'. If the learned doctors differ, one has to consult one's own conscience. Rules are made for man, and the conventions, not the moral principles, may be set aside in emergencies. A saint declared that he would eat beef if he chose, and another satisfied his hunger with dog's meat received from an impure low-caste man. 'A saint can eat anything', he said, 'and when a man is as hungry as I am, one kind of meat is as good as another'. He enunciates a rule that 'it is not a serious matter if one eats unclean food, provided one does not tell a lie about it'.[14] The former is a matter of convention, the latter relates to ethical life. The independence of the individual became fettered when the law with this four-fold basis became codified and required legislative enactments for changes.

The truth underlying the system is the conception of right action as a rightly ordered expression of the nature of the individual being. Nature assigns to each of us our line and scope in life according to inborn quality and self-expressive function. Nowhere is it suggested that one should follow one's hereditary occupation without regard to one's personal bent and capacities. The caste system is a degeneration of the class idea. It does not admit that the individual has the right to determine his future and pursue his interests. Though idealistic in its origin, beneficent in large tracts of its history, still helpful in some ways, it has grown out of harmony with our present conditions, owing to arrested development and lack of elasticity. The compulsory degradation of a large part of mankind is revolting to the refined natures who have a sense of the dignity of man and respect for the preciousness of human life. The right of every human soul to enter into the full spiritual heritage of the race must be recognised. Caste is a source of discord and mischief, and if it persists in its present form, it will affect with weakness and falsehood the people that cling to it.

THE FOUR STAGES OF LIFE

The Hindu scheme does not leave the growth of the individual entirely to his unaided initiative but gives him a framework for guidance. Human life is represented as consisting of four

[14] *Mahābhārata*, XII. 298.7.

cutive stages, of which the first three fall within the sdiction of class or caste.

Human offspring are the most helpless of all living creatures. In the absence of parental care, their chances of survival are little. The tending will have to be continued for a long period, till the child reaches the status of man. The higher the cultural level the longer is the period required for education.

The aim of education is not to pour knowledge into the resisting brain and impose a stereotyped rule of conduct on his struggling impulses: it is to help the child to develop his nature, to change him from within rather than crush him from without. The education imparted not only fits man for his role in life but gives him a general idea of the conditions of spiritual life.

By filling his place in social life, by helping its maintenance and continuity, the individual not only fulfils the law of his own being but makes his contribution to society. Man attains his full being only by living in harmonious social relationships. Sex is a normal human function concerned with the perpetuation of the race. Marriage, love, and motherhood are glorified. The wife has an equal position with the husband in all domestic and religious concerns. Every woman has a right to marry and have a home. Celibacy is the rarest of sexual aberrations. Any preoccupation with the flesh is in itself an evil even though it may be for purposes of crucifying it. Soul and body, however different, are yet closely bound together. The things of spirit are in part dependent on the satisfaction of the body. The physical and the economic, though they may not be important in themselves, are important as means to the life of spirit.

One must learn the social and spiritual lessons of the earlier stages before one can pass on to the later. One must learn to be sober before striving to become a saint. He who does not know what it is to love as a child or a husband or a parent cannot pretend to the love which contains them all. To withdraw the noblest elements of humanity from the married state to monkhood is biologically and socially unhealthy. The state of the householder is the mainstay of social life. It is said that the householder shall have his life established in the supreme reality, shall be devoted to the pursuit of truth, and shall dedicate to the Eternal Being whatever activities he undertakes. Hinduism does not demand withdrawal from life into mountain tops or gloomy caves as an essential condition for spiritual life. The way to a higher life is normally through the world.

To be, for man, is not merely to be born, to grow up, marry, earn his livelihood, found a family, and support it and pass away. That would be a human edition of the animal life. It is rather to grow upward exceeding his animal beginnings. By fulfilling his function in society, the individual begins to feel the greatness of the soul which is behind the veils of nature and longs to reach his true universality. When the children get settled and no more want his attention, he retires probably with his wife to a quiet place in the country to lead a life of enquiry and meditation and work out within himself the truth of his being, in an atmosphere of freedom from the strife of social bonds. The mystery of life, as of death, each one has to discover for himself. We can sing and taste with no tongues but our own. Though each one has to attain his purpose by his separate encounter, the result is of universal significance.

A *saññyāsin* renounces all possessions, distinctions of caste, and practices of religion. As he has perfected himself, he is able to give his soul the largest scope, throw all his powers into the free movement of the world and compel its transfiguration. He does not merely formulate the conception of high living but lives it, adhering to the famous rule, 'The world is my country; to do good my religion'. 'Regarding all with an equal eye he must be friendly to all living beings. And being devoted, he must not injure any living creature, human or animal, either in act, word, or thought, and renounce all attachments'. A freedom and fearlessness of spirit, an immensity of courage, which no defeat or obstacle can touch, a faith in the power that works in the universe, a love that lavishes itself without demand of return and makes life a free servitude to the universal spirit, are the signs of the perfected man. The *saññyāsin* is a supersocial man, a *parivrājaka*, a wandering teacher who influences spiritual standards though he may live apart from society. The difference between a

Brāhmin and a *saññyāsin* is that while the former is a full member of society, living with wife and children in a well-regulated but simple home, and performing religious rites, the latter is a celibate, homeless and wandering, if he does not live in a monastery, who has renounced all rites and ceremonies. He belongs neither to his language nor to his race but only to himself and therefore to the whole world. This order is recruited from members of all castes and both sexes. As the life of the *saññyāsin* is the goal of man, those who live it obtain the allegiance of society. Kālidāsa, the great Indian poet, describes this supreme ideal of life as 'owning the whole world while disowning oneself'.

Hinduism has given us in the form of the *saññyāsin* its picture of the ideal man. He carries within himself the dynamism of spirit, its flame-like mobility. He has no fixed abode and is bound to no stable form of living. He is released from every form of selfishness: individual, social, and national. He does not make compromises for the sake of power, individual or collective. His behaviour is unpredictable, for he does not act in obedience to the laws of the social group or the state. He is master of his own conduct. He is not subject to rules, for he has realised in himself the life which is the source of all rules and which is not itself subject to rules. The quietude of his soul is strange, for though he is tranquil within, everything about him is restless and dynamic. His element is fire, his mark is movement.

The ideal man of India is not the magnanimous man of Greece or the valiant knight of mediaeval Europe, but the free man of spirit who has attained insight into the universal source by rigid discipline and practice of disinterested virtues, who has freed himself from the prejudices of his time and place. It is India's pride that she has clung fast to this ideal and produced in every generation and in every part of the country from the time of the *ṛishis* of the Upaniṣads and Buddha to Rāmakṛishṇa and Gāndhi, men who strove successfully to realise this ideal.

The ideal of the *saññyāsin* has still an appeal to the Indian mind. When Gāndhi wants the political leaders to break all the ties that hold them to the world, to be ascetics owning nothing and vowed to celibacy, when he tells them that the prison should be their monastery, the coarse jail dress their religious habit, fetters and handcuffs their hair shirt and scourge, he is applying the ideal of renunciation in the political sphere.

The scheme of classes and stages is helpful but not indispensable. Mandana tells us that it is like a saddle horse which helps a man to reach his goal easily and quickly, but even without it man can arrive there. Life is a progress through stages. The race is a long one, and society should not lay on any one a burden too heavy to bear. The higher flights are not to be attempted until we train ourselves on the lower ones. We should not, however, be content to remain for all time on the lower stages. That would not be to live up to the ideal demanded of us. The goal is the vision of God and it is open to all. The world and its activities are no barriers to it but constitute the training ground.

IV

The scheme of the ends of life, classes, and stages has for its aim the development of the individual. It helps him to order and organise his life instead of leaving it as a bundle of incompatible desires. It looks upon him not as a mere specimen of a zoological species but as a member of a social group which reflects in its organisation the scheme of values for the realisation of which the group exists. By education and social discipline the individual is helped to develop the inner conviction essential for social stability. But throughout there is insistence on the fact that the highest values are supernational and truly universal. The activities and achievements of art and science, of morality and religion, are the highest manifestations of the human spirit assimilable and communicable across barriers of blood and race. This is not to deny or underrate the importance of the group life, but the highest values of art and literature, science and philosophy, have, in principle, a universal appeal. The higher the individual the more free is he of the social order. The highest is the most universal, having transcended the need for discipline by the social scheme (*ativarṇāśrami*). He is a king among men, being a king over himself, *svayam eva rājā*.

He is a citizen of the world and speaks a language that can be understood by all who call themselves men. Of the four ends the highest is spiritual freedom; of the four classes, the Brāhmin engaged in spiritual pursuits is the highest; of the four stages, that of *saññyāsa* is the most exalted. The meaning of human existence is in a larger consciousness which man does not enter so long as he remains confined in his individuality. The limitations of family life and social obedience embarrass the spirit in its main purpose of advancing into a life of unity with all being. The negative method of asceticism by which the individual mortifies his body, gives up all possessions, and breaks all social connexions is not the Hindu view, which requires us to grow into the larger freedom of spirit, the super-individuality, by developing each side of our life until it transcends its limits. In this fatal hour of twilight, of tragic conflict between light and darkness, it is the duty of the free men of the spirit, who have seen the real beyond the clouds, to do their best to ward off the darkness, and if that is not possible to light their lamps and get ready to help us to see when the night falls.

V

We are at a gloomy moment in history. Never has the future seemed so incalculable. With a dreary fatality the tragedy moves on. The world of nations seems to be like a nursery full of perverse, bumptious, ill-tempered children, nagging one another and making a display of their toys of earthly possessions, thrilled by mere size. This is true of all countries. It is not a question of East or West, of Asia or Europe. No intelligent Asiatic can help admiring and reverencing the great races that live in Europe and their noble and exalted achievements. His heart is wrung when he sees dark clouds massing on the horizon. There is something coarse at the very centre of our civilisation by which it is betrayed again and again. No civilisation, however brilliant, can stand up against the social resentments and class conflicts which accompany a maladjustment of wealth, labour, and leisure. Perpetual disturbance will be our doom if we do not recognise that the world is one and interdependent. If we do not alter the framework of the social system and the international order, which are based on force and the exploitation of the inferior individuals and backward nations, world peace will be a wild dream. While resolved to renounce nothing, this generation wishes to enjoy the fruits of renunciation.

The *Imitation* has a profoundly significant sentence. 'All men desire peace, but very few desire those things which make for peace'. We are not prepared to pay the price for peace, the renunciation of empires, the abandonment of the policy of economic nationalism, the rearrangement of the world on a basis of racial equality and freedom and devotion to world community. It is obvious common sense, but for it to dawn on the general mind, a mental and moral revolution is necessary. Peace demands a revolutionary desire, a new simplicity, a new asceticism. If men conquer their own inordinate desires, this inner victory will show forth in their outer relations. In the third century B.C. Aśoka succeeded to a realm more extensive than modern British India. He achieved in early life a reputation as a military hero. The spectacle of the misery caused by war filled him with remorse and he became a man of peace and an enthusiastic disciple of Buddha. The results of his conversion may be told in his own words as they appeared in the edicts which he caused to be carved on rocks and pillars throughout his vast empire. In one of them he tells us of his profound sorrow at the thousands who had been slain in his war on the Kalingas and at the misery inflicted on the non-combatants. 'If a hundredth or a thousandth part of these were now to suffer the same fate, it would be a matter of deep sorrow to his majesty. Though one should do him an injury, his majesty now holds that it must be patiently borne, so far as it can possibly be borne'.[15] Here was a mighty emperor who not only repented of his lust for dominion but had his repentance cut in rocks for the instruction of future ages. If science and machinery get into other hands than those of warring Caesars and despotic Tamerlanes, if enough men and women arise in each community who are free from the fanaticisms of religion and of politics, who will oppose strenuously every kind of mental and moral tyranny, who will develop in place of an angular national spirit a rounded world view, what might not be done?

[15] Rock Edict XIII. See Vincent A. Smith, *The Edicts of Aśoka* (1909), p. 19.

Yoga

THE WAY OF *Karma* *

The purpose of human life. Everything that lives aims at its own specific perfection. The blade of grass, the flowering tree, the flying bird, the running deer, each one strives to reach the perfection of its nature. While the sub-human species work according to a predetermined pattern, man, on account of the possession of creative will, has to achieve his fulfilment by his effort and will. Descartes reduced the human self to the status of an object for purposes of scientific understanding. The self was, for him, a counterpart of the body. Spinoza felt that if bodily states were strictly determined, mental states were also subject to a strict determinism. Mind and body became objects of scientific treatment only on the condition of a universal determinism. Freud and Marx adopt a similar objective view of the human self, that it is determined ultimately by unconscious impulses or relations of economic production.

Man is not completely a victim of circumstances. He can say 'no' to life whereas the animal always says 'yes' even when he is in the throes of terror and revulsion. Man can deliberately reject satisfaction at one level for the sake of satisfaction at another, higher level. He can impose discipline on his nature and check the drive of desire. He can create a new nature in which the different elements of his being are harmonised.

Each individual is not one but many, an assemblage of different factors. He must reach unity through inner development. External events impinge on us, emotions are suddenly aroused and become dominant and soon they give way to others which in turn try to govern us. There is a strain in human life which impels us to introduce peace and order into the swarm of

* From *The Brahma Sūtra* (New York: Harper and Brothers, 1959), pp. 151–223.

impulses, emotions, and notions, incongruous and often contradictory. This is a lifetime job, perhaps a job for many lives. There is in man the ache for unity, the anguish for beatitude.

Man's quest for perfection consists in organising the things of body, mind, and soul into a whole. The activities of the human spirit are interrelated, the artistic and the ethical, the religious and the rational. Man is a miniature of the universe in which he lives. Man, as he is, is a transitional being, an unfinished experiment. When he is awakened, he is at peace with himself, he thinks and acts in a new way. For this awakening, man has to take another step in his evolution. The Kingdom of Heaven is the highest state attainable by man. So long as our nature is not integrated, our actions are confused and contradictory. In an integrated man, thought, speech, and action are of one piece. The *Mahābhārata* says that there is no thief so dangerous as the hypocrite who says one thing and does another, for his is the sin of the deepest dye. When Jesus attacks the Pharisee, he is attacking the man of pretences who keeps up appearances, who pretends to be good when he is not. The Lord is merciful to the sins of the flesh but wrathful against those of the spirit. We must recognise that evil is in us though such a recognition may wound and shame our pride and presumption. There is only one thing of which we have to be ashamed, i.e., unwillingness to recognise the truth. The lie is the great evil of which the Pharisees are guilty.

Different ways to fulfilment. There is an old saying that there are as many ways to God as there are souls on earth. Each person is unique and his way to fulfilment is also unique. It is also true that there is so much in common among human beings that we can distinguish certain broad ways to man's realisation, the *karma-mārga*, the way of work, *bhakti-mārga*, the way of devotion, the *dhyāna-mārga*, the way of meditation. All these lead to *jñāna*, wisdom or enlightenment. All *yoga* is one and includes the different aspects of work, devotion, and knowledge.

Dharma in a wide sense is used to connote all the means for the achievement of the different ends of life. Samantabhadra says that *dharma* is that which leads people out of the woes of the world and fixes them in the highest bliss.

The primacy of ethics. Man is the bridge between nature and spirit. His destiny drives him on to the spirit. Through agonies and ecstasies he has to reach his fulfilment. The programme of duties laid down in *dharma śāstras* is intended to help man to reach his goal. The spiritual goal and the ethical means are bound up with each other and not externally related. The moral law within us is evidence of our citizenship in the world of spirit. Moral discipline makes for spiritual insight. Their relationship is not adventitious. To reach the goal is to perfect the means to it. We cannot by-pass the ethical. Almost all the religious classics of India insist on ethical conduct as an indispensable means for spiritual life. Ethics is the basis of spiritual life and its substance. Aśoka's *dharma,* for example, emphasises *śīla* or conduct, not creed or doctrine, worship or ceremony. In his Rock Edict 7, Aśoka says that 'all sects wish [to acquire] self-control and purity of mind'. He calls those without these qualities mean indeed, *nīcāḥ*.

Rock Edict 11 says there is no such gift as *dharma-dāna*. *Dharma* is defined as proper behaviour towards slaves and servants, respect for father and mother, gifts to friends and relatives, to *Brāhmaṇas* and ascetics, non-killing of creatures.

Śankara says that one should undertake enquiry into Brahman only after he acquires self-control, detachment, etc., what he calls *viveka, vairāgya, ṣaṭ-sampatti* and *mumukṣutva.* Moral life is an essential condition for the pursuit of wisdom. Ethical conduct is different from ceremonial piety. The latter is of no use to those who are morally impure. Speaking the truth is much better than performing many sacrifices. There is a popular verse which says that people want the fruits of *dharma* and not *dharma* itself. There is a general insistence on truth in inward nature and not merely conformity in outward conduct.

Freedom of will. The integration of the individual has to be achieved by a conscious effort. If God had desired to create a world of automata there would have been no evil, no failure, God could have eliminated evil if he had so wished by denying us freedom of choice. Evil is there because we sometimes abuse free will. If the world is a machine, then the human individual has no meaning. Man in so far as he is made in the image of God is a creator. He is not free until he is capable of creative activity. While animals are creatures men are creature-creators. There is no animal delinquency. Evil is not passivity but activity. Without creative freedom man cannot produce either a paradise or a desolation on earth. God permits evil because he does not interfere with human choice.

Man is subjected to different sets of laws. He cannot disobey the law of gravitation. If he is unsupported in mid-air he must fall to the ground like a stone. As a living organism he is subject to various biological laws which he cannot violate. These laws he shares with the animals but there is a law which he does not share with animals, a law which he can disobey if he so chooses. It is the law of *dharma* or right and wrong. Religion is essentially a passion for righteousness.

The complaint of world-negation. It is said that for the Hindu all true existence is non-material, unchangeable, and eternal and therefore the material, changeable, temporal existence is false. So it is said that the good of man consists not in transforming the world which is a vale of woe but in transcending it. It is not his aim to change the world but turn away from it. If the Hindu adopts an exalted morality, it is not founded on Hindu metaphysics but is inconsistent with it.

The world is not a deceptive façade of something underlying it. It is real though imperfect. Since the Supreme is the basis of the world the world cannot be unreal. *Māyā* has a standing in the world of reality. Śankara says that after filling our sight with wisdom let us see the world as Brahman. Such a vision is fruitful, not the vision which looks solely at the tip of the nose.

The world of multiplicity is acknowledged even by those who attempt to explain it away. Heidegger, for example, emphasises the finiteness and contingency of man's condition. Human life is a brief span of existence between original nothingness and death. It is constantly passing away and tends to return to non-being. The threat of nothingness is the source of that fundamental anguish which the existentialists emphasise. Some existentialists like Jaspers and Marcel, following the lead of Kierkegaard, find the counterpoise to the world of nothingness in the reality of God. In Hindu thought, *māyā* is not so much a veil as the dress of God. The destiny of the world is to be transformed into the perfect state of the Kingdom of God. The concept of *brahma-loka*, the Kingdom of God, is known to the Vedic seers, the Hebrew prophets, and Zarathustra. If we are to share the new existence, we must achieve perfection. We must renounce self-interest and dedicate ourselves to the doing of good. We must work for better conditions for the material and spiritual development of human beings, for civilisation is material and spiritual progress for both the individual and society. The aim is *lokasaṁgraha*, in the words of the *Bhagavadgītā*.

Man is a social animal. He loves those with whom he lives in close association. Latterly the small social groups have been broken up by the forces of industrialism but new opportunities for larger groups are now available. The whole of society requires to be reconstructed on the principle of social solidarity. Society is approaching what seems to be the final stage of economic evolution. We have passed beyond the hunting and the fishing stages, the pastoral, the agricultural, and the industrial stages with their different phases.

Unfortunately, the contemporary world situation where two rival power systems are facing each other is leading to the emergence of a narrowly secular, materialistic, extraverted mass-state. Sensitive people deplore the disintegration, the superficial materialism, the lack of creative vision, and the uncontrolled technocracy which are the alarming symptoms of a disease eating at the heart of our modern way of life. Our best attempts are incapable of remedying the disease of which we are all obscurely aware. The crisis which faces us is a spiritual one and what we need is a recovery of spiritual awareness, a new and transforming contact with the inner sources of spiritual inspiration which once animated the soul of our civilisation and produced and maintained its indefeasible unity of consciousness, in other words a healing of the divorce between the outward resources of power which are assuming frightening proportions and the inward resources of the spirit which are decaying or dead. Materialism is the height of unintelligence. The *Bhagavadgītā*, when it calls upon us to work for a world community, calls us back to the Indwelling Spirit which is in us as in others. Such a faith will help us to bring love where there is hatred, hope where there is despair, light where there is darkness, joy where there is sorrow. We must give if we wish to receive. We shall be able to serve if we are ourselves saved, integrated.

The world is the place where the human individual has to attain his integration, his fulfilment. We are called upon to participate in the life of the world. It is through time that time is conquered.

The transitoriness of earthly possessions is used to emphasise the imperative necessity of the practice of *dharma*. There is a well-known verse which reads: 'Our bodies are not permanent, our prosperity is fleeting; death is always near to us. Therefore one should take to *dharma*'. The goal is a reorientation of human personality, where the self assumes control over cravings and desires. These latter are not to be destroyed but transformed. The kind of life one leads has an importance both for oneself and the world. This world is our home and our lives are dedicated to action. We are not strangers in the world, required to develop indifference to it. Each individual appears to be isolated but we soon realise that there is a living substance from which all emerge.

We are called upon to act in a disinterested way, free from egotism. We should not become victims of material interests and vulgar appetites. We should not be preoccupied with our own salvation. The soul is bound so long as it has a sense of mineness; with the absence of the sense of mineness it is liberated. If God is to live in us pride must die in us. For the cultivation of detachment, it is not essential to become a *saññyāsin*. It is possible to cultivate *vairāgya* or detachment even as householders.

There is a popular impression that Hindu ethics requires us

to treat the body with contempt. It is well known that the body is regarded as the instrument for righteous living, *dharma-sādhanam.* We are not called upon to fear bodily desires or hate the body. If we adopt fasting and other physical discipline, it does not mean that the fasts and the physical exercises are ends in themselves. The practitioners of *Haṭha Yoga* are not the exponents of the best type of sanctity. The body must be disciplined in order that it may serve the ends of righteousness. We must be ready to cast off unnecessary burdens and travel light. Bodily discipline helps us to see the face of God and hear his voice. It helps us to see the needs of people, and undertake fresh acts of service, visit the sick, care for the poor, and put an end to injustice wherever we see it.

Ethical rules. The different virtues of fortitude, justice, love, compassion, self-control are not separate qualities but are the different facets of the personality. Inward awareness, *satya,* and life of compassion, *ahiṁsā,* are the two principal sides of a spiritual life. We must be truthful in our words and deeds. To know the truth we are taken out of the world but only temporarily. We are again brought back to it. The Divine is expressed in nature as an impersonal, non-ethical creative power and as ethical consciousness in human life.

When we realise that the Divine is expressed in us as in others we feel the obligation to help others. Thereby the individual spirit becomes enriched. *Ahiṁsā* is reverence for all life, active devotion to and a sense of union with all that exists. There is no infinite being except being in its infinite manifestations. If we believe in God, we will adopt the principle of *ahiṁsā.* The Qurān says: 'The servants of the merciful are those who meekly walk upon this earth and if the fools speak to them, they say "peace"'.[1] Again 'If you forgive and practise forbearance and pardon, verily Allāh is also forgiving and merciful'.[2] The individual is required to treat humanity as his kindred. We must cultivate in our hearts the sentiments of affection and trustfulness. Compassion is the one good that is never exhausted even if the whole world is pursuing it.

[1] XXV. 64.
[2] LXIV. 14.

The *Mahābhārata* says that 'nothing is wholly good and nothing is wholly bad. The two, good and evil, pervade the world throughout'. We must be careful before we judge others. The possessions we have are a trust for others. The *Bhāgavata* gives the proper attitude to wealth: 'Living beings have a right only up to what is necessary for satisfying their hunger; he who thinks of acquiring more is a thief and deserves punishment'. This is the basic principle of a socialist order of society. The Creative God is the source of all beings. He is infinite and unfathomable yet we can enter into spiritual relations with him by devoting ourselves to all living beings within the range of our help. In the *Rāmāyaṇa*, Rāma asks Lakṣmaṇa 'How shall we seek to please the Divine, who is not within our reach, when we neglect father, mother and teacher who are with us'? When we pierce through the confusions of the world to the strength and certainty of its basis we accept every man as brother and show sympathy, understanding, and patience in our dealings with others.

When *ahiṁsā* is said to be the supreme moral law, it is not merely negative abstention from injury to living beings, but positive love for them all. Sympathy and compassion are its expressions. Charity with kind words, knowledge without pride, courage with forbearance, and wealth with renunciation, these four are difficult to attain, but they make for man's progress.

Social institutions. Whereas the utterances of the founders of religions have a claim on our allegiance, this is not true of the institutions built round them. These must be flexible enough to be altered to suit progress in human thought. It is said that many pernicious customs pass for religious duties under the influence of ignorant persons of bad character. They are generally adopted out of greed, more often out of inertia.

The main obstacle to social progress in India is conformity. We wish to belong and not be isolated or lonely. Unless we belong to a social whole we feel that we are powerless, insignificant. So we adhere to absurd and degrading customs, because they relate us to others. Whereas the principal demands of truth and love, *satya* and *ahiṁsā*, are absolute, their application depends on the concrete situation. Changes of place, time, and circumstance cause changes in *dharma* also. There is one law for men in time of peace and another in time of distress. There is no single law for all time So *dharma* is known to depend on circumstances. No law has been found which is of help to all. Therefore it is changed for one that seems better and it is again found harmful demanding change. Therefore we see non-unity among customs at all times

The caste system. The vocation of a person is that which manifests his inner nature. It must accord with his temperament. In its origin the caste system represented the division of men into classes according to their capacity and function, *guna* and *karma*. Later it became mixed up with heredity. The *Mahābhārata* says: 'Austerity, learning, birth, these make the Brāhmin; he who lacks austerity and learning is a Brāhmin by birth alone'. Some of the great leaders of Indian civilisation were of mixed origin. Krishna Dvaipāyana Vyāsa was the son of a Brāhmin father and a non-Aryan mother. Kṛishṇa Vāsudeva Vārṣṇeya was the son of a Kṣatriya prince, Vasudeva, and a non-Aryan princess, Devakī, the sister of Kaṁsa. The system of caste whatever its historical significance has no contemporary value. Today it injures the spirit of humanity and violates human dignity. To offer a cup of water is a sign of friendship, not of defilement. "I consider to be a Brāhmin that Śūdra who is ever endowed with self-restraint, truthfulness and righteousness. A man becomes a Brāhmin by his conduct" If these characteristics be found in a Śūdra and if they be not found in a Brāhmin, then such a Śūdra is not a Śūdra and such a Brāhmin is not a Brāhmin'.

There is a story that when Śankara, in spite of his non-dualism, asked an outcaste to clear the way for him, the outcaste who was God himself asked: 'Do you wish my body to leave your body or my spirit to leave your spirit'? If democracy is to be seriously implemented, then caste and untouchability should go.

Women and family life. We are not called upon to suppress human desires, reject human pleasures, renounce the world and all its ways, and thus freeze the human spirit. The state of the householder is an exalted one. From early times, marriage has been treated as a sacrament and its purpose has been the production of offspring, especially a son. In the *Aitareya Brāhmaṇa*, we read: 'Of what good is dirt, the deer-skin, the unshaven hair, austerities, of what [good are they]? O Brāhmin, desire a son. He verily is the blameless source of enjoyment'. Manu says: 'One should direct one's mind to renunciation after discharging the three debts. He who, without discharging [them], practises renunciation goes below'.

In some periods of our history, women were not treated with fairness and dignity. The dominant ideal, however, has been one of perfect equality. When Janaka gives Sītā to Rāma, he asks him to treat her as his companion in all duties.

It would be wrong to hold that Madhva denied *mokṣa* or final release to women, Śūdras, and fallen Brāhmins and non-Hindus. He denied to them one particular method of attaining release. Other ways were prescribed for them which will lead to the same goal of final release. This exclusion, whatever justification it may have had at the time the commentaries were written, has no excuse today.

In the Vedas we find reference to women seers who are *brahma-vādinīs*. They, of course, had a right to *brahma*-knowledge, *brahma-vidyādhikāra*.

Brahmacarya, or chastity of body and mind, is insisted on. It is said in the *Brahma Purāṇa* that a woman who is addressed as mother in speech should be truly looked upon as mother. *Dharma* is a witness to this as also the wise.

Saññyāsa—sometimes renunciation of the world is exalted. What is meant is the spirit of renunciation.

Saññyāsa is sometimes prescribed as a preparation for service. There are some who take to *saññyāsa* when they feel lonely, inadequate, and incomplete and in their shock of loneliness and isolation wish to turn back on the world. That, however, is not the proper spirit. We cannot grow as individuals apart from one another.

The order of the *saññyāsins* presents itself to the modern world as a scandal. There was a time when it was taken for granted. People's lives were directed beyond the quest of wealth and pleasure, *artha* and *kāma*, and devoted to an invisible God. The true *saññyāsins* realise human unity and brotherhood in their souls. Even a *parivrājaka* who abandons the world absolutely has to sustain his life and do the duties that are allotted to him. The *saññyāsins* work in the world so long as their fellow-men are insensitive and irresponsible and so are unfree. In a sense until all men become free no one is absolutely free.

Beyond ethics. When one attains the spiritual level, he rises above the ethical, not that he repudiates it but he transcends it. Śankara says 'this is indeed an ornament to us that, when there is the realisation of *Brahman*, there is the destruction of all obligations and the accomplishment of everything that is to be accomplished'.

When we undergo the ethical discipline, there is a change in the inward man which makes us practise good in an effortless, spontaneous way. Freedom from obligation is only for those who have cast off their self-sense. 'I do nothing of myself. The Father that dwelleth in me, he doeth the works'. [3] 'If ye be led of the Spirit, ye are not under the law'.[4] Whoever is born of God cannot sin.[5] When Jesus tells us that our righteousness should be different from that of the Scribes and the Pharisees, he points out that our conduct should be not one of mere conformity to duty with an effort. We must cease to be men of external piety and become men of inner understanding. Then we break the inertia of habit. We become different and act not from expectation of reward or fear of consequences but because the act is good in itself. Jesus says of John the Baptist that he is the highest man born of woman but the least in the Kingdom of Heaven is greater than he. John stands for salvation through moral life. He tells us what to do but we

[3] John 8:28; 14:10.

St. François De Sales says: 'Tell me, I pray you, Theotimus, if a drop of water, thrown into an ocean of some priceless essence, were alive and could speak and declare its condition, would it not cry out with great joy: "O mortals I live indeed but I live not myself, but this ocean lives in me and my life is hidden in this abyss" '.

[4] Gal. 5:18.

[5] I John 3:9.

cannot gain release unless we change our nature, become different, are inwardly transformed. John asks us to become better men and Jesus asks us to become new men. There is a stage in which we accept the world, another in which we reject it, a third in which we accept it, gratefully acknowledging its place in the divine scheme.

Those who have full mastery over their natures sometimes do things which may appear wrong to the conventional people. John the Baptist was uneasy when he heard that Jesus and his disciples ate and drank and did not fast. They plucked the ears of corn on the Sabbath day. The *Bhāgavata* says: '*Iśvaras* or masters are sometimes seen to transgress rules of conduct with courage. These are not faults among those with *tejas* or radiance, even as the all-devouring fire is not affected [by the impurities it consumes]. He who is lacking in such control [*anīśvarāḥ*] should not even think of imitating such conduct for it can only bring destruction to him even like swallowing poison in imitation of *Śiva*'. Fire may consume a forest or Śiva drink poison without any harmful consequences. But ordinary men cannot transgress rules until they have shaken off all selfishness and established control over their nature.

It is easier to fight non-human nature, forests and woods and wild beasts. It is more difficult to fight the passions, the sub-rational elements in human nature. This is a more arduous struggle. We cannot extinguish selfish desire by the mere force of intellect. We have to develop the power of will. The different elements in human nature are divided in a disintegrated man but in an integrated life they are held in harmony. An integrated personality is incapable of doing anything wrong. The ethical man, the economic man, and the artistic man are all abstractions obtained by our intellect from the concrete unity of our being. These values are complementary. A great artist may be a great moral force. An ideal personality would be all these, a man of wisdom and holiness, sanity and sanctity.

THE WAY OF *Bhakti*

Need for religious devotion. It is often said that man is incurably religious. He must have some object or person or cause on which to fix his devotion. The instinct, if we may call it by that name, may become perverted and abused but the need is there. It must be turned to an ideal which is genuine, grounded in truth, an ideal that touches the deepest springs of man's inner life. What a man believes has a determining influence on his character.

There are some thinkers both in the East and the West who feel that man's capacity for integration, for the growth of the individual into a person would be unintelligible unless we have a Divine Personality. McTaggart's notion of a community of personalities living in a kind of spiritual void is not tenable, for the direct apprehension of value which transforms the individual into a person implies an ideal personality who embodies the value apprehended.

It is possible for atheists and agnostics to lead virtuous lives. They may be unaware or unmindful of the divine source of all. Existentialists of the school of Sartre struggle to seek some meaning for human life in a godless universe. If we grant that the world has meaning, it means that it has a purpose. The reality of God does not, however, depend on our views. Our irreligion does not entail the suspension of divine acting.[6]

Bhakti. *Bhakti* is conscious recognition of and wholehearted response to the source of all goodness, the Divine. It is said 'in this world, not vows, not pilgrimages, not *yoga* practices, not study of Scriptures, not sacrificial rites, not philosophical discourses; only devotion can give us freedom'.

The *Bhāgavata Purāṇa* is treated as the standard work on *bhakti*. 'It is the quintessence of the Vedānta philosophy. He who has tasted its nectar-like juice will not be attracted by anything else'. As we have seen, while God is transcendently infinite he is also greatly loving. He takes up human creatures into his range of action if they respond to his call. 'Behold, I stand at the gate and knock. If any man shall hear my voice and open to me the door, I will come in to him, and will sup with him and he with me'. God is the reward of those who

[6] Cf. St. Augustine: 'Thou hast always been with me but I have not always been with myself'.

wait on him. He helps his devotees to act in this world as partners in his divine work. Our one prayer is that God should increase in us true religion.

Śāṇḍilya Sūtra says *bhakti* is the highest attachment to God, *parānurakti*. In the *Viṣṇu Purāṇa* Prahlāda expresses the wish that he may have that attachment to God that is experienced with regard to sense-objects. One must find one's supreme pleasure in God. Love of man and woman is used to illustrate love of man for God. 'As maid delights in youth and youth in maid, so may my mind rejoice in Thee'. 'When the lovers are together, they are afraid of being separated; when they are not together, they have a painful desire for union'.

The clean of heart shall see God. If we sin against the light we will be left in darkness. Devotion implies obedience to the will of the Supreme in all our activities. It brings deliverance from anxiety about the necessities of life. There is a popular verse which says: 'In vain does the devotee worry about food and other necessities of life. Can God who sustains the whole creation ever forget his own devotees'? A devotee is not elated by praise or depressed by censure. In the name of God he does service to the world.

Bhakti and knowledge. *Bhakti* opens the way to illumination. Rāmānuja regards *bhakti* as a kind of knowledge. *Nārada Bhakti Sūtra* says: 'When adored with love God speedily manifests himself and gives his devotees perception'.

Praise of the devotee. The devotee is praised as the highest of all. 'What speciality is there in being born a member of the highest class? What does it matter even if one possesses learning that includes enquiry into all the systems of thought? In all the three worlds who is there more blessed than the person whose heart is always steeped in devotion to the Supreme Lord'?

The *Bhāgavata Purāṇa* says: 'The devotees are my heart and I am the heart of the devotees. They know no one else than me; I know no one else than them'.

Liberty of worship. From early days Hindu tradition has held that truth is a pathless land and cannot be organised.

When organised it cripples the individual mind and prevents it from growing. When our minds get incarcerated within the narrow confines of dogma, the spirit of free adventure is checked. Devotion to the Supreme opens our hearts to the new life. Spiritual life is the end. That is why the Hindu permits each individual to worship the aspect of Godhead which appeals to him most. The radiance of reality is mirrored variously according to the mediums in which it is reflected. The different aspects we adore are pointers, not halting places.

Whatever name we may give to the Supreme, it is addressed to the Ultimate Reality. 'I do not mind who he is, *Viṣṇu* or *Śiva*, *Brahmā* or *Indra*, the Sun or the Moon, the blessed *Buddha* or any saint. Whoever he be, that one who is free from the disease of being poisoned by craving and hatred, who is endowed with all noble qualities and is ever ready to act compassionately towards all creatures, to him I bow down always'.

Śankara, the great teacher of non-dualism, manifests a spirit of devotion to the different aspects of the Godhead. There are devotional hymns ascribed to him to Bhavānī; to Viṣṇu, to Śiva. Madhusūdana Sarasvatī, a great teacher of Advaita, says: 'I know not what truth there is beyond *Kṛishṇa*'. The Maharastrian saint-poet Eknath identifies *Viṭhoba* of Pandharpur with the Buddha.

Mystics of other religions and some leading thinkers tend to adopt an attitude of respect for other forms of worship than their own. The Word came and dwelt among us, not for the first and last time at Bethlehem but from the moment man was born into the world in the likeness of the divine image and as such distinct from other creatures. As Eternal Wisdom it was and is before all creation in its pure creativeness. For many Christian mystics, Christ is not limited to the historic personality of Jesus. He is the eternal Logos who comes to birth in men whenever they are inwardly united with God.

Justin Martyr in his *Apologia* and *Dialogue with Trypho* presents God as the Primordial Cause of the world, eternal, unchangeable, and accessible to reason. Before all creation, from the indefinable Father and Lord of the universe a force emanated called Logos which means Word and Reason. This Logos is the Son generated before all creation, the divine wisdom of Proverbs 8. He spoke through the Prophets and manifested his action also outside Israel.

To justify universal claims for the Logos, Justin argues that those outside the biblical tradition who have developed spiritual life like Heracleitus, Socrates, and his own contemporary Musonius all belong to the Christian fold. If they were called atheists and condemned to death, the Christians also suffered the same fate. Justin says: 'Everything good and beautiful taught by thinkers and poets is ours'. For all that is Christian is due to the working of the Logos. Justin presents Christianity as a philosophical religion which uses Greek ideas, specially the Stoic, in a biblical garb. Both Clement and Origen were Christian thinkers who wished to express Christian truth through Greek philosophical categories. They believe in the Eternal Logos. They speak about the ultimate oneness of God and man. The deepest self of all rational beings is divine. Every individual attains his fulfilment through unification with the Logos. By imitating Christ the Logos, every one can obtain the same power as the Logos.

William Law says that the Christ of God is 'the light and life and holiness of every creature that is holy'. He argues: 'Hence it was that so many eminent spirits, partakers of a divine life have appeared in so many parts of the heathen world. . . . These were the apostles of a Christ within'. 'As many as are led by the Spirit of God, these are the sons of God'. Man in his deepest being is one with God. The goal of life is to enter into the realisation of this hidden unity. Boehme asks 'were we not in the beginning made out of God's substance? Why should we not also abide therein'? William Penn said: 'It is better to be of no Church than to be bitter for any'. Kabīr says that he is 'a child of *Allāh* and *Rām*'. He did not find it necessary to identify himself with any religious faith but was devoted to spiritual realisation.

Religious intolerance does not make for world unity. Religions which aim at the conversion of the whole world to their own doctrines aim at the religion of power which amounts to sacred egoism, to spiritual pride. Reason should teach us to doubt our own infallibility. Unless we do it there is no chance for toleration in the world. If we are convinced of the absolute truth of our revelation and the falsity of others, how can we tolerate those who spread error and lead others astray? It is essential for us to note that while we are convinced of the infallibility of the truth we adopt, others may be equally convinced of the infallibility of their own doctrines. From ancient times, Hinduism adopted a view which would not hurt the religious susceptibilities of others. It enabled the Hindus to welcome the Jews, the Christians, the Parsees, and the Muslims.

The Hindu believes that, varied as all these religions are, behind them all is the same fire. The experience of the fire, though it speaks with many tongues, carries the same message. They all speak of the one realm of spiritual being. Of course, there are characteristic differences among the great religions. They do not all teach the same doctrines of God or of man or of the world or provide the same kind of ritual, myth, or norm of behaviour. But these differences are not enough to justify discord and strife. There may be mutual education among religions if they peacefully co-exist and there is no doubt that all the religions have helped to produce saints of an exalted character. We should be lacking in charity, even piety, if we denied the high character of sanctity in other religions than our own. Many of the living faiths are passing through self-criticism, are getting infected with secularism and humanism and the loss of the vision of God. Many of the leaders regard themselves as the priests of a new religion. We need not a new religion but a creative vitality in the practice of the old, the recognition that the Kingdom of Heaven lies within man, in his depths, in his integrity, in his inmost truth. God is the potentiality of every man.

Image worship. There is such a thing as *pratīkopāsanā* or symbol worship. This is an aid to worship. The symbolic is not the imaginary. Slowly we get beyond the symbol to the object symbolised. Until we reach the Highest, we gain rewards great or small, according to our aims and objects. Śaṅkara observes that on account of our imperfections we connect the Omnipresent Lord with limited abodes. 'Image worship is the first, doing *japa* and chanting *mantras* is the middle; meditation or mental worship is superior; reflection on one's own true nature is the highest of all'. Image worship is a means to realisation. When we gain our ends, the means fall away. Lamps are useful so long as we live in darkness, but when the sun arises they cease to be of any help. Kabīr sings: 'There is nothing but water at the holy bathing places; and I know that they are useless, for I have bathed in them. The images are all lifeless, they cannot speak; I know for I have cried aloud to them. The *Purāṇa* and the *Qurān* are mere words; lifting up the curtain, I have seen'.

The avatāras. The theory of *avatāras* assumes divine concern for human endeavour. God is the light in the soul; our part is to open our being to the Divine Light which is ever shining in us. When the Light in us comes to possess our being we speak of the birth of God in us. The Incarnation is not a special event but a continuous process of self-renewal.

The *avatāras* are born not only to put down evil but to teach us mortals. Great souls appear for the well-being and spiritual enlightenment of creatures. They tell us how to remould our lives so as to serve the purpose of the Divine. Deification is the transfusion of human nature by the Indwelling Spirit of the Divine. Rāma says: 'I look upon myself as a man, *Rāma*, the son of Daśaratha. May the Lord [*Brahmā*] tell me who I am, where I belong and whence I come'. Kṛishṇa by the repeated practice of meditation, by uninterrupted concentration for a long period, attaining through intuition of Brahman lordship similar to his over the world is seen to reveal that to Arjuna in the *Bhagavadgītā*. The devotee is slowly transformed into the likeness of the Divine. He becomes what he is called to be. He realises the meaning of his existence. It is said that devotion to the Supreme, experience of the Highest, and detachment from other things, all these three occur at the same time.

THE WAY OF *Dhyāna*

Yoga system. If we study the history of religions we will note that there is a broad stream of spiritual knowledge which requires us to grow to a higher level of being. It refers to an inner quickening and growth in our nature. The All-pervading Self abides in every heart. Those who turn from him, seeking outside, are inferior creatures. 'God is neither in temple nor in mosque', says Kabīr. He would add today: 'neither in Church nor in synagogue'. He is found in the heart of man. God is not doomed to be perpetually overwhelmed by an uncomprehending darkness. Nānak says that we should ascend to the *satya-loka,* the kingdom of truth, the abode of eternal life.

'Lead us from darkness into light' is the prayer of the Upaniṣads. We must be awakened out of the sleep of the natural world-view. We must break through the surface in which we live and move. Imprisoned in history we become restricted to the narrow limits of existence. We must be lifted out of this confinement and become aware of our historicity. We must grasp the real which is before all phenomena, before all time, and which is equally after all phenomena and all time. Yet it is neither before nor after. It is that which does not become, that which is, real, unhistorical being itself. We cannot think it, enclose it within categories, images, and verbal structures. But we know more than we can think and express in historical forms. By discipline of mind we should strive to apprehend the Real. 'True knowledge which is produced by the means of true knowledge and is comparable to its object can neither be brought about by hundreds of injunctions nor be checked by hundreds of prohibitions. For it does not depend on the will of man, but merely on what really and unalterably exists'. A rigorous discipline of mind, heart, and will is necessary. Our vision becomes obscure if it is dimmed by vice or weakness. The *Mahābhārata* says the Supreme is visible only to those who have overcome anger and mastered their senses.

To use Plato's words, we should not be bound to the shadows of the cave but get to see the reality. For this an illuminating revelation, a saving transformation is necessary; an opening of the eyes is essential. We cannot get this experience by detached observation, logical analysis, and inference. We must encounter truth as a matter of existential concern, participate in the Ultimate Mystery. It is not an intellectual state but a state of being when we are filled with the Spiritual Presence.

As the Upaniṣads declare the state can be gained by *śravaṇa,* hearing, *manana*, reflection, and *nididhyāsana* or concentration. *Dhyāna* is *anavaratānusandhāna*, constant meditation. To learn concentration one should learn to be alone with oneself, without reading or listening to the radio or other pre occupation. It is to be able to be alone with oneself. It is in moments of meditation that we become self-aware. We do not lose the sense of the eternal in the inevitable distractions of life. We acquire a trust in the foundations of things, a trust that sustains us in the most terrible catastrophes, a firm loyalty to truth in the midst of passions and lures.

The *yoga* system describes the processes by which our consciousness grows into the life divine by the control of the thinking mind. The cultivation of states of mind and body which permits the full realisation of the ultimate truth requires disciplined effort. The *Yoga Sūtra* says 'that [discipline of mental functioning] practised for long, unintermittently and with *satkāras* [i.e., self-control, austerity, faith, ceremonial piety] is the sure means of realising the truth'.

Boehme in his imaginary dialogue between a disciple and his master in *The Signature of All Things* makes the disciple ask the master what prevents him from apprehending the ultimate truth and the master answers that it is his 'thinking of Self and his willing of Self'. Our confusion of the real Self with the outward selves prevents our awareness of the true Self. Boehme said that we could come into a new reality of our being and perceive everything in a new relation 'if we can stand still from self-thinking and self-willing and stop the wheel of imagination and the senses'. The aim of *yoga* is to help us to discern the being that is at the back of all becoming. It is difficult to reach it, but one should concentrate on that which exists of itself above and continues to be such as it is in itself.

Stages of the journey. The ascent to union with the Supreme is hard and steep. It is a personal adventure. The categories of metaphysics are verified by states of consciousness. The soul must pass through the period of purgation. We must strip away the merely natural life and wake up to the importance of the spiritual life. The stripping process begins with the withdrawal from the bustle of earthly things. We must become free and unattached. God is the soul's guide on the journey with the purgative, the illuminative, and the unitive stages. The soul should realise the nothingness of temporal things and learn to understand that the spiritual world alone is real. With the practice of detachment, spiritual freedom occurs.

Speculation is vision, an intuitive mode of apprehension. It is not irresponsible meandering of the mind. Yājñavalkya says that *samādhi* is equanimity. We must steady the mind, concentrate on the truth by which one is intellectually convinced until it culminates in direct experience. By contemplation on a particular form we become one with it. The *Gāyatrī mantra, dhiyo yo naḥ pracodayāt*, inspire our understanding, is meditated on so that we may see the truth. When the seeker sees the truth he becomes spiritually free. All experience becomes ordered and unified. We do not prove the truth of an idea by merely demonstrating that its author lived centuries ago and was of a saintly disposition. The truth lies in our experience of it when it enters into us. Without the knowledge of oneself, no release is possible even in many ages.

Solitary meditation. There is an emphasis on a solitary life of meditation in a monastery or a hermitage but this does not mean a turning away from life. The *Bhagavadgītā* speaks to us of the way in which *dhyāna yoga* should be practised. We do not seek for rewards but aim at transforming our nature. Let a man lift himself by himself. *Vīramitrodaya-paribhāṣā-prakāśa* quotes *Aṅgiraḥ Smṛti* to the effect that excepting efforts for attaining self-knowledge, whatever one does out of his own personal desire is like child's play and unnecessary. We must get into the house of our innermost self, shut the door on everything outer and pray from that inner self. It is said of Mohammad that in his fortieth year he desired solitude. He withdrew to a cave on Mount Hira near Mecca and practised religious austerities.

By undergoing the disciplines of *karma, bhakti*, and *dhyāna*, the mind gets purified and truth dawns and ineffable peace is experienced. Whatever action we perform is illumined by knowledge and dedicated to the glory of God.

Samādhi when it is *sa-vikalpa* is a state of contact with a

Personal Being not evident to the senses, a Person discerned as divine. In *nir-vikalpa samādhi*, the reality is super-personal, the one that changes not, the deepest self in one which is also the Eternal. The state is one of unalterable bliss, freedom from self-sense, serenity, and transcendent peace. Those who attain *samādhi* claim that their experience is far richer and deeper than the most intense satisfaction of this world.

When Śankara says that no amount of temporal activity can take us to the heart of the Eternal, he is emphasising that the distinction between time and eternity is a qualitative one. Our thought must be lifted to another order of being. Time is everlasting but Reality is eternal. Though we may spend all our life doing good deeds, we do not cross from time to eternity. A glimpse of eternity is different from an endless series of finite things. To know the Self we must leap into another dimension. We are then released from the rules of conventional religion. 'The sun of consciousness shines always in the sky of the heart. There is neither rising nor setting of it. How shall I perform the *sandhyā* prescribed in the *sāstras*'?

Dionysius the Areopagite says: 'The simple, absolute and immutable mysteries of Divine Truth are hidden in the super-luminous darkness of that silence which revealeth in secret. For this darkness, though of deepest obscurity, is yet radiantly clear; and though beyond touch and sight, it more than fills our unseeing minds with splendours of transcendent beauty'.

The original meaning of theory is vision. Every philosophy is the exposition and justification of an experience.

By means of the three methods of work, devotion, and contemplation (which are not exclusive of each other), we are reborn into the world of spirit. Religion by the use of symbols and metaphors indicates to us the goal of our quest. The festival of Easter, for example, was a pagan one marking the awakening of nature to new life. The Christian Easter refers to the resurrection of Jesus. But even for those who are not disposed to accept the historical evidence, it has a meaning that we can all be made new. We must become what we are. The festival of Easter is not a commemoration of a past event but the recognition of a present reality.

The cosmic process has for its goal the kingdom of free

spirits where the son of man becomes the son of God. The first fruits of the new species of spiritual personality are already manifest on earth in the saints and the sages of the different religions who have risen from the disruption of being to its articulation, integration.

In the spirit of the Vedānta, the Buddha speaks of human fulfilment as the transition from ignorance and craving to enlightenment and compassion. The aim of religion is to release us from the tornness of our life. We must grow from the status of the creature, given to inertia, distractedness, corruption, selfishness to integrality with its unswerving devotion.

The Jews tell us that sin is the isolation of the selfish individual; it is lovelessness. When we turn away from it, our self-alienation, self-estrangement is gone. 'Return ye and make you a new heart and a new spirit'. 'Create me a clean heart, O God, and renew a steadfast spirit within me'. 'A new heart will I give you, and a new spirit will I put within you'. 'Turn me, O Lord, that I may turn'. Religion is a question of turning and renewal. For the Jews, 'The spirit of man is the candle of the Lord'. When the Lord lights the candle, darkness disappears. All the darkness in the world cannot put out the light of the candle.

Speaking of the mystery religions of Greece, Aristotle observes: 'The initiated do not learn anything so much as feel certain emotions and are put in a certain frame of mind'. To live one must first die to his old life. Orpheus believed that the soul was 'the son of the starry heaven', that its dwelling in a body was a form of original sin, its earthly life was a source of corruption, and its natural aim was to transcend this life. Each human being is a reflection of the celestial light and has his roots below. This view is at the heart of Plato's idealism. Plato tells us in his image of the cave in the *Republic* that we are all prisoners living in shadows. One philosopher shattered his fetters and saw the sun shining of which the fire in the cave was a small reflection.

PART V. THE UNIVERSAL VIEW: INDIA AND THE WORLD COMMUNITY

Rabindranath Tagore *

Let me express at the outset my grateful appreciation of the kindness which the Organising Committee have shown me by enabling me to participate in the events of this week and preside over the Conference to-day. While I regret that one more competent and familiar with the works of the poet in the original Bengali is not in my place, I am grateful for this opportunity to pay my homage to his important work and profound influence on the country and the world at large.

I. THE GREATNESS OF LITERATURE

It is the peculiar glory of great literature that it lasts much longer than kings and dynasties. History bears witness to the power of the human spirit, which endures longer than dynasties or creeds. The political world of Homer is dead while his song is living to-day. The splendour of Rome has vanished but the poetry of Virgil is yet vital. The dreams of Kālidāsa still move us like the cry of a living voice, with their poignant sense of tears in human relations, while the Ujjain of which he was the ornament has left her memory to his keeping. The great mediaeval potentates are forgotten, but the song of Dante is still cherished; and the Elizabethan Age will be remembered as long as the English language lives on account of its Shakespeare. When our lords and leaders pass into oblivion, Tagore will continue to enchant us by his music and poetry; for though he is an Indian, the value of his work lies not in any tribal or national characteristics, but in

* Presidential Address at the General Conference in connection with the Seventieth Birthday Celebrations of Rabindranath Tagore, held in Calcutta, December, 1931. Reprinted in *East and West in Religion* (London: George Allen & Unwin, 1958), pp. 129–143.

those elements of universality which appeal to the whole world. He has added to the sweetness of life, to the stature of civilisation.

II. EMPHASIS ON THE SPIRITUAL

To many a young Indian in these changing times Rabindranath's voice has been a comfort and a stimulus. When we are weighed down by the burden of defeated hopes and stand dazed at the conquests of science and organisation, when our minds lose their moorings and sense of direction, he comes to us instilling hope into our hearts and courage into our minds. He points out that though our heads are bleeding they are not bowed down, and the value of success need not be judged by standards of wealth and power. The true tests of civilisation are spiritual dignity and power of suffering. Wealth, power, and efficiency are the appurtenances of life and not life itself. The significant things are the personal ones which are beyond the reach of science and organisation.

In his insistence on the supremacy of spiritual values as central to good life and social order, Rabindranath is at one with the long tradition of Indian thinkers. In him we find the eternal voice of India, old and yet new. In spite of the vicissitudes of fortune and the driftings of history, India has kept her essential spirit alive. The self of man is not to be confused with the physical body or the intellect. There is something deeper than intellect, mind, and body:—the real self, which is one with the self of all goodness, truth, and beauty. To aim at that and make it a living presence is the purpose of religion; to train oneself through purity, love, and strength into conformity with that conception is the aim of ethics; to mould oneself to the pattern of that eternal being is the consummation of our aesthetic nature. One has to achieve not merely technical efficiency but greatness of spirit.

When we walk into the night and see the stars keeping their eternal watch, we experience a sense of awe before their remoteness, of annihilation before their immutability, of utter insignificance before their immensity. The heart stops beating, breathing is suspended, and our whole being receives a shock. Our petty interests and anxieties look pitifully small and sordid. There is a similar perturbation, a similar break in the breath, when we listen to great poetry or gaze into a human soul. Philosophy and religion, art and literature, serve to heighten this spiritual consciousness. It is because we have ignored this aspect of life that we find to-day so much instability, conflict, and chaos in spite of intellectual advance and scientific progress. For over three centuries scientific inventions and discoveries have produced increased prosperity. Famines have practically disappeared, population has increased, and the grimmer incidents of life like plagues and pestilences have been brought under control. As the sense of confidence and security about the social order spread over the world, the spirit of curiosity and exploration, which was mainly responsible for the triumphs in the scientific and the technical regions, became extended to the deeper things of life. The world was soon robbed of its mystery and romance. A strange new world of hardness and brutality, of science and big business arose, which prejudiced the order of love, beauty, and happiness so very essential for the growth of the soul. Scepticism and agnosticism have become attractive to the modern mind. In the struggle between the sceptics and agnostics who doubt whether there is anything behind the universe, and the spiritual positivists who affirm that the most vital reality is behind the universe, Rabindranath is with the latter.

There is a story about the visit of an Indian philosopher to Socrates. It comes not from Plato or Xenophon but from Aristoxenus of the third century B.C. He relates that Socrates told the Indian stranger that his work consisted in enquiring about the life of men, and the Indian smiled and said that none could understand things human who did not understand things divine. For the whole Western tradition, man is essentially a rational being, one who can think logically and act upon utilitarian principles. In the East, spiritual understanding and sympathy are of more importance than intellectual ability. For thousands who talk, one can think; for thousands who think, perhaps one sees and understands. What distinguishes man is this capacity for understanding.

Physical growth and intellectual efficiency cannot satisfy us. Even if we have extensive agriculture and efficient transportation and every one possesses his own aeroplane and radio set, if all disease is eradicated, if workmen receive doles and pensions and every one lives to a green old age, there will still be unsatisfied aspirations, wistful yearnings. Man does not live by bread alone or by learning alone. We may reorganise the world on the most up-to-date and efficient scientific lines, and make of it a vast commercial house where all the multiple activities of the human atoms are arranged for, so that we have in it every group from the scullery-maids and the errand boys doing their work in the basement cellars, up to the women of fashion making up their faces in the beauty parlours on the top floor, and may even succeed in transforming a society of human beings into a swarm of ants; yet there will be unsatisfied longings, a thirst for ultimates. Even in that new world-order, children will continue to laugh and cry, women to love and suffer, men to fight and struggle. The real greatness of man is due to his failure, to his moving about in worlds unrealised, with vague misgivings. Man is a creature with a dual status. He partakes of the characters of both the seen and the unseen worlds. While he is a part of the natural order, he has in him the seed of spirit which makes him dissatisfied with his merely natural being. He is truly 'a creature of the borderland', with animal desires and spiritual yearnings; and a life which is entirely given over to the former cannot give him rest.

In his daily life of work and toil, when he tills the soil or governs the state, when he seeks wealth or pursues power, man is not himself. In such activities things are in the saddle. The making of money and the tending of families absorb all the time and strength. Things eternal and unseen get no chance. And yet events occur which disturb the complacency of superficial minds, events with which the sense of mystery and the feeling of uncertainty return. When in the sorrow of death or the suffering of despair, when trust is betrayed or love desecrated, when life becomes tasteless and unmeaning, man stretches forth his hands to heaven to know if perchance there is an answering presence behind the dark clouds; *mahāntam puruṣam ādityavarṇam tamasah parastāt*—it is then that he comes into touch with the supreme in the solitude of his consciousness, in the realm of the profound and the intense. It is the world of light and love in which there is no language but that of silence. It is the world of joy that reveals itself in innumerable forms, *anandarūpaam amrtam yad vibhāti.*

The poetry of human experience, the realities of life as distinct from its mere frills, are achieved in solitude. When we move away from the self, we move away from the only reality which is accessible to us. Man is himself in his religion and in his love. Both these are strictly personal and intimate, peculiar and sacred. If our society attempts to invade even this inner sanctuary, life will lose all its worth and genuineness. A man can share his possessions with others, but not his soul.

We have become so poor to-day that we cannot even recognise the treasures of spirit. In the rush and clamour of our conscious life we do not pay attention to the less audible elements of our being. The sudden thrills, the disturbing emotions, the flashes of insight, it is these that reveal to us the mystery we are, and by these we apprehend the truth of things.

Only the man of serene mind can realise the spiritual meaning of life. Honesty with oneself is the condition of spiritual integrity. We must let in the light to illumine the secret places of the soul. Our pretensions and professions are the barriers that shut us away from truth. We are more familiar with the things we have than with what we are. We are afraid to be alone with ourselves, face to face with our naked loneliness. We try to hide from ourselves the truth by drugs or drunkenness, excitement or service. It is with an effort that we have to pull ourselves together, cultivate the inner life, and abstract from the outer sheaths of body, mind, and intellect. We then see the soul within and attain to a stillness of spirit. The discovery of inwardness is the essential basis of spiritual life.

So long as we lead outward lives, without being touched to our inward depths, we do not understand the meaning of life or the secrets of the soul. Those who live on the surface naturally have no faith in the life of spirit. They believe that they do their duty by religion if they accept the letter of faith. Such spiritual dependence is inconsistent with true religious life, of which the foundation is utter sincerity. A life without independent thought cannot comfort a spiritual being. It is lack of spiritual confidence that impels us to accept what others say about religious truth. But when once the individual in his freedom of spirit pursues truth and builds up a centre in himself, he has enough strength and stability to deal with all that happens to him. He is able to retain his peace and power even when he is faced by adverse conditions. Absolute serenity of spirit is the ultimate goal of human effort, and this is possible only for one who has deep faith in the creative spirit and is thus free from all petty desires. Naturally orthodox religion, whether as dogma or ritual, means almost nothing to him.

III. INSISTENCE ON LIFE

But to dwell in the realm of spirit does not mean that we should be indifferent to the realities of the world. It is a common temptation, to which Indian thinkers have fallen victims more than once, that spirit is all that counts while life is an indifferent illusion, and all efforts directed to the improvement of man's outer life and society are sheer folly. Frequently the ideal of the cold wise man who refuses all activity in the world is exalted, with the result that India has become the scene of a culture of dead men walking the earth which is peopled with ghosts. No one who holds himself aloof from the activities of the world and who is insensitive to its woes can be really wise. To practise virtue in a vacuum is impossible. Spiritual vision normally issues in a new power for good in the world of existence. The spiritual man does not turn his back on the realities of the world, but works in it with the sole object of creating better material and spiritual conditions. For spiritual life rises in the natural. Being a poet, Rabindranath uses the visible world as a means of shadowing forth the invisible. He touches the temporal with the light of the eternal. The material world becomes transparent as his spirit moves in it.

The world is not a snare nor its good a delusion. They are opportunities for self-development, pathways for realisation. This is the great tradition which has come down from the seers of the Upaniṣads and the author of the *Bhagavadgītā*. They delight in life. For since God has taken upon Himself the bonds of creation, why should we not take upon ourselves the bonds of this world? We need not complain, if we are clothed in this warm garment of flesh. Human relationships are the mainspring of spiritual life. God is not a Sultan in the sky but is in all, through all, and over all. We worship Him in all the true objects of our worship, love Him whenever our love is true. In the woman who is good, we feel Him; in the man who is true, we know Him. Tagore's Hibbert Lectures on *The Religion of Man* (1931) ask us to realise the supreme in the heart of us all.

The great of the world work in it sensitive to its woes. When Buddha preaches *maitri* and the *Bhagavadgītā* teaches *sneha* for all, they mean that we can understand others only through love. To look upon life as an evil and treat the world as a delusion is sheer ingratitude. In his play *Saññyāsi or the Ascetic*, Rabindranath points out how outraged nature had her revenge on the ascetic who tried to gain a victory over her by cutting away the bonds of human desires and affections. He attempted to arrive at a true knowledge of the world by cutting himself off from it. A little girl brought him back from this region of abstraction into the play of life. No asceticism is ever equal to the task of suppressing living beauty. The ascetic's inmost defences went down before the rapture of beauty, and clamant life compelled him to fling open the doors. The Saññyāsi discovered that 'the great is to be found in the small, the infinite within the bounds of form and the eternal freedom of the soul in love'. We must bring heaven down to earth, put eternity into an hour and realise God in this world. Ascetics are like cut flowers in metal vases. They are beautiful to contemplate for a while but they soon wither, being without nourishment from the soil. To be firm and rooted, man must consent to be nourished of life. Asceticism, however necessary it may be for the growth of the person, cannot be confused with a mere refusal of the nourishment by which the growth is helped. The saints do not refuse to sit at the rich man's table; nor do they object to the scent of precious ointment.

It is foolish to fancy that God enjoys our sorrows and sufferings, our pains and fasts, and loves those who tax themselves to the uttermost. Life is a great gift, and those who do not love it are unworthy of it. Those who lay waste their souls and call it peace cannot obtain the support of Tagore for their action.

One need not enter a convent or become an ascetic to reject life. Many of us reject life by surrounding ourselves with taboos and prohibitions. Interpreting the main intention of Hindu thought, Tagore insists on a loyal acceptance of life. We must face life as an adventure and give full play to its possibilities.

Religion speaks to us in many dialects. It has diverse complexions. And yet it has one true voice, the voice of human pity and compassion, of mercy, of patient love, and to that voice we must do all we can to listen. Naturally, a sensitive soul is bound to be outraged by the social order which is at the end of one age and the beginning of another. We say that there is a revolution in Russia or Spain; but there is one in our country too. We also have our guillotines and our victims, though many of those who suffer still go about with their heads on their shoulders. We have become mere walking and talking phantoms. With our languid paleness and lack of depth, which we try to cover by paint and pose, our lives remind us of the mannequins displayed in the shop windows of Chowringhee.

Our deepest passions are debased by the conditions imposed by society. Add to this the appalling poverty and ignorance in which many people live. If they are somewhat sensitive in temper, they are compelled to spend perturbed nights of anguish and long monotonous days of struggle measuring time by the throbs of pain and the memories of bitterness. When dim thoughts of suicide rush through their overcrowded heads, they stare at the ceiling and smoke a cigarette. Rabindranath has not much sympathy with the prevalent view that social service consists simply in joining leagues to stop cigarette smoking or to advance the practice of birth control. It consists in enabling people to live with intensity of being.

As a poet he despises organisation and believes in each man living his own life in his own way. He is the champion of the individual in his age-long struggle against the mass tyranny which crushes him. The fate of one who sets himself against the established order is abuse and criticism, persecution and fierce solitariness. Tagore is the poet of sorrow and suffering. The pathos of men's striving, the bitterness of life submerged in the shadows, the waste and loneliness of women's lives have found few more profoundly moved spectators. To this audience it is scarcely necessary to refer to the innumerable instances where the poet reveals the anguish that is implicit in common situations.

The most sacred of all human relationships is love; and whatever our scriptures may say, our practice is immoral because it demands the beauties of self-control and self-abnegation from only one sex. So long as our women are treated as mere servants and toys of the undisciplined male, the social order will continue to be corrupt. The convention that a woman's virtues are chastity and submissiveness to man is altogether too flimsy an excuse for masculine tyranny. What is virtue in a man is virtue in a woman. It is unfortunate that there are many among us who are cold-blooded libertines who unscrupulously use women as instruments of their lust. They are the human animals, the slaves of sense.

The body is the temple of the spirit, the apparatus for spiritual growth. To regard the body or any part of it as indecent or vile is the sin of impiety. To treat it as cheap and vulgar is equally impious. Physical union without love is the essence of prostitution. This is true within as without marriage. A woman who gives herself to a man for whom she has no love, as a mere act of duty just because she is his wife, is as cruelly abusing herself as the husband who insists on his rights. Love is spiritual and aesthetic, a matter of conscience and good taste and not one of law or codes. Married life without love is like slave labour. Obedience to ecclesiastical pundits or social rules is a form of self-indulgence, even as action in obedience to one's deepest being is the imperative command of life. As beauty is higher than harmony, as truth is higher than consistency, so is love higher than law. Like fire it purifies everything.

In his play *Sati*, Uma refuses to accept the man who never won her love even though he was her chosen husband, whatever pledges others may have given for her. When she cuts herself away from Jivaji to whom she was sacredly affianced and accepts another, she defends herself by saying, 'my body was yielded only after love had given me'. When her mother says, 'Touch me not with impure hands', she replies, 'I am as pure as yourself'. Her eloquent and dignified bearing cuts her father to the quick and he says: 'Come to me, my darling child! mere vanity are these man-made laws, splashing like spray against the rock of heaven's ordinance'. Our legal providers and protectors do not realise that our women possess souls, yearning for understanding, for some one to share their dreams and their longings; and when a man and a woman offer to each other, not their strength or rank or fortune but their weakness, their desolation, their heart's need, they enter into a region which is not built by the labour of human hands but by the love of their hearts. Their union is consecrated though it may not be approved.

IV. CONCLUSION

In all Rabindranath's work three features are striking: (1) The ultimateness of spiritual values to be obtained by inward honesty and cultivation of inner life; (2) the futility of mere negation or renunciation and the need for a holy or a whole development of life; and (3) the positive attitude of sympathy for all, even the lowly and the lost. It is a matter for satisfaction to find an Indian leader insisting on these real values of life at a time when so many old things are crumbling away and a thousand new ones are springing up.

Mahātmā Gāndhi: His Message for Mankind *

Civilisation is based on a dream. Its codes and conventions, its way of life and habits of mind are poised on a dream. When the dream prevails, civilisation advances; when the dream fails, civilisation goes down. When life becomes cluttered with things, when the vanities and follies of the world overtake us, when we see all around the murderous interplay of destructive forces and unnatural strivings, when we fail to see any purpose in it all, it is time that we probe the human situation and find out what is wrong with it. Though we have been warned by the last war that our civilisation is fragile and will break down if the present trend of human cupidity wedded to scientific genius is not checked, we seem to be confused and hesitant about the need to change the direction in which human history has been moving. When a prophet soul who is not enslaved by his environment, who is filled with compassion for suffering humanity, calls upon us to turn our backs on the present world with its conflicts and competitions, class distinctions and wars, and seek the upward path, narrow and difficult, the human in us comes alive and responds. To a world lost in error and beset by the illusions of time, Gāndhi announces the value of the timeless principles of the truth of God and love of fellow-men as the only basis for establishing right human relationships. In his life and message we see the dream of civilisation come true. Centuries have gone to his making and his roots are established in the ages. No wonder the world was shocked with horror and smitten with grief when it heard that the great soul, rare in any age but amazing in ours, was

* From S. Radhakrishnan (ed.), *Mahātmā Gāndhi: Essays and Reflections on His Life and Work* (2nd ed.; London: George Allen & Unwin, 1949), pp. 336–361.

struck down. President Truman said that a giant among men had fallen. This little man, so frail in appearance, was a giant among men, measured by the greatness of his soul. By his side other men, very important and famous men big in their own way, big in their space and time, look small and insignificant. His profound sincerity of spirit, his freedom from hatred and malice, his mastery over himself, his human, friendly, all-embracing charity, his strong conviction which he shared with the great ones of history that the martyrdom of the body is nothing compared with the defilement of the soul, a conviction which he successfully put to the test in many dramatic situations and now in this final act of surrender, show the impact of religion on life, the impact of the eternal values on the shifting problems of the world of time.

I. RELIGION AND LIFE

The inspiration of his life has been what is commonly called religion, religion not in the sense of subscription to dogmas or conformity to ritual, but religion in the sense of an abiding faith in the absolute values of truth, love, and justice and a persistent endeavour to realise them on earth. Nearly fifteen years ago I asked him to state his view of religion. He expressed it in these words: 'I often describe my religion as Religion of Truth. Of late, instead of saying God is Truth, I have been saying Truth is God, in order more fully to define my religion. . . . Nothing so completely describes my God as Truth. Denial of God we have known. Denial of Truth we have not known. The most ignorant among mankind have some Truth in them. We are all sparks of Truth. The sum-total of these sparks is indescribable, as yet unknown Truth which is God. I am being daily led nearer to It by constant prayer'. [1]

In the Upaniṣads, the Supreme is said to be Truth, Knowledge and Eternity, *satyam, jñānam, anantam, Brahma.* God is the Lord of Truth, *satyanārāyana.* 'I am', says Gāndhi, 'but a seeker after Truth. I claim to have found the way to it. I

[1] Radhakrishnan and Muirhead, *Contemporary Indian Philosophy* (1936), p. 21.

claim to be making a ceaseless effort to find it. To find Truth completely is to realise oneself and one's destiny, in other words, to become perfect. I am painfully conscious of my imperfection and therein lies all the strength I possess. I lay no claim to superhuman powers: I want none. I wear the same corruptible flesh that the weakest of my fellow-beings wears and am therefore as liable to err as any'. Through prayers and fasts, through the practice of love, Gāndhi tried to overcome the inconsistencies of his flesh and the discursiveness of his nature and to make himself a fitter instrument for God's work. He felt that all religions at their best prescribe the same discipline for man's fulfilment. The Vedas and the Tipitaka, the Bible, and the Qurān speak to us of the need for self-discipline. The place of prayers and fasts in the lives of the Hindu sages, the Buddha, and Jesus is well known. The voice of the Muezzin which breaks the silence of the early dawn with the summons that has echoed for nearly fourteen centuries: Allāhu Akbar, God is great, affirms that prayer is better than sleeping and that we should start our day with thoughts of God. The follower of Islam is called upon to pray five times a day at set hours and in prescribed words and acts and to fast one month in each year, the month of Ramadan, from sunrise to sunset without partaking of any food whatsoever.

Gāndhi was convinced that all religions aim at the same goal. The inner life, the life of the spirit in God, is the great reality. All else is outside. We make much of the accessories of religion, not of religion itself, not of the temple of God in the human spirit but of the props and buttresses which we have built round the temple for fear that it should fall. These details are moulded by the external conditions and adapted to the traditions of the people.

Hindu religious classics emphasise our duty to see all human beings in our own self, to admit their value and not judge them by external standards. India never attempted to suppress the longings of soul or the patterns of life of communities who have settled there and contributed to the richness of Indian culture. Gāndhi recalls us to the age-old tradition of India, the tradition not of mere tolerance but of profound respect for all faiths, and warns us that we should not squander away the spiritual patrimony which generations of our ancestors have built for us with so much assiduity and abnegation. When he was asked to define Hinduism, he said, 'though he was a *sanātani* Hindu he was unable to define Hinduism. As a layman (who was not learned in the science of religion) he could say that Hinduism regarded all religions as worthy of all respect'.[2] 'Tolerance', says Gāndhi, 'implies a gratuitous assumption of the inferiority of other faiths to one's own, whereas *ahiṁsā* teaches us to entertain the same respect for the religious faiths of others as we accord to our own, thus admitting the imperfections of the latter'. Gāndhi does not claim exclusive validity for Hinduism and does not grant it to other religions. 'It was impossible for me to believe that I could go to heaven or attain salvation only by being a Christian . . . It was more than I could believe that Jesus was the only incarnate Son of God'. Truth belongs to God and ideas belong to men and we cannot be certain that our ideas have assimilated the whole truth. Whatever our religious ideas may be, we all seek to climb the hill and our eyes are fixed on the same goal. We may choose different paths and follow different guides. When we reach the top, the roads leading to it matter little if only we keep on ascending. In religion what counts is effort.

The conception of the Indian State as a non-communal one does not mean that it aims only at the secular ends of life, material comfort, and success. It means that the State will accord free and equal treatment to all religions, to profess, practise, and propagate their faiths so long as their beliefs and practices are not repugnant to the moral sense. The equal treatment of all religions imposes an obligation on the members of the different religions to practise mutual tolerance. Intolerance is a proof of incomprehension. In January, 1928, Gāndhi said to the Federation of International Fellowships: 'After long study and experience I have come to these conclusions, that (i) all religions are true, (ii) all religions have some error in them, (iii) all religions are almost as dear to me as my own Hinduism. My veneration for other faiths is the same as for my own faith. Consequently the thought of conversion is im-

[2] *Harijan*, February 1, 1948, p. 13.

possible. . . . Our prayer for others ought never to be "God, give them the light thou hast given to me", but "give them all the light and truth they need for their highest development". My faith offers me all that is necessary for my inner development, for it teaches me to pray. But I also pray that every one else may develop to the fullness of his being in his own religion, that the Christian may become a better Christian and the Mohammadan a better Mohammadan. I am convinced that God will one day ask us only what we are and what we do, not the name we give to our being and doing'. At the prayer meeting on January 21, 1948, Gāndhi said that he 'had practised Hinduism from early childhood. His nurse had taught him to invoke Rāma when he feared evil spirits. Later on he had come in contact with Christians, Muslims and others, and after making a fair study of other religions had stuck to Hinduism. He was as firm in his faith to-day as in his early childhood. He believed God would make him an instrument of saving the religion that he loved, cherished, and practised'. [3]

Even though Gāndhi practised this religion with courage and consistency, he had an unusual sense of humour, a certain light-heartedness, even gaiety, which we do not associate with ardent religious souls. This playfulness was the outcome of an innocence of heart, a spontaneity of spirit. While he redeemed even the most fugitive and trivial moment from commonness, he had all the time a remote, a far-away look. The abuses and perversities of life did not shake his confidence in the essential goodness of things. He assumed, without much discussion, that his way of life was clean, right, and natural, while our way in this mechanised industrial civilisation was unnatural, unhealthy, and wrong.

Gāndhi's religion was an intensely practical one. There are religious men who, when they find the troubles and perplexities of the world too much for them, wrap their cloaks around them, withdraw into monasteries or mountain-tops and guard the sacred fires burning in their own hearts. If truth, love, and justice are not to be found in the world, we can possess these graces in the inviolable sanctuary of our souls. For Gāndhi, sanctity and service of man were inseparable.

[3] *Harijan*, February 1, 1948, p. 11.

'My motive has been purely religious. I could not be leading a religious life unless I identified myself with the whole of mankind; and this I could not do unless I took part in politics. The whole gamut of man's activities to-day constitutes an indivisible whole, you cannot divide social, political, and purely religious work into watertight compartments. I do not know any religion apart from human activity. My devotion to truth has drawn me into the field of politics; and I can say without the slightest hesitation, and yet with all humility, that those who say that religion has nothing to do with politics do not know what religion means'. Many of us who call ourselves religious maintain the stage-set of religion. We practise mechanically its rites, acquiesce passively in its dogmas. We conform to the forms as such conformity brings us social advantages or political privileges. We invoke the name of God and despise our neighbours. We deceive ourselves with empty phrases and mental clichés. For Gāndhi religion was a passional participation in the life of spirit. It was intensely practical and dynamic. He was keenly sensitive to the pain of the world and longed 'to wipe every tear from every eye'. He believed in the sanctification of all life. 'Politics divorced from religion' was, for him, 'a corpse, fit only to be burned'.

He looked upon politics as a branch of ethics and religion. It is not a struggle for power and wealth, but a persistent and continuous effort to enable the submerged millions to attain the good life, to raise the quality of human beings, to train them for freedom and fellowship, for spiritual depth and social harmony. A politician who works for these ends cannot help being religious. He cannot ignore the formative share of morality in civilisation or take the side of evil against good. Owing no allegiance to the material things of life, Gāndhi was able to make changes in them. The prophets of spirit make history just by standing outside history.

II. INDIA'S STRUGGLE FOR FREEDOM

It is impertinent for any man to set about reforming the universe. He must start his work from where he is. He must take up the work that lies nearest to hand. When, on his return from South Africa, he found the people of India suffering from mortified pride, want, pain, and degradation, he took up the task of their emancipation as a challenge and an opportunity. It is wrong for the weak to submit to oppression and wrong for the strong to be allowed to oppress. No improvement, he felt, was possible without political freedom. Freedom from subjection should be won not by the usual methods of secret societies, armed rebellion, arson, and assassination. The way to freedom is neither by abject entreaty nor by revolutionary violence. Freedom does not descend upon a people as a gift from above, but they have to raise themselves to it by their own effort. The Buddha said: 'Ye who suffer, know ye suffer from yourselves; none else compels'. In self-purification lies the path to freedom. Force is no remedy. The use of force in such circumstances is foul play. The force of spirit is invincible. Gāndhi said: 'The British want us to put the struggle on the plane of machine-guns. They have weapons and we have not. Our only assurance of beating them is to keep it on the plane where we have the weapons and they have not'. If we could combine perfect courage to endure wrong while resisting it with the perfect charity which abstains from hurting or hating the oppressor, our appeal to the human in our oppressor would become irresistible. To a people oppressed for centuries by outsiders, he gave a new self-respect, a new confidence in themselves, a new assurance of strength. He took hold of ordinary men and women, men and women who were an incredible mixture of heroism and conceit, magnificence and meanness, made heroes out of them, and organised an unarmed revolt against British rule. He weaned the country from anarchy and terrorism and saved the political struggle from losing its soul. There were occasions in India's struggle for freedom when he adopted measures which were unintelligible to the mere politician. There are great leaders who know how to bend and flatter in order to draw other men unto them. While they keep their eyes fixed upon the goal, they do not scruple about the means to reach the goal. Not so Gāndhi. 'If India takes up the doctrine of the sword she may gain a momentary victory, then India will cease to be the pride of my heart. I believe absolutely that India has a mission for the world; however, India's acceptance of the doctrine of the sword will be the hour of my trial. My life is dedicated to the service of India through the religion of non-violence, which I believe to be the root of Hinduism'. He ordered the suspension of the movement of non-co-operation when he saw that his people were not able to conform to his high standards. By his withdrawal he exposed himself to the derision of his opponents. 'Let the opponent glory in our humiliation and so-called defeat. It is better to be charged with cowardice than to be guilty of denial of our oath and sin against God. It is a million times better that I should be the laughing-stock of the world than that I should act insincerely towards myself. . . . I know that the drastic reversal of practically the whole of the aggressive programme may be politically unsound and unwise but there is no doubt that it is religiously sound'. What is morally wrong cannot be politically right. On the evening of August 8, 1942, when what is known as the 'Quit India' resolution was passed by the All-India Congress Committee, Gāṇdhi said: 'We must look the world in the face with calm and clear eyes, even though the eyes of the world are bloodshot to-day'. When the naval disturbances started in Bombay he scolded those who organised it: 'Hatred is in the air and impatient lovers of the country will gladly take advantage of it, if they can, through violence to further the cause of independence. I suggest that it is wrong at any time and everywhere. But it is more wrong and unbecoming in a country whose fighters for freedom have declared to the world that their policy is truth and non-violence'. He had great faith that the spirit of violence 'is a survival which will kill itself in time. It is so contrary to the spirit of India'. 'I have striven all my life for the liberating of India. But if I can get it only by violence, I would not want it'. The means by which freedom is attained are as important as the end itself. An India made free through immorality cannot be really free. He conducted the struggle with the established government in India as in South Africa, without any trace of racial feeling, with civilised dignity. The transfer of power on August 15, 1947, marked the end of that struggle. It has ended in a settlement reached in a spirit of good temper and friendliness.

Freedom for Gāndhi was not a mere political fact. It was

a social reality. He struggled not only to free India from foreign rule but to free her from social corruption and communal strife. 'I shall work for an India in which the poorest shall feel that it is their country in whose making they have an effective voice; an India in which there shall be no high class and low class of people; an India in which all communities shall live in perfect harmony. There can be no room in such an India for the curse of untouchability or the curse of intoxicating drinks and drugs. Women will enjoy the same rights as men. Since we shall be at peace with all the rest of the world, neither exploiting nor being exploited, we shall have the smallest army imaginable. All interests not in conflict with the interests of dumb millions will be scrupulously respected. Personally, I hate the distinction between foreign and indigenous. This is the India of my dreams'.[4]

Political freedom does not represent the fulfilment of a nation's dreams. It only provides scope and opportunity for the renewal of a nation's life. A free India must be made a country of discerning people, cherishing the values of true civilisation, peace, order, good will between man and man, love of truth, quest of beauty, and hatred of evil. When we scramble for power over our fellows, for power to make money, for power to make life more ugly than it is, it means that we have lost the grace of life and the dignity of civilisation.

Anxious to make the Indian society a truly free one, Gāndhi put at the centre of his constructive programme the spinning-wheel, the removal of untouchability, and communal harmony. Freedom is a mockery so long as men starve, go naked, and pine away in voiceless anguish. The *charka* or the spinning-wheel will help to redeem the common man from the evils of poverty and ignorance, disease and squalor. 'Political freedom has no meaning for the millions if they do not know how to employ their enforced idleness. Eighty per cent. of the Indian population are compulsorily unemployed for half the year; they can only be helped by reviving a trade that has fallen into oblivion and making it a source of new income'. Gāndhi stressed the use of the spinning-wheel as an occupation supplementary to agriculture.

[4] *Young India*, September 10, 1931.

It also serves as a check against the increasing mechanisation of life. In a highly industrialised society men's minds act like machines and not as living organisms. They are dependent on large and complicated forms of organisation, capitalist combines and labour unions and they cannot influence their decisions much. Again, natural creative impulses are suppressed in millions of human beings who do one little piece of work and not the whole. There is not the sense of satisfaction in the work we do, when we do not act as responsible individuals in the society to which we belong; our lives become tiresome and meaningless and we take to wild forms of compensation for excitement and vital experience. The rich and the poor both seem to suffer in a mechanised society. The rich, men and women, seem as though they have an almost physical sense of spiritual death with their souls still and rigid. Old men starve to death condemned to work until they can work no longer, and women are forced to undertake the most exhausting labours.

Gāndhi struggled to retain the traditional rural civilisation which expressed the living unity of a people harmoniously interacting on a certain soil swayed by a common feeling about life, the earth, and the universe. The ambitious spirit of man feels itself strong and free in the villages with their open spaces and green belts rather than in overcrowded cities with their darkness and squalor, foul smell and stagnant air, fevers and rickets. In the village community men feel that they are responsible individuals effectively participating in its life. When these villagers move to towns they become restless, spiritless, and hopeless. The peasant and the weaver are displaced by the mechanic and the business man, and to compensate for the boredom of life exciting amusements are devised. No wonder the spirit of man becomes lost in this wilderness of living. If we are to humanise society and bring moral significance to acts and relationships we should work for a decentralised village economy where machinery could be employed so long as it does not disturb much the fundamental framework of society and the freedom of the human spirit.

Gāndhi does not reject machinery as such. He observes: 'How can I be against all machinery when I know that even this body is a most delicate piece of machinery? The spinning-wheel is a machine; a little toothpick is a machine. What I object to is the craze for machinery, not machinery as such. The craze is for what they call labour-saving machinery. Men go on "saving labour" till thousands are without work and thrown on the open streets to die of starvation. I want to save time and labour, not for a fraction of mankind but *for all.* I want the concentration of wealth, not in the hands of a few, but in the hands of all. To-day, machinery merely helps a few to ride on the backs of millions. The impetus behind it all is not the philanthropy to save labour, but greed. It is against this constitution of things that I am fighting with all my might. The machine should not tend to atrophy the limbs of man. . . . Factories run by power-driven machinery should be nationalised, state-controlled. The supreme consideration is man.

'If we could have electricity in every village home, I should not mind the villagers plying their instruments and tools with the help of electricity. But then the village communities or the state would own power houses, just as the villages have their grazing pastures. . . . The heavy machinery for work of public utility which could be undertaken by human labour has its inevitable place, but all that would be owned by the state and used entirely for the benefit of the people'.

As a religious and social reformer Gāndhi pricked us into a new awareness of the social evils from which we have been suffering. He exhorted us to rid religion of the many accretions with which in its long history it became encumbered, notably untouchability. Hinduism has paid a heavy price for its neglect of social responsibilities. The draft constitution for the new India aims at establishing an equitable social order in which ideals of virtue and freedom will inspire economic and political, social and cultural institutions.

Under the leadership of Gāndhi, the Indian National Congress worked for friendly relations among the different religions and communities of India, for the establishment of a non-communal democratic state. He strove for a free and united India. The hour of his triumph proved to be the hour of his humiliation. The division of the country is a grievous wrong we have suffered. Our leaders, caught in a mood of frustration, tired of communal 'killings', which disgraced the country for some months past, anxious to give relief to the harassed, distraught multitudes, acquiesced in the partition of India against their better judgement and the advice of Gāndhi. No amount of regret will bring back a lost opportunity. Mistakes of an hour may have to be atoned for by the sorrow of years. We cannot, however, build as we will but only as we can. It will take centuries of history to enable such a momentous decision as the partition of India to be properly appreciated. We have not the gift of penetrating the future. For the present, however, the price of partition has not yielded communal peace, but has actually increased communal bitterness. The New Delhi celebrations on August 15, Gāndhi would not attend. He excused himself and was engaged in his lonely trek in the villages of Bengal, walking on foot, comforting the poor and the homeless, entreating them to remove from their hearts every trace of suspicion, bitterness, and resentment. The large migrations, the thousands of people wandering to and fro, weary, uprooted, heavy laden, the mad career of communal violence, worst of all the spiritual degradation all around, suspicion, anger, doubt, pity, grief, absence of hope, filled Gāndhi with deep sorrow and led him to devote the rest of his life to the psychological solution of this problem. His fasts at Calcutta and Delhi had a sobering effect, but the evil was too deep to be cured so easily. On his seventy-eighth birthday, October 2, 1947, Gāndhi said: 'With every breath I pray God to give me strength to quench the flames or remove me from this earth. I, who staked my life to gain India's independence, do not wish to be a living witness to its destruction'.

When last I met him, early in December, 1947, I found him in deep agony and determined to do his utmost to improve the relations among the communities or die in the process. Announcing his decision to undertake the fast, Gāndhiji said at his prayer meeting on January 12, 1948, at Delhi, '. . . No man, if he is pure, has anything more precious to give than his life. I hope and pray that I have that purity in me to justify the step. I ask you all to bless the effort and to pray for me and with me. The fast will end when and if I am satisfied that there is a reunion of hearts of all communities brought about without any outside pressure, but from an awakened sense of duty. The reward will be the regaining of India's dwindling prestige and her fast-fading sovereignty over the heart of Asia and then through the world. I flatter myself with the belief that the loss of her soul by India will mean the loss of the hope of the aching, storm-tossed and hungry world. I urge everybody dispassionately to examine the purpose and let me die, if I must, in peace, which I hope is ensured Death for me would be glorious deliverance rather than that I should be a helpless witness of the destruction of India, Hinduism, Sikhism, and Islam. Just contemplate the rot that has set in in beloved India, and you will rejoice to think that there is a humble son of hers who is strong enough and possibly pure enough to take the happy step. If he is neither, he is a burden on earth. The sooner he disappears and clears the Indian atmosphere of the burden, the better for him and all concerned'. He met his death while engaged in this great work. It is the cross laid on the great-hearted that they exhaust themselves in sorrow and suffering so that those who come after them may live in peace and security.

We are too deeply entangled in our own past misdeeds; we are caught in the web we had ourselves spun according to the laws of our own twisted ethics. Communal differences are yet a wound, not a sepsis. But wounds have a tendency to produce sepsis. If this tendency is to be checked we must adhere to the ideals for which Gāndhi lived and died. We must develop self-restraint; we must refrain from anger and malice, intemperance of thought and speech, from violence of every kind. It will be the crown of his life work, if we settle down as good neighbours and adjust our problems in a spirit of peace and goodwill. The way to honour his memory is to accept and adopt his way of approach, the way of reconciliation and sympathetic adjustment of all differences.

III. *Satyāgraha*

When the strife of these days is forgotten, Gāndhi will stand out as the great prophet of a moral and spiritual revolution without which this distracted world will not find peace. It is said that non-violence is the dream of the wise while violence is the history of man. It is true that wars are obvious and dramatic and their results in changing the course of history are evident and striking. But there is a struggle which goes on in the minds of men. Its results are not recorded in the statistics of the killed and the injured. It is the struggle for human decency, for the avoidance of physical strife which restricts human life, for a world without wars. Among the fighters in this great struggle, Gāndhi was in the front rank. His message is not a matter for academic debate in intellectual circles. It is the answer to the cry of exasperated mankind which is at the cross-roads—which shall prevail, the law of the jungle or the law of love? All our world organisations will prove ineffective if the truth that love is stronger than hate does not inspire them. The world does not become one simply because we can go round it in less than three days. However far or fast we may travel, our minds do not get nearer to our neighbours. The oneness of the world can only be the oneness of our purposes and aspirations. A united world can only be the material counterpart of a spiritual affinity. Mechanical makeshifts and external structures by themselves cannot achieve the spiritual results. Changes in the social architecture do not alter the minds of peoples. Wars have their origins in false values, in ignorance, in intolerance. Wrong leadership has brought the world to its present misery. Throughout the world there seems to be a black-out of civilised values. Great nations bomb one another's cities in order to obtain the victory. The moral consequences of the use of the atom bomb may prove to be far more disastrous than the bomb itself. The fault is not in our stars but in ourselves. Institutions are of little avail unless we are trained to obey our conscience and develop brotherly love. Unless the leaders of the world discover their highest human dignity in themselves, not in the offices they hold, in the depth of their own souls, in the freedom of their conscience, there is no hope for the ordered peace of a world-community. Gāndhi had the faith that the world is one in its deepest roots and highest aspirations. He knew that the purpose of historical humanity was to develop a world-civilisation, a world-culture, a world-community. We can get out of the misery of this world only by exposing the darkness which is strongly entrenched in men's hearts and replacing it by understanding and tolerance. Gāndhi's tender and tormented heart heralds the world which the United Nations wish to create. This lonely symbol of a vanishing past is also the prophet of the new world which is struggling to be born. He represents the conscience of the future man.

For Gāndhi, *satya* or truth is the Reality. It is God in the soul of man. It is more potent than the sword. Truth and non-violence, *satya* and *ahiṁsā* are related to each other as two sides of one coin. If we recognise the superiority of spirit to matter and the supremacy of the moral law, we must be able to overcome evil through the moral power. Violence is the ultimate expression of personality at the farthest remove from the spirit of truth. When anyone takes to it as a first rather than a last resort, he is deemed mad or criminal or both. Non-violence is not limited to physical life. It is a frame of mind. To think ill of others, to tell lies is an act of violence.

Satyāgraha, or non-violence, is not for Gāndhi a quiescent or negative attitude. It is positive and dynamic. It is not non-resistance or submission to evil. It is resistance to it through love. *Satyāgraha* is belief in the power of spirit, the power of truth, the power of love by which we can overcome evil through self-suffering and self-sacrifice. It gives a new meaning to the temporal strivings for freedom and peace. We must impose suffering on ourselves and not inflict it on others. '*Satyāgraha* is self-dependent. It does not require the assent of our opponent before being brought into operation. It manifests its power most strongly against an opponent who offers resistance. It is therefore irresistible. A *satyāgrahi* does not know what defeat is, for he fights for truth without losing any of his strength. Death in the struggle is release and prison a gateway wide open to liberty. And as a *satyāgrahi* never injures his adversary and always appeals to his reason by gentle argument or to his heart by sacrifice of self, *satyāgraha* is twice blessed; it blesses him who practises it and him against whom it is put in practice.

'My creed of non-violence is an extremely active force. It has no room for cowardice or room for weakness. There is hope for a violent man to be some day non-violent but not for a coward. I have therefore said more than once in these pages that, if we do not know how to defend ourselves, our women, and our places of worship by the force of suffering, i.e. non-violence, we must, if we are men, be at least able to defend all of them by fighting'.[5] 'The world is not entirely governed by logic. Life itself involves some kind of violence, and we have to choose the path of least violence'.[6] We will fight for what we believe to be right rather than abstain from violence through weakness or cowardice or selfish love of ease.

Gāndhi organised an Indian ambulance corps which he led as a sergeant major in the Boer War. He formed a stretcher-bearer unit in the Zulu rebellion of 1906. He did so because he felt convinced that the claims of Indians to the rights of citizenship entailed corresponding responsibilities. In World War I he took part in a recruiting campaign for soldiers on the ground that many of them refrained from joining up not because they believed in non-violence but because they were cowardly. He had always argued that death whilst fighting with courage was far better than refraining from its risks through fear. But for him non-violence is the heart of religion and his many experiences strengthened his faith.

In 1938 Gāndhi said: 'Behind the death-dealing bomb there is the human hand that releases it, and behind that still is the human heart that sets the hand in motion. At the back of the policy of terrorism is the assumption that terrorism, if applied in a sufficient measure, will produce the desired result, namely, bind the adversary to the tyrant's will. . . . I have an implicit faith—a faith that burns to-day brighter than ever, after half a century's experience of unbroken practise of non-violence—that mankind can only be saved through non-violence, which is the central teaching of the Bible as I have understood the Bible. Ultimately force, however justifiably used, will lead us into the same morass as the force of Hitler and Mussolini. There will be just a difference of degree. Those who believe in non-violence must use it at the critical moment. We must not despair of touching the heart even of gangsters, even though for

[5] *Young India*, September 16, 1927.

[6] *Ibid.*, September 28, 1934.

the moment we may seem to be striking our heads against a blind wall'.

It is difficult to persuade the 'advanced' nations to believe that political success can be achieved by peaceful weapons. Upton Sinclair said: 'My own forefathers got their political freedom by violence; that is to say, they overthrew the British Crown and made themselves a free Republic. Also by violence they put an end to the enslavement of the black race on this continent. . . . If there is any chance of oppressed peoples getting free by violence I should justify the use of it'. Bernard Shaw points out that violence has been the scientific method of history: 'It is idle in the face of history to deny these facts; it might as well be said that tigers have never been able to live by violence and that non-resistance will convert tigers to a diet of rice'. But these advanced thinkers who are members of the powerful nations now realise that the next war of atomic weapons will lead to the extermination of the human race, to the destruction of all that they wish to conserve. Wars in which lives are lost, hearts broken, and minds unhinged by the million among nations which claim to be in the right—a claim which is repudiated by the enemy—are an evil and a denial of God and humanity. If Gāndhi's attempts to effect changes peacefully do not succeed, we need not be disturbed. 'What does it matter, then, if we perish in the attempts to apply the principle of non-violence? We shall have lived and died for a great principle'.

Gāndhi recognised that his followers accepted his lead for the struggle for independence but were not pledged to the adoption of non-violence in all circumstances as he himself was. Political action has to take into account the limitations of ordinary human nature and Gāndhi felt that the Indian National Congress was again and again obliged to reach political decisions which did not conform to his deep convictions. When once we begin to compromise, there is no knowing where we will end. If an adherence to truth is not absolute, anything can be justified in the name of expediency. Gāndhi understood the risks of adaptation of truth to the exigencies of political life and so declined to make himself responsible for the Congress decisions. He resigned his formal membership in the Congress and severed his connexion with it, though he had offered advice to the Congress and assistance to it when it agreed to uphold his uncompromising honesty and truth in its actions.

Violence, *hiṁsā,* is not to be confused with coercive force, or *daṇḍa.* There is a difference between the use of force in a state and the use of force in wars between states. The use of force is permissible when it is ordered in accordance with law by a neutral authority in the general interest and not in the interest of one of the parties to the dispute. In a well-ordered state we have the rule of law, courts of justice, and police and prisons, but we have no international law, no international courts of justice, and no international police. It is anarchy and gangster rule that prevail. Each belligerent country claims to be in the right. We may think that our cause is just. It only reflects the goodness of the human heart which seeks instinctively what is good and rejects what is bad. Even Hitler appealed to the German people in the name of the German cause, which to them seemed good. It shows the dominance in the world of the good over the evil motive. Hitler was defeated possibly because his cause was worse than ours, bad as it was. Where there is no world government, where there is no impartial court to determine what is just, no one has a right to use force to make his cause prevail over that of his neighbour. In a world where might is the basis of right, the use of force is violence and is wrong.

The root cause of wars is the anarchical world. Hitler himself is a product, not an original cause. Unless we have belief in a purpose beyond the state, the state itself is unjustly constituted. Belief in the state as the supreme object of the citizens' service may inspire a feverish fury of fanaticism but it cannot, in the present stage of human evolution, yield anything like a permanent inspiration. Supreme power is not above law. The highest law of *dharma* is that of which the states are the servants. When we have a world-government, with its courts of law and police, even Gāndhi would permit the use of a police force on behalf of the world-government. Just as in a civilised national state, judgements of law and submission to established procedures are enforced by coercive methods, a world-government may have to restrain the aggressor nations by force. Even then Gāndhi would hold that such a world-government should be able to non-co-operate with law breakers in a non-violent manner as a resisting people can against a tyrannical government.

Gāndhi has expressed in his life and teaching the ancient distinction between the functions of the teacher and the administrator, the Brāhmin and the Kṣatriya, the dreamer and the organiser. The teacher, the prophet, the Hindu *saññyāsin*, the Buddhist monk, the Christian priest, should express unreservedly the truth as they see it. They should abstain from the use of force in any circumstances. They should not kill, for it is their duty to reconcile enemies and expel hate. For them non-violence is the law of life, even in the physical sense of abstaining from the use of force. Their roots go deeper than those of the ordinary run of men, for they draw their strength from the perception of the inner beauty and purpose of things, from the invisible life which lies beyond the life of this world but which alone ennobles and explains it. But the wicked cannot be put down by a mere show of moral goodness unsupported by physical force. Christ on the Cross draws all men to himself, but that culminating act of moral steadfastness unsupported by force did not prevent the crucifixion. Gāndhi's case, along with a few others in history, shows that the highest wisdom is to turn the other cheek, but there is nothing to warrant the assumption that it will not be smitten. Until the whole world is redeemed there will be the soulless, and the maintenance of the social order imposes on us the obligation to execute justice. It must be executed by spiritual persuasion where possible and by the use of force where necessary. While the teachers who accept the monastic discipline arouse us to the divine possibilities of human nature, we should also have judges and police who use force not for its own sake or for their private advantage or from a desire for revenge. They employ force under just authority and are imbued with the spirit of true non-violence or compassion. The distinctions of conduct, the complete abstention from force of the teacher who is educating us in ancient charity and disciplined co-operation and the use of force under just authority by the judges and the police, arise from the distinction of functions. Charity and justice have both a place in the imperfect human society.[7]

IV. MARTYRDOM

Gāndhi has paid the penalty of all who are ahead of their time, misunderstanding, hatred, reaction, violent death. 'The light shineth in darkness and the darkness comprehendeth it not'. The struggle between light and darkness, between love and hate, between reason and unreason, which is at the heart of the cosmic is shown up by this most moving tragedy of our age. We made Socrates drink death; we nailed Jesus to the Cross; we lighted faggots that burnt the mediaeval martyrs. We have stoned and killed our prophets. Gāndhi has not escaped the fate of being misunderstood and hated. He has met his death facing the forces of darkness, of ultimate unreason, and through it has increased the powers of light, love, and reason. Who knows if Christianity would have developed had Jesus not been crucified? Years ago Romain Rolland declared that he regarded Gāndhi as a 'Christ who only lacked the Cross'. We have now given him the Cross also. Gāndhi's death was a classical ending to his life. He died with the name of God on his lips and love in his heart.[8] Even as he received the bullet wounds he greeted his murderer and wished him well. He lived up to what he preached.

Possessed and inspired by the highest ideals of which human nature is capable, preaching and practising fearlessly the truth revealed to him, leading almost alone what seemed to be a forlorn hope against the impregnable strongholds of greed and

[7] See Radhakrishnan, *The Bhagavadgītā* (1948), pp. 68–69.

[8] Cf. Gāndhi's earlier statements, 'The self-sacrifice of one innocent man is a million times more potent than the self-sacrifice of a million men who die in the act of killing others'. 'I hope that there will be non-violent non-co-operators enough in India of whom it will be written "they suffered bullets without anger and with prayer on their lips even for the ignorant murderer"' *Harijan*, February 22, 1948. On January 20, 1948, when a misguided youth threw a bomb, Gāndhi told the Inspector-General of police ' "not to harass him in any way. They should try to win him over and convert him to right thinking and doing. . . ." Gāndhi warned his hearers against being angry with the accused' *Harijan*, February 1, 1948, p. 11.

folly, yet facing tremendous odds with a calm resolution which yielded nothing to ridicule or danger, Gāndhi presented to this unbelieving world all that is noblest in the spirit of man. He illumined human dignity by faith in the eternal significance of man's effort. He belongs to the type that redeems the human race.

If Gāndhi was able to rid himself of all rancour and hatred, to develop that flame of love which burnt up all impurities, if he feared no evil even though he walked in the valley of the shadow of death, if he represented to us the eternal voice of hope, it is because he believed in the heritage of India, the power of the inward life of spirit. When problems material and spiritual crowded upon him, when conflicting emotions shook him, when troubles oppressed him, he retired at will into the retreats of the soul, into the secret corridors of the self to gain strength and refreshment. His life has revived and refreshed our sense of the meaning and value of religion. Such men who are filled with spiritual poise and yet take upon themselves the burden of suffering humanity are born into the world at long intervals.

We have killed his body, but the spirit in him which is a light from above will penetrate far into space and time and inspire countless generations for nobler living.

yad-yad vibhūtimat sattvam
śrīmad ūrjitam eva vā
tat-tad eva'vagaccha tvam
mama tejo aṁśasambhavam

Whatever being there is endowed with glory and grace and vigour, know that to have sprung from a fragment of My splendour.

Bhagavadgītā, X. 41.

Nehru *

FRIENDS: Tomorrow it will be a year since we lost our great leader. He was incomparably the greatest figure after Gāndhi in our history—a man of dynamic force, intellectual power, and profound vision. To these he added a feminine sensitiveness to atmosphere. He spent lavishly his rich and varied gifts for the cause of human freedom. He was involved in the major events of his time, national and international. He participated in them all while maintaining the highest standards of public conduct. Though he is no more with us, the qualities he possessed and the ideals he cherished remain with us.

Nehru had a sense of history. He looked not only to the past but into the future. This endowed him with the vision without which true greatness is not possible. In the Constituent Assembly he said: 'Whether we are men and women of destiny or not, India is a country of destiny'. What is this destiny? Civilisations are kept alive when their values are re-created in men's minds. The principal values of Indian civilisation are the freedom of the human spirit and the unity of mankind.

Nehru was essentially a free being. This freedom is a matter of mind and heart. If the mind is narrow and the heart bitter, there is no freedom, whatever else we may have. No individual is complete until he develops a sense of belonging to humanity. We are human first and foremost and not simply Indian or Chinese, American or Russian, Christian or Jew. At no moment in one's life could one say with certainty, 'I am the whole man; I have reached my fulfilment'. We are never complete. There is always more to come and that more is incalculable.

* Broadcast to the nation, May 26, 1965.

The social and political forms of family and class, race and creed, nation and society are there between the simple unity of man and the supreme unity of mankind; they are artificial, contingent, and transitory, and not absolute. Yet they are valuable in so far as they contribute to the unity of the world, to human fellowship. The growing inter-dependence of nations is upon us. Nations, religions, and races cannot run away from one another, even if they wish to.

We have not lacked thinkers who rose above national feuds and religious clashes and put humanity above everything else. In our own age we had, among others, Tagore, Gāndhi, and Nehru.

Nehru was a student of science and looked upon it as the means for the liberation of man. Science and the understanding it brings are the enemies of prejudice and of inert traditional ideas. Science liberates us from past institutions, from past assumptions, from past binding customs. Science and technology help to establish a free society based on economic justice and opportunities for all, a society which aims at the cultivation of spiritual values, of the spirit of service, of unselfishness. The spread of the scientific outlook and the industrialisation of the country are due, to no small extent, to the influence of Nehru who strove to free the common people from the shackles of poverty, disease, illiteracy, and discrimination. In this endeavour he succeeded to a large extent, though we have yet to wear down our superstitious traditions, break our selfishness, and awaken our social conscience.

Nehru was a deeply spiritual man though he did not uphold any particular form of religion. He sometimes delighted in calling himself a pagan. This only meant that he was opposed to the formal, dogmatic, sectarian aspects of religion. Possessed of a scientific temper, he was interested in the empirical route to Reality. The Ultimate *ānanda* which takes over the other categories of *anna, prāṇa, manas, vijñāna,* is the mystery in the heart of time. In the depths of the spirit is the pathway to the Supreme. Our strength is in the silence where utterance is not and where definition is unknown. A fundamental reticence marks the seers.

anakṣarasya dharmasya śrutiḥ kā deśanā ca kā

God's ways cannot be confined within the human grasp; otherwise we will make God in our own image. Religion is self-discovery, or perhaps recovery. It is the soul's dialogue with itself. Its secret is inwardness, self-scrutiny, inner cleansing, change of heart, renunciation, the unceasing attempt to create through love a new social order. We lived for generations sheltered lives, comfortable, indulgent, and soft. We forgot the everlasting aims that matter for any people, self-respect, dignity, honour, and sacrifice. In each generation we have to earn our heritage through blood, toil, and tears.[1] We have to change the moral climate of our people.

Religion is not an escape from social struggle. Spiritual wisdom and social affairs must be brought into intimate relationship. One cannot be irrelevant to the other. Nehru fought all prejudices with passion and deeply distrusted all absolute philosophies and dogmas. He believed in a priesthood which is spread over all lands and religions, which interprets religion in terms of a 'spiritual' realisation of the Kingdom of God on Earth. He worked for the spread of such a liberal, spiritual religion among the people of India. The communal conflict which disfigured our life gave him acute pain. He strove his utmost to remove the fanaticism which led to communal strife. We must grow out of our slavery to what is called orthodoxy.

If we are to live other than on sufferance, we have to put forth a united national effort. At a time like this when we are threatened by enemies within and without, national unity and discipline are our greatest needs.

The creativity operating within human life commits us to democracy, to the belief in the worth of the individual person.

[1] Nehru observed: 'Fortunately Indian thought, philosophy, can be easily separated from the superstitious and dogmatic part. They are not inextricably intertwined, though for many people they might be. It is not as if you must accept a basic dogma if you are to remain true to your faith. No such thing in India. You can discard every dogma and yet be true to your religion'. Jawaharlal Nehru, Personal Interview, New Delhi, February 25, 1960.

Democracy is not merely a form of government or a code of laws. It is a scheme of life, a set of values and standards. We must defend democracy not merely with our heads but also with our hearts. He who is a fanatic at heart cannot be a true democrat.

Jawaharlal had a deep reverence for parliamentary institutions and he used to attend Parliament as his first duty. Though sometimes he was irritated by the heated behaviour and crude personal attacks of some members, he never lost respect for parliamentary institutions. He was deeply hurt by the activities of a few demagogues who tried to reduce democracy to mob rule but he never lost hope for the future of democracy in India. Plato told us centuries ago: 'The penalty that good men pay for refusing to take part in government is to live under the government of bad men'. Nehru wished us to be forward-looking and imaginative and to dream and make a new India based on freedom for all people and equality of opportunity for all. It is our duty to treat the parliamentary institutions with dignity and do nothing which is likely to impair their proper functioning. This does not mean that all our opinions are to be regimented. We have a right to disagree; only the disagreements will have to be honest.

While Nehru had a versatile, penetrating, and gracious mind, this did not exclude a tender heart. He loved life and was a man of intense feeling. He never lacked compassion for others. He was free from the cant, squeamishness, hypocrisy, and self-deception of many people in regard to human relations. When complaints reached him about the misdemeanours of people, he took a tolerant view and made allowance for the credulity of the mind, the vulnerability of the heart, and the discursiveness of human nature. He understood frustrated, unhappy neurotics who found themselves incapable of facing up to the standards and restraints of the social order. He would not judge human beings by stripping them of their humanity. This attitude is not the result of a simple naiveness or a strange innocence but of deep humility and gentle understanding of human nature. In the name of preserving the standards of society which have come down to us, we sometimes make ourselves responsible for many personal tragedies. No social institutions are too venerable for change. We are in the midst of a world revolution which affects every aspect of our life. Industrial development, educational progress, social and physical mobility of peoples, improved standards of living, and opportunities for all individuals, these compel radical changes.

Gāndhi and Nehru raised the status of women in the social, political, economic, and educational fields though we have yet a long way to go.

Nehru was essentially a man of peace. He hated war not as an abstraction but for what it did to man. He loathed the instincts of fear and hatred which caused wars, the suffering it inflicted and the degradation of values it resulted in. Weapons of defence have now become weapons of universal destruction. Nehru understood the facts and implications of nuclear weapons. He worked for the abolition of nuclear weapons which meant death to millions and disease to more. Nuclear war is a catastrophe in which every one loses; ending the threat of war is a victory for mankind. Peace was Nehru's passion and he believed that it was essential for the growth of humanity.

This world is today a madhouse where individuals exaggerate their racial superiority, religious pride, or national egotism, and thus become the victims of moral and spiritual blindness. If violence, which is a cowardly escape from the rule of reason, is rampant, the answer to it is the growth of decency and compassion. We have to view the world as one whole, a single community, a fellowship of human beings who have the same instincts of hunger and sex, the same aspirations of generosity and fellow-feeling, the same faith in the Unseen. We are marching towards this goal of a world community in spite of blind alleys and setbacks.

Nehru tried to apply ethical principles to political problems. Under his guidance, India took a leading part in the peace-keeping operations of the United Nations—in Korea, Gaza, and the Congo. He was acknowledged to be a leader of the uncommitted and emerging nations of the world. He tried to prevent the division of the world into two warring camps. Non-alignment is not moral indifference. It is to keep the doors open for talks however aggrieved or angry we may be.

The great powers must learn to live together in peace and friendly co-operation.

Limitless is human folly in politics. When some years ago T. S. Eliot was asked about the future of our civilisation, he said, 'Internecine fighting . . . people killing one another in the streets'.[2] Civilisation seemed to him a crumbling edifice destined to fall to pieces and perish in the flames of war. This despair of life cannot be the end of things. The tragedy of the human condition imposes on us the opportunity and the obligation to give meaning and significance to life, to develop human dignity and work for the future and believe in the young. This is the cause we have to serve and the cause which must win if humanity worth the name is to survive.

There is a moral force, which, as the human race advances, more and more strengthens and protects those who possess it. If we allow the moral force which our country has long exerted, especially in the period of Gāndhiji, to become diminished, or perhaps even destroyed for the sake of the costly, dangerous military apparatus, we take a fatal risk. The nuclear developments have changed everything except our ways of thinking and acting. We have to make a great effort to transform our minds and social conditions.

We have to remember on this first anniversary of Nehru's passing away that humanity is one and our commitment to humanity requires sacrifices of our personal prejudices and national passions. The road ahead is long, difficult, and dangerous but the breath of spring is in the air. Jawaharlal taught us to be courageous and unafraid. 'I am not afraid of the future. I have no fear in my mind, and I have no fear, even though India, from a military point of view, is of no great consequence. I am not afraid of the bigness of Great Powers, and their armies, their fleets and their atom bombs. That is the lesson which my Master taught me. We stood as an unarmed people against a great country and a powerful empire. We were supported and strengthened, because throughout all this period we decided not to submit to evil. . . . I think if we banish this fear, if we have confidence, even though we may take risks of trust rather than risk violent language, violent

[2] *Encounter*, April, 1965, p. 8.

actions and in the end war, I think those risks are worth taking'.[3]

This most lovable and magnanimous of men is an earnest of the age to come, the age of world men with world compassion. The best way to honour his memory is to get on with the work which he left unfinished, his work for peace, justice, and freedom at home and abroad.

[3] Speech to the United Nations General Assembly, Paris, November 3, 1948.

Religion and Religions *

Sectarian divisions. The Report on the *Conversion of England* deplores the unhappy divisions, the lack of charity among particular congregations, which obscure the fellowship of the Christian Church and calls upon the different Christian sects to continue and co-operate in the task of the conversion of England. It asks us to adopt the principle of unity in variety, which is not only a profound spiritual truth but the most obvious sense.

The need for comprehension. If we accept this principle seriously we cannot stop at the frontiers of Christianity. We must move along a path which shall pass beyond all the differences of the historical past and eventually be shared in common by all mankind. Belief in exclusive claims and monopolies of religious truth has been a frequent source of pride, fanaticism, and strife. The vehemence with which religions were preached and the savagery with which they were enforced are some of the disgraces of human history. Secularism and paganism point to the rivalries of religions for a proof of the futility of religion. A little less missionary ardour, a little more enlightened scepticism will do good to us all. Our attitude to other religions should be defined in the spirit of that great saying in a play of Sophocles, where Antigone says, 'I was not born to share men's hatred, but their love'. We must learn the basic principles of the great world religions as the essential means of promoting international understanding.

* From "Fragments of a Confession," ed. Paul Arthur Schilpp (New York: Tudor Publishing Company, 1952), pp. 72–82. Now published by The Open Court Publishing Company, La Salle, Illinois.

Besides, Whitehead observes that 'the decay of Christianity and Buddhism as determinative influences in modern thought is partly due to the fact that each religion has unduly sheltered itself from the other. They have remained self-satisfied and unfertilised'. A study of other living religions helps and enhances the appreciation of our own faith. If we adopt a wider historical view we obtain a more comprehensive vision and understanding of spiritual truth. Christian thinkers like St. Thomas Aquinas were willing to find confirmation of the truths of Christianity in the works of pagan philosophers. We live in a world which is neither Eastern nor Western, where every one of us is the heir to all civilisation. The past of China, Japan, and India is as much our past as is that of Israel, Greece, and Rome. It is our duty and privilege to enlarge our faculties of curiosity, of understanding, and realise the spaciousness of our common ground. No way of life is uninteresting so long as it is natural and satisfying to those who live it. We may measure true spiritual culture by the comprehension and veneration we are able to give to all forms of thought and feeling which have influenced masses of mankind. We must understand the experience of people whose thought eludes our categories. We must widen our religious perspective and obtain a world wisdom worthy of our time and place.

Religious provincialism stands in the way of a unitary world culture which is the only enduring basis for a world community. 'Shall two walk together except they have agreed'? To neglect the spiritual unity of the world and underline the religious diversity would be philosophically unjustifiable, morally indefensible, and socially dangerous.

The arrogant dislike of other religions has to-day given place to respectful incomprehension. It is time that we accustom ourselves to fresh ways of thinking and feeling. The interpenetration of obstinate cultural traditions is taking place before our eyes. If we have a sense of history we will find that human societies are by nature unstable. They are ever on the move giving place to new ones. Mankind is still in the making. The new world society requires a new world outlook based on respect for and understanding of other cultural traditions.

Religious education. The procedure suggested here provides us with a basis for inter-religious understanding and co-operation. It involves an abandonment of missionary enterprises such as they are now. The 'compassing of sea and land to make one proselyte' is not possible when our ignorance of other peoples' faiths is removed. The main purpose of religious education is not to train others in our way of thinking and living, not to substitute one form of belief for another, but to find out what others have been doing and help them to do it better. We are all alike in need of humility and charity, of repentance and conversion, of a change of mind, of a turning round. The missionary motives are derived from the conviction of the absolute superiority of our own religion and of supreme contempt for other religions. They are akin to the political motives of imperialist countries to impose their culture and civilisation on the rest of the world. If missionary activities such as they are now are persisted in, they will become a prime factor in the spiritual impoverishment of the world. They are treason against Him who 'never left himself without a witness'. St. Justin said: 'God is the word of whom the whole human race are partakers, and those who lived according to Reason are Christians even though accounted atheists . . . Socrates and Heracleitus, and of the barbarians, Abraham and many others'. St. Ambrose's well-known gloss on I Corinthians 3:3, 'all that is true, by whomsoever it has been said, is from the Holy Ghost', is in conformity with the ancient tradition of India on this matter. 'As men approach me, so I do accept them, men on all sides follow my path' says the *Bhagavadgītā*. 'If the follower of any particular religion understood the saying of Junayd, "The colour of the water is the colour of the vessel containing it", he would not interfere with the beliefs of others, but would perceive God in every form and in every belief', says ibn-ul-'Arabi. Our aim should be not to make converts, Christians into Buddhists or Buddhists into Christians, but enable both Buddhists and Christians to rediscover the basic principles of their own religions and live up to them.

Progress in religions. Every religion is attempting to reformulate its faith in accordance with modern thought and criticism. Stagnant and stereotyped religions are at variance with the psychology of modern life. If, in the name of religion, we insist on teaching much that modern knowledge has proved to be untrue, large numbers will refuse to accept devitalised doctrines. Aware of this danger, religions are emphasising the essential principles and ideals rather than the dogmatic schemes. For example, the moral and spiritual truths of Christianity, faith in the Divine Being, in the manifestation of the spiritual and moral nature of the Divine in the personality of Jesus, one of the eldest of many brothers, faith that we can receive strength and guidance by communion with the Divine, are regarded as more important than beliefs in the miraculous birth, resurrection, ascension, and the return of Jesus as the judge of mankind at the end of human history. The *Report of the Commission on Christian Doctrine* appointed by the Archbishops of Canterbury and York, made it permissible for the English Churchmen to hold and to teach the Christian faith in accordance with the verified results of modern scientific, historical, and literary criticism. Other religions are also attempting to cast off the unessentials and return to the basic truths. Whereas the principles of religions are eternal, their expressions require continual development. The living faiths of mankind carry not only the inspiration of centuries but also the encrustations of error. Religion is a 'treasure in earthen vessels' (St. Paul). These vessels are capable of infinite refashioning and the treasure itself of renewed application in each succeeding age of human history. The profound intuitions of religions require to be presented in fresh terms more relevant to our own experience, to our own predicament. If religion is to recover its power, if we are to help those who are feeling their way and are longing to believe, a restatement is essential. It is a necessity of the time. 'I have many things to say unto you, but ye cannot bear them now; when he, the Spirit of

Truth, is come, he will guide you into all the truth'.[1] Every religion is growing under the inspiration of the Divine Spirit of Truth in order to meet the moral and spiritual ordeal of the modern mind. This process of growth is securing for our civilisation a synthesis on the highest level of the forces of religion and culture and enabling their followers to co-operate as members of one great fellowship.

Fellowship, not fusion. The world is seeking not so much a fusion of religions as a fellowship of religions, based on the realisation of the foundational character of man's religious experience. William Blake says: 'As all men are alike (though infinitely various), so all Religions, as all similars, have one source'. The different religions may retain their individualities, their distinctive doctrines and characteristic pieties, so long as they do not impair the sense of spiritual fellowship. The light of eternity would blind us if it came full in the face. It is broken into colours so that our eyes can make something of it. The different religious traditions clothe the one Reality in various images and their visions could embrace and fertilise each other so as to give mankind a many-sided perfection, the spiritual radiance of Hinduism, the faithful obedience of Judaism, the life of beauty of Greek Paganism, the noble compassion of Buddhism, the vision of divine love of Christianity, and the spirit of resignation to the sovereign lord of Islam. All these represent different aspects of the inward spiritual life, projections on the intellectual plane of the ineffable experiences of the human spirit.

If religion is the awareness of our real nature in God, it makes for a union of all mankind based on communion with the Eternal. It sees in all the same vast universal need it has felt in itself. The different religions take their source in the aspiration of man towards an unseen world, though the forms in which this aspiration is couched are determined by the environment and climate of thought. The unity of religions is to be found in that which is divine or universal in them and not in what is temporary and local. Where there is the spirit of truth

[1] John 16:12f.

there is unity. As in other matters, so in the sphere of religion there is room for diversity and no need for discord. To claim that any one religious tradition bears unique witness to the truth and reveals the presence of the true God is inconsistent with belief in a living God who has spoken to men 'by diverse portions and in diverse manners'. God is essentially self-communicative and is of ungrudging goodness, as Plato taught.[2] There is no such thing as a faith once for all delivered to the saints. Revelation is divine-human. As God does not reveal His Being to a stone or a tree, but only to men, His revelation is attuned to the state of the human mind. The Creative Spirit is ever ready to reveal Himself to the seeking soul provided the search is genuine and the effort intense. The authority for revelation is not an Infallible book or an Infallible Church but the witness of the inner light. What is needed is not submission to an external authority but inward illumination which, of course, is tested by tradition and logic. If we reflect on the matter deeply we will perceive the unity of spiritual aspiration and endeavour underlying the varied upward paths indicated in the different world faiths. The diversity in the traditional formulations tends to diminish as we climb up the scale of spiritual perfection. All the paths of ascent lead to the mountain top. This convergent tendency and the remarkable degree of agreement in the witness of those who reach the mountain top are the strongest proof of the truth of religion.

Different traditions of religion. Religious life belongs to the realm of inward spiritual revelation; when exteriorised it loses its authentic character. It is misleading to speak of different religions. We have different religious traditions which can be used for correction and enrichment. The traditions do not create the truth but clothe it in language and symbol for the help of those who do not see it themselves. They symbolise the mystery of the spirit and urge us to move from external significations, which reflect the imperfect state of our consciousness and social environment, to the thing signified. The symbolic character of tradition is not to be mistaken for reality.

[2] *Timaeus*, 29B.

These are second-hand notions which fortify and console us so long as we do not have direct experience. Our different traditions are versions in a series, part of the historical and relative world in which we live and move. If we cling to these historically conditioned forms as absolute they will not rescue us from slavery to the momentary and the contingent. They leave us completely immersed in the relative. It does not mean that there is nothing central or absolute in religion. The unchanging substance of religion is the evolution of man's consciousness. The traditions help to take us to the truth above all traditions and of which the traditions are imperfect, halting expressions. If we love truth as such and not our opinions, if we desire nothing except what is true and acceptable to God, the present religious snobbery and unfriendliness will disappear. If we open ourselves up unreservedly to the inspirations of our age, we will get to the experience of the one Spirit which takes us beyond the historical formulations. Averroes, the Arab philosopher, distinguished between philosophic truth (*secundum rationem*) and religious views (*secundum fidem*). No single religion possesses truth compared with philosophic knowledge, though each religious view may claim to possess a fragment of the truth. 'Yet every priest values his own creed as the fool his cap and bells'. Our quarrels will cease if we know that the one truth is darkened and diversified in the different religions. If we are to remove the present disordered, divided state of the world, we have to adopt what William Law called

> a catholic spirit, a communion of saints in the love of God and all goodness, which no one can learn from that which is called orthodoxy in particular churches, but is only to be had by a total dying to all worldly views, by a pure love of God and by such an unction from above as delivers the mind from all selfishness and makes it love truth and goodness with an equality of affection in every man, whether he is Christian, Jew or Gentile.

William Law says also;

> The chief hurt of a sect is this, that it takes itself to be necessary to the truth, whereas the truth is only then

> found when it is known to be of no sect but as free and universal as the goodness of God and as common to all names and nations as the air and light of this world.

Maitrī Upaniṣad says:

> Some contemplate one name and some another. Which of these is the best? All are eminent clues to the transcendent, immortal, unembodied Brahman; these names are to be contemplated, lauded and at last denied. For by them one rises higher and higher in these worlds; but where all comes to its end, there he attains to the unity of the Person.

In the midst of the travail in which we are living we discern the emergence of the religion of the Spirit, which will be the crown of the different religions, devoted to the perfecting of humanity in the life of the spirit, that is, in the life of God in the soul. When God is our teacher, we come to think alike.

Freedom from dogma. The thought of the Upaniṣads, the humanism of Confucius, the teaching of the Buddha are marked by the comparative absence of dogma, and their followers are, therefore, relatively free from the evils of obscurantism and casuistry. This is due to the fact that there is greater emphasis in them on the experience of Spirit. Those whose experience is deepest do not speak of it because they feel that it is inexpressible. They feel that they are breaking, dividing, and betraying the experience by giving utterance to it. By their attitude of silence they affirm the primacy of Being over knowledge with the latter's distinction of subject and object. In the deepest spiritual experience we are not self-conscious. When we describe it, it is by way of second reflection, in which we turn the inward presence into an object of thought. We take care to observe that the truth goes beyond the traditional forms. Ruysbroeck says about the reality known by the seer: 'We can speak no more of Father, Son and Holy Spirit, nor of any creature, but only of one Being, which is the very substance of the Divine Persons. There were we all one before our creation, for this is our super-essence. There the Godhead is in simple essence without activity'. A devout Catholic of the Counter-Reformation period, J. J. Olier, observes: 'The holy light of faith is so pure, that compared with it, particular lights are but impurities: and even ideas of the saints, of the Blessed Virgin and the sight of Jesus Christ in his humanity are impediments in the way of the sight of God in His purity'. When the seers try to communicate their vision in greater detail they use the tools put into their hands by their cultural milieu. Jesus interprets his experience in terms of notions current in contemporary Jewish thought. We perhaps owe the doctrine of the world's imminent dissolution to the Jewish circle of ideas. So long as we are on earth we cannot shake off the historical altogether.

The mystery of spiritual life. Sometimes we exteriorise the mystery of spiritual life. Religions which believe in the reality of spiritual life interpret the dogmas with reference to it. Religious views are not so much attempts to solve the riddle of the universe as efforts to describe the experience of sages. The concepts are verbalisations of intense emotional experience. They are lifted out of their true empiricism and made historical rather than experimental, objective instead of profound inward realisation. Christ is born in the depths of spirit. We say that he passes through life, dies on the Cross, and rises again. These are not so much historical events which occurred once upon a time as universal processes of spiritual life, which are being continually accomplished in the souls of men. Those who are familiar with the way in which the Kṛishna story is interpreted will feel inclined to regard Christhood as an attainment of the soul; a state of inward glorious illumination in which the divine wisdom has become the heritage of the soul. The annunciation is a beautiful experience of the soul. It relates to the birth of Christhood in the soul, 'the holy thing begotten within'. The human soul from the Holy Breath, *Devakī* or *daivī prakṛti,* divine nature is said to be the mother of Kṛishṇa. Mary, the mother of the Christ child, is the soul in her innermost divine nature. Whatever is conceived in the womb of the human soul is always of the Holy Spirit.

Universal religion. The mandate of religion is that man must make the change in his own nature in order to let the divine in him manifest itself. It speaks of the death of man as we know him with all his worldly desires and the emergence of the new man. This is the teaching not only of the Upaniṣads and Buddhism but also of the Greek mysteries and Platonism, of the Gospels and the schools of Gnosticism. This is the wisdom to which Plotinus refers, when he says, 'This doctrine is not new; it was professed from the most ancient times though without being developed explicitly; we wish only to be interpreters of the ancient sages, and to show by the evidence of Plato himself that they had the same opinions as ourselves'.[3] This is the religion which Augustine mentions in his well-known statement: 'That which is called the Christian Religion existed among the Ancients, and never did not exist, from the beginning of the human race until Christ came in the flesh, at which time the true religion, which already existed, began to be called Christianity'.[4] This truth speaks to us in varying dialects across far continents and over centuries of history. Those who overlook this perennial wisdom, the eternal religion behind all religions, this *sanātana dharma*, this timeless tradition, 'wisdom uncreate, the same now that it ever was, and the same to be forevermore',[5] and cling to the outward forms and quarrel among themselves, are responsible for the civilised chaos in which we live. It is our duty to get back to this central core of religion, this fundamental wisdom which has been obscured and distorted in the course of history by dogmatic and sectarian developments.

At the level of body and mind, physique and temperament, talents and tastes, we are profoundly unlike one another; but at the deepest level of all, that of the spirit which is the true ground of our being, we are like one another. If religion is to become an effective force in human affairs, if it is to serve as the basis for the new world order, it must become more inward and more universal, a flame which cleanses our inward being and so cleanses the world. For such a religion the historical ex-

[3] *Enneads* V, 1.8.

[4] *Librum de verà religione*, Chapter 10.

[5] St. Augustine.

pressions of spiritual truth and the psychological idioms employed by religions to convey the universal truth cease to be rocks of offence. The barriers dividing men will break down and the reunion and integration of all, what the Russians call *sobornost,* an altogetherness in which we walk together creatively and to which we all contribute, a universal church will be established. Then will the cry of St. Joan in Bernard Shaw's epilogue to that play be fulfilled: 'O God that madest this beautiful earth, when will it be ready to receive thy saints'? Then will come a time when the world will be inhabited by a race of men, with no flaw of flesh or error of mind, freed from the yoke not only of disease and privation but of lying words and of love turned into hate. When human beings grow into completeness, into that invisible world which is the kingdom of heaven, then will they manifest in the outer world the kingdom which is within them. That day we shall cease to set forth God dogmatically or dispute about his nature but leave each man to worship God in the sanctuary of his heart, to feel after him and to possess him.

While I never felt attracted to travelling for its own sake, I have travelled a great deal and lived in places far from home, in England and France, America and Russia. For some years, I have spent long periods in England and the qualities of the English people such as their love of justice, their hatred of doctrinairism, their sympathy for the underdog, made an impression on me. All Souls College, which has provided a second home for me all these years, has given me an insight into English intellectual life with its caution and stability, confidence and adventure. Whatever one may feel about the character of the Russian Government, the people there are kindly and human and their lives are filled as anywhere else with jokes and jealousies, loves and hates. Though I have not been able to take root in any of these foreign countries, I have met many, high and low, and learned to feel the human in them. There are no fundamental differences among the peoples of the world. They have all the deep human feelings, the craving for justice above all class interests, horror of bloodshed and violence. They are working for a religion which teaches the possibility and the nccessity of man's union with himself, with nature, with his fellow-men, and with the Eternal Spirit of which the visible universe is but a manifestation and upholds the emergence of a complete consciousness as the destiny of man. Our historical religions will have to transform themselves into the universal faith or they will fade away. This prospect may appear strange and unwelcome to some, but it has a truth and beauty of its own. It is working in the minds of men and will soon be a realised fact. Human unity depends not on past origins but on future goal and direction, on what we are becoming and whither we are tending. Compared with the civilisation that is now spreading over the earth's surface, thanks to science and technology, the previous civilisations were restricted in scope and resources. Scientists claim that organic life originated on this planet some twelve hundred million years ago, but man has come into existence on earth during the last half million years. His civilisation has been here only for the last ten thousand years. Man is yet in his infancy and has a long period ahead of him on this planet. He will work out a higher integration and produce world-minded men and women.

The eternal religion, outlined in these pages, is not irrational or unscientific, is not escapist or a-social. Its acceptance will solve many of our desperate problems and will bring peace to men of good will.

This is the personal philosophy which by different paths I have attained, a philosophy which has served me in the severest tests, in sickness and in health, in triumph and in defeat. It may not be given to us to see that the faith prevails; but it is given to us to strive that it should.

Creative Religion *

While Europe is threatened with new dangers, Asia and Africa are being transformed by the impact on them of Western ideas and technical skill. The world is becoming increasingly interconnected and cultures and civilisations are mingling. To think that any one way of life is the only way seems to be the height of egocentricity. The different geniuses of the people need not be reduced to a dead level of uniformity. They reveal different qualities. Our task is not to displace one way of life by another but to share the treasures of which each is the guardian.

There are no fundamental distinctions between the East and the West. Each one of us is both Eastern and Western. East and West are not two historical and geographical concepts. They are two possibilities which every man in every age carries within himself, two movements of the human spirit. There is tension in the nature of man between his scientific and religious impulses. This tension or tumult is not a disaster but a challenge and an opportunity.

Each one of us is both religious and rational. There have been outstanding scientific contributions from the East and notable religious gifts from the West. At best it is only a difference of emphasis. Mind and spirit are both qualities of human nature. They have not yet attained an equilibrium. There is today a schism in the soul between mind and spirit. A society is stable when its different components, economic and political, cultural and social, are in harmony. If these elements fall into discord, the social order disintegrates.

* From *East and West* (New York: Harper and Brothers, 1956), pp. 120–131.

The hopeful and the distressing features of our age are world-wide and not peculiar to the East or the West. If the purpose of the world is to be realised, all nations require to go through a process of inner renewal. World unity cannot be achieved only through the United Nations Organisation and its agencies. Local solutions are not enough. Everything hangs together. Only total peace can prevent total war. There is the religious view for which the East has stood, and which is not unknown in the West, that man with his sense of values is the most concrete embodiment of the divine on earth. This view has suffered from a misunderstanding of the spirit of science which has resulted in the intellectual devastation of spiritual life, the drying out of creative energies.

Great spiritual revivals occur through the fusion of different traditions. In Clement's metaphor the Christian Church itself was the confluence of two rivers, the Hellenistic and the Jewish. The impact of Christianity converted the disintegrating Graeco-Roman world into a new community. The common enclosure of all beings in space and time, through the occupation of the earth's surface gives us the physical basis and makes possible the unity of mankind. This latter is not a fact but a task. The diffusion of ideas and implements is making for intellectual unity. But human solidarity and coherence are possible only through the radiant moments of the profound revelations of spirit which work like a ferment in the course of history. They constitute the goal and justification of the human endeavour for world coherence. The meeting of East and West today may produce a spiritual renaissance and a world community that is struggling to be born.

The present conditions of the world, the universal acceptance of the scientific method, studies in comparative religion, the challenge of world unity are producing in all religions a movement of religious creativity. Progressive thinkers of different faiths are getting together in a common endeavour to realise the good life through truth and love. The world is groping not for the narrow, stunted religion of the dogmatic schools, not one of fanaticism that is afraid of the light but for a creative spiritual religion. It should not be inconsistent with the spirit of science. It should foster humanist ideals and make for world unity.

A true understanding of science supports a religion of spirit. Science is not an entirely self-moving process or an unconscious instrument of historical change. The development of science is due to the genius of the individual who has knowledge, skill, and values. Man is not master of the universe because he can split the atom. He can split the atom because he has that in him which is far superior to the atom. The material achievements stand as witnesses to what the human spirit can accomplish. Again, these achievements are the outcome of severe mental and moral discipline, disinterested devotion to truth, a spirit of dedication as well as creative imagination.

The conflict between science and religion is due to historical circumstances. In the past scientists have suffered from religious and political tyrannies. Giordano Bruno was burnt at the stake, Galileo was imprisoned and threatened and even today scientists are discouraged by threats of political inquisition or moral ostracism from speaking the truth. If the release of nuclear energy is not welcomed as opening a new era in man's mastery of nature and its powers for the common good but is looked upon as a new threat to mankind, it is because of the overpowering influence of nationalist dogmas. Scientists must stand against all tyranny, determined to preserve the integrity of science and prevent its perversion from its proper beneficent use, and save civilisation from misusing science for its own destruction. God is truth and the service of truth is the service of God.

Both religion and science affirm the unity of nature. The central assumption of science is the intuition of religion that nature is intelligible. When we study the processes of nature we are impressed by their order and harmony and are led to a belief in the divine reality. St. Thomas put it, 'By considering what God has made we can—first of all—catch a glimpse of the divine wisdom which has in some measure impressed a certain likeness to itself upon them'. We should see in the order and constancy, the beauty and pattern of nature, the divine wisdom and not in the exceptional and the bizarre. To suggest that the whole course of history is bound up with some unique event which happened at one time and in one place in a universe which has had nearly six thousand million years of existence may strain the scientific conscience of even ordinary people. Heaven mingles with earth from the very start.

Goethe tells us that Faust investigated all branches of human knowledge, found no answers that would satisfy him and reached the place of *nothing* in his quest for truth. He exclaims: 'And here I am at last, a very fool, with useless learning curst, no wiser than at first'. His learning proves useless, his quest meaningless. He is faced with despair. He opens an ancient book and his eyes fall on the seal of Solomon—the two triangles placed upside down, signifying the interpenetration of lower and higher nature. A change comes over him and he exclaims: 'Ha, what new life divine, intense, floods in a moment every sense. I feel the dawn of youth again. . . . Was it a God who wrote these signs?' Earth and heaven are intermingled. He has a new understanding of the visible world. Even at the moment when his journey had led him to darkness, a new light is revealed.

Science is empirical; it is non-dogmatic. It is open-minded. Religious truths which are commended to us should not be mixed up with incredible dogmas. They must be based on experience, not of the physical world but of the religious reality. Even the concepts of science acquire their validity in experience. Experience is not limited to perceptual experience or the data of introspection. It should take into account para-normal phenomena and spiritual insights.

If scientific truth is what works in experience, religious truth also can be put to the same test. If we take the raw material of human nature and process it through detachment, humility, and love, knowledge of God is attained. Religious exercises are intended to produce religious results. Albert Schweitzer observes: 'Rational thinking which is free from assumptions ends in mysticism'.

The Eastern emphasis on religion as experience or life is being increasingly accepted by the religious people of all denominations. It is not faith but works that are needed. Not all those who say Lord, Lord, but those who do the will of God. Talmud has it: 'Would that they had forgotten my name and done that which I commanded of them'. The utterly superficial character of our religious faith was given a practical demonstration in World War II when adherents of religions dragged themselves down to incredible depths.

To conform to the will of the Supreme, personal sanctification is necessary. The flame of spirit must be kindled in each human soul. 'Thus saith the Lord God . . . I will put a new spirit within you; and I will take the stony heart out of their flesh and will give them an heart of flesh'. The way to this spiritual change is through detachment which develops the qualities of truth and honesty, chastity and sobriety, mercy and forgiveness. So long as we are dominated by our own passions and desires we will flout our neighbour, never leave him in peace, build institutions and societies which mirror our violent impulses, aggression, and greed. The change from self-centredness to God-centredness brings with it a peace and radiance of living. We reach the deepest vision into the nature of the Real by devotion, contemplation, and detachment. The basic element in religion is not the intellectual acceptance of dogmatic principles or historic events. These are but the preparation for the experience which affects our entire being, which ends our disquiet, our anguish, the sense of the aimlessness of our fragile and fugitive existence. St. Ambrose says 'Not by dialectic did it please the Lord God to save His people'. Religion is not mere contemplation of the truth but suffering for it. The human mind is sadly crippled in its religious thinking by the belief that truth has been found, embodied, standardised, and nothing remains for man to do but to reproduce feebly some precious features of an immutable perfection. Such a view of rationalistic self-sufficiency overlooks the quality of religion as spiritual adventure. In the Eastern religions, the fulfilment of man's life is an experience in which every aspect of his being is raised to its highest extent. We pass from darkness to light. We feel caught up in a universal purpose. Our being is integrated, our solitude is ended. We are no longer the victims of the world around us but its masters. Every religious seer from the moment he has the vision and is moved to the depths of his being launches on a new path. The Buddha or Jesus is a redeemer or saviour only in so far as he calls upon us to be born anew. In their life and teaching they set us examples of conversion whereby we break the bonds that are laid on us by our first birth and by nature and rise above our original imperfection. When our consciousness is raised above the normal, when *meta-noia* occurs, we apprehend the unknowable and experience a joy so extreme that no language is adequate to describe the ravishment of the soul, when it meets in its own depths the ground of its own life and of all reality.

This awareness of Absolute Being which the seers speak of is ineffable. The Ineffable which we encounter can be *shown* but not said, in the words of Ludwig Wittgenstein.[1] Whitehead has some excellent words on this subject: 'It is characteristic of the learned mind to exalt words. Yet mothers can ponder many things which their lips cannot express. These many things which are thus known constitute the ultimate religious evidence beyond which there is no appeal'.[2] When the experience is communicated through symbols, there is variety in the latter which are shaped by the knowledge and beliefs of the seers. The basic experience is, however, the same whether we deal with Hindu, Buddhist, Christian, and Sufi mystics. The late Dean Inge said that 'whatever their creed, date or nationality, the witness of the mystics is wonderfully unanimous'.[3]

When the integral insight or the experience of the whole self is interpreted for purposes of communication by intellectual symbols, the latter are only symbolic. Eternity cannot be translated fully into categories of time, awareness of being cannot be adequately expressed in terms of existence, in spatio-temporal symbols. Yet they are not unrelated. Some of the religious ideas are results of profound insight. The symbols and images are used as aids to the worship of God, though they are not objects of worship themselves.

When we frame theories of religion we turn the being of the soul into the having of a thing. We transform what originally comprehended our being into some object which we ourselves comprehend. The total experience becomes an item of knowledge. The notions of God formed by men are not God Him-

[1] *Tractatus Logico-Philosophicus*, E.T. 56. 522, p. 187.
[2] *Religion in the Making*, p. 67.
[3] *The Philosophy of Plotinus*, Vol. II, p. 143.

self. The theories of God are tested by the facts or experiences of religion which prompted them. We should not take them as final and universally binding.

The Absolute which is beyond the distinctions of subject and object, as the divine subject illumines the plane of cosmic objectivation, sustains and absorbs it. The world which science studies is the revelation of spirit. All nature and life are sacramental.

When we say that God wills this world, it does not mean that His will is capricious. It only suggests that universal possibility is limitless and unpredictable. It also means that the created world cannot assume an absolute character. Were it so, then the relative would be absolute. Even as human beings are conformed to God, made in His image—otherwise they would not exist—the world is the reflection of God. Even as we are different from God, the world is different from God.

Love of neighbour is taught by all religions but the capacity to love is difficult to attain. Growth in spiritual life is the only force which gives us the capacity to love our neighbour, even when we are not naturally inclined to do so. In the Epistle of St. James, it says: 'Whence come wars and fightings among you? Come they not hence, even of your desires, that war in your members'. Conflicting desires within men lead to strains and conflicts among men. We must be at harmony within ourselves. The words of St. Teresa are full of meaning. 'Christ has no body now on earth but yours; yours are the feet with which He goes about doing good; yours are the hands with which He blesses'. William Law, the great eighteenth-century mystic said: 'By love I do not mean any natural tenderness, which is more or less in people according to their constitution; but I mean a larger principle of soul, founded in reason and piety which makes us tender, kind and gentle to all our fellow creatures as creatures of God and for His sake'. This world has long suffered and bled from religious intolerance. Even the political intolerance of our time which has become as despotic, as universal, and as bitter as any religious conflict has assumed a religious garb reminding us of the Crusades of the Middle Ages. The motive that impelled the Christian armies to march eastward was faith. But sincerity of faith is not a security against wild intolerance. The Crusaders thought that they were fighting for the Christian God against the Muslim God. They could not conceive it to be possible that the God of Islam might be the same God on whom they themselves relied.[4] All too often men feel that their loyalty to their religious society absolves them from the restraints they would impose on their private actions. We become ambitious not for ourselves but for our religious organisations. The phenomenon is described by William Law as 'turning to God without turning from self'. All the lusts and prejudices of the heart are retained but identified with some supposedly religious cause. 'Pride, self-exaltation, hatred and persecution, under a cloak of religious zeal will sanctify actions which nature, left to itself, would be ashamed to own'. We are prepared to burn and torture in the name of the love of God. Mankind seems to be involved in a corporate system of evil to which it seems to be in bondage. It appears as though some monster had taken charge of it, which possesses men and situations, making the best endeavours of honest men and using their good impulses for evil purposes. If God is love, He cannot be a jealous God. With the jealous God goes the doctrine of the chosen people. If God's light is the light that lighteth every man that He left not Himself without witness, the adherents of religions other than our own are not shut out from the love of God. There are alternative approaches to the mystery of God.

At its depth, religion in its silences and expressions is the same. There is a common ground on which the different religious traditions rest. This common ground belongs of right

[4] The historian of the Crusades, Mr. Steven Runciman, concludes his account with very significant words which have a bearing on the contemporary world situation: 'In the long sequence of interaction and fusion between Orient and Occident out of which our civilisation has grown, the Crusades were a tragic and destructive episode. The historian, as he gazes back across the centuries, must find his admiration overcast by sorrow at the witness that it bears to the limitations of human nature. There was so much courage and so little honour, so much devotion and so little understanding. High ideals were besmirched by cruelty and greed, enterprise and endurance by a blind and narrow self-righteousness; and the Holy War itself was nothing more than a long act of intolerance in the name of God, which is the sin against the Holy Ghost'. *A History of the Crusades*, Vol. III (1954), p. 480.

to all of us, as it has its source in the non-historical, the eternal. The same elements appear in the experiences of the seers of the different religions. We all seek the same goal under different banners. When we get across the frontiers of formulas and the rigidities of regulations, the same spiritual life is to be found. The universality of fundamental ideas which historical studies demonstrate is the hope of the future. It emphasises the profound truth which Eastern religions had always stressed, the transcendent unity underlying the empirical diversity of religions.

There have been in the Christian world too, many profound thinkers who did not believe in spiritual exclusiveness. Nicholas of Cusa was prepared to recognise elements of truth in non-Christian religions. According to him Christianity should give as well as receive. He believed in the *coincidentia oppositorum,* i.e., everything lives and takes effect by reason of being the point of intersection of two opposite forces. God is all-embracing infinity and is found in even the smallest thing. Professor Arnold J. Toynbee [5] writes that he would 'express his personal belief that the four higher religions that were alive in the age in which he was living were four variations on a single theme, and that, if all the four components of this heavenly music of the spheres could be audible on earth simultaneously, and with equal clarity, to one pair of human ears, the happy hearer would find himself listening, not to a discord, but to a harmony'. He does not believe that any one religion is an exclusive and definitive revelation of spiritual truth. To deny to other religions that they may be 'God's chosen and sufficient channels for revealing Himself to some human souls, is for me, to be guilty of blasphemy'. He quotes Symmachus who says. 'the heart of so great a mystery can never be reached by following one road only'.[6] Archbishop William Temple puts

[5] *A Study of History,* Vol. II (1954), p. 428.

[6] Professor Toynbee explains his position in clear terms: In our spiritual struggle, he says 'I guess that both the West and the world are going to turn away from man—worshipping ideologies—Communism and secular individualism alike—and become converted to an Oriental religion coming neither from Russia nor from the West. I guess that this will be the Christian religion that came to the Greeks and the Romans from Palestine, with one of two elements in traditional Christianity discarded and replaced by

it in a different way: 'All that is noble in the non-Christian systems of thought or conduct or worship is the work of Christ upon them and within them. By the Word of God—that is to say, by Jesus Christ—Isaiah and Plato and Zoroaster and (the) Buddha and Confucius conceived and uttered such truths as they declared. There is only one divine light, and every man in his measure is enlightened by it. Yet, each has only a few rays of that light, which needs all the wisdom of all the human traditions to manifest the entire compass of its spectrum'.

The history of Christianity shows how in its great days it was capable of giving as well as receiving. It has been perpetually changing its emphasis and even surrendering its dogmas. It adapted itself to the needs of the Roman Empire when it converted it, of the barbarian world which had its own cultural traditions and social institutions. The mediaeval Catholic belief in the impossibility of salvation outside the Church has faded away. I do not think there are many today who support the clear-cut ruling of Lateran IV, *De Fide Catholica:* 'There is only one universal Church of the faithful and outside it none at all can be saved'. In this changing world even dogmas change. Take, for example, the mediaeval doctrine of the eternal perdition of unbaptised infants. Take Augustine's words: 'Hold fast to this truth, that not only men of rational age but even babes who die without the sacrament of baptism in the name of Father, Son and Holy Ghost, pass from this world to be punished in eternal fire'. According to the *Catholic Encyclopaedia*, as late as A.D. 1100, 'St. Anselm was at one with St. Augustine in holding that unbaptised children share in the positive sufferings of the damned'. The authoritative '*Catechism of the Council of Trent*' (1566) holds that unbaptised children are 'born to eternal misery and perdition'. Catholics do not accept this dogma today.

---

a new element from India. I expect and hope that this avatar of Christianity will include the vision of God as being Love. But I also expect and hope that it will discard the other traditional Christian vision of God as being a jealous god, and that it will reject the self-glorification of this jealous god's "chosen people" as being unique. This is where India comes in, with her belief (complementary to the vision of God as Love) that there may be more than one illuminating and saving approach to the mystery of the universe'. *Times Literary Supplement*, April 16, 1954, p. 249.

We should not insist on an objective, universally valid doctrinal content. Where everybody thinks alike nobody thinks at all. In a world community each individual will have freedom to evolve his own realisation of the Supreme and the historical faiths will remain free to grow according to their own genius. Each religion contributes to the richness of the whole even as each note contributes to the complexity and harmony of the music of the symphony. In the present crisis, the spiritual forces of the world must come together and the great religious traditions should transcend their differences of form, underline their basic unity and draw from it the strength necessary to counter materialistic determinism. The type of religion here outlined is scientific, empirical, and humanistic. It fosters the full development of man which includes the spirit in man. It will not be silent in the face of man's inhumanity to man.

Islam attracted attention because it complained about the theological controversies in which Christians lost themselves neglecting the social problems. Communism again is attracting attention because it condemned the otherworldly and reactionary character of religion. Truly religious souls will identify themselves with the social and human revolution that is afoot and guide the aspirations of mankind for a better and fuller life.

Christ is the second Adam, the first born of a new race of men, who, as the spiritual kingdom is spread on earth, will achieve a unity of nature and supernature, comparable to our present union of mind and animal nature but transcending it as rational life transcends the sentient life below it. The effort of man to remake himself and remake the world in the pattern of a divine order gives greatness and significance to his failures. The Christian hope is the creation of a new species of spiritual personality of which the first fruits had already been manifested in Jesus and the saints. They are the heralds of truth on earth, the instruments of the Divine for the spread of spiritual religion. The process of creation is still going on. It is not complete. It is in the process of completion.

CONCLUSION

We are living at the dawn of a new era of universal humanity. There is a thrill of hope, a flutter of expectation as when the first glimmer of dawn awakens the earth. Whether we like it or not we live in one world and require to be educated to a common conception of human purpose and destiny. The different nations should live together as members of the human race, not as hostile entities but as friendly partners in the endeavour of civilisation. The strong shall help the weak and all shall belong to the one world federation of free nations. If we escape from the dangers attendant on the control by irresponsible men, of sources of power hitherto unimaginable, we will unite the peoples of all races in a community, catholic, comprehensive, and co-operative. We will realise that no people or group of peoples had had a monopoly in contributing to the development of civilisation. We will recognise and celebrate the achievements of all nations and thus promote universal brotherhood. Especially in matters of religion we must understand the valuable work of the sages of other countries and ages.

Peace is not the mere absence of war; it is the development of a strong fellow-feeling, an honest appreciation of other people's ideas and values. Distinctions of a physical character diminish in importance as the understanding of the significance of the inner life of man increases. We need, not merely a closer contact between East and West, but a closer union, a meeting of minds and a union of hearts.

Mankind stems from one origin from which it has figured out in many forms. It is now striving towards the reconciliation of that which has been split up. The separation of East and West is over. The history of the new world, the one world, has begun. It promises to be large in extent, varied in colour, rich in quality.

The World Community *

I

The human race is involved in a new stage of history. Profound and striking changes are spreading over the whole world. These changes recoil on our thought and behaviour. The world is too small for nuclear weapons. They have to be brought under control in the interests of world community. A great cultural and social transformation is taking place. People are restless, alternating between faith and doubt, hope and anxiety.

In World War I, of the ten million people who were killed, 95 per cent. were soldiers and 5 per cent. civilians. In World War II, over fifty million were killed of whom 52 per cent. were soldiers and 48 per cent. civilians. In the Korean War, of the nine million killed, 84 per cent. were civilians and 16 per cent. soldiers. In these circumstances, it is difficult to believe that war that has degenerated into the mass murder of the defenceless, non-combatants, women and children, is a legitimate instrument of politics.

Nuclear developments have given enough power to the great countries to annihilate the human race many times over. Politicians have become indifferent to the growing danger and speak of the balance of terror. The apathy of the masses and the indifference of the classes have resulted in a creeping paralysis of the people. If we do not wish to shut our eyes to the devastation which the building of nuclear armaments means, the destruction of cities, the ruin of countries, the sufferings of millions of human beings who are as good as ourselves, the demoralisation of the world which acquiesces in a conspiracy of silence about the effects of nuclear explosions, radioactive fallout, the annihilation of human beings, we must acquire a

* From *Religion in a Changing World* (New York: Humanities Press, ?), pp. 155–182.

Radhakrishnan addressing the United Nations, with President John F. Kennedy and Secretary-General U Thant in the background. Photograph courtesy of City News Bureau, Inc.

little quietude and think deeply. We should fight the immorality and unreasonableness which still govern the world. We must protest against the suppression of those who wish to enlighten the public about the realities of nuclear warfare. We should realise that there is no protection from nuclear weapons through shelters or emergency regulations.

In a world, where peace is becoming more and more precarious, the great powers have a special responsibility. With calmness, deliberateness, and patience they have to face and meet problems. We need not assume that human nature is unchangeable and since there had always been wars, there would always be wars. World peace is not a dream in a shrinking world. It is a necessity, an essential condition for the survival of the human race. Can we attain this goal with the threat or the use of force?

William James in a famous essay on *The Moral Equivalent of War* proposed a 'substitute for war's disciplinary functions'. He held out other ways of preserving martial virtues as 'the ideals of honour and standards of efficiency'. But it is not enough to propose equivalents for military virtues, we have to devise alternatives for the military methods. Issues which were hitherto decided through wars should hereafter be decided by other means. As long as there are nations, there will be disputes and they should be decided by peaceful means. In political life as in social life, we cannot exclude conflicts altogether. These have to be settled by a world organisation, an international authority. Kant, in his essay on *Perpetual Peace,* did not suggest a world state but a group of states, observing minimal rights of civilised behaviour. He proposed a notion of world citizenship, a common fabric of legal behaviour without the support of an overall sovereignty. The interpenetration of states is the growing practice. World control by a single authority is an illusion. No democracy can become a world state. The latter may easily turn out to be a tyranny or a dictatorship. A federal solution is the way out, a world community which substitutes the processes of law for armed conflicts. The alternative to international anarchy is a world-wide system of justice, law, and order. *Dharma* in Indian thought means a gathering in, a binding together, integration; *adharma* its opposite, is a scattering out, a falling away, disintegration. The world has to be bound together. A world federal government with powers limited to those necessary for establishing and maintaining law and order among the nations of the world is a practical way of achieving just and lasting peace. Regional and political loyalties may stand against a world authority. We cannot abolish existing social structures without providing alternative ways of fulfilling functions discharged by them. We must have means to protect them against tyranny and aggression if they are not to submit to these evils. An international authority does not mean absence of wars. It will have coercive power to use, when necessary, against rebellious units. Within nation states we have rebellious citizens and groups, civil wars and revolutions.

World War I was fought, to use President Wilson's words 'to make the world safe for democracy'. The League of Nations did not satisfy the American people who stood aloof from it.

A world authority to be effective is a consequence of a world understanding or world community. The present moral, social, and political conditions of the world have to be altered before we can have a world community. We should work for a world community, for the alternatives are chaos or world tyranny.

II

From the beginnings of human history, poets, prophets, and philosophers have asked us to grow equal to our destiny, to regenerate and transform ourselves by religious devotion, spiritual contemplation, and moral courage. The Hammurabi code of the Babylonians, and the Egyptian Book of the Dead contain suggestions of the Ten Commandments of the Israelites. One of them reads 'Thou shalt not oppress the stranger for ye were once strangers in Egypt'. Hosea, Isaiah, and Hillel emphasised compassion, mercy, forgiveness, piety, and love. The prophet Isaiah states the promise of God. 'I will gather all nations and tongues; and they shall come and see my glory'.

Alexander was struck greatly by the austerity of life and profound philosophic wisdom of the Indian teachers. He approached them without prejudice and acknowledged their greatness. Plutarch says that Alexander brought together into one body all men everywhere, uniting and mixing in one great loving cup as it were, men's lives, their characters, their marriages, their habits of life. He looked upon the whole inhabited world as his fatherland. All good men are of this; the wicked are the aliens. Aśoka, Harsa, and Akbar represent this view of life. Aśoka cut into rock the central lessons of the Buddha. By continually dwelling on the selfishness of others, we ourselves become more selfish. Not by accusing others do we get out of our selfishness but by purifying ourselves. The way from passion to peace is not by hurling charges against others but by overcoming oneself.

Jesus was trained in a context which could not accept the primitive morality of an 'eye for an eye'. For Jesus God was love and compassion as well as righteousness. 'Thou shalt love thy neighbour as thyself'. 'Return good for evil'. 'Bless those that curse you'.

Professor Max Mueller, who did a great deal for the interpretation of Indian religion to the Western world, thought that he was a Christian Vedāntist even as some Christians are Christian Platonists. The aim of human existence was for him, as for many others, world community. 'Where the Greeks saw barbarians, we see brethren; where the Greeks saw nations, we see mankind, toiling and suffering, separated by oceans, divided by language, and severed by national enmity—yet evermore tending, under divine control, towards the fulfilment of that inscrutable purpose for which the world was created, and man placed in it, bearing the image of God'.

Science has broken down the barriers of space and time. The independence of nations and the growth of the international community are felt the world over. The dream of conquering the vastness of space, of economic partnership across the frontiers of countries, of education for all our children, of employment for all who seek and need them are common to all.

The real force working for world unity is man's inborn compassion for others. It is the basis of life and requires to be organised. Our enemies are lack of courage, lack of imagination, indolence, and inertia. We have to lead man towards civilisation.

III

There is a deeper ethic, which calls every human being to eliminate the sources of conflict, the causes of war, to join with others to reform the institutions and relationships which lead to wars. Human reason and creative imagination should evolve the kind of education, mutual aid, and collective security by which the nations will be able to resolve their differences peacefully. We should use cultural and ideological differences to enrich our wisdom and produce a higher international ethics.

The sovereignty of the world community comes before all others, before the sovereignty of classes and groups, tribes and nations. Every individual by his birth into the human family has the right to live and grow, breathe unpoisoned air and water on uncontaminated soil. Earth, water, and air, now outer space and the celestial bodies are the common property of all mankind.

IV

The unification of the world is in process though it is struggling against many difficulties. Even as individuals are bound by the laws of the nation to which they belong, nation states should be bound by international law. Just as there are individuals who break the law, there are nations who break the law and commit aggression. The law of nations should be based on the federation of free states.

A society becomes cohesive if its members share large hopes, ideals, and desires. If the world is to become a community, all the peoples should share common ideals and purposes even though they are separated by barriers, physical and psychological. All history is the story of remarkable individuals dramatically engaged in mastering the hostile environment. A few in every nation, in every part of the world, amid the uproar of nations and empires hear the voice of the future, the gentle stirring of life and hope. It is not one nation or one man. It is a new spirit that is awakened, revived and nourished by seemingly helpless but convinced and committed solitary individuals, to adapt the words of Albert Camus, whose deeds and works negate frontiers and breathe the oneness of humanity. As the result of their sufferings and sacrifices the vision of the threatened truth that each one of us belongs to the whole and should build for all becomes manifest. None of the differences which separate the governments of the world is as important as their membership in the family of nations.

The central problem is the development of loyalty to the world community. The greatest era of human history on earth is within reach of all mankind. To achieve this ideal, we have to discover our moral strength, define our purposes, and direct our energies.

In facing this task, we come up against the crudest implications of history, that war is the maker of nations. Though, in previous epochs we waged wars which brought misery, destruction, and ruin in their wake, we pointed out that defensive wars were better than shameful submission to barbaric aggressors who wished to achieve greatness and power by dominating the whole world. The two wars, the most ghastly in history, were waged by men of our generation. The leaders of the civilisation who brought about these wars, in their moments of cool reflection, hate themselves for their responsibility. The world was full of oppressions and cruelties, stupidities and delusions and we thought we would remove them by resorting to violence. The nations today feel a genuine sense of guilt and shame. There is a widespread consciousness of the folly and wickedness in which most people and governments are involved. In spite of our earnest desire to get rid of wars, the fear of them, the baseness and savagery which that fear engenders are there raising the question, whether there is any hope for this perverted and criminal generation. Is there any hope that man can civilise himself? History is a dreadful warning. A few individuals suffer from mental derangements and some nations pass through nervous breakdowns resulting in excitement, violence, and hatred.

The great powers are engaged in a struggle to capture the souls of the emerging peoples who have been released from colonial domination. These nations are in a state of inner turmoil. One conflict leads to another. Irrational feeling, racial hatred, primitive tribalism, poverty, hunger, suffering, intrigues, plots, and counter-plots make of them a seething mass, mysterious and unpredictable. The new nations will have no peace, for the great powers are fighting on the soil of small emerging nations.

V

Our aim is to establish a world community based on a universal moral order.[1] It is possible only with a commitment to the ideal and practice of democracy based on the dignity of the individual. Even the most powerful nation or ruler must say with Shakespeare's Richard II:

> I live with bread like you, feel want
> Taste grief, need friends; subjected thus
> How can you say to me I am a king.

Democracy aims at achieving its ideals through persuasion, love, example, and moral force. Violence and the machinery of intolerance are inconsistent with the spirit of democracy. The organisers of evil take a part of the blame and the many who acquiesce in it have to share a large part. We must emancipate human beings from the meshes they have woven round themselves, free them from the organisations of national selfishness. Even the Fascist system claims to be democratic. Gentile, the Italian philosopher, sets forth the Fascist claim in these words: 'Democracy consists in giving the people what they want; they do not know what they want; the Leader tells them and then processes it for them'.

The United Nations Organisation is the nearest we have to world government. It attempts to the best of its ability to eliminate the causes of conflicts. It affirms that international disputes should be resolved not by force of arms but by reasonable negotiations. It helps nations to remain in communication with one another for any co-operative or creative action. It uses moral force as a check on the aggressiveness and harass-

[1] Cf. Professor W. E. Hocking: 'Religion . . . is the forerunner of international law because it alone can create the international spirit, the international obligation'. To this was added a footnote: 'We require a world religion just because we do not require, nor wish, a world state'.

The Meaning of God in Human Experience

ment of others. The United Nations Organisation tries to free nations from political domination, racial oppression, and economic exploitation. The right of a nation to survive depends not on the extent of its territory or the size of its population or its military might but its integrity and adherence to law. We aim at a family of nations to which each member will bring its unique gifts. All nations are sacred to themselves and so to each other and to the whole. The world should become an international commonwealth based on disinterested nationalism. Selfishness is sin whether in individuals or in nations.

Freedom from political exploitation is essential for human dignity. Freedom demands to be shared. The nation or the individual who enjoys freedom should make its bounds wider yet. Freedom is a spiritual quality. It overcomes all bounds and crosses all barriers. Freedom is universal in its application. Nationalism at one stage integrated people in Europe. The main spring of nationalism is the will of the people to be members of an independent sovereign state. Those who dominate other nations invent a thousand excuses for their conduct. They preach a doctrine of malice and intolerance towards the subject peoples. They carry a highly infectious disease which kills decent people. These merchants of hate drape themselves in a cloak of self-righteousness. They exploit peoples' ignorance, prejudice, and bigotry and destroy their ideals which they claim to uphold. Decolonisation processes may be regarded as slow but they are steadily reversing the political subjection of peoples. It is no use telling people who are subjected to colonial domination that they are given education, health, the end of tribal feuds, but in exchange they get humiliation.

Racial oppression is anti-democratic. There is only one race, the human race. It is above considerations of politics and nationality. Even the best of men subordinate racial evil to national interest.

Abraham Lincoln said, 'My paramount object in this struggle is to serve the Union, and is not either to save or to destroy slavery. If I could save the Union without freeing any slave, I would do it; and if I could save it by freeing all the slaves, I would do it; and if I could save it by freeing some and leaving others alone, I would also do that. What I do about slavery and the coloured race, I do because I believe it helps to save the Union; and what I forbear, I forbear because I do not believe it would help to save the Union. I have here stated my purpose according to my view of official duty; and I intend no modification of my oft expressed personal wish that all men everywhere could be free'. Civil rights are guaranteed in democratic constitutions. They imply the existence of an organised society maintaining public order without which liberty itself would be lost in the excesses of unashamed licence. Every democracy should fight race discrimination.

Nationalism has lost its drive. The people of Europe wish to feel and think as Europeans. Many in Europe and other parts of the world hope to live under a universal system which no theorist foresees. More than half the population of the world suffer from hunger, malnutrition, and disease. A world in which such things are permitted is a world of wilful insanity. We have brains to evaluate facts but we do not use them. Every area can be made fertile and habitable, every disease can be removed and every scarcity can be conquered. These are attempted by the Food and Agricultural Organisation and the World Health Organisation.

If a fraction of the expenditure we incur on armaments is diverted to social welfare we can clothe every man, woman, and child and we will build schools for all of them. We will advance general health, housing, nutrition, culture, and other ingredients of social well-being. This will help to eliminate fear, hatred, and bigotry among nations. We will promote ethical enlightenment, spiritual freedom, development of artistic possibilities. We will live by sound reason and not by blind emotion or primitive instincts.

If the communist faith has won the allegiance of millions of people, it is not because of their acceptance of Marxist theory but because of the sense of hope it gives to millions of its adherents by the advocacy of the overthrow of reactionary governments and the end of exploitation, racial, economic, and political. It pleads for the economic progress of the common people, equality of economic opportunities. It attempts to abolish the distinction of rich nations and poor ones. It promises a rational allocation of resources and the establishment of world brotherhood. Those whose privileges and positions are challenged, are tempted to withdraw, emigrate inwardly to another state where they find security. The spread of communism has led to modification in the capitalist system and what was forecast as the inevitable collapse of capitalism did not happen. The system was greatly modified by the inspiration of communist doctrine or the trade union spirit. The middle classes did not merge into the proletariat but the latter rose to the rank of the middle classes. State planning and the government's responsibility for basic welfare became generally accepted. Technology made the workers not poorer but more prosperous.

We should wage a war against poverty. A true democrat should identify himself with the poor and the outcast. We must work for the social revolution.

VI

Men of imagination appreciate what is different from themselves. Homer and Shakespeare, St. Paul and Francis are as much ours as Kālidāsa and Vālmīki. We are the heirs of all times and with all nations we share our inheritance.

The intellectually gifted are not ethically superior to the common people in the bitterness and injustice of their feelings. They are excellent as individuals but as members of groups they are as bad as others. Even intellectuals are getting demoralised by accepting the view that truth is reached by statistical observations or empirical experiments. The pursuit of a meaning in life or purpose in conduct is dismissed as a romantic passion. They overlook that human beings have a conscience, have values, have imagination through which they create art and literature. If we wish to co-operate, we must learn about each other and each other's art and history. UNESCO's range is wider. The artists, the thinkers, and the scientists, whose works move multitudes, should know one another, understand one another and work together and lay the foundations for that great republic of beauty, truth, and human brotherhood. We should work not only for our national aims, however just and reasonable they may be, but for the healing of discords of the political and economic world by the magic of that inward community of spiritual life which, in spite of difficulties, reveals to us our brotherhood and high destiny. Goethe said to Eckermann: 'As a man and a citizen, the poet will love his fatherland but the fatherland of his poetic powers and his poetic activity is the good, the noble, the beautiful which is the property of no particular person and no particular land. This he seizes upon and forms whenever he finds it'. Gāndhi says: 'I am wedded to India because I believe absolutely that she has a mission for the world. . . . My religion has no geographical limits. I have a living faith in it which will transcend even my love for India herself'. 'I do not want my house to be walled in on all sides and my windows to be stuffed. I want the culture of all lands to be blown about my house as freely as possible. . . . But I refuse to be blown off my feet by any of them. . . . Mine is not a religion of the prison-house. It has room for the least among God's creations. But it is proof against insolent pride of race, religion or colour'.

VII

There has been a steady progress in the democratic way, which is the way of non-violence. We were once cannibals, then we became nomadic hunters, and later settled down to agriculture. These are signs of increasing non-violence and diminishing violence.

Great forces are at work bringing about a relaxation of tensions. These include the rising pressures in both democratic and communist countries for a more abundant life, the fear of mutual annihilation in a nuclear war, civilised leadership in the great countries. The whole direction of political society is towards freedom, the dignity of the individual, and political democracy. Even totalitarian systems are moving relentlessly towards an open society. No dogma can for ever close the mind of the human being. The communist society is getting gradually democratised. The Soviet Union has passed through stages of development. It is capable of co-operating co-existence. Though the communist states exploit revolutionary situations by the use of force, they do not rely entirely on force. Even this may disappear. Many states today need revolutionary changes for appeasing popular demands. Communism means modernisation and a high degree of social justice. Stalin's Constitution of 1936 indicates a positive step in the direction of the recognition of human rights. In 1943, finding it difficult to uproot religion, the Soviet Union allowed the election of a Metropolitan of Moscow. Stalin announced that the party 'could no longer deprive the Russian people of their Church and freedom of worship'. Envoys were exchanged with Western powers, with the United States in 1933. In 1945 the Soviet Union was a founder-member of the United Nations. If war is the breakdown of dialogue or conversation, to continue conversation is to accept the presuppositions of conversation, agreement, brotherhood, and ethical principles. Dialogue or conversation means mutual understanding.

Rumania affirmed some years ago the right of each communist state to build socialism according to its own interests and desires. She is questioning the need for the Warsaw Pact, the military organisation headed by the Soviet Union and comprising the six East European Nations including Albania. The French and the Rumanians both believe that times have changed since the two pacts were created, NATO in 1949 and the Warsaw Pact in 1955. Each country wishes to control its own forces. The Rumanian leader, Nicholae Ceausescu said on May 7 this year (1966) that the pacts were 'an anachronism incompatible with the independence and national sovereignty of the peoples and normal relations among States'. The Rumanians, a Latin nation in a Slav alliance, share President De Gaulle's view of a 'Europe of nations from the Atlantic to the Urals'.

Eighteen years ago, Yugoslavia resisted Soviet domination. Marshal Tito is trying to free Yugoslavia from the shackles of party bureaucracy whose vision is narrow and to harness to the business of government and production new forces and new talents. He wishes to broaden the base of government by enlisting the active participation of men of ability, who have no use for party doctrine and intrigue. Yugoslavian society is opening to new ideals and influences. Yugoslavia and the

Vatican have entered into an agreement and are exchanging envoys.

The Soviet Union and the East European States are becoming more nationalist and democratic. China is preparing for a new leap forward. Indonesia is attempting to have the rule of law and democratic government.

We do not have capitalism or communism today as we had in 1917. The changes taking place in them are necessary and convergent. The communist states are striving to devise the right machinery for passing on power, for making a peaceful transition from one leader to another in a democratic way. When Mr. Khrushchev was defeated in the party presidium, he appealed successfully to the party's Central Committee in June, 1957. However, in 1964, he was made to retire.

After the war, we marched up to the brink in Greece and Turkey, Iran and Berlin, the Congo and Cuba. We marched down again. The signing of the Nuclear Test Ban Treaty is a step towards peace and away from war, towards reason. The combination of toughness and restraint saved the world. It is a hopeful sign that the Soviet Union has made proposals to the United Nations similar to those made by the United States in regard to the exploration of outer space.

International co-operation is accepted the world over. Woodrow Wilson, in his second inaugural address, said: 'The greatest thing that remains to be done must be done with the whole world for a stage and in co-operation with the wide and universal forces of mankind'.

We are conscious of living in a tragic age. We aim at lucidity and scepticism but hold our views with passionate intensity and enhanced sensibility. A truly religious man by his life and work sows the seeds of love and tolerance.

Our duty is to subdue the irrational and stabilise the international equilibrium. We are still growing, striving, looking confidently to an age when men will not be born into emptiness. The mantle of greatness belongs today not to those who make wars but to those who prevent wars. We must wake up into a world free of fear, myth, and prejudice. Immediately after World War II, the East European States came under the influence of the Soviet Union. All of them adopted what is called a people's democracy, a one-party system and the absence of civil liberties for the sake of the triumph of the proletariat. The countries of Western Europe, jealous of their freedom, sought the help of the United States. This entailed a relative loss of independence. The necessity of relative submission to the United States was felt to be humiliating and unwholesome and was resented by the former big powers, the United Kingdom and France and even the smaller ones with legendary memories of past history. Whenever danger arose and the Soviet Union intensified the 'cold war', the leadership of the United States became more pronounced. The Berlin blockade resulted in the Atlantic Pact. NATO's integration and the West German re-armament can be traced to the Korean War. The 'cold war' started between Soviet domination and the leadership of the United States.

VIII

India gained her independence in 1947 immediately after World War II and, under the leadership of Jawaharlal Nehru, adopted the policy of non-alignment. A military approach is somewhat foreign to India. We are pledged to the principles of freedom and justice. The pursuit of peace, the liberation of subject peoples, the elimination of racial discrimination, and international co-operation have been India's objectives. Any policy involving entangling alliances would have endangered Indian unity after independence, and would have made impossible the very limited economic development we have achieved.

This policy of peaceful co-existence is in accord with the spirit of India's genius:

ye yathā māṁ prapadyante
tāṁs tathai 'va bhajāmy aham
mama vartmā 'nuvartante
manuṣyāḥ pārtha sarvaśaḥ.

As men approach me, so do I accept them: men on all sides follow my path, O Pārtha (Arjuna).

Bhagavadgītā, IV. 11.

Though beliefs and practices are varied, the goal of spiritu[al] fulfilment is the same.

Aśoka in one of his edicts instructs those who were to carry the *dharma* to other countries: 'Remember that everywhere you will find some root of faith and righteousness, see that you foster this and do not destroy it'. He dreamed of the whole world to be federated by ideas, by the striving towards absolute truth and right conduct. It is the way to bind the diversity of races. His Rock Edict XII is an expression of this spirit:

> King Priyadarśī honours men of all faiths, members of religious orders and laymen alike, with gifts and various marks of esteem. Yet he does not value either gifts or honours as much as growth in the qualities essential to religion in men of all faiths.
>
> This growth may take many forms, but its root is in guarding one's speech to avoid extolling one's own faith and disparaging the faith of others improperly or, when the occasion is appropriate, immoderately.
>
> The faiths of others all deserve to be honoured for one reason or another. By honouring them, one exalts one's own faith and at the same time performs a service to the faith of others. By acting otherwise, one injures one's own faith and also does disservice to that of others. For if a man extols his own faith and disparages another, because of devotion to his own and because he wants to glorify it, he seriously injures his own faith.
>
> Therefore, concord alone is commendable, for through concord, men may learn and respect the conception of *dharma* accepted by others.

This spirit influenced Islam also. Abul Fazl describes the spirit of Akbar's Universal Faith in these words:

> O God, in every temple I see people that seek Thee, and in every language I hear spoken, people praise Thee. Polytheism and Islam feel after Thee: each religion says, 'Thou art One, without equal'. If it be a mosque, people murmur the holy prayer and if it be a Christian Church, people ring the bell from Love to Thee. Sometimes I frequent the Christian cloister, sometimes the mosque. But it is Thou whom I search from temple to temple. Thy elect have no dealings with either heresy or orthodoxy for neither of them

> stands behind the screen of Thy truth. Heresy to the heretic; and religion to the orthodox. But the dust of the rose petal belongs to the heart of the perfume seller.

Rammohun Roy founded the Brahmo Samaj in the year 1830 and its trust deed contains the following:

> A place of public meeting of all sorts and descriptions of people without distinction as shall behave and conduct themselves in an orderly, sober, religious and devout manner for the worship and adoration of the Eternal, Unsearchable and Immutable Being who is the author and preserver of the Universe but not under or by any other name, designation or title peculiarly used for and applied to any particular being or beings by any man or set of men whatsoever.

This spirit is opposed to the view that only one religion is valid:

> I am the Lord thy God . . . Thou shalt have no other gods before me. Thou shalt not make unto thee any graven image, or any likeness of any thing that is in heaven above, or that is in the earth beneath, or that is in the water under the earth: Thou shalt not bow down thyself to them, nor serve them: for I the Lord thy God am a jealous God, visiting the iniquity of the fathers upon the children unto the third and fourth generation of them that hate me.

Non-alignment does not mean non-commitment. It is active commitment to peaceful co-existence, peace, and disarmament. It gives freedom of action in international affairs. Non-alignment is not neutrality. Jawaharlal Nehru made this quite clear when he said at Columbia University, New York, October 17, 1949, that 'when man's liberty or peace is in danger, we cannot and shall not be neutral, neutrality then would be a betrayal of what we have fought for and stand for'.

We do not accept the thesis that every country has to choose one or the other group. The United States has a long record of non-involvement in other people's affairs. The foreign policy of the United States was for a century and a half dominated by President Washington's farewell address. He said:

> The nation which indulges towards another an habitual hatred or an habitual fondness, is in some degree a slave. It is a slave to its animosity or to its affection, either of which is sufficient to lead it astray from its duty and its interest.
>
> Europe has a set of primary interests which to us have none or a very remote relation. Hence she must be engaged in frequent controversies, the causes of which are essentially foreign to our concerns. Hence, therefore, it must be unwise in us to implicate ourselves, by artificial ties, in the ordinary vicissitudes of her politics, or the ordinary combinations and collusions of her friendships, or enmities. Our detached and distant situation invites and enables us to pursue a different course. . . . Why by interweaving our destiny with that of any part of Europe, entangle our peace and prosperity in the toils of European ambition, rivalship, interest, humor or caprice? It is our true policy to steer clear of permanent alliances with any portion of the foreign world.

Washington expressed his conviction that 'if we remain one people under an efficient government the period is not far off . . . when we may choose peace or war as our interest guided by our justice shall counsel'. Jefferson was only re-emphasising this policy when in his first inaugural address on March 4, 1801, he advocated 'peace, commerce and honest friendship with all nations—entangling alliances with none'.

We have adopted the policy which was so well formulated by the leaders of the United States. A non-aligned country is not afraid to express its views. It is not neutral between good and evil, between right and wrong. Non-alignment is not isolationism. India participated in collective actions in Korea, Indo-China, the Middle East, and the Congo. Non-alignment gives us the right, if not the authority, to influence the two great super-powers.

The non-aligned nations which are not committed to either military group—communist or anti-communist—are unwilling to adopt an oversimplified attitude of black or white. They do not wish to divide the world into two camps—the wolves and the sheep. They recognise the intermediate shades and are willing to admit that both sides have elements of reason and justice. They also feel that the two systems are undergoing drastic changes. The Western powers are becoming more socialist in character and the Soviet Union is becoming more liberal in outlook. The United Kingdom, the Scandinavian countries, and even the United States of America are not what they were at the beginning of the century. Lenin's Russia, Stalin's Russia, and Khrushchev's Russia are different from one another. The Soviet Union has been changing from the old international ideal of world communism to the government of a great power. At the time of the Russo-American rapprochement in 1959, Mr. Khrushchev, forgetting for the moment his role as the leader of the world communist movement and speaking as a Russian, said, 'if only Russia and America could agree, the peace of the world would be ensured, for between them the two great powers could stop any war anywhere'. Besides, there are different types of communism in the Soviet Union, in China, in Poland, and in Yugoslavia. Communist states are aiming at a radical liberalisation of their regimes and the establishment of a new kind of socialist state. We must fight the ideologies which affirm the infallibility of their doctrines and divide the world into irreconcilable camps. The two systems have to live together if the threat of war posed by the nuclear and other weapons of mass destruction is to be removed. If the disarmament discussions are still continuing, it is because the great powers are increasingly aware of the dangers of nuclear war. We should try to increase confidence between nations. If we assume that war and capitulation are the only alternatives, it is due to the failure of imagination, to a sense of helplessness. We are so overwhelmed, even overawed, by the danger threatening us, that we have lost the capacity to think afresh and to act differently.

IX

International peace can be achieved by the self-discipline of sovereign states and not by the removal or abolition of states. We cannot have peace without law and law must be based on justice and not power. Only the spirit of justice can unite the whole human race. Through the gift of patience, spiritual wisdom, we should show the way to the solution of the problem which faces all the peoples of the world. In spite of racial and national differences, we must evolve a relationship, a unity of mind and heart, a feeling which will bring us intimately close to one another. We must strengthen the forces of sanity in society. Every truly religious man whose nature is freed from dogmatic rigidity realises that all prayers flow into one Supreme. We must create new men who will stay our doom, and build a new humanity. It is inevitable that a new spirit of oneness will take hold of the human race. Wars and revolutions may retard but the final unification is clear. Nations should progress slowly to remove the barriers that separate them and test each other's sincerity at every step so that in time mutual confidence is created.

World government may be a long way off but we must continue at an ever increasing rate to blunt the edges of national sovereignty. Nations should compete peacefully with one another in establishing the reign of truth and justice. This has to be done with effort.

We should free the concept of the Divine from all objective and anthropomorphic attributes. Man becomes aware of his potential identity with the Divine. Hindu thought emphasises the importance of the divine character of the human being—*tat tvam asi*—that art thou. The Boddhisattva, the nature of enlightenment is in all. Jeremiah's last words are to the effect: 'I will put my law in their inward parts, and write it in their hearts; and will be their God and they shall be my people'. Christianity which affirms, 'Behold, I make all things new', uses the concept of the Holy Spirit as 'the spirit of truth', 'the bearer of witness', and 'the promise of the Father'. 'The Kingdom of God is within you'. 'The truth shall make you free'. 'The true light which lighteth every man that cometh into the world'. 'God is a spirit: and they that worship Him must worship Him in spirit and in truth'. In Christian theology the emphasis is on God the spirit. It is this that is manifesting itself in the strivings for peace, the struggle for civil rights and social justice by men of all faiths.

The knowledge of God in the human being is possible through the withdrawal of the senses and mind from the world of outer experience and concentrating these energies on the inward reality. Man realises his true nature through this inward penetration. When the individual gains the knowledge of the self, he becomes illumined, the bonds of the heart are destroyed, and his finiteness is transcended.

The discipline of religion is to make this potential into actual. This identification of the Divine is not a matter of history but of personal experience of the individual. At the centre of our being we encounter a world where all things are at rest and the differences which divide us fade into insignificance. This experience is through the cultivation of man's inward life. Man has to devote himself for a few minutes each day to the best that is in him. We must cleanse the soul of self-delusion. Until the human individual explores the contents of his consciousness and with deliberation and effort makes himself one with the Divine and affirms with conviction, 'I and my Father are one', the Divine is transcendent, the 'wholly other'.

In our conduct of affairs the effect of unreason is so obvious that mind itself becomes a wilderness. 'Wrath is cruel and anger is outrageous'. Thomas Jefferson wisely counselled 'when angry, count ten before you speak, if very angry, an hundred'. We should bring our temper under control before it blazes forth in harsh words and unjust accusations, before our excited emotions make it difficult for us to judge wisely. We must develop self-control through brotherly love which confers a tranquil frame of mind that is difficult to overthrow. If we take man as he is, we will be in despair; if we take him for what he ought to be, we will help him to become that. Man's understanding of himself leads to a life of disciplined disinterestedness and of love for all. The brotherhood of man is a present possibility. New men with a new instinct to unify, to share, serve, and sacrifice are possible. If mankind is released from the pressure of population, if the waste of warfare is avoided, if the sources of wealth are organised by the community, people will become free and adventurous and not lead lives of routine and indolence.

In man and his future we must have confidence. The ideal of world community, our obvious destiny and duty, is at once a summons to creative endeavour, and a call to co-operative action.

Glossary and Index of Important Names and Terms

This glossary includes all of the names and terms that are important for an understanding of the selections in this volume, as well as some terms that do not appear in this volume but are important in books by and about Radhakrishnan (very few of which have a glossary). An asterisk indicates words defined in the glossary.

Adhyāsa superimposition; according to Advaita Vedānta,* refers to the mistaken habit of seeing something differently from what it really is—e.g., seeing the phenomenal world as if it were a self-sufficient reality; *adhyāsa* is due to, and ultimately equivalent to, *māyā* * and *avidyā* *.

Advaita "non-dual," a school of Vedānta* philosophy that teaches the absolute oneness or non-duality of Brahman.* According to Śankara,* the chief exponent of the advaitic system, Brahman is unqualified by attributes or particulars; the existence of the phenomenal world is due to the superimposition (*adhyāsa* *) of reality on the self and on the phenomenal world.

Ahimsā "non-injury," one of the fundamental Hindu obligations, based on the sacredness of all life; fostered by Gāndhi.*

Ānanda happiness or bliss; one of the three attributes of Brahman (*sat**-*cit**-*ānanda*).

Aśrama the four periods or stages of life of the three highest Hindu classes or *varnas.** See pp. 214–219.

Ātman Supreme Self or Brahman; *ātman*, self or soul. See pp. 132–137.

Aurobindo, Sri Aurobindo Ghose (1872–1950), prominent nationalist until 1910 when he founded an ashram at Pondicherry and devoted the rest of his life to yogic meditation and to the writing of religious and philosophical treatises.

Avidyā — Ignorance or unwisdom; a metaphysical or ontological ignorance of the true nature of reality, i.e., a failure to realize that the self and all particulars are nothing other than the Absolute Brahman.* In effect, equivalent to *māyā.** See 138–147 and 153–160.

Bhagavadgītā — "Song of the Lord," the sacred book of the Hindu tradition originally comprising the twenty-fifth to the forty-second chapters of the section on Bhimsa in the *Mahābhārata.** The *Gītā* is a synthesis of several strains, including the three *yogas* *: *jñāna,** *karma,** and *bhakti.** Indian thinkers such as Śankara,* Rāmānuja,* Aurobindo,* Gāndhi,* and Radhakrishnan offer slightly different interpretations of the *Gītā,* but generally agree that its message involves the ideal of selfless action, true knowledge of reality, and devotion to the Lord.

Bhakti — fervent devotion to God; a religious discipline or *yoga* * for worshipping a personal God (e.g., worship of Vishnu * and Śiva,* or their personifications, such as Kṛishṇa * or Kali). See pp. 232–238.

Brahmā — the Creator God, the first person of the Hindu triad (of which Vishnu * and Śiva * are the other two). Also called *Hiraṇya-garbha.**

Brahman — non-dual or absolute divine reality; in itself, Brahman is *nirguṇa,** or without qualities; but from the human perspective, or within *māyā* * and *avidyā,** Brahman is referred to as *saguṇa,** or with qualities. See pp. 114–131.

Brahmā-loka — the Plane or Heaven of Brahmā; according to Radhakrishnan, it is not beyond the empirical world, but the furthest limit of the empirical wherein liberated souls see each other in the light of Absolute Brahman.* See pp. 182–183.

Brahma-Sūtra a sacred treatise by the second-century B.C. philosopher, Bādarāyaṇa; the Commentary by Śankara * is an interpretation of Bādarāyaṇa's rendering of the Upanishads * as a non-dualist system, and Radhakrishnan's Commentary follows Śankara's. Rāmānuja * interprets the *Brahma-Sūtra* in terms of a qualified non-dualist system, and Madhva * offers a dualistic interpretation.

Brāhmin strictly "Brahman," the first of the four Hindu *varnas* (traditional classes); priests and teachers of the Brāhmanical and Hindu religious traditions; a highly privileged class because they were believed to be of pure Aryan blood and to have had a divine mission as protectors and perpetuators of all Vedic * knowledge.

Buddha Siddhartha of the Gautama clan of the Sakya tribe, achieved Bodhi or Enlightenment, and thereafter taught the Four Noble Truths and the Eightfold Path leading to salvation. Radhakrishnan tends to treat Gautama and the Buddhist tradition as an elaboration of the Upanishadic view, but most scholars of Indian Buddhism reject this interpretation.

Caste system Radhakrishnan defends the system of the four traditional *varnas* or classes (popularly called "castes"), Brāhmin,* Kṣatriya,* Vaiśya,* and Śūdra,* but criticizes such characteristics of the caste system (consisting of *jatis*, or "caste" in the technical sense of the term) as heredity, endogamy, and commensal relations. See pp. 193–214.

Cit, or chit consciousness; one of the three attributes of Brahman * (*sat* *-*cit-ānanda* *).

Dharma the full range of social, moral, and religious obligations in the Hindu tradition. See pp. 191–192.

Dhyāna-yoga discipline of meditation or contemplation. See pp. 238–243.

Darśana a philosophical insight or school; according to Radhakrishnan, philosophy or *darśana* combines empirical research, logical analysis, and spiritual insight.

Gāndhi, Mohandas K. (1869–1948), called Mahātmā or great-soul, leader of the Indian Independence movement, prophet of *ahiṁsā,** and symbol of Hindu asceticism. See pp. 257–277.

Hinduism the term used to designate the vast complex of texts, beliefs, and practices of the religious traditions that constitute four thousand years of Indian religious history.

Hiraṇya-garbha equivalent of Brahmā,* and the first creation of Brahman *; the world is its manifestation. See pp. 130–131.

Iśvara the Lord, or Saguṇa * Brahman * in its personal aspect; also God, or Brahman, from the perspective of *māyā.** See pp. 122–125.

Jīva the individual soul which, under the influence of *māyā,** appears to be an independent existent but is in reality the Absolute Brahman.* See pp. 148–149.

Jīvan-mukti deliverance of the soul from *avidyā* * or from the effects of *māyā* * before death (cf. *videha-mukti*, or deliverance after death). See p. 176.

Jñāna knowledge, primarily spiritual knowledge or the knowledge of Brahman,* which liberates the soul from spiritual bondage; also the discipline or *yoga* * by which this liberation is achieved. See pp. 157 and 160.

Karma the principle or law of morality such that all action inexorably bears a credit or debit value on the scale of existence; also refers to the discipline or *yoga* * by which individuals can progress spiritually according to the ideal of selfless action. One of the three most important *yogas.** See pp. 221–232.

Kṛishṇa "black," one of the most popular deities

of the Hindu pantheon; believed to be the eighth incarnation of Vishnu.*

Kṣatriya the second *varna* or class in Hindu society, traditionally the military and governing castes.*

Madhva thirteenth-century exponent of dualism, and critic of the Advaita * Vedānta * system of Śankara.* See pp. 113–114.

Mahābhārata one of the two great epics of India (the other being the *Rāmāyana*); a compilation of history, folklore, ethics, and some philosophical sections, one of which constitutes the *Bhagavadgītā.**

Mantra a sacred formula, chant, or incantation addressed to a deity, or used as a way of acquiring superhuman power.

Māyā the mystery of all existence, which is mistakenly seen as distinct from Brahman *; *māyā* is *avidyā* * or the failure to see that the self and the entire created world are really the Absolute Brahman.* See pp. 140–141.

Mokṣa liberation or release from *saṁsāra* * or the bonds of existence and rebirth.

Nehru, Jawaharlal (1889–1964), with Gāndhi, leader of the Nationalist movement; Prime-Minister, 1947–64; urbane and pragmatic (in contrast to Gāndhi's Hindu piety and asceticism). See pp. 278–283.

Nirguṇa Brahman Brahman devoid of qualifying attributes (cf. Saguṇa * Brahman).

Patanjali author of the *Yoga-Sūtras*, the most systematic presentation of *yoga*,* probably in the second century B.C.

Prakṛti "unformed non-being" or "the formless substrate of things"; with the influence of its complementary pole, *puruṣa* * or spirit, *prakṛti* is potentially all things.

Puruṣa "man," a human being, the male principle of the cosmos; ultimately, the Absolute Brahman.*

Rāmānuja, or Rāmānujāchārya the eleventh-century South Indian exponent of *Viśishtādvaita* or the qualified non-dualist system of advaita.*

Ṛishis sage or singer of the Vedas *; inspired authors or conveyors of Vedic texts and Vedic knowledge.

Saguṇa Brahman — the Absolute Brahman as viewed from the perspective of creation or *māyā* *; includes God, souls, world, and all that falls short of Nirguṇa * Brahman, or Brahman without qualities.

Samādhi — in *yoga*,* the union of the individual mind with the Supreme or Cosmic Consciousness.

Saṁsāra — the world as a perpetual flow of events in which the soul is subject to a succession of rebirths until it achieves *mokṣa* * or liberation.

Sankara, or Śankarāchārya — the ninth-century philosopher and saint, greatest exponent of the Advaita * Vedānta * system.

Sāmkya — one of the six Indian systems of philosophy considered orthodox (i.e., based on the Vedas *); emphasizes the plurality of *puruṣas* * or selves and the unity of *prakṛti* * or nature. Patanjali's * *raja-yoga* is based on the Sāmkya system.

Saññyāsa — the fourth *aśrama* * or stage of life; *saññyāsin*, an ascetic who renounces earthly concerns and devotes himself to the study of sacred texts and meditation.

Sat — being or existence; one of the three attributes of Brahman (*sat-cit**-*ānanda**).

Satchidānanda — *ṣat**-*cit**-*ānanda*,* the three attributes of Brahman.

Satyāgraha — according to Gāndhi, means "truth-force" and by extension, "nonviolent resistance."

Śiva — the third god of the Hindu triad (with Brahmā * and Vishnu *); god of destruction and of all cosmic processes and rhythms, consequently called Natarāja or Lord of the Cosmic Dance.

Smrti — the entire collection of sacred writings and prescriptions of human origin in the Vedic * tradition (excludes *śruti* *).

Sruti — the oral and inspired transmission of Vedic * knowledge and texts through generations of Brāhmins * (cf. *smṛti*).

Sūdra — the fourth *varna* or class in the Hindu social structure; primarily menial servants.

Tagore, Rabindranath (1861–1941), Bengali author, musician, and artist; broadly Vedāntist * but primarily a humanist. See pp. 247–256.

Upanishads a collection of philosophical texts, believed to number between one and two hundred, but most interpreters deal with slightly more than the ten on which Sankara * commented. Radhakrishnan follows Śankara's suggestion that " 'Upanishad' means Brahmā-knowledge by which ignorance is loosened or destroyed."

Vaiśya the third *varna* or class in the Hindu social structure; primarily traders and farmers.

Vedānta the end or acme of the Vedas,* first formulated as an advaitic * or nondual system by Bādarāyaṇa in the *Brahma-Sutra,** and fully developed by Śankara in his commentary on this work, on the Upanishads * and on the *Bhagavadgītā.** See pp. 111–113.

Vedas knowledge identical with or derived from the Vedic Hymns (including the Upanishads), which form the basis of most Hindu philosophical and religious systems: Ṛg-Veda, Yajur-Veda, Sāma-Veda, and Atharva-Veda; each Veda is comprised of a *Mantra* * and a *Brāhmaṇa* part and the various Upanishads.*

Vidyā knowledge; in contrast to *avidyā.** See pp. 153–160.

Vishnu the second person of the Hindu triad (the other two being Brahmā * and Siva *), conceived primarily as the pervader or sustainer of the universe; Kṛishṇa * is counted among Vishnu's many incarnations.

Yoga as formulated by Patanjali * and based on the Sāmkya * system, a physical, mental, and spiritual discipline leading to *samādhi* *; more generally, any one of several disciplines such as *karma-yoga,** *jñāna-yoga,** *bhakti-yoga*, and *dhyāna-yoga*. See pp. 221–243.

Bibliography

Paperback [illegible] [illegible] [illegible] [illegible] [illegible]; the [illegible] [illegible] [illegible] refers to the [illegible] [illegible] [illegible].

[illegible]

Bibliography

Paperback editions are marked by an asterisk; the date in parentheses refers to the original date of publication.

I RADHAKRISHNAN'S PRINCIPAL WORKS

1. Books

Ed. and tr. *The Bhagavadgītā*. London: George Allen and Unwin, 1948 *.

Ed. and tr. *The Brahma-Sūtra*. New York: Harper and Brothers, 1959.

East and West. New York: Harper and Brothers, 1956.

East and West in Religion. London: George Allen and Unwin, 1958 (1933).

Eastern Religions and Western Thought. New York: Oxford University Press, 1959 * (1939).

Fellowship of the Spirit. Cambridge, Massachusetts: The Center for the Study of World Religions, 1961.

Freedom and Culture. Madras: G. A. Natesan and Company, 1936 *.

Great Indians. Bombay: Hind Kitabs Ltd., 1956 * (1949).

The Heart of Hindustan. Madras: G. A. Natesan and Company, 1936.

The Hindu View of Life. New York: Macmillan Company, 1962 * (1926).

An Idealist View of Life. London: George Allen and Unwin, 1957 * (1932).

India and China. Bombay: Hind Kitabs Ltd., 1944.

Indian Philosophy. 2 vols. New York: Macmillan Company, 1962 (1923, 1927).

Kalki—or The Future of Civilization. Bombay: Hind Kitabs Ltd., 1956 * (1948).

Ed. *Mahātmā Gāndhi: Essays and Reflections on His Life and Work*. (2nd ed.). London: George Allen and Unwin, 1949 (1939).

Occasional Speeches and Writings. First Series (1952–56); Second Series (1956–57); Third Series (1959–62). New Delhi: Publications Division, Government of India, 1956–63.

On Nehru. New Delhi: Publications Division, Government of India, 1965.

President Radhakrishnan's Speeches and Writings. New Delhi: Publications Division, Government of India, 1965.

The Philosophy of Rabindranath Tagore. London: Macmillan Company, 1918.

Ed. and tr. *The Principal Upanishads*. London: George Allen and Unwin, 1953 *.

Recovery of Faith. New York: Harper and Brothers, 1955.

The Reign of Religion in Contemporary Philosophy. London: Macmillan Company, 1920.

Religion and Society. London: George Allen and Unwin, 1959 (1947).

Religion in a Changing World. New York: Humanities Press, 1967.
With MOORE, CHARLES A., ed. *A Source Book in Indian Philosophy.* Princeton: Princeton University Press, 1957 *.
With MUIRHEAD, J. H., ed. *Contemporary Indian Philosophy.* (2nd ed.). London: George Allen and Unwin, 1958.
With others, ed. *History of Philosophy Eastern and Western.* 2 vols. London: George Allen and Unwin, 1952, 1953.
With RAJU, P. T., ed. *The Concept of Man: A Study in Comparative Philosophy.* London: George Allen and Unwin, 1966.

2. *Other Writings*

"Fragments of a Confession," *The Philosophy of Sarvepalli Radhakrishnan*, ed. PAUL ARTHUR SCHILPP. Library of Living Philosophers. New York: Tudor Publishing Company, 1952.
"The Indian Approach to the Religious Problem," in *Philosophy and Culture—East and West*, ed. CHARLES A. MOORE. Honolulu: University of Hawaii Press, 1962; reprinted in *The Indian Mind: Essentials of Indian Philosophy and Culture*, ed. CHARLES A. MOORE. Honolulu: East-West Center Press, 1967.
"My Search for Truth," in *Religion in Transition*, ed. VIRGILIUS FERM. London: George Allen and Unwin, 1937.
"Religion and World Unity," in *The Hibbert Journal* (April, 1951), pp. 218–225.
"Reply to Critics," in *The Philosophy of Sarvepalli Radhakrishnan*, ed. SCHILPP.
"The Role of Philosophy in the History of Civilization," in *Proceedings of the Sixth International Congress of Philosophy*, ed. E. S. BRIGHTMAN. New York: Longmans, Green and Company, 1927.
"Spirit in Man," in *Contemporary Indian Philosophy*, eds. RADHAKRISHNAN and MUIRHEAD.
"The Voice of India in the Spiritual Crisis of Our Time," *The Hibbert Journal*, XLIV (July, 1946), pp. 295–304.

II NOTES ON FURTHER READING

1. *Radhakrishnan*

Although there are no distinct stages, periods, or areas in the development of Radhakrishnan's works, there is considerable range of subject matter and technicality. Among the most readable introductions to his thought are *The Hindu View of Life*, the first three chapters of *The Idealist View of Life*, "Fragments of a Confession" in Schilpp's *The Philosophy of Sarvepalli Radhakrishnan*, and *Religion in a Changing World.* For an understanding of the Indian root of Radhakrishnan's philosophical view, see his 240-page Introduction to his edition of *The Brahma-Sūtra.* For a synthesis of Indian and Western philosophical elements, see his most systematic and critical work, *An Idealist View of Life.*

Radhakrishnan's religious thought is best expressed in *Recovery of Faith* and in the first two chapters of *Religion and Society.* Among his many works on Indian ideals, the sections on India in *Eastern Religions and Western Thought* are the most carefully developed; although this lengthy work contains a host of references to historical personalities and events which may be unfamiliar to the average reader, it is Radhakrishnan's most comprehensive comparative study of Indian and Western religious and cultural ideals. *East and West* is insightful and perhaps more readable, but is not easily available.

The most important secondary source on every aspect of Radhakrishnan's thought is Schilpp's *The Philosophy of Sarvepalli Radhakrishnan.* In addition to excellent critical articles by Charles A. Moore, Charles Hartshorne, Joachim Wach, P. T. Raju, T. R. V. Murti, F. S. C. Northrop, D. M. Datta, and others, this volume contains Radhakrishnan's fifty-page "Reply to Critics" and an eighty-page intellectual "Confession." It also contains a complete bibliography up to 1952 (the preceding list includes all of Radhakrishnan's books and articles from 1952 to the present).

The most useful full-length study of Radhakrishnan's philosophy is J. G. Arapura, *Radhakrishnan and Integral Experience* (New York: Asia Publishing House, 1966). C. E. M. Joad, *Counter-Attack from the East: The Philosophy of Radhakrishnan* (London: George Allen and Unwin, 1933) was written before the publication of Radhakrishnan's major works. S. J. Samartha, *Introduction to Radhakrishnan* (New York: Association Press, 1964 *) is extremely elementary and uncritical. S. K. Roy, *The Political Thought of President Radhakrishnan* (Calcutta: Firma K. L. Mukhopadhyay, 1966) compares Radhakrishnan with a catalogue of Western historical figures. Rajendra Pal Singh, *Radhakrishnan: The Portrait of an Educationist* (Delhi: Sterling Publishers, 1967) gleans a philosophy of education from Radhakrishnan's philosophical writings. For a critical study of Radhakrishnan's philosophical method, see my unpublished dissertation, "Radhakrishnan's Comparative Philosophy," Boston University, 1969.

There are several excellent article-length studies of various aspects of Radhakrishnan's thought. See: P. T. Raju, *Idealist Thought of India* (London: George Allen and Unwin, 1953), pp. 331–350; R. S. Srivastava, *Contemporary Indian Philosophy* (Delhi: Munshi Ram Manohar Lal, 1965), pp. 257–338; Ram Pratap Singh, "Radhakrishnan's Substantial Reconstruction of the Vedānta of Śankara," *Philosophy East and West,* XVI (January–April 1966), pp. 5–32. See also my article, "Radhakrishnan and Comparative Philosophy," *International Philosophical Quarterly* (Fall, 1970). Most of the articles dealing with Radhakrishnan in J. P. Atreya (ed.), *Dr. S. Radhakrishnan Souvenir Volume* (Moradabad: Darshana International, 1964) and K. Iśwara Dutt (ed.), *Sarvepalli Radhakrishnan: A Study of the President of India* (New Delhi: Popular Book Services, 1966) are laudatory rather than expository or critical.

2. The Indian Tradition

There are an increasing number of excellent and inexpensive introductions to Indian culture. A. L. Basham's *The Wonder That Was India* (New York: Grove Press, 1959 *) (1954) is still the most comprehensive and informative; O. L. Chavarria-Aguilar (ed.), *Traditional India* (Englewood Cliffs, N.J.: Prentice-Hall, 1964 *) contains brief but authoritative essays on every aspect of Indian culture. The most valuable source book is Wm. Theodore de Bary (ed.), *Sources of Indian Tradition* (New York: Columbia University Press, 1964 *) (1958).

For primary material in classical Indian philosophy, the most useful anthology is Radhakrishnan's and Moore's *Source Book* *; unfortunately, some of the selections are extremely abridged and some of the Editors' notes reveal a Vedāntist bias. Radhakrishnan's *The Principal Upanishads* includes an extremely useful "Introduction," extensive commentary, and a translation which is still representative of the present stage of Sanskrit scholarship. Swami Nikhilananda's edition of *The Upanishads* (New York: Harper and Row, 1964 *), though abridged, is nevertheless an excellent, and an inexpensive, introduction to the Upanishads. Eliot Deutsch's *The Bhagavadgītā* (New York: Holt, Rinehart and Winston, 1968) is probably the most accurate and readable translation; although it is generally regarded as the standard edition, Franklin Edgerton (trans.), *The Bhagavadgītā* (New York: Harper and Row, 1964 *) (1944) is so literal that it is frequently obscure.

For Indian Buddhism, see E. A. Burtt (ed.), *The Teachings of the Compassionate Buddha* (New York: New American Library, 1955 *) and Henry Clarke Warren, *Buddhism in Translations* (New York: Atheneum, 1963 *) (1896).

Among the excellent surveys and interpretations of Indian philosophical and religious thought, see especially: Louis Renou, *Religions of Ancient India* (New York: Schocken Books, 1968 *); Kenneth Morgan (ed.), *The Religion of the Hindus* (New York: The Ronald Press Company, 1953); Heinrich Zimmer, *Philosophies of India*, ed. Joseph Campbell (New York: The World Publishing Company, 1964 *); M. Hiriyanna, *Outlines of Indian Philosophy* (London: George Allen and Unwin, 1964 *); Charles A. Moore (ed.), *The Indian Mind* (Honolulu: East-West Center Press, 1967); Karl H. Potter, *Presuppositions of India's Philosophies* (Englewood Cliffs, New Jersey: Prentice-Hall, Inc., 1963); P. T. Raju, *Idealist Thought of India* (London: George Allen and Unwin, 1953); Chandradhar Sharma, *Indian Philosophy: A Critical Survey* (New York: Barnes & Noble, Inc., 1962 *); V. S. Naravane, *Modern Indian Thought* (New York: Asia Publishing House, 1964).

3. Comparative Studies

The East-West Philosophers' Conferences, held in Hawaii, in 1939, 1949, 1959, 1964, and 1969, under the direction of Charles A. Moore until his death in 1967, have been the moving force behind the growing interest and competence among Westerners in Asian and comparative philosophy. The Proceedings of these Conferences are collected in four excellent volumes edited by Professor Moore: *Philosophy—East and West* (Princeton: Princeton University Press, 1944); *Essays in East-West Philosophy* (Honolulu: University of Hawaii Press, 1951); *Philosophy and Culture—East and West* (Honolulu: University of Hawaii Press, 1962); *The Status of the Individual in East and West* (Honolulu: University of Hawaii Press, 1967). The other indispensable source for comparative philosophy is *Philosophy East and West: A Quarterly Journal for Asian and Comparative Philosophy*, also founded by Professor Moore, and edited by him until 1967 when he was succeeded by Eliot Deutsch.

P. T. Raju, a protegé of Radhakrishnan, has written an informed and incisive study of the content and method of comparative philosophy, *Introduction to Comparative Philosophy;* Radhakrishnan and Raju (eds.), *The Concept of Man: A Study in Comparative Philosophy* (London: George Allen and Unwin, 1966) contains seven essays on "The Concept of Man" by scholars representing the Greek, Jewish, Chinese, Indian, Christian, Islamic, and Marxist traditions. W. R. Inge, and others (eds.), *Radhakrishnan: Comparative Studies in Philosophy Presented in Honour of His Sixtieth Birthday* (London: George Allen and Unwin, 1951) contains excellent essays on comparative philosophy by E. A. Burtt, Charles A. Moore, A. R. Wadia, D. M. Datta, F. S. C. Northrop, and P. T. Raju.

Although it is limited to Asia, and concentrates on Buddhism as the constant in the comparison of the four Asian traditions, Hajime Nakamura's *Ways of Thinking of Eastern Peoples* (Honolulu: East-West Center Press, 1964) is nevertheless a uniquely important study of Asian thought (see review, *Philosophy East and West*, XV [April, 1965], pp. 161–182). For a brief introduction to Asian thought patterns, see Thomas Berry, "Oriental Philosophy and World Humanism," *International Philosophical Quarterly*, I (February, 1961), pp. 5–33, reprinted as *Five Oriental Philosophies* (New York: Magi Books, 1968).

Two recently published collections are also noteworthy: P. T. Raju and Albury Castell (eds.), *East West Studies on the Problem of the Self* (The Hague: Martinus Nijhoff, 1968), and Ram Jee Singh (ed.), *World Perspectives in Philosophy, Religion and Culture: Essays Presented to Professor Dhirendra Mohan Datta* (Patna: Bharati Bhavan, 1968).

4. *Bibliographies*

An indispensable bibliography on every phase of Asian studies, organized by country and discipline, is published annually, usually in the fall, by the *Journal of Asian Studies.* J. Michael Mahar's *India: A Critical Bibliography* (Tucson: University of Arizona Press, 1964 *) is comprehensive and helpfully annotated. The Asia Society (112 East 64 Street, New York 10021) has published *Asia: A Guide to Basic Books* * and *Asia: A Guide to Paperback Books**, both of which are well annotated and organized according to country and discipline.

a lengthy bibliography on the entire range of Indian philosophy. Useful bibliographies are also in Zimmer, *Philosophies of India* *, and Sharma, *Indian Philosophy* *. Karl Potter's *Bibliography of Indian Philosophies* will soon be published by Motilal Banarsidass, Delhi. On Indian religons, helpful bibliographical information follows each article in Benjamin Walker's two-volume encyclopedic survey of Hinduism, *The Hindu World* New York: Praeger, 1968).

COMPLETE
JAICO CATALOGUE

ORIENTAL CLASSICS

J

J-1 THE RUBAIYAT OF OMAR KHAYYAM Rs. 25

J-3 PANCHATANTRA Rs. 55

JATAKA TALES Rs. 50

J-242 THE RAMAYANA Rs. 12

J-243 THE MAHABHARATA Rs. 13

7 THE PROPHET Rs.25/-

J-519 KING VIKRAM & THE GHOST Rs. 36

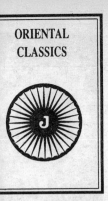

J-532 TALES FROM 1001 ARABIAN NIGHTS Rs. 150

J-545 IMMORTAL TALES FROM KALIDASA Rs. 32

J-547 THE GREAT THRONE OF KING VIKRAMADITYA Rs. 15

J-611 MAHABHARATA (II PARTS) Rs Pe

J-611 MAHABHARATA (II PARTS) Rs. 25 Per Set

J-666 RAMAYANA OF GOSWAMI TULSIDAS Rs. 85

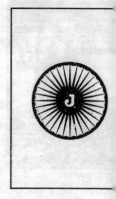

INDIAN
LITERATURE

J-26 THE GOLDEN BOAT Rs. 25

J-27 NECTAR IN A SIEVE R

FAREWELL MY FRIEND & THE GARDEN Rs. 30

J-52 GODAN Rs. 45

J-207 CHEMMEEN Rs. 25

POSSESSION Rs. 15

J-317 OUR UNIVERSE Rs. 25

J-318 LIPIKA Rs. 25

J-339 SRIKANTA Rs. 20

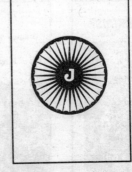

J-439 THE KHALIL GIBRAN READER Rs. 55

J-490 THE HEAD OF KAY'S Rs

J-491 THE POTHUNTERS Rs. 24

J-492 A PREFECT'S UNCLE Rs. 24

J-493 THE WHITE FEATHER Rs

J-494 THE GOLD BAT Rs. 25

J-511 KIDNAPPED Rs. 15

J-512 THE ADVENTURES OF ROBINSON CRUSOE Rs

13 20,000 LEAGUES UNDER THE SEA Rs. 15

J-514 AROUND THE WORLD IN EIGHTY DAYS Rs. 15

J-520 THE COMPLETE LONG STORIES OF SHERLOCK HOLMES Rs. 65

-522 THE COUNT OF MONTE CRISTO Rs. 15

J-523 OLIVER TWIST Rs. 15

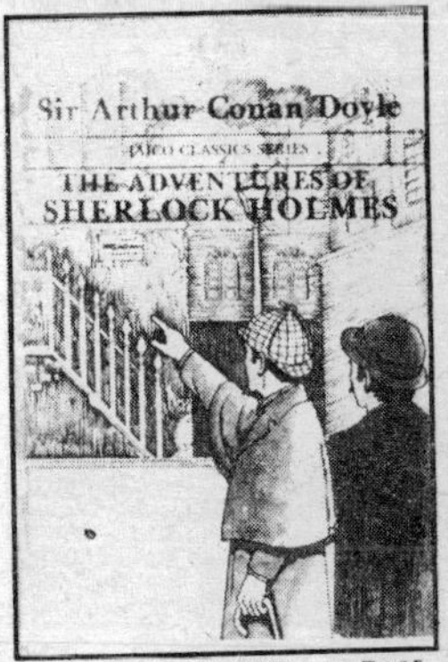

J-524 THE ADVENTURES OF SHERLOCK HOLMES Rs. 15

-525 THE STRANGE CASE OF DR. JEKYLL & MR. HYDE Rs. 15

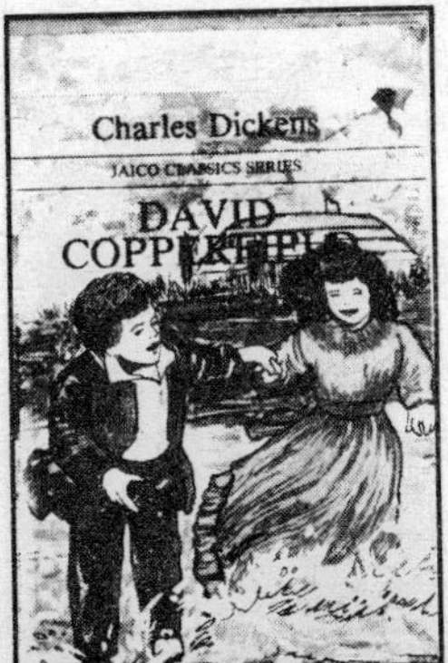

J-526 DAVID COPPERFIELD Rs. 15

J-527 TREASURE ISLAND Rs. 15

J-528 THE ADVENTURES OF. Rs. 15
TOM SAWYER

J-529 THE MAN IN THE IRON Rs. 15
MASK

J-530 THE COMPLETE Rs. 135
SHORT STORIES OF
SHERLOCK HOLMES

J-544 LADY CHATTERLEY'S Rs. 40
LOVER

J-548 A TALE OF TWO CITIES Rs. 15

J-551 THE HOUND OF Rs. 15
BASKERVILLES

J-568 THE HUNCHBACK OF Rs. 15
NOTRE-DAME

J-572 THE PRISONER OF Rs. 15
ZENDA

J-573 ADVENTURES OF Rs. 15
ROBIN HOOD

THE GREATEST WORKS OF KAHLIL GIBRAN Rs. 180

J-595 IVANHOE Rs. 15

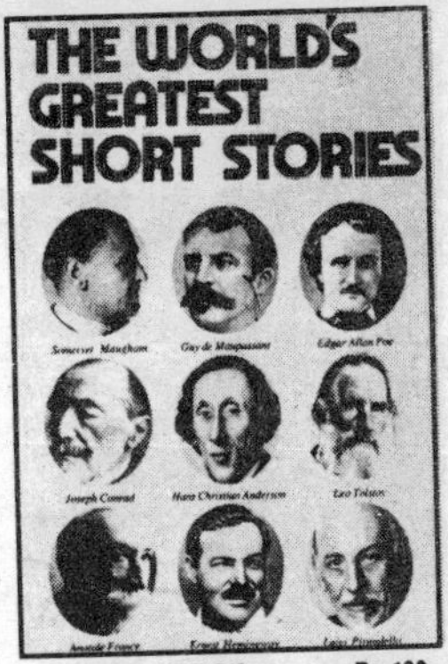

J-598 THE WORLD'S GREATEST SHORT STORIES Rs. 130

HIS LAST BOW Rs. 35

J-603 THE CASE-BOOK OF SHERLOCK HOLMES Rs. 35

J-604 THE MEMOIRS OF SHERLOCK HOLMES. Rs. 35

THE ADVENTURESOF SHERLOCK HOLMES Rs. 35

J-606 THE RETURN OF SHERLOCK HOLMES Rs. 35

J-616 ADVENTURES OF DON QUIXOTE Rs. 15

J-639 THE INVISIBLE MAN - Rs. 15

J-644 THE BOOK OF GREAT MYSTERIES Rs. 150

J-694 THE WORLD'S GREATEST LOVE STORIE[S] R[s]

JB-522 THE COUNT OF MONTE CRISTO (BENGALI) Rs. 15

JB-525 THE STRANGE CASE OF DR. JEKYLL & MR. HYDE (BENGALI) Rs. 15

JB-548 A TALE OF TWO CITIES (BENGALI) R

JB-573 ADVENTURES OF ROBINHOOD (BENGALI) Rs. 15

JB-616 ADVENTURES OF DON QUIXOTE (BENGALI) Rs. 15

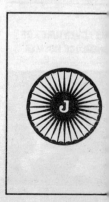

AUTOBIOGRAPHIES AND BIOGRAPHIES

J

J-41 MAHATMA GANDHI **Rs. 75**
(ESSAYS & REFLECTIONS)

J-71 NAPOLEON **Rs. 80**

-2 JAWAHARLAL NEHRU **TOP**

J-175 SUBHASH CHANDRA **Rs. 45**
BOSE

J-196 AUTOBIOGRAPHY **Rs. 46**
OF A YOGI (ENGLISH)

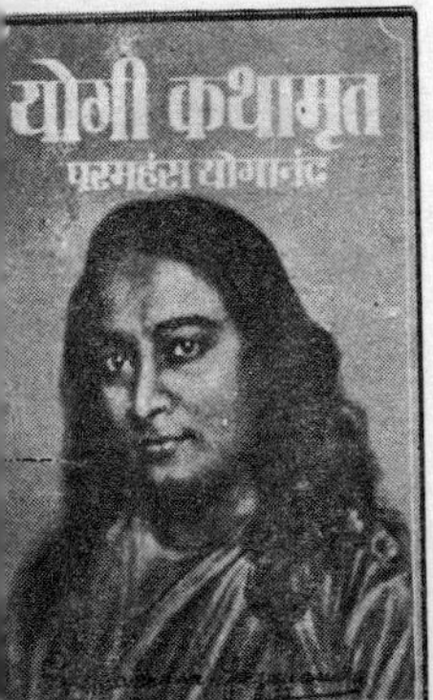

-196 YOGI KATHAMRIT **Rs. 50**
(HINDI)

JT-196 YOGI ATMAKATHA **Rs. 65**
(TELGU)

J-208 AUTOBIOGRAPHY OF **Rs. 75**
AN UNKNOWN INDIAN

J-316 A TAGORE TESTAMENT Rs. 30

J-412 ADOLF HITLER Rs. 35

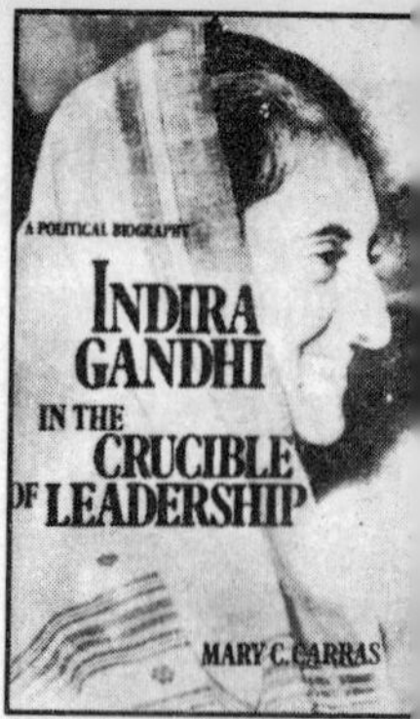

J-475 INDIRA GANDHI IN THE CRUCIBLE OF LEADERSHIP Rs. 175 (
Rs. 15 (

J-510 MEJDA: SRI PARAMAHANSA YOGANANDA - HIS FAMILY & EARLY LIFE Rs. 40

J-541 MEIN KAMPF Rs. 125

HISTORY, POLITICS AND SOCIOLOGY

J-247 THE CONTINENT OF CIRCE Rs. 60

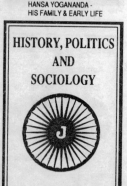

J-464 WAR OF THE SPRINGING TIGERS Rs.

8 HOW MOSCOW Rs. 40(PB)
3 SEES KASHMIR Rs. 125(HB)

JH-58 PRINCELY INDIA & LAPSE OF BRITISH PARAMOUNTCY Rs. 220

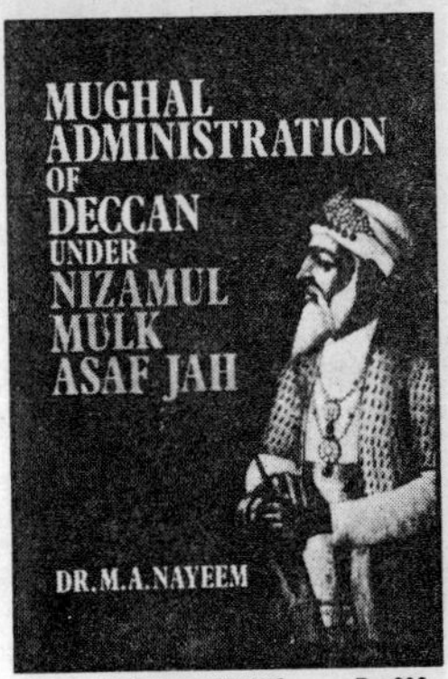

JH-59 MUGHAL ADMINISTRATION OF DECCAN UNDER NIZAMUL MULK ASAF JAH Rs. 300

60 THE SPLENDOUR OF HYDERABAD Rs. 650

JH-67 THE RANI OF JHANSI Rs. 200

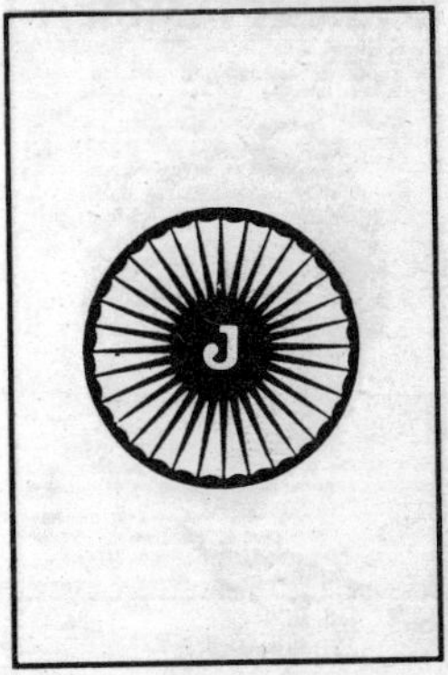

J-33 THE WISDOM OF INDIA Rs. 75

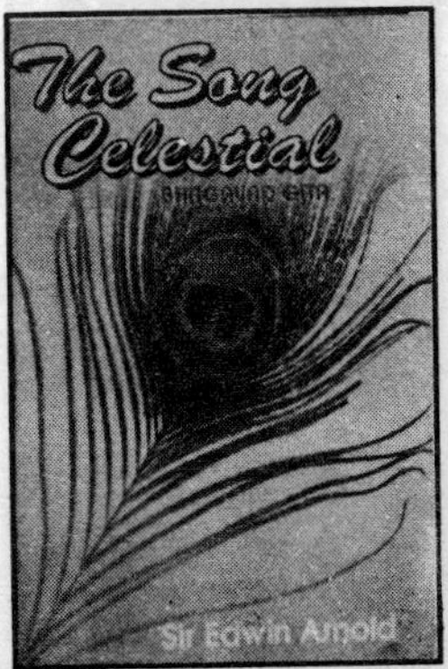

J-64 THE SONG CELESTIAL BHAGAVAD GITA Rs. 35

J-124 GLIMPSES OF WORLD RELIGIONS Rs. 55

J-126 RAMANA MAHARSHI THE PATH OF SELF-KNOWLEDGE Rs. 45

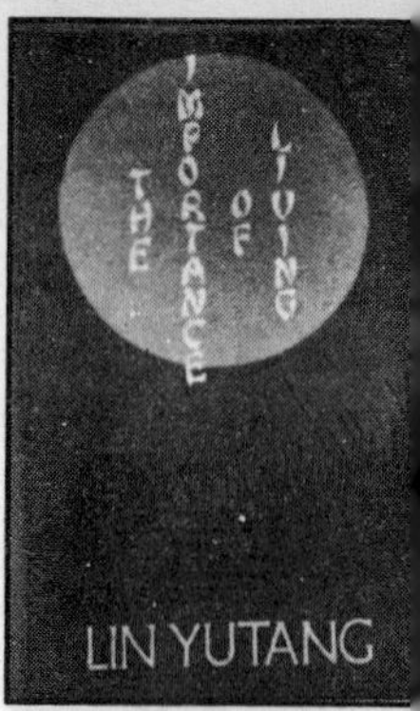

J-176 THE IMPORTANCE OF LIVING T

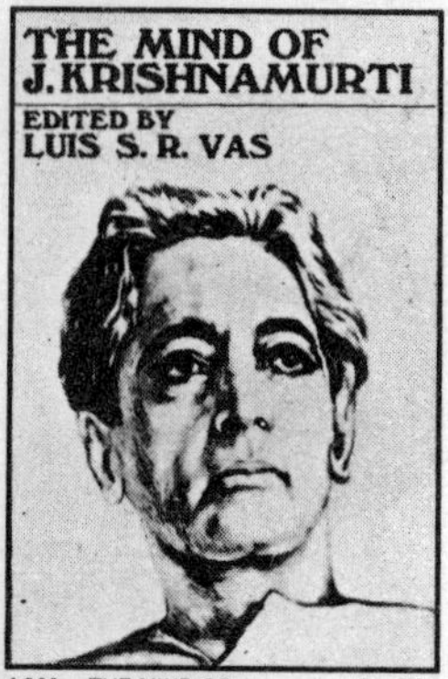

J-363 THE MIND OF J.KRISHNAMURTI Rs. 55

J-384 THE BASIC WRITINGS OF S. RADHAKRISHNAN Rs. 40

J-411 THE MIND OF SWAMI VIVEKANANDA Rs.

J-429 BEGONE GODMEN Rs. 35

J-430 THE MIND OF ADI SHAKARACHARYA Rs. 30

J-452 GODS, DEMONS & SPIRITS Rs. 4

KRISHNA: MYTH OR REALITY Rs. 12

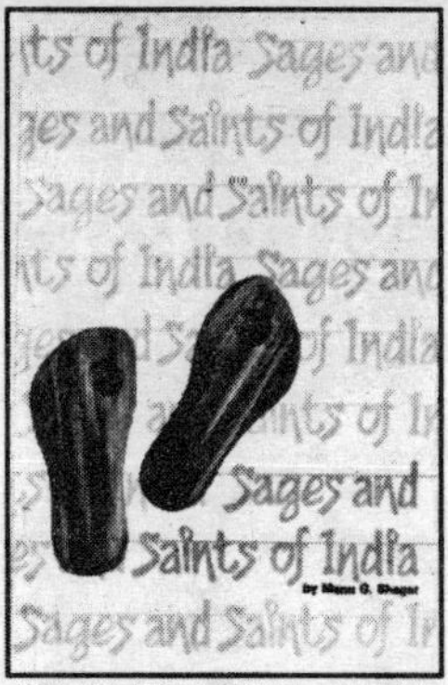

J-488 SAGES & SAINTS OF INDIA TOP

J-495 MUSLIM MIRACLE MAKERS Rs. 20

HE BHAGAVATAM TOP

J-509 TREASURY OF SPIRITUAL TRUTHS Rs. 20

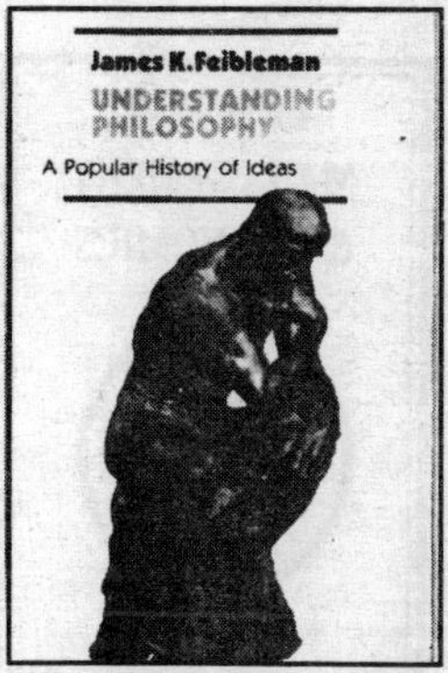

J-557 UNDERSTANDING PHILOSOPHY Rs. 45

RISHNA : THE AN & HIS PHILOSOPHY Rs. 140

J-600 HINDU PHILOSOPHY Rs. 45

J-661 SAI BABA OF SHIRDI Rs.110

J-561 FUTURE CRIME Rs. 35

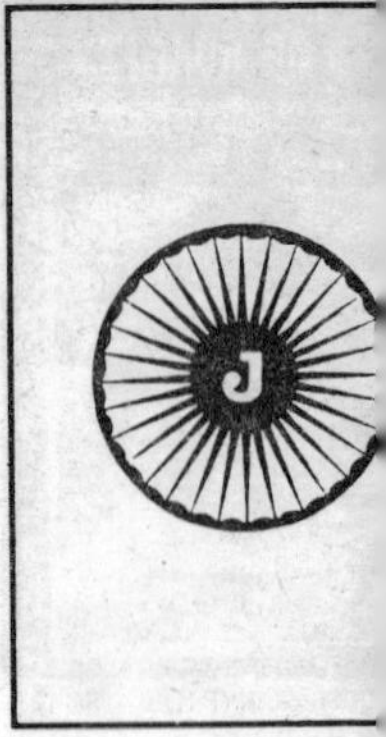

J-460 HOW TO FIGHT DIRTY AGAINST MANAGEMENT Rs.40

J-462 HOW TO CUT OFFICE COSTS

J-515 THE MAGIC OF RATIOS Rs. 35

J-531 BACK TO BASICS: PLANNING Rs. 35

J-533 YOU CAN NEGOTIATE ANYTHING

4 CORPORATE COMBAT **Rs. 40**

J-538 INDUSTRIAL PURC-HASE ING& MATERIALS MANAGEMENT **Rs. 75**

J-539 ACCOUNTING & FINANCE FOR MANAGERS **Rs.140**

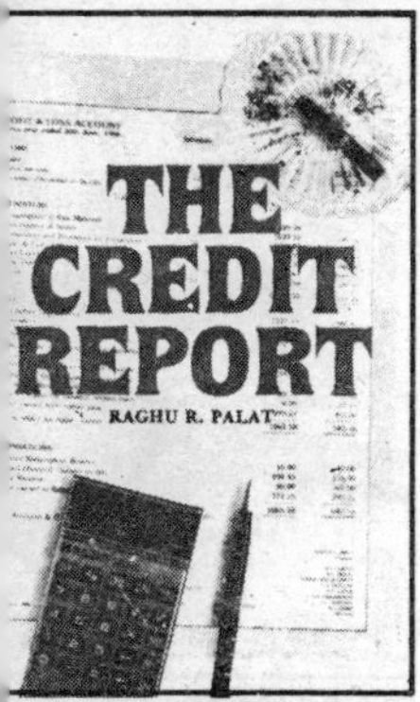

3 THE CREDIT REPORT **Rs. 35**

J-546 MATERIALS MANA- **Rs.75(PB)**
JH-69 GEMENT & INVEN- **Rs.195 (HB)**
TORY CONTROL

J-720 TAX PLANNING FOR THE SALARIED EMPLOYEE (Revised Edition 1993/94) **Rs. 40**

) THE GREATEST MANAGEMENT PRINCIPLE IN THE WORLD **Rs.35**

J-559 MANAGEMENT BY COMMON SENSE **Rs. 55**

J-567 PROMOTING SALES **Rs. 40**

J-570 THE LAST WORD ON MANAGEMENT Rs. 55

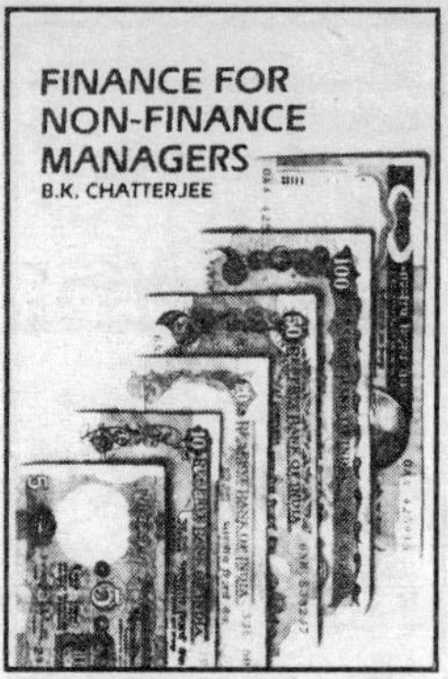

J-587 FINANCE FOR NON-FINANCE MANAGERS Rs. 75

J-588 COSTING & MANAGERIAL ACCOUNTING Rs.

J-617 HOW TO READ ANNUAL REPORTS Rs. 65

J-634 TELEMARKETING THAT WORKS Rs. 90

J-656 UNLOCKING CREATIVITY Rs.

J-657 STEPS TO STRATEGIC MANAGEMENT Rs. 55

J-662 THE ACTION CENTRED LEADER Rs. 50

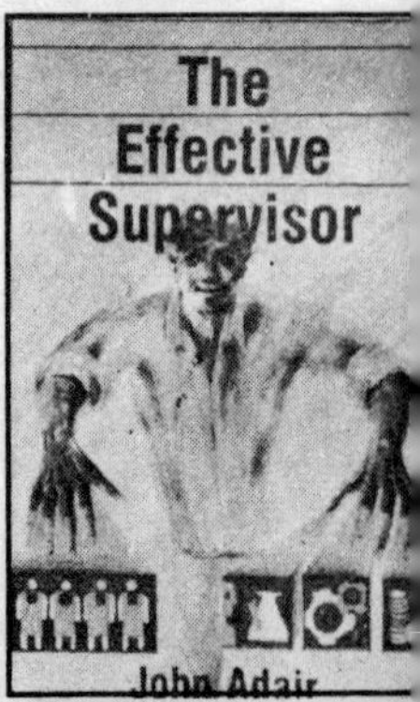

J-664 THE EFFECTIVE SUPERVISOR Rs.

Techniques of **FINANCIAL ANALYSIS**

Latest SEVENTH Revised Edition

J-678   TECHNIQUES OF   **Rs. 120**
FINANCIAL ANALYSIS

OTC EXCHANGE OF INDIA

THE STOCK EXCHANGE FOR YOU AND ME

NIPUN S. MEHTA

J-695   OTC EXCHANGE OF   **Rs. 50**
INDIA

JAICO'S wonderworld OF investments

Raghu R Palat

J-734   JAICO'S WONDER
WORLD OF INVESTMENTS
(Revised Edition 1993/94)

A COMPLETE GUIDE FOR **NON-RESIDENT INDIANS**

KULDEEP NAJELA

J-735   A COMPLETE GUIDE   **Rs. 80**
FOR NON-RESIDENT
INDIANS (1993/94)

COMPENSATING YOUR SALES FORCE

HOW TO USE COMMISSIONS • DRAWS •
BONUSES • PERKS • CONTESTS •
TERRITORIES AND QUOTAS TO MOTIVATE
THE SALES TEAM AND INCREASE SALES

J-696   COMPENSATING   **Rs. 90**
YOUR SALES FORCE

Handbook of service conditions for Workmen in Banks

FIFTH EDITION INCORPORATING
SUPPLEMENTARY THIRD BIPARTITE
SETTLEMENT AND FOURTH BIPARTITE SETTLEMENT

HOSHANG DOONGAJI

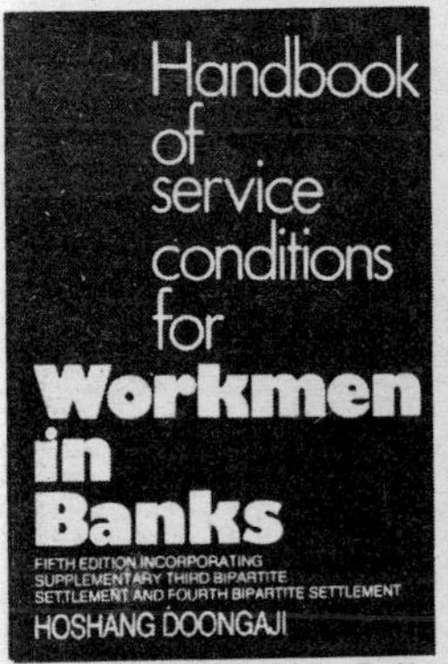

JH-7   HANDBOOK OF SERVI-   **Rs. 60**
CE CONDITIONS FOR
WORKMEN IN BANKS

PERSONNEL MANAGEMENT

V. G. KARNIK

JH-24   PERSONNEL   **Rs. 55**
MANAGEMENT

PERSONNEL MANAGEMENT

An Overview
Anand S Agarwal

JH-43   PERSONNEL MANAGE   **Rs. 30**
MENT-AN OVERVIEW

Marketing Management

A FINANCE EMPHASIS

S.K. Chatterjee

JH-45   MARKETING MANAGE   **Rs. 75**
MENT : A FINANCE
EMPHASIS

JH-55 HOW TO DELEGATE- A GUIDE TO GETTING THINGS DONE Rs. 160 (HB) Rs. 65 (PB)

JH-56 NON-RESIDENTS : TAX-ATION & INVESTMENT IN INDIA Rs. 350

JH-57 THE NEW MANAGE-RIAL GRID Rs. 200 (HB) Rs. 75 (PB)

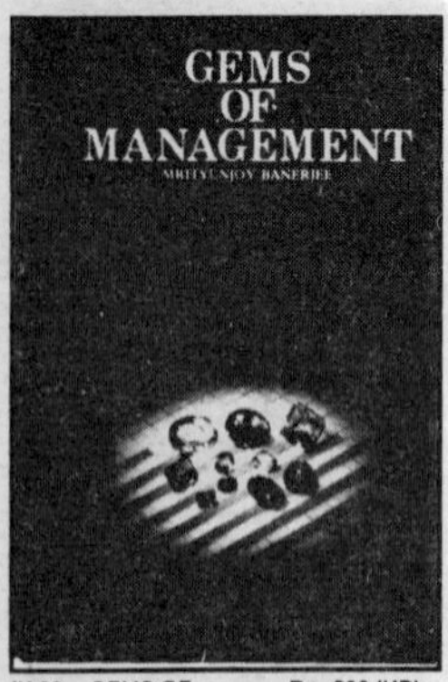

JH-63 GEMS OF MANAGEMENT Rs. 200 (HB) Rs. 55 (PB)

JH-65 AN EXECUTIVE'S COACHING HAND BOOK Rs. 225

JH-66 SOCIAL VIEW OF INDUSTRIAL RELATIONS Rs. 175

JH-68 PROUT & ECONOMIC REFORM IN INDIA & THE THIRD WORLD Rs. 150

JH-74 THE MAKINGS OF A MILLIONAIRE Rs. 200

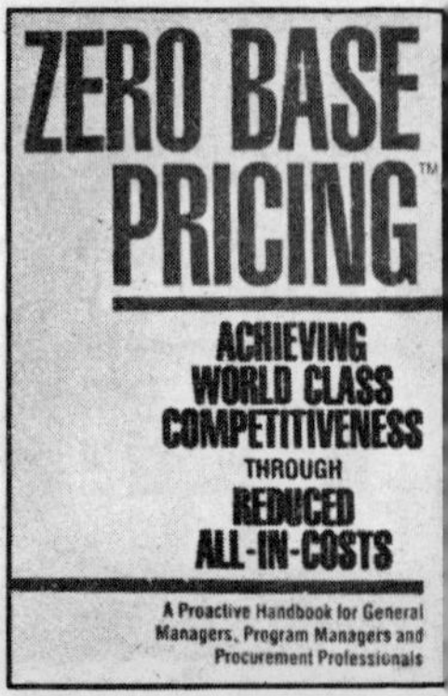

JH-75 ZERO BASE PRICING Rs. 410

H-79 IMPROVING ORGANISATIONAL EFFECTIVENESS **Rs. 250**

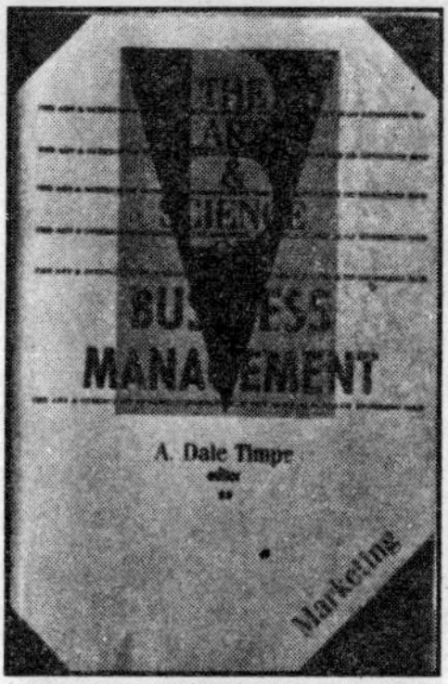

JH-80 THE ART & SCIENCE OF BUSINESS MANAGEMENT (in 7 Vols.) **Rs. 3500** (Per Set)

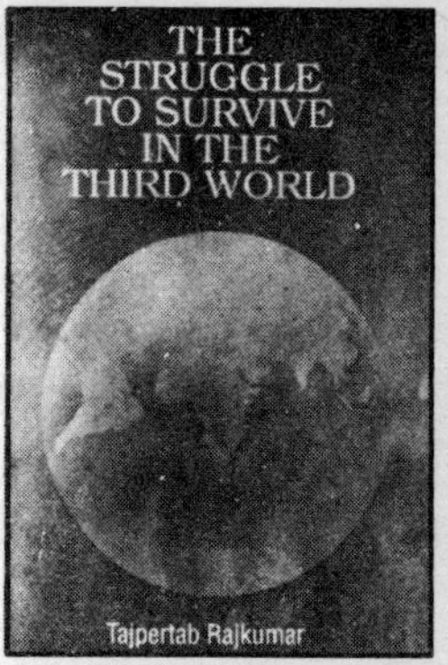

JH-86 THE STRUGGLE TO SURVIVE IN THE THIRD WORLD **Rs. 225**

-87 PROJECT COST CONTROL FOR MANAGERS **Rs. 300**

JH-88A COST REDUCTION HANDBOOK **Rs. 650**

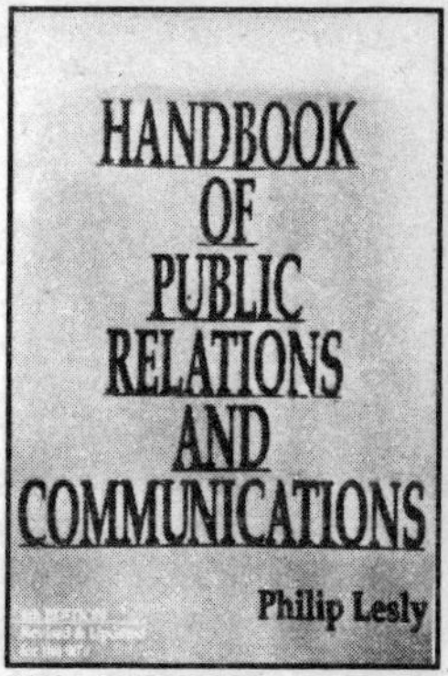

JH-90 HANDBOOK OF PUBLIC RELATIONS & COMMUNICATIONS **Rs.1350**

JH-91 SAFETY MANAGEMENT IN INDUSTRY **Rs. 975**

BOOKS FOR
EVERYDAY USE

J-372   WOMAN'S WORLD   Rs. 24

J-403   CONVERSATIONAL   Rs. 15
          HINDI

J-408   HINDUSTANI FOR   Rs. 15
          THE TOURIST

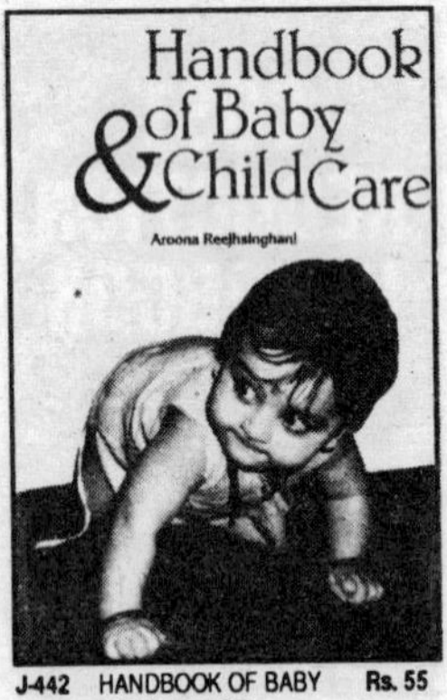

J-442   HANDBOOK OF BABY   Rs. 55
          & CHILD CARE

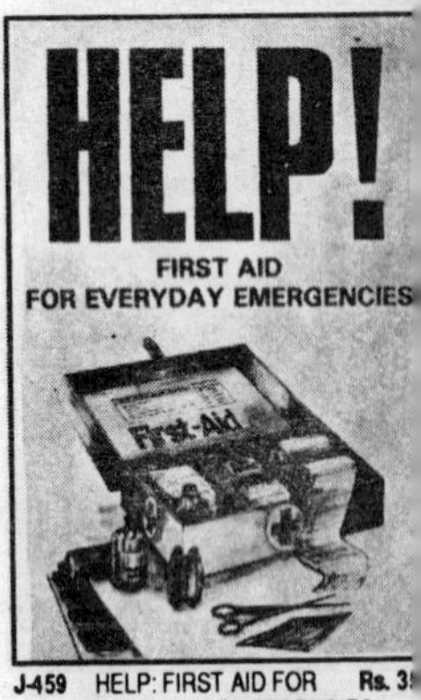

J-459   HELP: FIRST AID FOR   Rs. 3!
          EVERYDAY EMERGENCIES

J-461   UNDERSTANDING   TOP
          ELECTRONICS

J-499   ARABIC FOR   Rs. 35
          EVERYDAY USE

HANDBOOK
OF
ENGLISH
USAGE
for Editors,
Writers and
Executives

J-537   HANDBOOK OF   Rs. 4
          ENGLISH USAGE FOR
          EDITORS, WRITERS. . . .

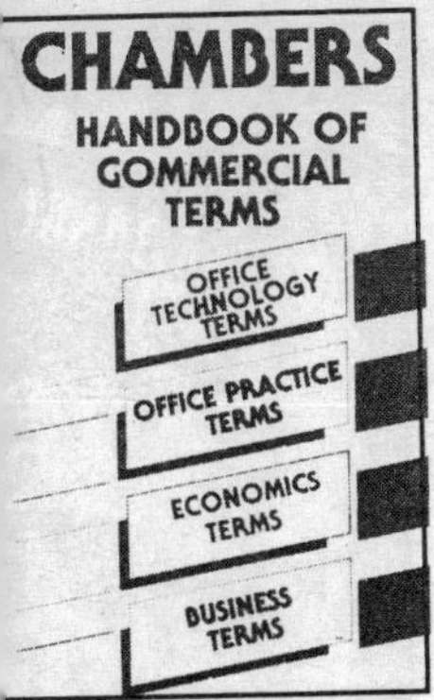

562 CHAMBERS HANDBOOK OF COMMERCIAL TERMS Rs. 60

We welcome manuscripts from Heads of Departments, Professors and Academicians for publication in fields of Management, Computers, Engineering, Technical and other related fields.

Should you be interested in recieving regularly our catalogue and forthcoming information of new books, do send us your full name and proper address.

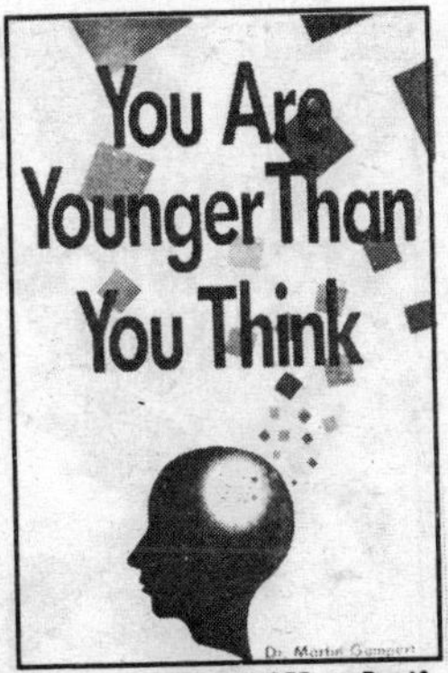

J-102 YOU ARE YOUNGER THAN YOU THINK Rs. 40

J-179 HINTS FOR SELF-CULTURE Rs. 40

J-192 1001 WAYS TO IMPROVE YOUR CONVERSATION & SPEECHES Rs. 45

J-463 REMEMBERING MADE EASY. Rs. 25

J-472 RAPID READING Rs. 36

J-536 ANGER: HOW TO LIVE WITH & WITHOUT IT Rs. 70

J-614 THE ART OF RELAXATION Rs. 40

J-655 HOW TO BE SELF-CONFIDENT Rs.

J-672 DYNAMICS OF MIND MANAGEMENT Rs. 60

JH-64 ATTITUDE FORMATION & CHANGE Rs.450

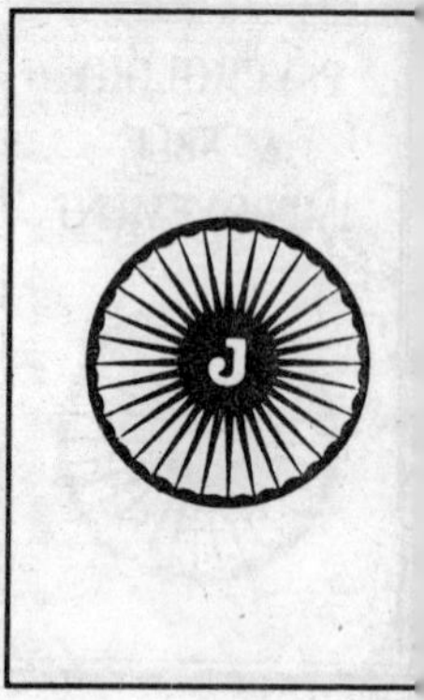

J-199 SPEAKER'S ENCYCLOPAEDIA OF HUMOUR Rs. 48

J-224 SPEAKER'S HAND BOOK OF HUMOUR Rs. 4

LOVE IS A MAN'S AFFAIR Rs. 4

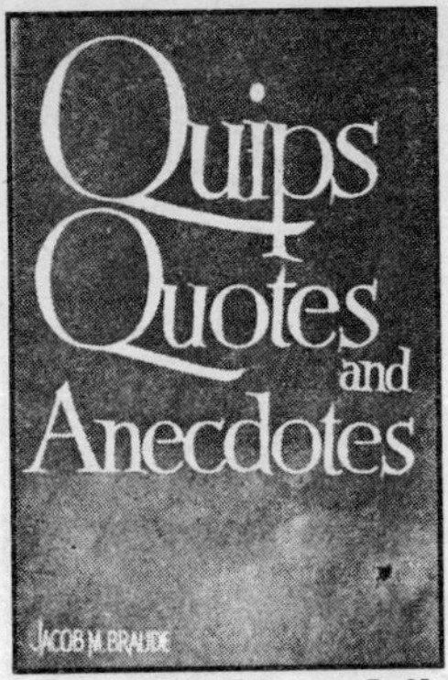

J-236 THE SPEAKER'S ENCYCLOPAEDIA OF QUIPS, QUOTES & ANECDOTES Rs. 65

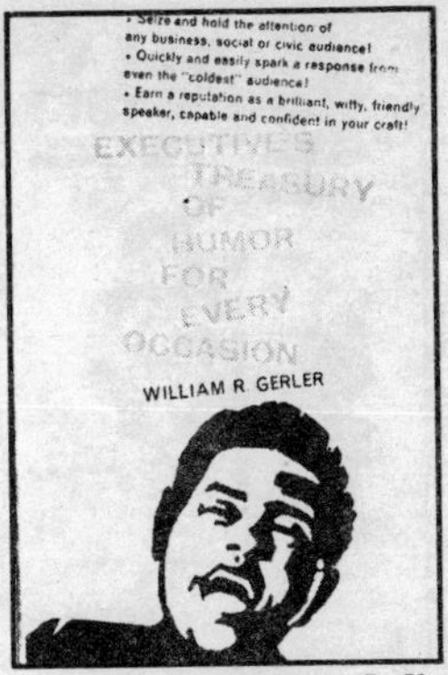

J-275 EXECUTIVE'S TREASURY OF HUMOUR FOR EVERY OCCASION Rs. 50

BRAUDE'S TREASURY OF WIT & HUMOUR Rs. 50

J-371 NEW TREASURY OF STORIES, SPEAKING & WRITING FOR EVERY OCCASION Rs. 65

J-383 THE BEST JOKES OF ALL TIME & HOW TO TELL THEM Rs. 50

SEX CAPADES Rs. 10

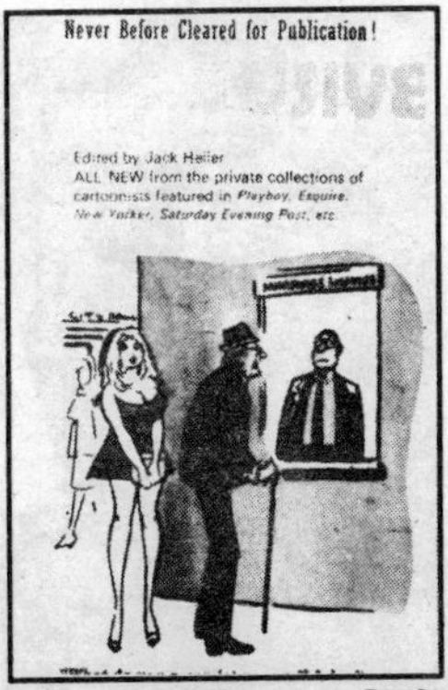

J-469 SEXCLUSIVE Rs. 10

J-470 SUPER SEX Rs. 10

J-471 DO I HAVE A GIRL FOR YOU Rs. 15

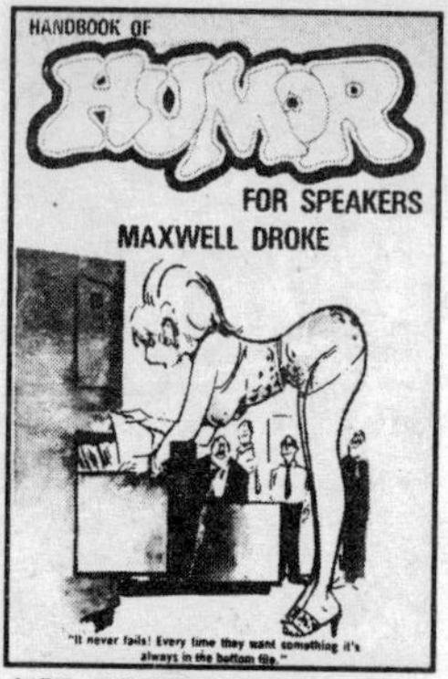

J-474 HANDBOOK OF HUMOUR FOR SPEAKERS Rs. 45

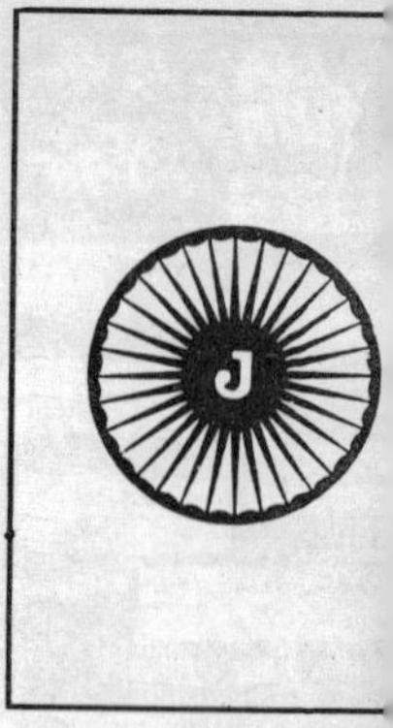

J-186 THE ART OF LOVE MAKING Rs. 45

J-191 KAMASUTRA OF VATSYAYANA (ILLUSTRATED) F

J-202 SEX IN MARRIAGE Rs. 45

J-365 SECRETS OF SEX Rs. 40

J-377 SENSOUS MAN R

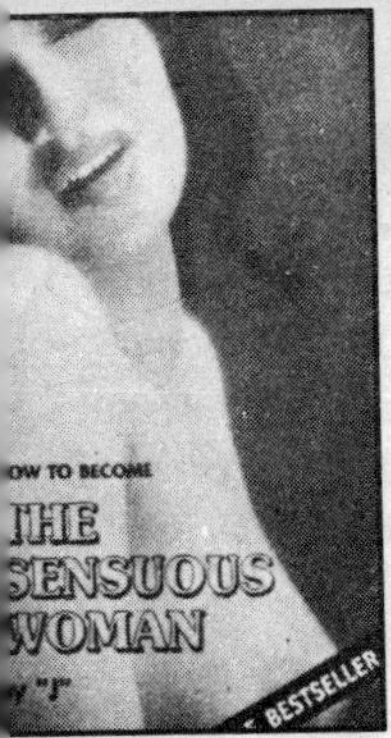

SENSOUS WOMAN Rs. 40

J-423 TANTRA: THE SECRET POWER OF SEX Rs. 35

J-431 YOUR GUIDE TO LOVE & SEX. Rs. 35

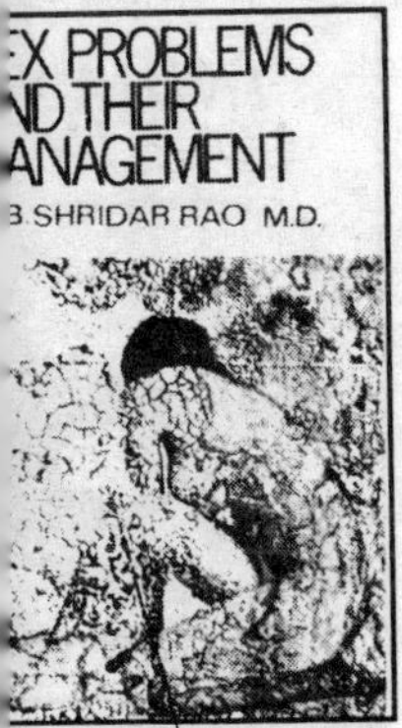

SEX PROBLEMS & THEIR MANAGEMENT Rs. 8

J-465 EXPERT LOVEMAKING Rs. 35

J-485 TANTRA : THE KEY TO SEXUAL POWER & PLEASURE Rs. 45

THE SOCIAL POWER OF SEX Rs. 35

J-540 HOW TO MANAGE YOUR HUSBAND TOP

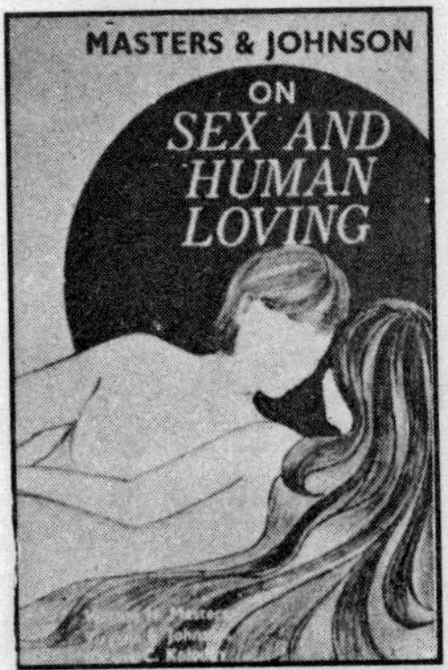

J-558 MASTERS & JOHNSON ON SEX & HUMAN LOVING Rs. 125

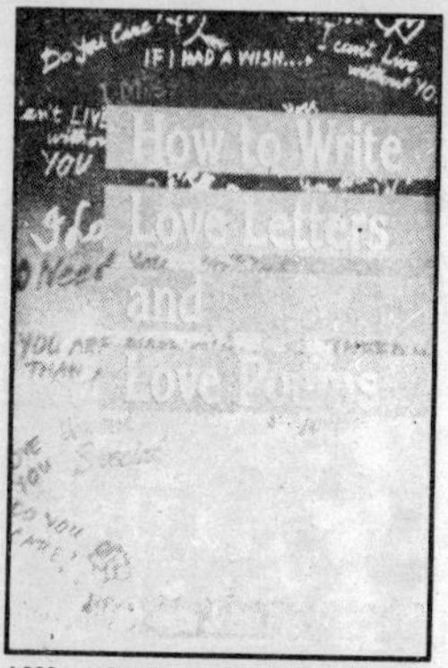

J-693 HOW TO WRITE LOVE LETTERS & LOVE POEMS Rs. 75

COOKERY

J-62 INDIAN COOKERY Rs. 35

J-187 INDIAN COOKING

J-189 CURRIES OF INDIA Rs. 35

J-268 THE ART OF VEGETARIAN COOKERY Rs. 36

J-300 GOOD FOOD FROM INDIA. R

NDIAN COOKERY Rs. 35

J-343 REGIONAL INDIAN RECIPES Rs. 40

J-344 SIMPLIFIED INDIAN COOKERY Rs. 35

DVENTURES IN NDIAN COOKING Rs. 50

J-392 HOUSEWIFE'S GUIDE TO CHINESE COOKING Rs. 35

J-404 ART OF SOUTH INDIAN COOKING Rs. 35

ELIGHTS FROM AHARASHTRA Rs. 35

J-422 DELICIOUS BENGALI DISHES Rs. 35

J-424 VEGETARIAN WONDERS FROM GUJARAT Rs. 35

J-445 COOKING THE PUNJABI WAY Rs. 35

J-451 PARTY RECIPES Rs. 35

J-496 TEMPTINGLY YOURS

J-497 101 RECIPES Rs. 35

J-501 DELICIOUSLY YOURS Rs. 35

J-516 APPETISINGLY YOURS

J-542 DELIGHTS FROM GOA Rs. 35

J-552 OIL-LESS COOKING Rs. 35

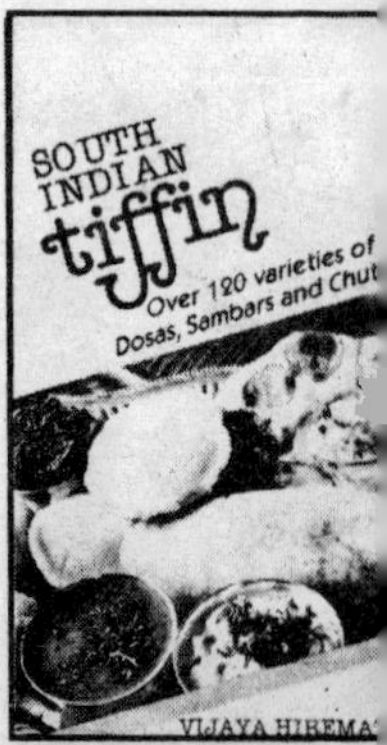

J-560 SOUTH INDIAN TIFFIN

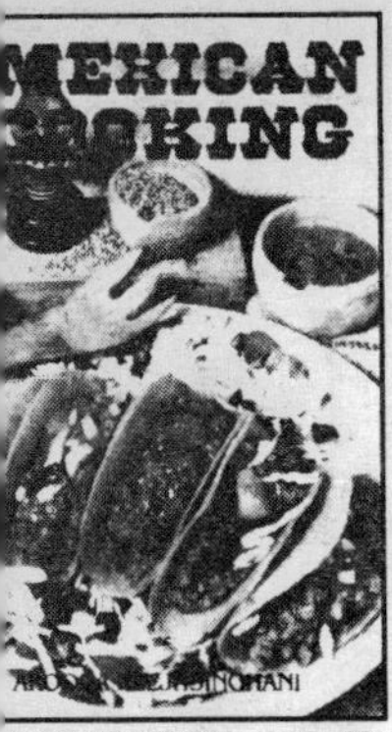

MEXICAN COOKING Rs. 35

FOR RECIEVING
REGULAR INFORMATION
ON BOOKS, CONTACT
OR WRITE TO US
WITH COMPLETE ADDRESS.

J-296 YOGA : THE TECHNIQUE OF HEALTH & HAPPINESS Rs. 25

J-308 YOGA FOR YOU Rs. 35

FOREVER YOUNG FOREVER HEALTHY Rs. 30

J-349 YOGA FOR PHYSICAL FITNESS Rs. 45

J-351 YOGA : THE KEY TO LIFE Rs. 45

J-397 YOGA : MEANING, VALUES & PRACTICE Rs. 30

J-414 YOGA: ILLUSTRATED DICTIONARY Rs. 45

J-446 ALL ABOUT CONTACT LENSES R

J-476 YOUR BODY IN HEALTH & SICKNESS Rs. 30

J-486 YOGA FOR HEALING Rs. 30

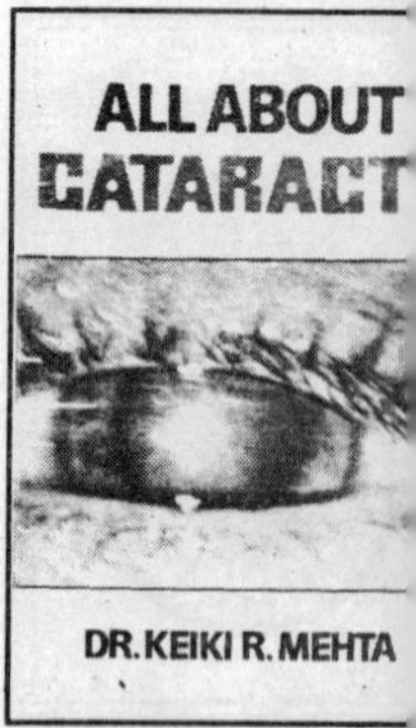

J-498 ALL ABOUT CATARACTS R

J-500 EYE CARE Rs. 25

J-508 YOGA & YOUR HEART Rs. 50

J-517 CONQUERING CONSTIPATION Rs

DEFEATING DEPRESSION **Rs. 30**

J-549 DIET CURE FOR COMMON AILMENTS **Rs. 50**

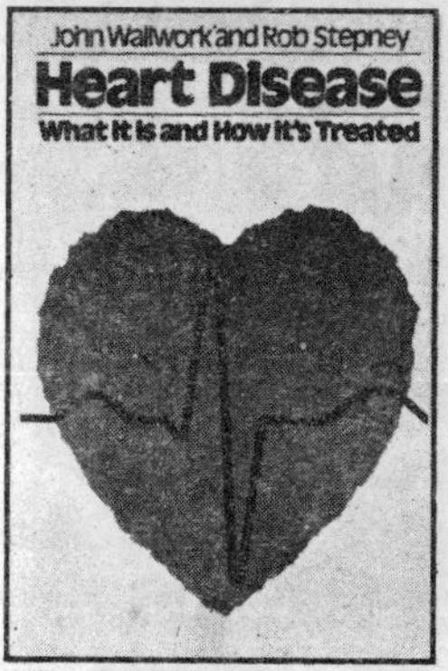

J-554 HEART DISEASE- WHAT IT IS & HOW IT'S TREATED **Rs. 50**

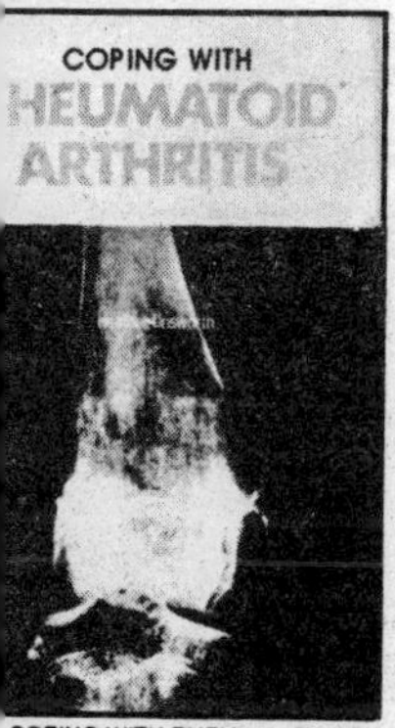

COPING WITH RHEU-MATOID ARTHRITIS **Rs. 25**

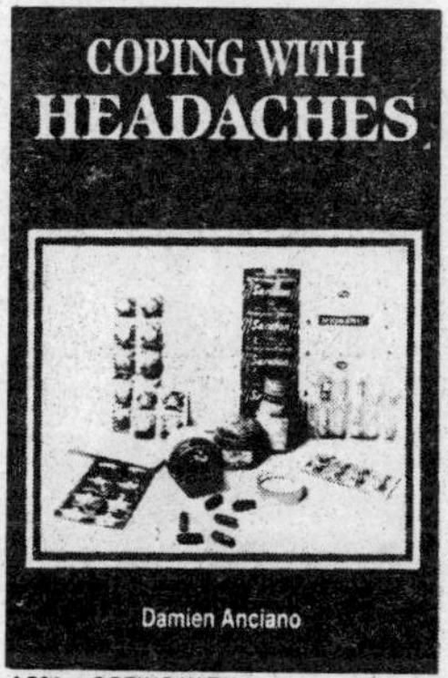

J-564 COPING WITH HEADACHES **Rs. 25**

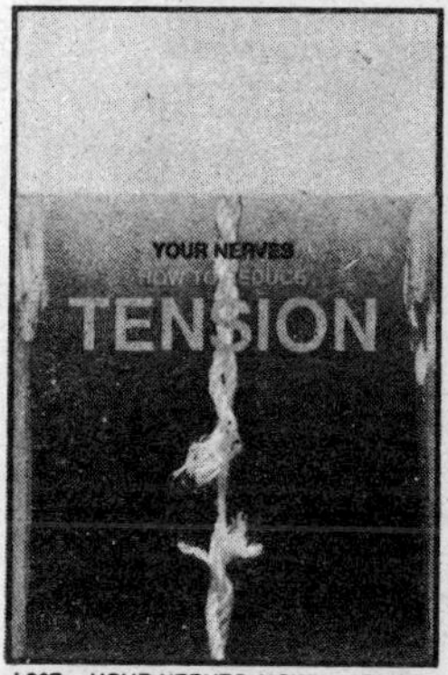

J-607 YOUR NERVES: HOW TO REDUCE TENSION **Rs. 20**

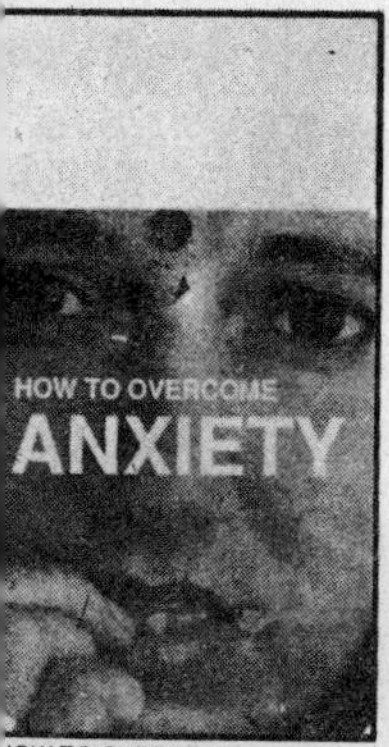

HOW TO OVERCOME ANXIETY **Rs. 20**

J-610 HANDBOOK OF MEDICINES FOR LAYMAN **Rs. 75**

J-618 A COMPLETE HAND-BOOK OF NATURE CURE. **Rs. 100**

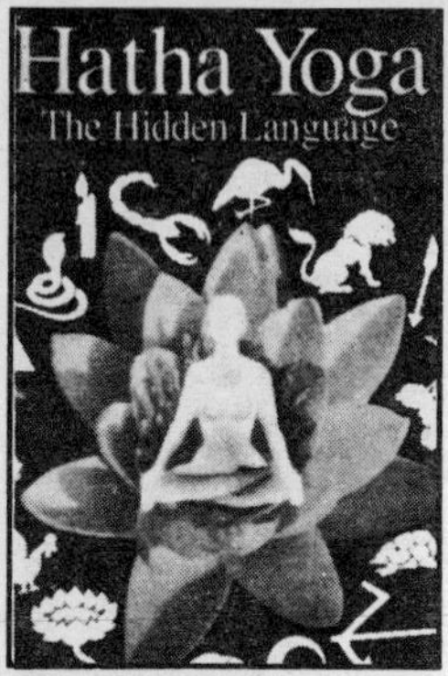

J-658 HATHA YOGA - THE HIDDEN LANGUAGE Rs. 150

We welcome manuscripts from Heads o Departments, Professors, Academicians & Professionals in fields of Management Computers, Engineering, Technology, etc.

BRITISH MEDICAL ASSOCIATION FAMILY SERIES

J

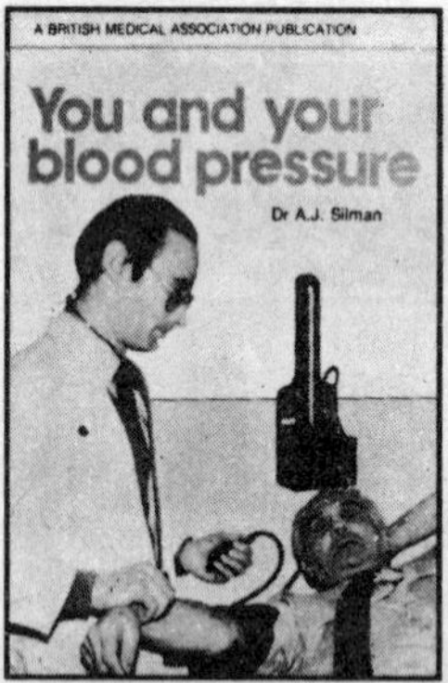

J-575 YOU & YOUR BLOOD PRESSURE Rs. 15

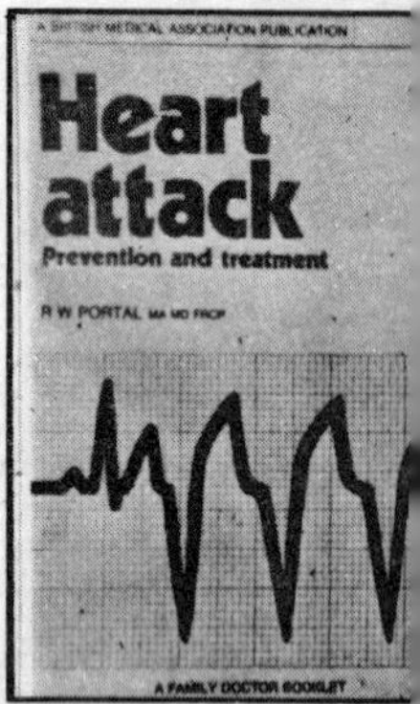

J-576 HEART ATTACK Rs.

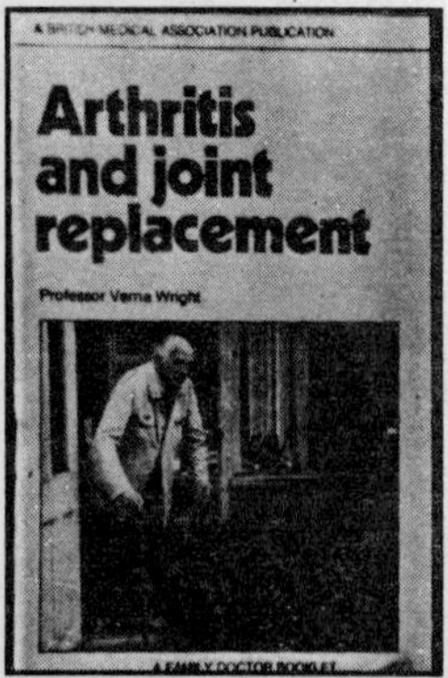

J-577 ARTHRITIS & JOINT REPLACEMENT Rs. 15

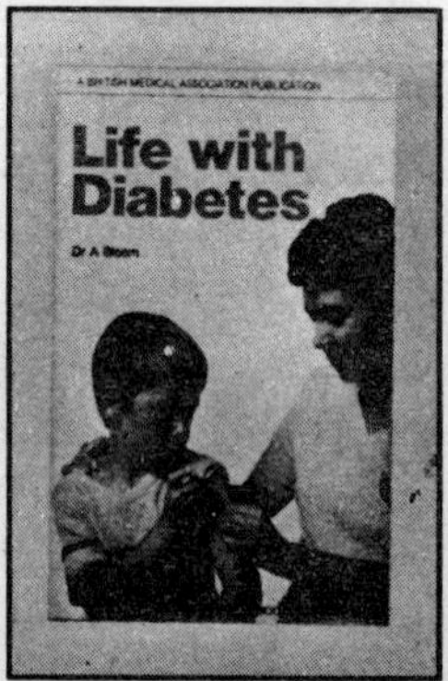

J-578 LIFE WITH DIABETES Rs. 15

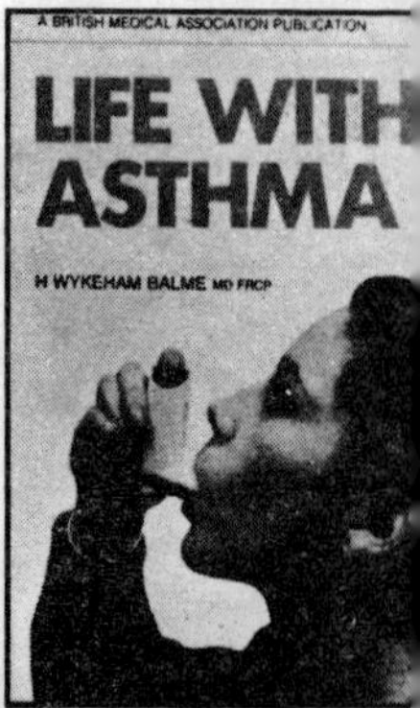

J-579 LIFE WITH ASTHAMA Rs.

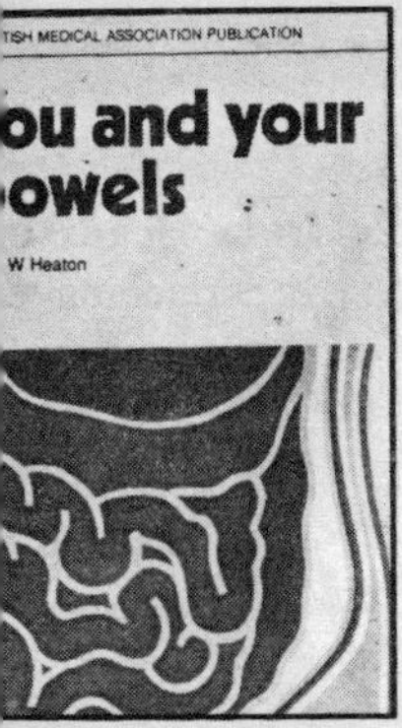

YOU & YOUR BOWELS Rs. 15

J-581 KNOWING ABOUT SEX Rs. 15

J-582 COPING WITH STRESS Rs. 15

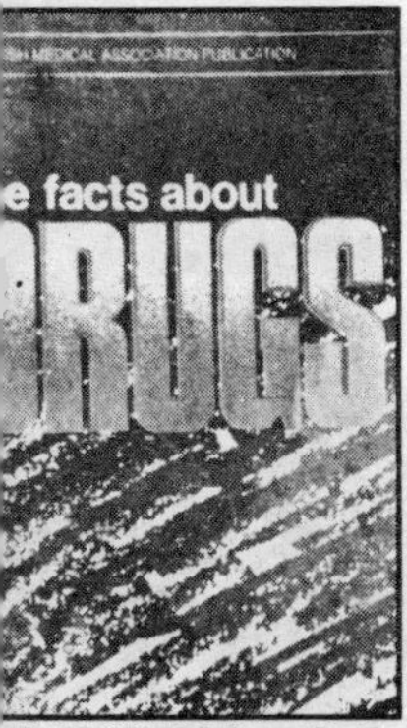

THE FACTS ABOUT DRUGS Rs. 15

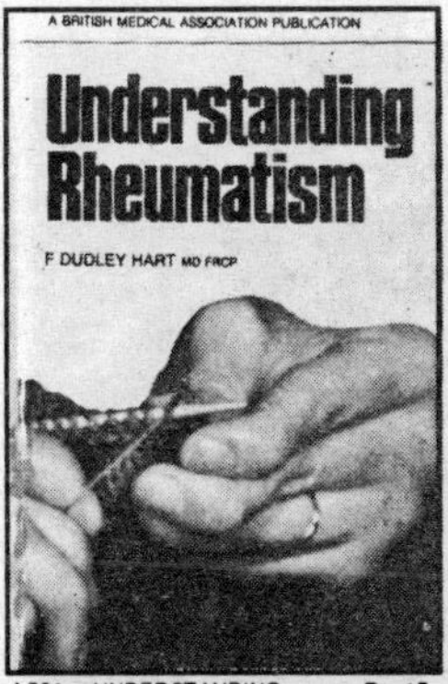

J-584 UNDERSTANDING RHEUMATISM Rs. 15

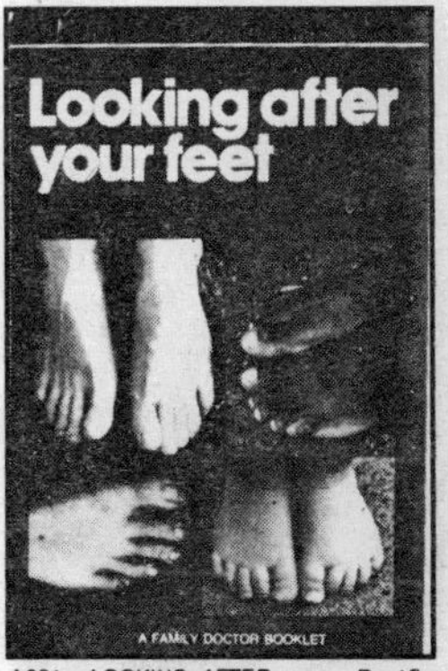

J-621 LOOKING AFTER YOUR FEET Rs. 15

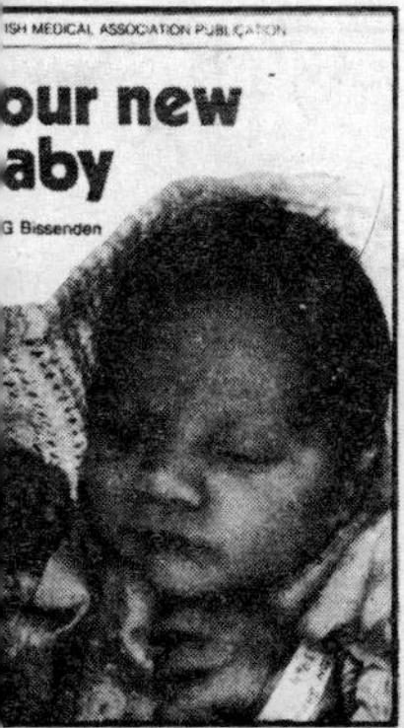

YOUR NEW BABY Rs. 15

J-623 AIDS Rs. 15

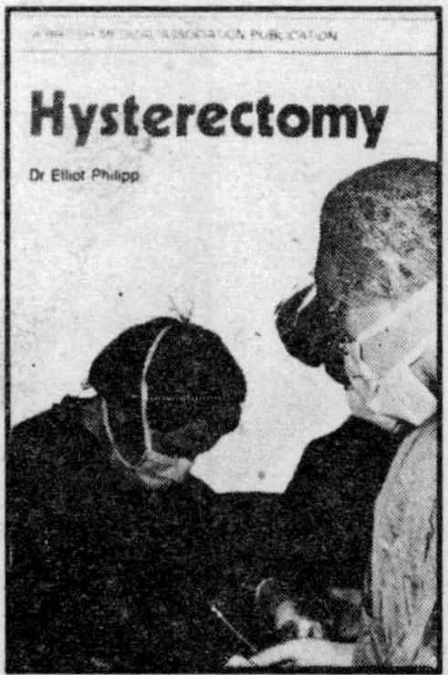

J-624 HYSTERECTOMY Rs. 15

J-625 LOOKING AFTER YOUR BACK Rs. 15

J-626 TODDLERS COMMON PROBLEMS Rs. 15

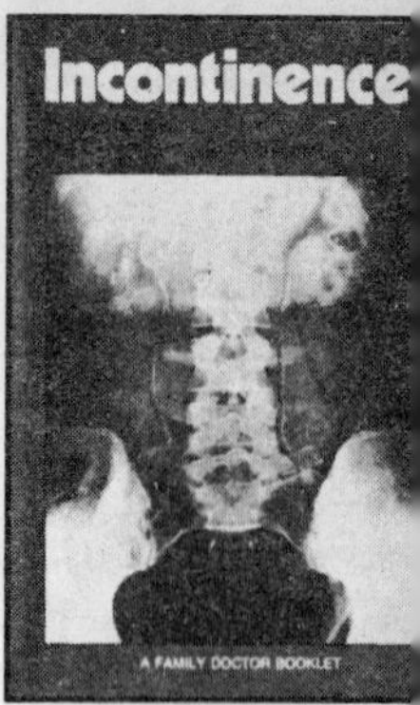

J-627 INCONTINENCE Rs.

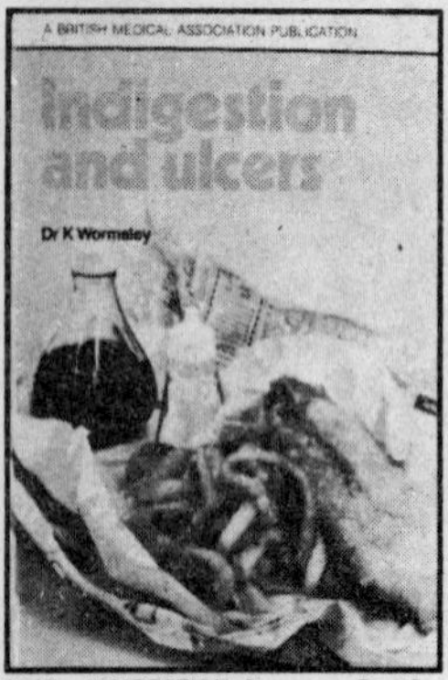

J-628 INDIGESTION & ULCERS Rs. 15

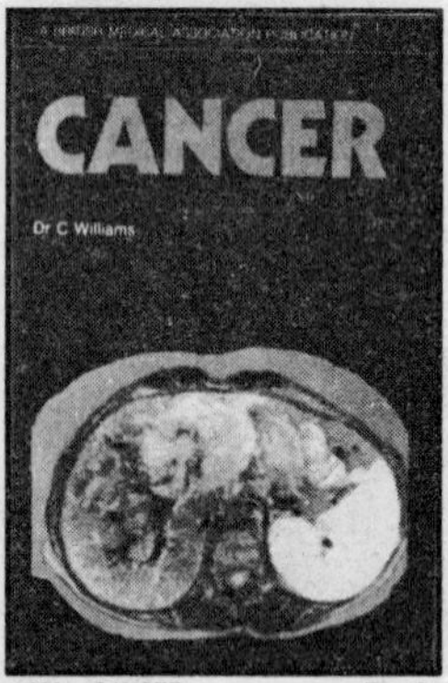

J-629 CANCER Rs. 15

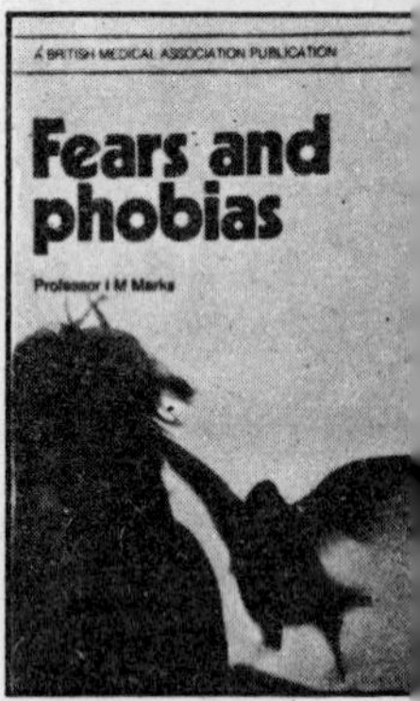

J-630 FEARS & PHOBIAS Rs.

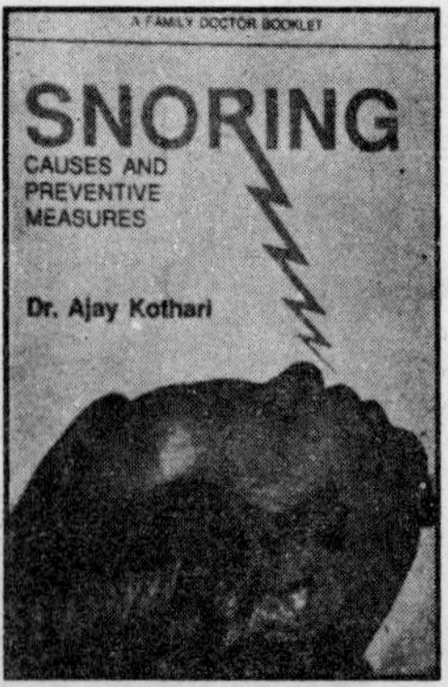

J-663 SNORING: CAUSES & PREVENTIVE MEASURES Rs. 15

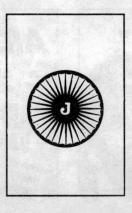

J-272 FOREST OF THE NIGHT Rs. 25

J-273 SHIKAR Rs. 25

HINTS ON TIGER SHOOTING Rs. 25

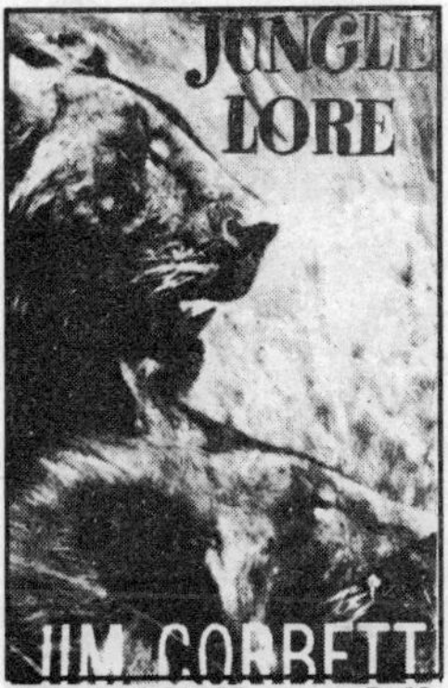

J-326 JUNGLE LORE Rs. 25

J-379 TALES OF SHIKAR TOP

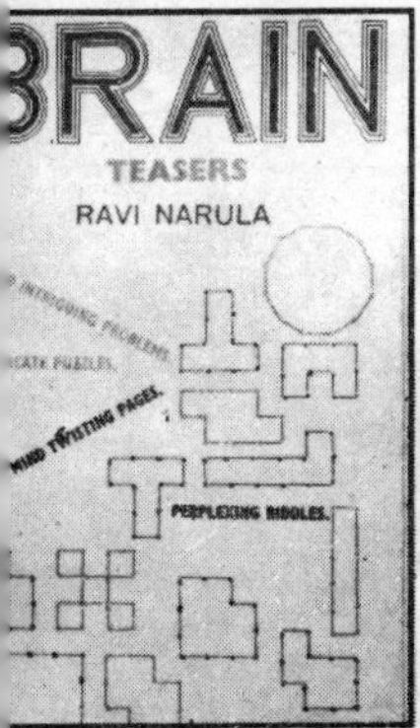

BRAIN TEASERS Rs. 50

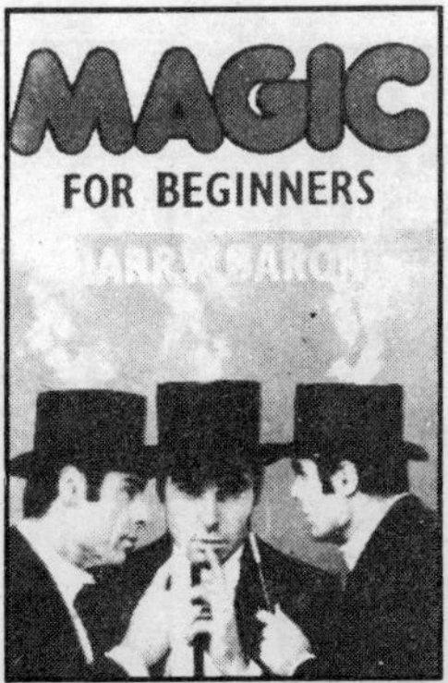

J-457 MAGIC FOR BEGINNERS Rs. 35

J-458 CARD TRICKS FOR BEGINNERS Rs. 35

J-487 KING OF KINGS: THE STORY OF SIR GARFIELD SOBERS Rs. 25

J-504 ALF GOVER'S CRICKET MANUAL Rs. 35

J-507 CRICKET'S UNFORGETTABLE CLIFF-HANGERS Rs

J-592 CHESS : A BEGINNER'S GUIDE Rs. 55

J-632 MIND TEASERS & MIND PUZZLERS Rs 45

J-676 THE WORLD'S BIGGEST RIDDLE BOOK IN THE WORLD Rs

J-692 THE WORLD'S BEST PARTY GAMES Rs. 50

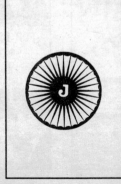

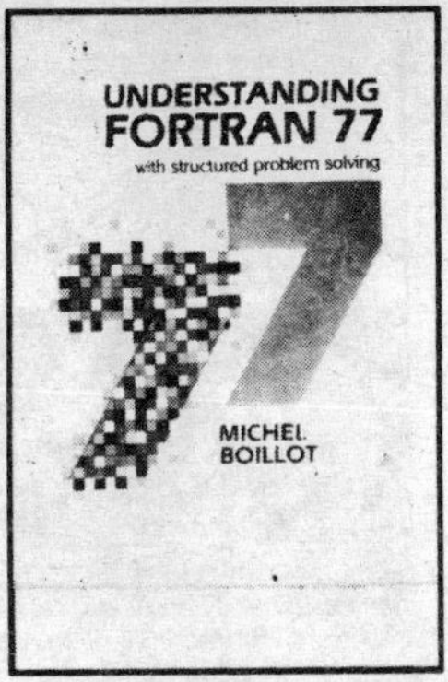

J-555 UNDERSTANDING FORTRAN Rs. 110

J-565 PROGRAMMING IN BASIC Rs. 100

566 THE SPIRIT OF C Rs. 120

J-589 A FIRST BOOK OF C Rs. 95

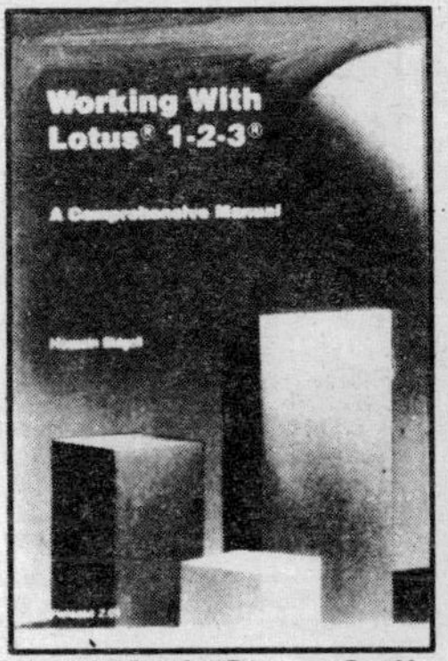

J-590 WORKING WITH LOTUS 1-2-3 Rs. 100

591 UNDERSTANDING & USING dBASE III PULS Rs. 60

J-593 PROGRAMMING & PROBLEM SOLVING WITH PASCAL Rs. 90

J-594 UNDERSTANDING & USING WORDSTAR 4.0 Rs. 65

J-601 REALTIME SOFTWARE FOR SMALL SYSTEMS Rs. 60

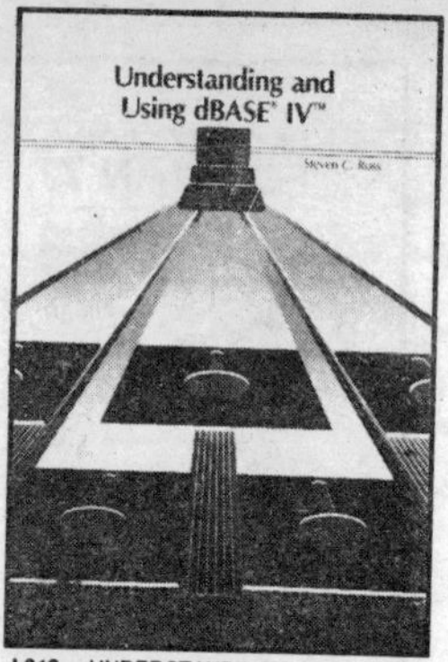

J-612 UNDERSTANDING & USING dBASE IV Rs. 125

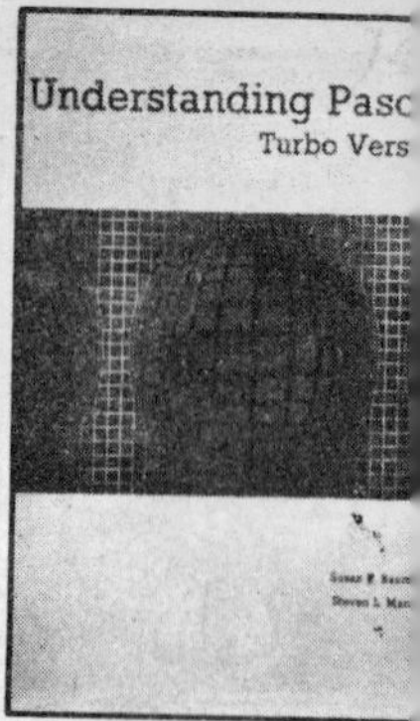

J-613 UNDERSTANDING PASCAL TURBO VERSION Rs

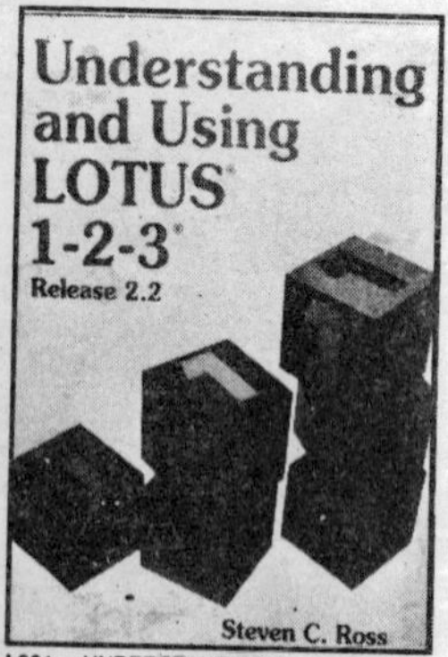

J-631 UNDERSTANDING & USING LOTUS 1-2-3 Rs. 90

J-635 ILLUSTRATED WORDSTAR PROFESS-IONAL RELEASE 5.0 Rs. 80

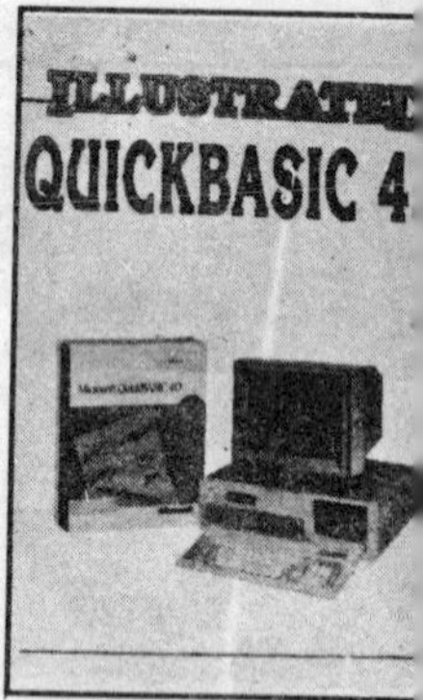

J-636 ILLUSTRATED QUICK BASIC 4.0 Rs.

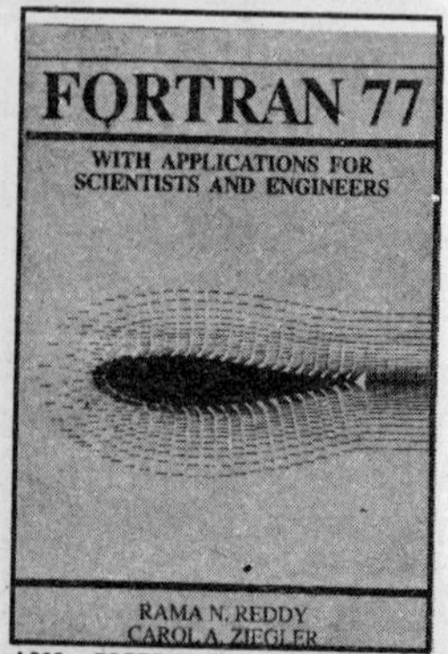

J-638 FORTRAN 77 Rs. 112

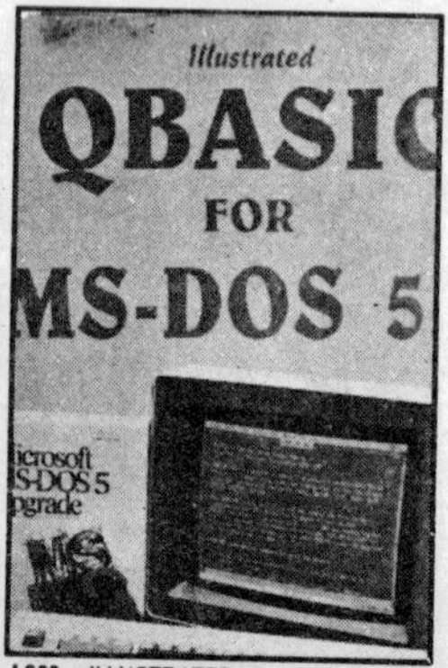

J-680 ILLUSTRATED Q BASIC FOR MSDOS 5.0 Rs. 125

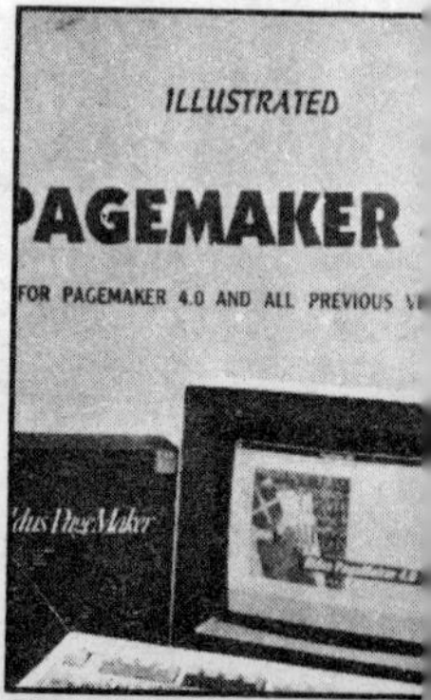

J-682 ILLUSTRATED PAGE MAKER 4.0 Rs. 11

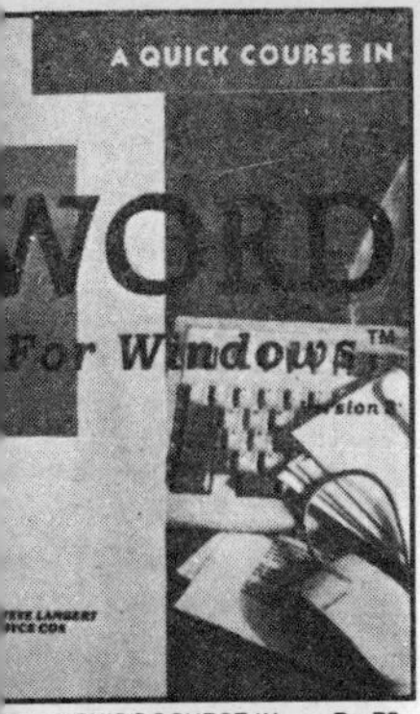

4 A QUICK COURSE IN WORD FOR WINDOWS Rs. 75

J-685 A QUICK COURSE IN LOTUS 1-2-3 Rs. 75

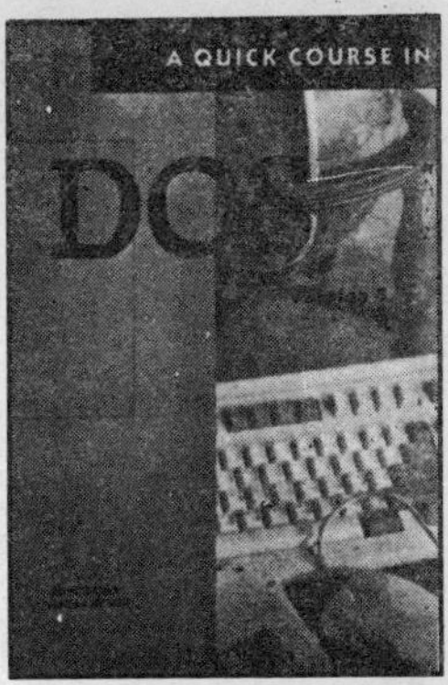

J-686 A QUICK COURSE IN DOS Rs. 75

7 A QUICK COURSE IN WINDOWS 3.1 Rs. 75

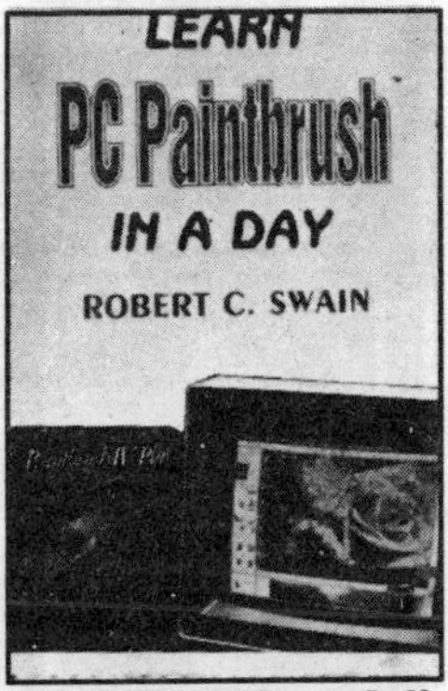

J-688 LEARN PC PAINT-BRUSH IN A DAY Rs. 55

J-689 A QUICK COURSE IN EXCEL-4 Rs. 75

0 LEARN PAL IN A DAY Rs. 85

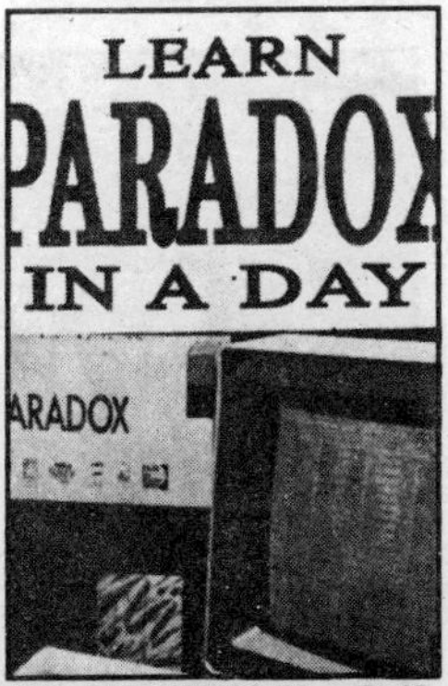

J-691 LEARN PARADOX IN A DAY Rs. 65

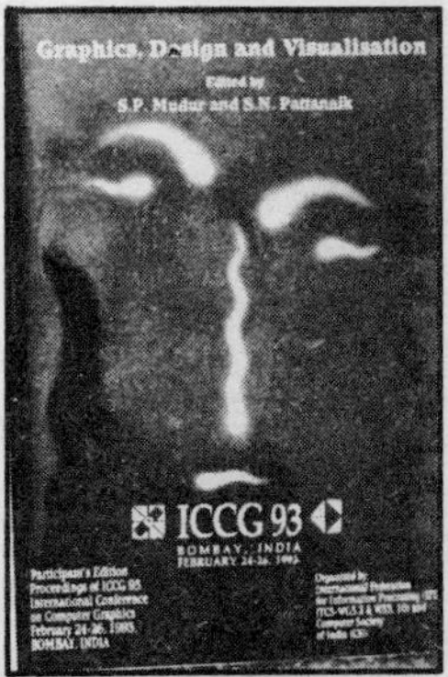

J-701 GRAPHIC DESIGN AND VISUALISATION

ENGINEERING & TECHNOLOGY

LABORATORY MANUAL IN ENVIRONMENTAL ENGINEERING

Prof. P.D. Kulkarni

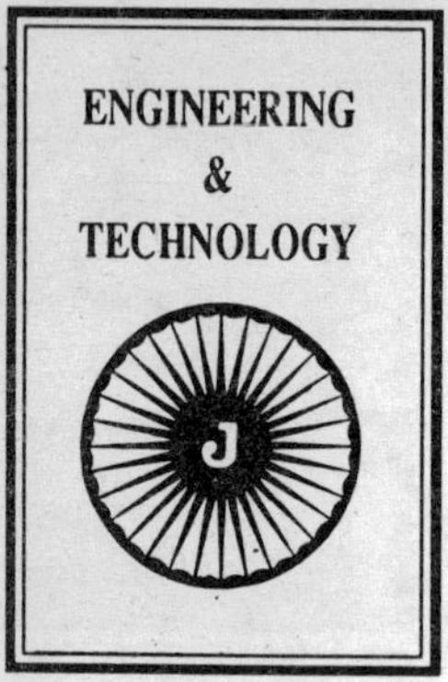

J-683 LABORATORY MANUAL **Rs. 35**
IN ENVIRONMENTAL
ENGINEERING

Automatic Control Systems

George J. Thaler

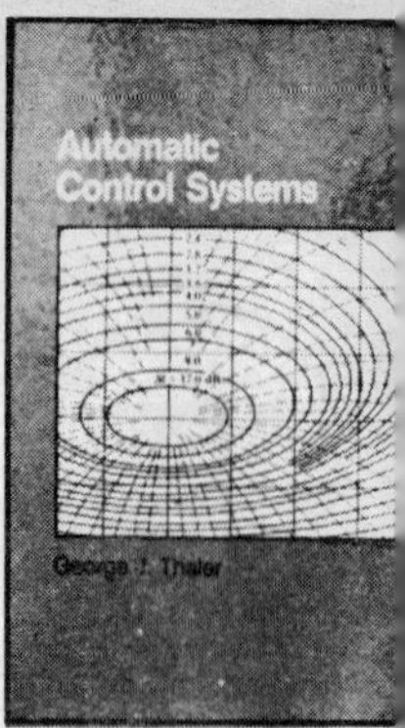

JH-77 AUTOMATIC CON- **Rs. 35(**
J-659 TROL SYSTEMS **Rs. 95(**

MACHINE COMPONENT DESIGN

William Orthwein

Vol. I

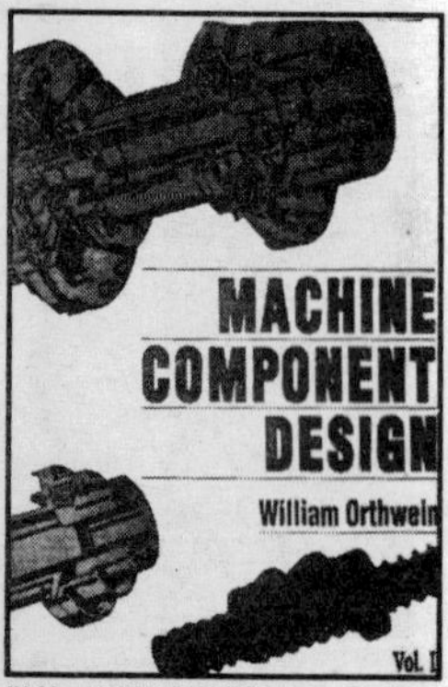

JH-88 MACHINE COMPO- **Rs. 750**
NENT DESIGN (2 VOLS.)

ELECTRONIC CIRCUIT ANALYSIS AND DESIGN

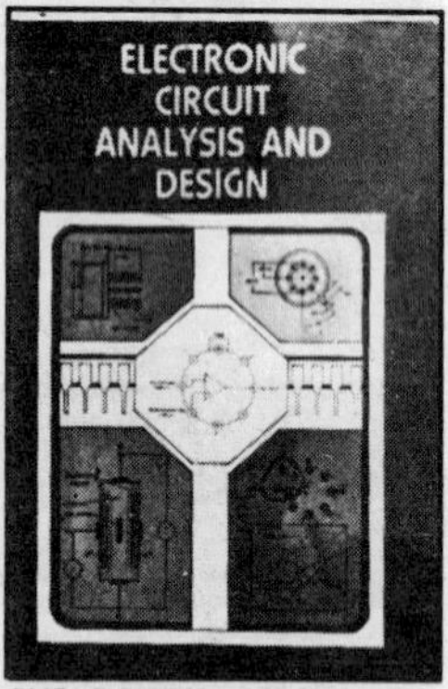

JH-97 ELECTRONIC CIRCUIT **Rs. 650**
ANALYSIS & DESIGN

PRINCIPLES OF COMMUNICATIONS

SYSTEMS, MODULATION AND N

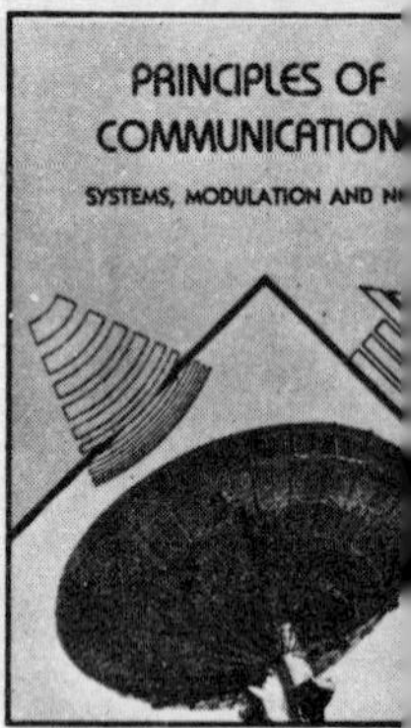

JH-98 PRINCIPLES OF **Rs**
COMMUNICATIONS

HYDRAULIC ENGINEERING

• ROBERSON
• CASSIDY
• CHAUDHRY

JH-99 HYDRAULIC **Rs. 900**
ENGINEERING

THE COMPLETE COMMUNICATION HAND BOOK

ED PAULSON

JH-102 THE COMPLETE **Rs. 495**
COMMUNICATIONS
HANDBOOK

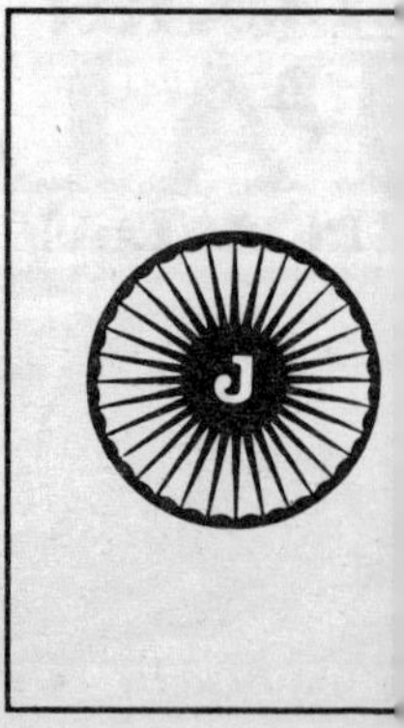

SPECIAL SUBJECTS

MASS COMMUNICATION IN INDIA

JH-15   MASS   TOP
COMMUNICATION IN INDIA
(Under Revision)

A PRACTICAL MANUAL OF COLON CLASSIFICATION: EDITION-7

Dr. SEWA SINGH

JH-74   A PRACTICAL MANUAL   Rs. 290
OF COLON CLASSIFICATION

LIBRARY USER STUDIES

A MANUAL FOR LIBRARIES
AND INFORMATION SCIENTISTS

P.S. KAWATRA

JH-89   LIBRARY USER   Rs. 390
STUDIES

DICTIONARY & ENCYCLOPAEDIA

MIZORAM

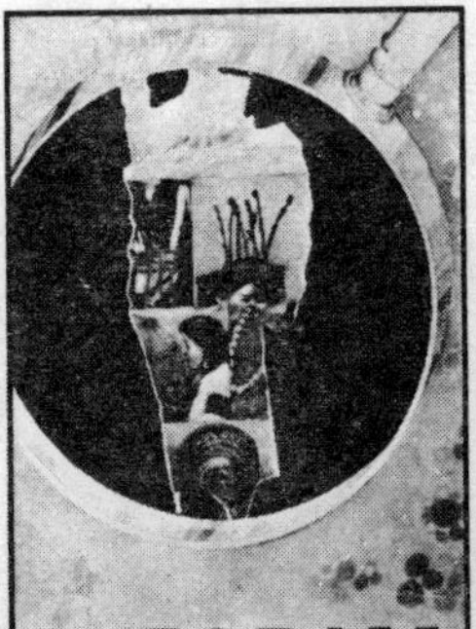

JH-73   MIZORAM ENCYCLO-   Rs. 875
PAEDIA

JAICO ILLUSTRATED ENCYCLOPAEDIA OF TECHNICAL TERMS

Vol. 2

Board of Editors

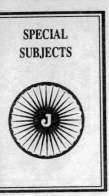

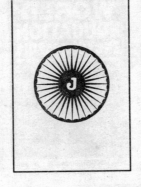

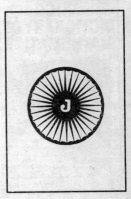

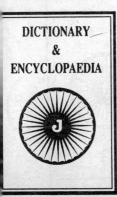

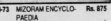

JH-81   JAICO ILLUSTRATED   Rs. 750(HB)
JH-671 ENCYCLOPAEDIA   Rs. 95(PB)
OF TECHNICAL TERMS (2 Vols.)

JH-82 JAICO DICTIONARY Rs. 450
J-668 OF COMPUTERS Rs. 75 (PB)

JH-83 JAICO ENCYCLO- Rs. 450 (HB)
J-670 PAEDIA OF BIOLOGICAL Rs. 95 (PB)
TERMS (2 Vols.)

JH-84 JAICO DICTIONARY Rs. 450(H
J669 OF CHEMISTRY Rs. 75 (P

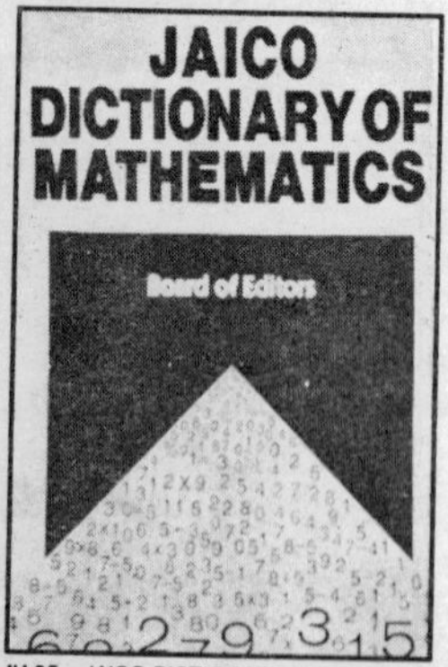

JH-85 JAICO DICTIONARY Rs. 450 (HB)
J-671 OF MATHEMATICS. Rs. 75 (PB)

JH-94 WORLD EDUCATION Rs. 3500
ENCLYCLOPEDIA (Per Set)
(3 Vols.)

JH-96 JAICO DICTIONARY Rs. 45
OF TELECOMMUNICATIONS

JH-101 WORLD POLITICAL Rs. 775
ENCYCLOPAEDIA

FICTION

J-597 THE BEST OF EDGAR WALLACE Rs. 95

J-641 MAMMOTH BOOK OF MURDER STORIES Rs. 100

THE MAMMOTH BOOK OF PRIVATE EYE STORIES Rs. 100

J-647 MAMMOTH BOOK OF SHORT HORROR NOVELS Rs. 100

J-648 THE MAMMOTH BOOK OF GOLDEN AGE SCIENCE FICTION Rs. 125

THE MAMMOTH BOOK OF CLASSIC SCIENCE FICTION Rs. 130

J-650 THE MAMMOTH BOOK OF SPY THRILLERS Rs. 100

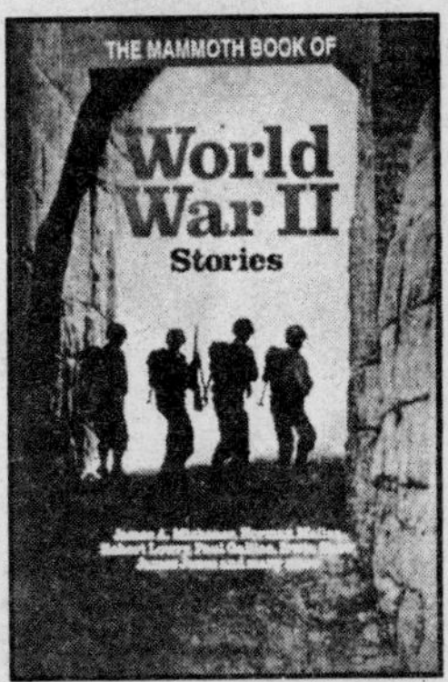

J-651 THE MAMMOTH BOOK OF WORLD WAR II STORIES Rs. 100

J-654 THE MAMMOTH BOOK OF GREAT DETECTIVE STORIES Rs. 100

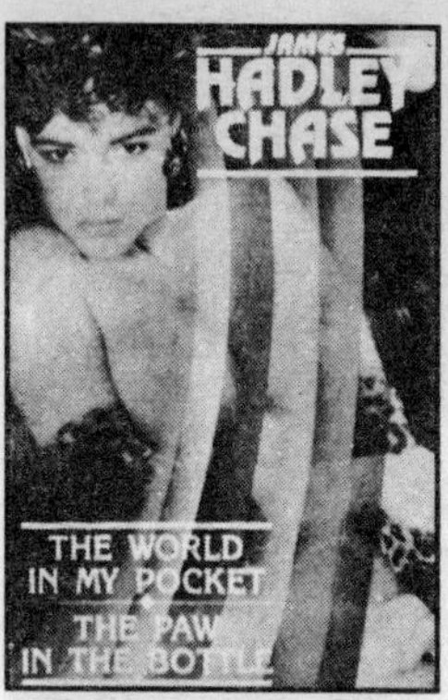

JH-92 THE WORLD IN MY POCKET & THE PAIN INTHE BOTTLE JAMES HADLEY CHASE Rs. 75

JH-93 YOU HAVE YOURSELF A DEAL; TELL IT TOTHE BIRDS JAMES HADLEY CHASE Rs. 7

MISCELLANEOUS

J

J-553 JAICO BOOK OF BABY NAMES WITH MEAN-INGS & EXPLANATIONS Rs 20
Rs. 120 (Boxed)

J-270 THE TIGER OF RAJASTHAN Rs. 2

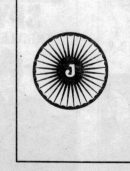

J-633 INTERPRET YOUR DREAMS Rs. 20

J

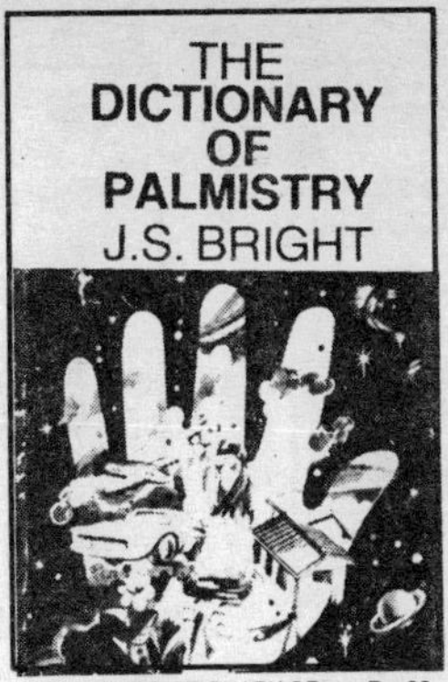

J-128 THE DICTIONARY OF PALMISTRY Rs. 30

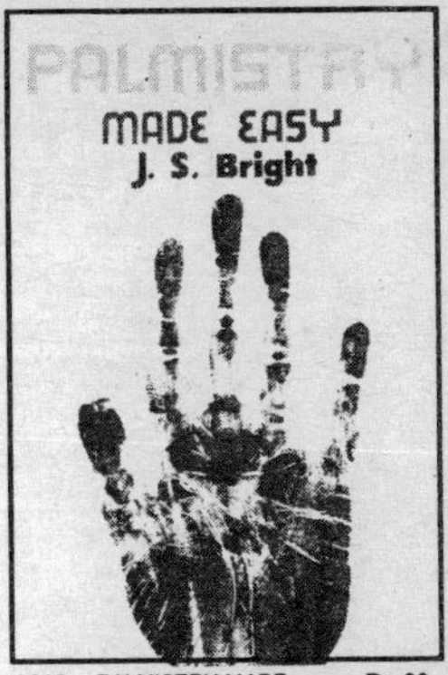

J-232 PALMISTRY MADE EASY Rs. 30

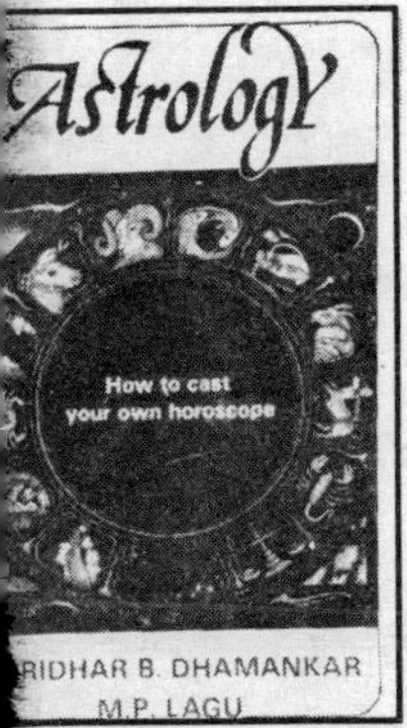

ASTROLOGY Rs. 25

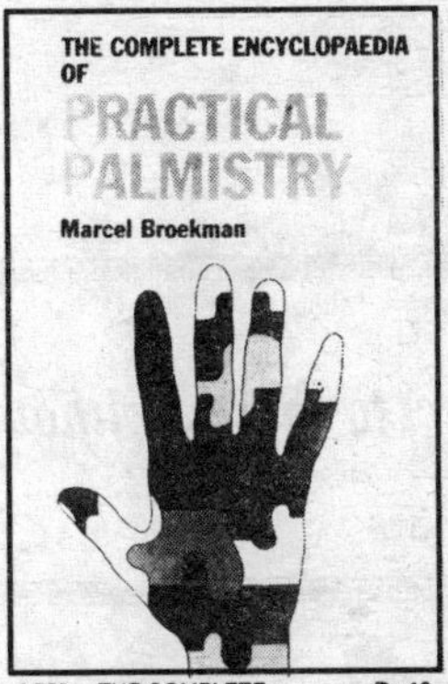

J-556 THE COMPLETE ENCYCLOPAEDIA OF PALMISTRY Rs.40

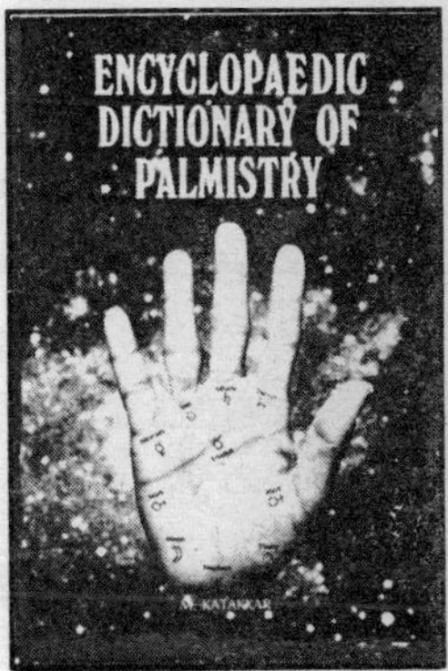

J-569 ENCYCLOPAEDIC DICTIONARY OF PALMISTRY Rs. 55

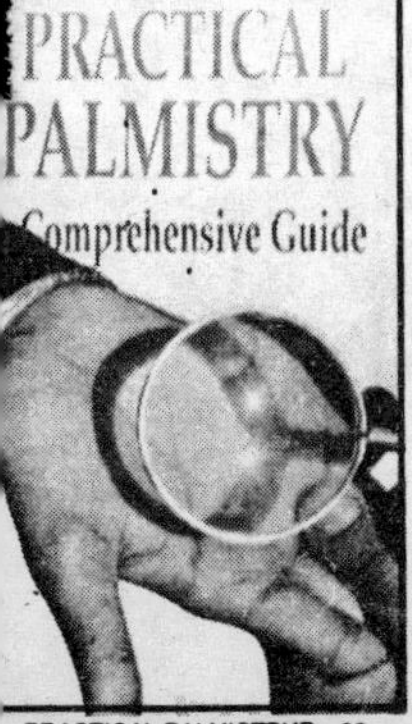

PRACTICAL PALMISTRYRs. 60
A COMPREHENSIVE GUIDE

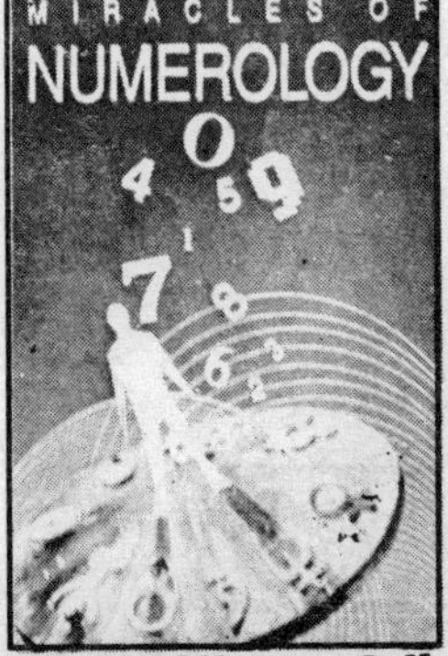

J-619 MIRACLE OF NUMEROLOGY Rs. 55

J-637 BEJAN DARUWALLA'S BOOK OF STAR SIGNS, NUMEROLOGY, CHINESE ASTROLOGY. Rs. 60

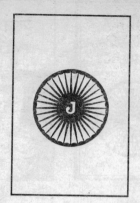

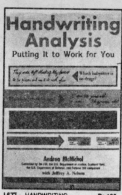